Melbourne • Oakland • London

Mara Vorhees

Moscow

The Top Five

1 Sanduny Baths
Sweat off your city smut at this opulent bathhouse (p150)

2 Lenin's Tomb
Pay your respects to Vladimir Ilych on Red Square (p63)

3 Izmaylovo (Vernisazh) Market
Bargain for trash and treasure with local artisans (p162)

4 Kremlin
Discover medieval Muscovy at this imposing fortress (p54)

5 Moscow metro
Take a ride through an underground art museum (p117)

Contents

Published by Lonely Planet Publications Pty Ltd
ABN 36 005 607 983

Australia Head Office, Locked Bag 1, Footscray,
Victoria 3011, ☎ 03 8379 8000, fax 03 8379 8111,
talk2us@lonelyplanet.com.au

USA 150 Linden St, Oakland, CA 94607,
☎ 510 893 8555, toll free 800 275 8555,
fax 510 893 8572, info@lonelyplanet.com

UK 72–82 Rosebery Ave, Clerkenwell, London,
EC1R 4RW, ☎ 020 7841 9000, fax 020 7841 9001,
go@lonelyplanet.co.uk

Printed by SNP Security Printing Pte Ltd, Singapore

The Author

Mara Vorhees

Often asked why she chose to study Russia, Mara is stumped for a satisfactory reply. Certainly, she admits, she sometimes wishes she had given more consideration to the cuisine and climate before making the decision.

Nonetheless, she has been travelling to Russia since the days of communism. She recalls the time when the lines inside GUM (State Department Store) were dwarfed only by the lines outside Lenin's tomb. Later, she spent two years working on a foreign-aid project in the Urals and fighting with the tax police. During this time, Moscow was a frequent destination for 'recovery trips'.

These days, Mara's time in Moscow is spent sipping coffees at Coffee Bean (p121) and seeking inspiration amid the architecture of Kitay Gorod (p114). She is the co-author of Lonely Planet's guides *Russia & Belarus* and the *Trans-Siberian Railway*, and her stories about Russia have appeared in the *Boston Globe* and the *Los Angeles Times*. She has even come to love Russia's cuisine and climate, a transformation she attributes to *solyanka*, a steamy, salty soup to delight any palate; and the *banya* (Russian bathhouse), an infallible antidote to Russian winters.

MARA'S TOP MOSCOW DAY

The best days in Moscow start off at Coffee Bean with the *Moscow Times*. After a leisurely latte, I hop on the metro to buy fresh fruit and hot *pirozhki* (Russian pastries) amid the sounds and smells of Dorogomilovsky Market (p122).

Then I ride the riverboat along the Moscow River, past the golden domes of Novodevichy Convent (p95) and the Stalinist skyscraper at Sparrow Hills (p106), getting off at Gorky Park (p99). Here, among babushkas pushing strollers and lovers kissing on park benches, I find a quiet corner to enjoy my picnic.

After lunch, I explore the art galleries and trolling for treasures in the Central House of Artists (p161). I don't miss the opportunity to stroll around the Sculpture Park (p100), where statues of Lenin, Stalin and others rest among flower-filled gardens.

For dinner, I have my heart set on the rich, spicy flavours of Georgian food, and that means Tiflis (p136). I sit out on the restaurant's grand terrace, sipping wine from the house vineyard, and toast a delightful day in Moscow.

PHOTOGRAPHER
Jonathan Smith

Raised in rural Aberdeenshire, Jon graduated from Scotland's St Andrews University in 1994 with an MA Honours in German and little idea of what to do with his life. After a spell teaching languages in newly independent Lithuania, he spent three years travelling around the former USSR, trying to carve himself a niche as a freelance travel photographer. Jon's byline has appeared in over 100 Lonely Planet titles and recent commissions have included Lonely Planet's *Edinburgh, Stockholm, Paris* and *St Petersburg* city guides. This is Jon's third assignment in Moscow and his first major digital shoot; the highlights of which he says were snapping *devushky* (young women) at the Creamfields festival, people-watching at the zoo and lodging with a host family. Indeed he would like to thank Marina and Slava for putting up with him and his smelly trainers for four weeks.

Introducing Moscow

Sunlight glints off the golden domes and catches your eye. The ancient, patchwork-patterned church is right in front of you, but you almost miss it because you are walking with your head down, shielding your face from the wind and employing all efforts to avoid slipping on hidden patches of ice. A steely-eyed babushka, laden with a heavy fur coat and an oversized shopping bag, still manages to negotiate the precarious pathway faster than your inexperienced feet.

You navigate around a pair of young lovers who have stopped to admire the lacy lingerie in a shop window. You stare, only for a moment, as a blonde – devastatingly gorgeous with impossibly long legs – emerges from a sleek, black sedan.

You resist the temptation to duck into a cosy café, where the din of casual conversation and clinking coffee cups invites you to warm your chilled bones. Instead, you follow the babushka inside the church. The heavy door closes behind you, blocking out the cacophony of honking horns and screaming sirens. Inside, the only sound is the whisper of prayers. As your eyes adjust to the darkness of the candlelit interior, you make out the familiar characters on the age-old icons, which adorn the whitewashed walls. You find yourself transported from the hustling, bustling modern capital across centuries to medieval Moscow, the mighty fortress and centre of Orthodoxy, where ancient Rus grew up.

Russia's earliest roots are in Moscow: the Kremlin still shows off the splendour of Muscovy's grand princes and St Basil's Cathedral still recounts the defeat of the Tatars. Moscow also recalls Russia's more recent past, still fresh in our memories. On Red Square, the founder of the Soviet state lies embalmed. And only a few kilometres away, a future leader rallied outside the White House, leading to the demise of the same state.

Moscow continues to make history. It is unfolding on every street corner, as Muscovites move into the 21st century, embracing the global culture of the modern era. With the same purposeful optimism that their predecessors looked 'forward to communism!', Muscovites today are looking forward to the opportunities promised by the New Russia. They are breaking down the barriers of generations past – political boundaries, cultural taboos and ideological stricture – and exploring the possibilities of consumerism, creativity and career.

LOWDOWN

Population 10,381,000
Time zone GMT/UTC + 3hr
Three-star double room R3000-4000
Coffee R60
Half a litre of beer R120
Metro fare R13
Don't Sit down on the metro escalator
Do Kiss on the metro escalator

Moscow is the epicentre of New Russia and everything that it represents. It boasts commerce and culture that most provincial Russians can only dream about. Plagued by soaring prices and riddled with corruption, it also epitomises the seamier side of postcommunist Russia. Nowhere are Russia's contrasts more apparent than in Moscow: ancient monasteries and ultramodern monoliths stand side by side, and New Russian millionaires and poverty-stricken pensioners walk the same streets.

The city is magnificent in late spring (May or June) and early autumn (September or October), when the city's parks are filled with flowering trees or colourful leaves. Moscow is spruced up for the May holidays and City Day, both festive times in the capital. But if you want to delve deep into the Russian soul, come in winter, when snow, cold and darkness muffle the modern noise.

Any time of year, Moscow evokes wonder. Even today, you will appreciate the words penned by Pushkin almost 200 years ago in *Eugene (Yevgeny) Onegin*: 'Already gleaming/ before their eyes they see unfold/the towers of whitestone Moscow beaming/with fire from every cross of gold./Friends, how my heart would leap with pleasure/when suddenly I saw this treasure/of spires and belfries, in a cup/with parks and mansions, open up.'

City Life

City Life

MOSCOW TODAY

The word of the day in Moscow is 'exclusive'. The hottest clubs have the most expensive drinks and the tightest 'face control'. Travelling by private car – preferably a big, black one – is way cooler than hoofing it or going by metro. Designer labels fly off the racks at pricey boutiques. Muscovites have taken to feasting on sushi instead of herring, and drinking French champagne instead of *Sovietskoe shampanskoe*. There is even a new brand of 'elite' tea, *Elitny Chai*, trying to cash in on this preoccupation with prestige.

For all of its status-consciousness, Moscow is a bourgeois city. Driving Hummers and dressing in Armani are privileges reserved for a small – albeit visible – elite. Nevertheless, most Muscovites are now also enjoying a disposable income that they never had before.

In 2005 over three million cars clogged Moscow's streets – a number that increases by 200,000 every year. There are plenty of Mercedes, but also Hondas, Citroens and good old-fashioned Ladas. New restaurants include cosy cafés and bohemian bars, not just overpriced, upscale eateries. Many nightclubs are branded 'exclusive', but others are considered 'democratic' and open to all. Even eating raw fish has become a populist experience, with the proliferation of all-you-can-eat sushi bars.

Perhaps this prosperity explains Moscow's apolitical attitude. While Rose and Orange Revolutions are taking place just next door, Russians stand by quietly and watch President Putin censor their press and eliminate their right to elect governors (see p20); Muscovites appear to be more concerned with the latest restaurant opening than the latest legislative debates. The exception is when their own comfort levels are threatened – as they were in 2005, when the proposed monetisation of pension benefits provoked thousands of pensioners to take to the streets in protest.

HOT CONVERSATION TOPICS

Here is what you might overhear while sipping your cappuccino in a Moscow café:

- How long did it take you to get through the traffic jam on the Garden Ring?
- Does the new Hotel Moskva really look better than the old Hotel Moskva?
- Which 'oligarch' will be arrested next?
- Which celebrities will shag on *Dom Tri*?
- Have you tried the new sushi/steak/seafood restaurant around the corner?

Partisan statues at Belorusskaya metro station (p117)

One issue that cannot be ignored is the ongoing war in Chechnya. Muscovites have been forced to face the bleak reality of the conflict, as bombs have exploded on their own streets. The terrorist attacks of recent years affected the nation's capital in an infinite number of ways; some are obscure while others are in-your-face, such as the metal detectors in the Bolshoi Theatre and the ubiquitous document-checking police in front of every metro station.

Nonetheless, the capital remains upbeat. The optimism is pervasive. It is evident in the construction of skyscrapers, shopping malls, theme parks and theatres; in the 'world premiers' and 'grand openings'; and on the faces of shoppers, strollers, diners and drinkers on the crowded Moscow streets. Indeed (to borrow a communist slogan), 'the future is bright!'

CITY CALENDAR

Standout seasons to visit Moscow are late spring (May or June) and early autumn (September or October), when the city's parks are filled with flowering trees or colourful leaves. The city is spruced up for the May holidays and September's City Day, both festive times in the capital. It also gets fired up to ring in the New Year, when Muscovites emerge from their warm homes into the winter night for free concerts and fireworks.

Cultural festivals and special exhibits occur throughout the year for lovers of art, music, theatre and film. For additional information on events in Moscow, refer to the *Moscow Times* or *element* (see p222). For details on public holidays, see p220.

JANUARY

Though January represents the deepest, darkest days of winter, it is a festive month, kicked off by New Year's celebrations in the grandest tradition (see p11). The Orthodox Christmas, or Rozhdestvo, is celebrated on 6 January. Many offices and services are closed during the first week of January.

WINTER FESTIVAL

It's an outdoor funfest for those with anti-freeze in their veins (and you can bet plenty of people use vodka for this purpose). Teams compete to build elaborate ice sculptures in front of the Pushkin Fine Arts Museum and on Red Square. But the real nutters (or those who have *far* too much antifreeze in their veins) can be found punching holes in the ice on the Moscow River and plunging in for a dip. Do this and you're a member of the 'Walrus Club'.

FEBRUARY

Maslenitsa marks the end of winter, but it does seem premature. Temperatures con-

tinue to be cold, hovering around -10°C for weeks. Occasional southerly winds can raise temperatures briefly to a balmy 0°C. The city continues to sparkle with snow, and sledders and skiers are in seventh heaven.

MOSCOW BIENNALE OF CONTEMPORARY ART

www.moscowbiennale.ru/en/

This month-long festival is organised and partly funded by Russia's Ministry of Culture, with the aim of establishing the capital as an international centre for contemporary art. Venues around the city exhibit works by artists from around the world. In 2005 many of the exhibits were held at the former Central Lenin Museum (p65), offering a rare glimpse inside this old Soviet building, as well as an invigorating artistic display.

DEFENDER OF THE MOTHERLAND DAY

Celebrated on 23 February, this unofficial holiday traditionally honours veterans and soldiers. It has become a sort of counter-part to International Women's Day and is now better known as 'Men's Day'. Women are supposed to do nice things for the men in their lives, but the extent of the celebration is limited.

MASLENITSA

www.maslenitsa.com

Akin to Mardi Gras, this fête celebrates the end of winter and kicks off Orthodox

---

TOP FIVE CULTURAL EVENTS

- December Nights Festival (p11)
- Golden Mask Festival (p10)
- Interfest (p10)
- Moscow Biennale of Contemporary Art (right)
- Moscow Forum (p10)

Lent. 'Maslenitsa' comes from the Russian word for butter, which is a key ingredient in the festive treat, *bliny* (crepes). Besides bingeing on Russian crepes, the week-long festival features horse-drawn sledges, storytelling clowns and beer-drinking bears. The festival culminates with the burning of a scarecrow to welcome spring. Exact dates depend on the dates of Orthodox Easter, but it is usually in February or early March. Look out for events at Kolomenskoe (p104) and special *bliny* menus at local restaurants.

MARCH & APRIL

During the spring thaw – in late March and early April – everything turns to mud and slush.

INTERNATIONAL WOMEN'S DAY

Russia's favourite holiday was founded to honour the women's movement. These days, on 8 March, men buy champagne, flowers and chocolates for their better halves – and for all the women in their lives.

GOLDEN MASK FESTIVAL

www.goldenmask.ru

It involves two weeks of performances by Russia's premier drama, opera, dance and musical performers, culminating in a prestigious awards ceremony. The festival brightens up otherwise dreary March and April.

EASTER

The main holiday of the Orthodox Church is Easter, or Paskha. The date varies, but it is usually in April or early May – often a different date than its Western counterpart. Forty days of fasting, known as Veliky Post, lead up to the religious holiday. Easter Sunday kicks off with celebratory midnight services, after which people eat *kulichy* (special dome-shaped cakes) and *paskha* (curdcakes), and they may exchange painted wooden Easter eggs. Many banks, offices and museums are closed on Easter Monday.

MOSCOW FORUM

www.ccmm.ru

This is a contemporary music festival held every year since 1994. It features avantgarde musicians from Russia and Europe, who perform at the Moscow Tchaikovsky Conservatory (p145).

MAY

Spring arrives in the capital! Many services, offices and museums have limited hours during the first half of May, due to the run of public holidays. Nonetheless, it is a festive time, as the parks are finally green and blooming with flowers, and the streets are filled with people celebrating. Victory Day, on 9 May, hosts parades on Tverskaya ulitsa and other events at Victory Park (p106).

JUNE

June is Moscow's most welcoming month. Temperatures are mild, and days are long and sunny. Little girls wear giant white bows in their hair to celebrate the end of the school year.

INTERFEST

www.miff.ru

Interfest is short for the Moscow International Film Festival. This week-long event attracts filmmakers from the US and Europe, as well as the most promising Russian artists. Films are shown at theatres around the city, including Illuzion (p150) and Rolan Cinema (p150).

FASHION WEEK IN MOSCOW

www.rfw.ru

In recent years, Moscow's major fashion event has attracted as many as 60 designers from Russia and around the world. See innovative styles on display on catwalks around the city.

JULY & AUGUST

Many Muscovites retreat to their dachas (see boxed text, p186) to escape summer in the city, and the cultural calendar is quiet. Maximum temperatures are usually between 25°C and 35°C, although the humidity makes it seem hotter. July and August are also the rainiest months, although showers tend to be brief. While residents make themselves scarce, tourists flood the capital during this season. Train tickets and accommodation can be more difficult to secure, and attractions around Moscow tend to be overrun with visitors.

Summer is the time for outdoor music festivals, including huge rock events such as Krylya and Nashestviye, which take place out of the city. For more information, see p26.

SEPTEMBER & OCTOBER

Early autumn is another standout time to be in the capital. The heat subsides and the foliage turns the city splendid oranges, reds and yellows. October usually sees the first snow of the season.

CITY DAY

City Day, or *den goroda* in Russian, celebrates Moscow's birthday every year on the first weekend in September. The day kicks off with a festive parade, followed by live music on Red Square and plenty of food, fireworks and fun.

KREMLIN CUP

www.kremlincup.ru

This international tennis tournament is held every October at the Olympic Stadium, near the Renaissance Moscow Hotel (p167). Not surprisingly, Russian players have dominated this tournament in recent years.

NOVEMBER

Winter sets in. The days are noticeably short and temperatures are low. By now, the city is covered in a blanket of snow, which reflects the city lights and lends a magical air.

DAY OF RECONCILIATION & ACCORD

The former October Revolution day – 7 November – is still an official holiday, though it is hardly acknowledged. It still is, however, a big day for flag-waving and protesting by old-school Communist Party members, especially in front of the former Central Lenin Museum (p65) and on Tverskaya ulitsa. It makes for a great photo-op.

DECEMBER

Short days and long nights keep most people inside for most of the month. On 12 December, Constitution Day marks the adoption of the new constitution in 1993. But political holidays are not what they used to be, and no-one pays much attention.

DECEMBER NIGHTS FESTIVAL

It is held at the main performance halls, theatres and museums from mid-December to early January. Classical music at its best is performed in classy surroundings by the best Russian and foreign talent.

NEW YEAR

This event lures Muscovites out of their warm homes to watch fireworks over Red Square and warm their bones with vodka toasts to the coming year.

CULTURE

IDENTITY

While Moscow feels like a cosmopolitan European capital, it is conspicuously homogenous. Over 80% of the population is Russian: light-skinned, Slavic-looking, Russian-speaking people. Small numbers of Jews, Ukrainians, Belarusians and Tatars mix it up a little, but these ethnic groups each represent only about 3% of the population. People from the southern republics, such as Georgia, Kazakhstan and Armenia, each account for about 1%.

Among this Russian-dominant population the religion of choice is of course Russian Orthodoxy. After decades of church closure, confiscation of property and harassment of believers under the Soviet regime, the Russian Orthodox Church (Russkaya Pravoslavnaya Tserkov) is enjoying a remarkable revival. By 1991 it already had an estimated 50 million members, and that number has continued to grow. Today, closed and neglected churches are being restored all over the country and especially in Moscow. There are approximately 23,000 active churches in the country, up from 7000 in 1988. This

ESSENTIAL MOSCOW

- **Dorogomilovsky Market** (p122) Colourful produce and colourful people.
- **Patriarch's Ponds** (p84) A quiet corner of literary Moscow.
- **Pushkin Fine Arts Museum** (p91) Fabulous collection of impressionist and postimpressionist paintings.
- **Sculpture Park** (p100) Art and history come together in a moody, magical way.
- **Tiflis** (p136) A perfect place for a Georgian feast.

seems like an impressive comeback, but it still represents less than half of the churches that were operating in Russia in 1917.

These days, 90% of ethnic Russians identify themselves as Russian Orthodox, though many are not practicing. The increase in self-ascribed believers has been linked to the growth of Russian nationalism, as Orthodoxy is often considered an intimate part of what it means to be Russian.

While the renovation of churches seems like a positive development, Russian nationalism does have its ugly side. Neo-Nazi movements and violence against minorities are on the rise in big cities such as Moscow. Sadly, many of these acts often go unpunished. More common, but equally damaging, is the relentless harassment of non-Russians by police, who are always on hand to verify the documents of passers-by, especially those with darker skin tones.

Thousands of people, especially from ethnic minorities, live in Moscow without proper residency permits. It is the primary reason why official population figures for the capital are dubious – many estimates put the real total closer to 12 million. The capital's advantageous economic conditions prompt permitless Muscovites to tolerate frequent police document inspections and pocket-emptying bribes.

LIFESTYLE

Soviet workers used to joke that 'we pretend to work and they pretend to pay us'. It was funny because it was all too true. New Russia has a new work ethic, and nowhere is it more evident than Moscow. Eager young Muscovites are working long hours, so they too can partake of the good life they see going on around them. They are fighting traffic, working weekends, talking on mobile phones and breaking for a 'business lunch', just like their London and New York counterparts.

THE INSIDER'S GUIDE TO NEW RUSSIA

The reality of most Moscow lifestyles is a far cry from the images of free-spending *Novy Russkie* (New Russians) that dominate the media. Sure, the capital is home to 26 billionaires, but it is also home to some 10 million people who have considerably less money than that. Understandably, the conspicuous consumption of the upper echelons sparks a fair amount of curiosity – and envy – among middle-class Muscovites.

The autobiographical novel *Casual,* written by Moscow elite insider Oksana Robsky, became an instant bestseller when it was published in 2005. It provided a rare glimpse inside a world of gated mansions, bodyguards, luxury spas, chauffeured cars and all-night parties. It's a world that everybody sees – in the form of lanky lasses decked out in designer labels and sleek cars parked in front of fancy restaurants – but few people actually experience.

And it is worth it: Moscow restaurants are packed with merrymakers, charter flights to Turkey and Greece are filled with holidaymakers, and supermarkets are crowded with homemakers. Muscovites are working hard and enjoying the fruits of their labour.

However, they are also – often – supporting several generations in the one household. Older people are increasingly dependent on family members, as their pensions have become near worthless. Grandmothers (who live on average 14 years longer than their male counterparts) often live with their children, which turns out to be an effective system of childcare in this country where upwards of 90% of women of working age work outside the home.

In Russia, small families are the norm, multiple generations aside. This is especially so in Moscow where expensive real estate necessitates small flats. Most families have only one child (Russian families averaged 1.25 children in 2000); but still, living quarters are tight. Personal space overlaps with public space: living rooms convert into dining rooms each evening, and then into bedrooms come nightfall. It explains why you see so many young couples kissing on park benches – they probably have very little privacy at home.

It also explains why the average age at marriage continues to be relatively low, as young Russians are anxious to move out of their crowded homes. Early marriage and lack of social repercussions result in one of the world's highest divorce rates. According to *Divorce Magazine,* 65% of Russian marriages end in divorce.

JUDAISM IN MOSCOW

Lenin once said 'scratch a Bolshevik and you'll find a Russian chauvinist'. While the revolution provided a period of opportunity for individual Jews, the socialist regime was not tolerant toward Jewish language and customs. In 1930, Lazar Kaganovich, an ethnic Jew and Stalin crony, was made mayor of Moscow. He pleaded against the destruction of the Christ the Saviour Cathedral out of fear that he would be personally blamed and it would provoke popular anti-Semitism (both of which happened).

Anti-Semitism became official policy in the late Stalinist period. The Jewish quarter in the Dorogomilova neighbourhood was levelled for new building projects. Two huge apartment houses were constructed for the communist elite, at 24 and 26 Kutuzovsky prospekt, on top of the city's old Jewish cemetery. Systematic discrimination finally prompted the rise of a dissident movement, which battled Soviet officialdom for the right to leave the country.

In 1986 Mikhail Gorbachev announced that refusnik Anatoly Scharansky was permitted to emigrate, signalling a more relaxed official stance. Between 1987 and 1991, 500,000 Soviet Jews emigrated to Israel, and another 150,000 to the USA. Moscow's Jewish community fragmented as a result.

Today, Judaism in Moscow is enjoying a modest revival, as believers reconnect with their ancestry and traditions. As many as 57,000 Jews have returned to Moscow from Israel and the USA in the post-Soviet period. Jewish communities are flourishing, providing kosher restaurants and Hebrew-speaking service providers for the newcomers.

As in earlier times, the opportunities for Jews that have arisen in postcommunist Russia have also stirred anti-Semitic incidents and rhetoric. High-profile Jewish businessmen, such as Mikhail Khodorkovsky (see p37), have attracted resentment and very public political rants. Anti-Semitic graffiti, nationalist rallies and even violence against Jews have occurred on the streets of Moscow. Such harassment is negligible compared to the strife they endured in the old Soviet Union, though.

As Russian Jews return to Moscow, synagogues are slowly repaired and re-opened, and the community that has survived here for hundreds of years rebuilds itself.

FOOD

Seventy years of mistreatment by the Soviets has given Russian cuisine a bad rap. Now, many restaurants in Moscow allow the diner to experience Russian food as it is meant to be – exquisite *haute-russe* masterpieces once served at banquets and balls, as well as tasty and filling meals that have for centuries been prepared in peasant kitchens with garden ingredients.

Options for dining out during the Soviet period were so limited that Russians hardly ever did it. They might have taken lunch at the local *stolovaya* (cafeteria), but otherwise, they cooked, ate and drank at home; home-cooked meals tasted far better than the slab of meat and lump of potatoes served in most restaurants.

The past decade has done wonders for dining in Moscow. Now the options seem limitless, not only for traditional Russian fare, but also for sushi, pasta, coffee etc. Clever restaurateurs are inventing newer, more interesting ways to present food (see the boxed text, p131). Likewise, Muscovites are changing the way they eat. They may still take lunch at the *stolovaya*, but it is a modern *stolovaya* with a funky theme or an all-you-can-eat buffet. They go out for business lunches, for after-work drinks, for celebratory occasions and even just for dinner.

This does not mean that Muscovites no longer entertain at home; Russian hospitality has deep roots. If you visit a Muscovite at home, you can expect to be regaled with stories, drowned in vodka, receive many toasts and to offer a few yourself. You can also expect to eat an enormous amount of food off a tiny plate. Once the festivities begin, it is difficult to refuse any food or drink – you will go home stuffed, drunk and happy.

Should you be lucky enough to be invited to a Muscovite's home, bring a gift. Wine, confectionery and cake are all appropriate. Keep in mind that food items are a matter of national pride, so unless you bring something really exotic (eg all the way from home), a Russian brand will be appreciated more. Flowers are also popular, but make certain there's an odd number because even numbers are for funerals.

Staples & Specialities

Breakfast *(zavtrak)* in hotels can range from a large help-yourself buffet to a few pieces of bread with jam and tea. Traditional Russian breakfast favourites include *bliny* and *kasha*

TABLE SCRAPS FROM HEAVEN

According to Georgian legend, God took a supper break while creating the world. He became so involved with his meal that he inadvertently tripped over the high peaks of the Caucasus, spilling his food onto the land below. The land blessed by Heaven's table scraps was Georgia.

Darra Goldstein, from The Georgian Feast

Georgian Food

Moscow is the best place outside the Caucasus to sample the rich, spicy cuisine of Georgia. This fertile region – wedged between East and West – has long been the beneficiary (and victim) of passing merchants and raiders. These influences are evident in Georgian cooking, which shows glimpses of Mediterranean and Middle Eastern flavours.

The truly Georgian elements – the differences – are what make this cuisine so delectable. Most notably, many meat and vegetable dishes use ground walnuts or walnut oil as an integral ingredient, yielding a distinctive rich, nutty flavour. Also characteristic is the mix of spices, *khmeli-suneli,* which combines coriander, garlic, chillies, pepper and savoury with a saffron substitute made from dried marigold petals.

Georgian chefs love to prepare their food over an open flame, and grilled meat is certainly among the most beloved items on any Georgian menu. Traditionally, however, meat was reserved for special occasions, and daily meals revolved around vegetables and greens. The fertile Georgian soil yields green beans, tomatoes, eggplants, mushrooms and garlic, all of which make their delicious way to the table. Herbs such as coriander, dill, parsley and green onions are often served fresh, with no preparation or sauce – a palate-cleansing counterpoint to the other rich dishes. Fruits such as grapes and pomegranates show up not only as dessert, but also as tart complements to roasted meats.

Here are a few tried-and-true Georgian favourites to get you started when faced with an incomprehensible menu:

Basturma Marinated, grilled meat, usually beef or lamb.

Buglama Beef or veal stew with tomatoes, dill and garlic.

Chakhokhbili Slow-cooked chicken with herbs and vegetables.

Chikhirtmi Lemony, chicken soup.

Khachi puri Rich, cheesy bread, made with sour or salty cheese and served hot.

Kharcho Thick, spicy beef soup made from stale bread soaked in yogurt.

Khinkali Dumplings stuffed with lamb or a mixture of beef and pork.

Lavash Flat bread used to wrap cheese, tomatoes, herbs or meat.

Mkhali A vegetable puree with herbs and walnuts, most often made with beets or spinach.

Pakhlava A walnut pastry similar to baklava, but made with sour-cream dough.

Shilaplavi Rice pilaf, often with potatoes.

Tolmas Vegetables (often tomatoes, eggplant or grape leaves) stuffed with beef.

Georgian Wines

Wine is an essential part of any Georgian meal. At all but the most informal occasions, Georgians call on a *tamada,* or toastmaster, to ensure that glasses are raised and drinks topped up throughout the meal.

Georgian vintners utilise a process that is different from their European and New World counterparts. The grapes are fermented together with skins and stems, then stored in clay jugs, resulting in a flavour specific to the Caucasus. Noteworthy Georgian wines:

Kindzmarauli A sickeningly sweet, blood-red wine which, appropriately enough, was the favourite of Stalin.

Mukuzani A rather tannic red; it is the best known and oldest Georgian wine.

Saperavi A dark, full-bodied red produced from grapes of the same name.

Tsinandali Pale and fruity, the most popular Georgian white.

(porridge). Sunday brunch is an institution for many expats and wealthy Russians (see p136 for some of the best brunch options).

Russians prefer to have a fairly heavy early afternoon meal *(obed)* and a lighter evening meal *(uzhin)*. Meals (and menus) are divided into various courses such as *zakuski* (appetisers, often grouped into either hot or cold dishes); first courses (usually soups); second courses (or mains), also called hot courses; and desserts.

APPETISERS

A typical Russian meal starts with a few *zakuski,* which are often the most interesting items on the menu. The fancier *zakuski* rival main courses for price.

Russia is famous for its caviar *(ikra):* the snack of tsars and New Russians. Caviar is no longer the bargain it once was due to declining sturgeon populations and the good old market economy. The best caviar is black (sturgeon) caviar *(ikra chyornaya* or *zirnistaya),* and the much cheaper and saltier option is red (salmon) caviar *(ikra krasnaya* or *ketovaya).* Russians spread it on buttered bread or *bliny* and wash it down with a slug of vodka or a toast of champagne. Vegetarians can try ersatz caviar made entirely from eggplant or other vegetables.

Most restaurant menus offer a truly mind-boggling array of salads *(salat),* including standards such as *ovoshnoy salat* (vegetable salad, which contains tomatoes and cucumbers) and also *stolichny salat* (capital salad, which contains beef, potatoes and eggs in mayonnaise). Even if you read Russian, the salads are usually not identifiable by their often nonsensical names.

COURSES

Rich soups, offered as a first course, may well be the pinnacle of Slavic cooking. There are dozens of varieties, often served with a dollop of sour cream. Most are made using meat stock. The most common soups include borscht, *shchi* (cabbage soup), *okroskha* (cucumber soup with a *kvas* – a beer-like drink – base), and *solyanka* (a tasty meat soup with salty vegetables and hint of lemon).

The second course can be poultry *(ptitsa),* meat *(myaso)* or fish *(ryba),* which might be prepared in a few different ways (see p233). Russian dumplings *(pelmeni)* are usually filled with meat. However, they may also come with potatoes, cabbage or mushrooms. Often you must order a *garnir* (side dish) or you will just get a hunk of meat on your plate. Options here are usually potatoes *(kartoshki),* rice *(ris)* or undefined vegetables *(ovoshchi).* Bread is served with every meal. The Russian black bread (a vitamin-rich sour rye) is delicious and uniquely Russian.

> ## TOP FIVE UNDERRATED RUSSIAN FOODS
>
> - **Beets** Try the classic Russian salad *seld pod shuby,* or 'herring in a fur coat', a colourful conglomeration of herring, beets and carrots.
> - **Kasha** There are dozens of kinds of *kasha* (porridge), but they are all delicious when they are drowned in butter and brown sugar.
> - **Kefir** A sour yogurt drink, often served for breakfast. To adapt the wise words of Mary Poppins – just a spoonful of sugar helps the *kefir* go down.
> - **Pelmeni** Russian comfort food: dumplings stuffed with ground beef and topped with a dollop of sour cream.
> - **Soup** Hot and hearty, nothing beats a steaming bowl of goodness on a cold winter day.

Perhaps most Russians are exhausted or drunk by dessert time, because this is the least imaginative course. The most common options are ice cream *(morozhenoye),* super sweet cake *(tort)* or chocolate *(shokolat).*

DRINKS

'Drinking is the joy of the Rus. We cannot live without it.' With these words Vladimir of Kiev, father of the Russian state, is said to have rejected abstinent Islam on his people's behalf in the 10th century.

The word 'vodka' is the diminutive of the Russian word for water, *voda,* so it means something like 'a wee drop'. Russians sometimes drink vodka in moderation, but more often they tip it down in swift shots, followed by a pickle.

In Moscow, the Kristall distillery is considered to produce the finest vodka. Yuri Dolgoruki is the top of the line, while Zolotoe Koltso (Golden Ring) and Moskovskaya are also high-quality vodkas. Another favourite of the 'Vodkaphiles' Club' is Klassik. Its unique bottle is an authentic replica of a 300-year-old traditional style. Another brand gaining popularity is Smirnovskaya vodka, distilled in Chernogolovka, a small town not far from Moscow.

Beer has recently overtaken vodka as Russia's most popular alcoholic drink. The market leader is Baltika, a Scandinavian joint-venture with Russian management, based in St Petersburg. Baltika makes no less than nine excellent brews, fittingly labelled '1' to '9'. Tinkoff (see p135) is a national chain of microbreweries that has begun bottling its potent brews for sale in shops.

Russians drink sparkling wine, or *Sovietskoe shampanskoe*, to toast special occasions and to sip during intermission at the theatre. It tends to be sickeningly sweet, so look for the label that says *sukhoe* (dry).

Kvas is a mildly alcoholic, fermented, rye-bread water. Cool and refreshing, it is a popular summer drink that tastes something like ginger beer. In the olden days it was dispensed on the street from big, wheeled tanks. Patrons would bring their own bottles or plastic bags and fill up. The *kvas* truck is a rare sight these days, but this cool, tasty treat is still available from Russian restaurants.

TOP FIVE COOKBOOKS

- *Please, To the Table* (Anya Von Bremzen) is a tried and true authority on Russian cooking. Learn to make *bliny* (and just about every other Russian dish) like the babushkas.
- *Tastes and Tales from Russia* (Alla Danishevsky) presents each recipe accompanied by a folktale – a great way to introduce children to Russian cooking.
- *The Georgian Feast* (Darra Goldstein) is one of the few English-language cookbooks focusing on this spicy Caucasian cuisine.
- *A Year of Russian Feasts* (Catherine Cheremeteff Jones), part cookbook and part travelogue, describes the author's experiences with Russian traditions and customs, culinary celebrations and day-to-day life.
- *Classic Russian Cooking: A Gift to Young Housewives* (Elena Molokhovets) is more of a history lesson than a recipe book; this tome is based on the most popular cookbook from the 19th century.

FASHION

On first impression, conspicuous consumption seems to be the theme of Russian fashionistas (see the boxed text, opposite). Connoisseurs argue, however, that *la mode* in Moscow is becoming more sophisticated, creatively mixing well-known Western brands with up-and-coming local designers.

Russian models have certainly taken the fashion world by storm, with beauties such as Natalya Vodianova and Evgenia Volodina dominating the pages of *Vogue* and *Elle*. Moscow designers are also attracting increasing attention, both at home and abroad. Names to look out for include the controversial Yegor Zaitsev, son of the famed Slava Zaitsev and celebrated designer in his own rite. Igor Chapurin has earned international recognition, as well as winning the award for best women's-wear designer at the First Russian and Fashion Style Awards in 2005.

Since 2002, Moscow has hosted two major fashion events: Russian Fashion Week (see p10) and the smaller Fashion Week in Moscow, held in October.

Such high fashion is not so interesting to the average Ivan or Tatiana on the street, though. These days, most Russians shop at the same stores and wear the same clothes as their counterparts in the West: blue jeans, business suits, or anything in between. Moscow's many shopping centres are filled with the same stores that you might find anywhere in Europe.

Only winter differentiates Russian style, bringing out the best or the worst of it, depending on your perspective. Fur is still the most effective and most coveted way to stay warm. Some advice from a local fashion connoisseur: 'your protests that fur is cruel are likely to be met by blank stares and an uncomfortable shifting of feet. Don't come in winter if this offends you.'

PEDICURES, PANTIES & POODLES Alan & Julia Thompson

Olga and Masha, two New Russian women, meet at a party, clutching identical Prada handbags.

'Paris, US$300,' Olga confidently reports.

'Moscow, US$500!' Masha trumps.

This popular anecdote chides the perversely status-conscious New Russians, whose social world is awash with exclusive designer labels and conspicuous price tags. Russia's newly rich have abandoned the austerity of the old Soviet regime and become adoring patrons of Europe's fashion houses. So now Moscow boasts boutiques for Louis Vuitton, Jimmy Choo, Hermes, Cartier, Dior, Tiffany and more. In fact, Moscow's Armani store does more business than any other in the world, apart from Tokyo.

To view Moscow's show ponies in their natural habitat, check out Tretyakovsky proezd (p155). Here, the high fashionistas gather in full regalia. It is not always a pretty sight. The desire to coordinate often goes to extremes, even if it means head-to-toe Burberry plaid. Manicures, pedicures and lipstick, brassiers, panties and high heels, are all made to match as if by Milan-mandate. Keeping up with the Hiltons, temperamental lapdogs – sometimes supporting designer poodle-wear – have become an accessory essential.

And what of the New Russian man? He still lags somewhat behind his girlfriend. Taking his fashion cues from AC/DC, the New Russian man is 'Back in Black': black suit, black shoes, black Hermes tie, black belt, black sunglasses. Look for the Cartier watch to distinguish the New Russian man from ordinary security guards and doorman, for whom black is also the colour of choice.

SPORT

Russia's international reputation in sport is well founded, with athletes earning international fame and glory for their success in ice hockey, basketball, gymnastics and figure skating.

Anna Kournikova attracted the world's attention to Russian tennis, even though she became better known for her photogenic legs than her ripping backhand. More recently, Wimbledon champion Maria Sharapova leads a cohort of young Russians who currently figure highly in the women's game. Wimbledon champ Marat Safin remains one of the most explosive stars on the men's circuit. The Kremlin Cup is an international tennis tournament held in Moscow every year (see p11). The lesser-known women's tournament, the Federation Cup, attracted big names such as Venus Williams and Anastasia Myskina in 2005.

The most popular spectator sport in Russia is football (soccer), and five Moscow teams play in Russia's premier league (Vysshaya Liga). Currently, football is enjoying a boom pumped up by large sponsorship deals with Russian big business. Lukoil has thrown its considerable financial weight behind Russia's most successful club, Spartak, a Moscow team that has won the Russian premier league every year since 1996. Other teams in the 16-strong league to watch out for are the Moscow-based Lokomotiv, TsSKA (2005 UEFA Cup winners), Torpedo and Dinamo. These days, though, Russia's most famous football club is 'Chel-sky', billionaire Roman Abramovich's highly successful entry in the English premier league.

Despite (or maybe because of) its popularity, running a soccer club in Russia has become a risky business – in the post Soviet-era, seven soccer officials have been the targets of assassination attempts. Corruption is believed to be rife in the clubs with match fixing a particular problem.

Popular winter sports include ice hockey and basketball. Both of these sports lose many of their best players to the American professional leagues. Nonetheless, the top Moscow basketball team, TsSKA, is champion of the Russian league and it also does well in the European league.

In 2005 the National Hockey League (in North America) cancelled its season when players and management were unable to resolve a labour dispute. As a result, 72 players (many of them Russian) came to play in the Russian *super liga* – a windfall to have so many of the world's best ice-hockey players. Moscow hosts three teams, including champions Dinamo and their archrivals Spartak.

MEDIA

Newspapers

Though a far cry from the one-note news days of the Soviet era, most of Russia's biggest papers are, to some degree, mouthpieces for the various powerful bodies that own them, be they political parties or rich businessmen. The public, long used to reading between the lines, know how to take a bit from here, a bit from there, and construct a truth that's somewhere in between.

The most popular Russian dailies are *Izvestia, Kommersant* and *Komsomolskaya Pravda.* The government's official newspaper is the *Rossiyskaya Gazeta,* while the tabloids are represented by *Moskovsky Komsomolets Versiya* and *Sovershenno Sekretno.*

The weekly *Argumenty I Fakty* is one of the most popular papers in the country, selling over 30 million copies a week. Reputed to be relatively free from outside influences, it covers politics, economics and the social scene.

Novaya Gazeta is a liberal rag, well known for its column by Russia's most famous investigative reporter, Anna Politkovskaya. She gained notoriety after playing an active role in negotiations with Chechen rebels during the 2002 Nord-Ost crisis in Moscow (see p36). She claims that later attempts to act as a neutral go-between got her poisoned by Kremlin thugs. Her controversial book, *Putin's Russia,* was published in the UK in 2004.

Television

He who controls the TV, controls the country – and no-one understands this better than President Putin. In 2000 his administration conducted a heavy-handed legal attack on the owners of NTV, a channel that came closer than others to matching the professional, unbiased news standards more associated with the West (see the boxed text, below). Now, in terms of independent journalism, there's little to distinguish NTV from the state-owned channels.

Not that Russian TV is managed by some Soviet-styled spooks. In fact the heads of the main state channels – Channel 1 and Rossiya – were among those young journalists who

THE VOICE OF MOSCOW *Leonid Ragozin*

A Soviet verse says that the quiet light of the Kremlin's ruby stars can reach the furthest corners of the country – a metaphor that is sweet for some Russians and horrible for others. But there is another tower in Moscow whose emanations reach almost every Russian home – very literally – via a complicated network of terrestrial installations and satellites. It is the Ostankino TV tower.

Putin's unexpected accession to the highest post in Russia was accompanied by a dramatic TV war. The country's most-watched channel, ORT, then controlled by oligarch Boris Berezovsky, pounded Putin's potential competitors with accusations of corruption and incompetence. The main evening news bulletin was followed by a 10-minute comment by notorious journalist Mikhail Leontyev, whose wicked irony crossed all conceivable ethical borders.

The NTV channel owned by another oligarch, Vladimir Gusinsky, answered with unfounded allegations that Putin's security forces might be behind terrorist attacks in Moscow and offered no less jaw-dropping satire. One political puppet show restaged Ernst Hoffmann's fairy tale *Klein Zaches,* in which a fairy takes pity on a boy born a freak, physically and mentally. She makes the whole town believe that the boy is a genius of staggering beauty and infinite talents. The Zaches puppet looked very much like Putin, and the fairy closely resembled Berezovsky.

Soon after Putin became the president, NTV's main creditor, the state-owned gas monopoly Gazprom, launched a legal crusade against the channel culminating in its full takeover and a change of management. Gusinsky was forced into exile. Half of NTV's journalists left the channel and were taken on board by TVS. This new channel was run by none other than Berezovsky – a fairy now rather disenchanted with and unloved by the product of his own magic.

But now the magic wand was in someone else's hands. Very soon the oil giant Lukoil came up with a rather dubious legal suit and – surprise, surprise – forced TVS into oblivion. Berezovsky turned into another fugitive-oligarch.

So what are the Ostankino emanations telling people now? They say there is no worse evil than an orange revolution, that human rights and freedom of speech are nice words with little meaning, that Russia is regaining its former strength, but those (unnamed, but certainly westward) forces who don't want to reckon with it, are waging a campaign of political sabotage.

gave Russian audiences a taste of editorial freedom in the 1990s. Many faces on the screen are still the same, but news and analysis are increasingly transforming into ideological brainwashing. Only RenTV, a channel owned by the state power grid, has coverage that somewhat deviates from the party line.

LANGUAGE

In prerevolutionary Russia, France was considered the epitome of high culture, and this was reflected in cuisine, music and language. Indeed, among the well-educated upper classes, French was spoken more commonly than Russian.

All this changed in the 20th century, when the language of the people – solid, working-class Russians – became the language of the state. Western influences were generally frowned upon, in any case, and French in particular was derided for its classist pretences. In Russia, one spoke Russian. Indeed, in Ukraine, Belarus, Georgia etc, one also spoke Russian. Muscovites could travel far and wide from their capital, and never leave the boundaries of their Russian-speaking region.

TOP FIVE QUESTIONS TO ANSWER 'CHUT-CHUT'

If you learn only one phrase in Russian, let it be *chut-chut* (pronounced 'choot-choot'), meaning 'a little bit'. Here are just a few questions you are sure to field, and you will be grateful you know the appropriate response:

- *Vy gavariti pa-russky?* Do you speak Russian?
- *Vam nravitsa svyokla?* Do you like beets?
- *Skol'ka u vas stoit kvartira/mashina/visshe abrazavanie?* How much does a flat/car/higher education cost?
- *Nu, tam luchshe?* So, is it better 'over there' (meaning wherever you are from)?
- *Davai vypim vodku!* Let's drink vodka!

The legacy of this is that today everyone in Moscow speaks Russian. You can expect English to be spoken only at the finest hotels and restaurants and at a few hostels and agencies that cater to international backpacker types. The city is becoming a bit more foreigner-friendly, with some signs in Roman script and menus and maps in English at major tourist attractions. But you are advised to learn – at least – the Cyrillic alphabet and a few friendly phrases, before setting out on your own (see p230).

ECONOMY & COSTS

Experts estimate that the average Muscovite earns about R16,800 a month, far in excess of the average of R6020 earned elsewhere in the country. However, this figure is misleading, as 70% of the population earns less than the average. Large portions of people are on fixed wages and pensions that may not top R5000 a month.

Moscow is one of the most expensive cities in the world, up there with London and Hong Kong. Expect to pay at least R600 a head for a meal in a restaurant. If you self-cater or dine at cafeterias, you can probably get by on R500 a day for meals.

The logo of the Nikulin Circus (p149)

Prices for lodging are also high, as the city has a shortage of comfortable, cheap hotels. With a few exceptions, the cheapest accommodation is usually not less than R1200 per day. Expect to pay at least R3000 for a double room in a decent three-star hotel (for suggestions see p164). Prices for top-end hotels start at R5000 and go all the way up.

Although dual pricing for hotels and transport tickets no longer exits, as a foreigner in Russia you'll still often find yourself paying more than a Russian for museums. The mark-up for foreigners is extreme – often as much as 10 times the price that Russians pay (although you may be able to avoid it if you have student identification). Take heart that the extra money you shell out is desperately needed to protect the very works of art and artefacts you've come to see.

HOW MUCH?

Admission to the Kremlin R350

All-you-can-eat sushi R600

Bottle of Baltika beer R30

Cappuccino R60

Hard Rock Cafe Moscow T-shirt R570

Litre of bottled water R15-30

Litre of petrol R16-18

One hour online R60

Souvenir matryoshka doll R500

Take-away bliny R20

Two-room flat (one month) US$1200

GOVERNMENT & POLITICS

In December 1993, two years after the collapse of the Soviet Union, Russia finally adopted a new constitution. The circumstances of its enactment were less than desirable. Russia's early transition away from Communist Party rule was marked by power conflicts between the president, Boris Yeltsin, and parliament, as well as between central and regional governments.

In the autumn of 1993, the contest turned violent, when Boris Yeltsin ordered the defiant parliament to be shut down. Under siege in their offices in Russia's White House (p86), Yeltsin's left-wing opponents issued a nationwide summons for people to take to the streets in protest. But their call to arms went unheeded, and their resistance was bombarded into submission. The president had prevailed.

The resultant 1993 Constitution created a strong executive system. The president is charged with selecting the prime minister and forming the government, and he is entitled to bypass the legislature and rule by executive decree if deemed necessary. Moreover, the president possesses access to a wide array of bureaucratic, economic and coercive resources with few restraints. President Yeltsin's leadership style was to broker deals with his political rivals, using force only in exceptional cases. President Putin, on the other hand, has been more willing to use the coercive powers inherent in the office to cower his would-be opponents.

The parliament, or Federal Assembly, contains a lower house, or Duma (p65), based on popular representation, and an upper house, or Senate (p55), based on regional representation. Despite its limited powers, the parliament does not act as a mere rubber stamp. Under the polarising and unpredictable Yeltsin, the Duma made the most of its mandate, opposing the president's policies and organising impeachment inquiries. But under the popular and determined Putin, the legislature has become a more compliant branch, passing the president's initiatives while fearing his retribution.

The Constitution also established a federal system composed of 89 territorial subjects, including the city of Moscow. During Yeltsin's tenure, Russia's regions enjoyed greater autonomy over local political and economic affairs. But this trend was reversed under Putin; after a brief experiment with direct elections, the president has reassumed the right to appoint and dismiss regional governors.

The 1993 Constitution created the institutional framework of a democratic system, but it also contained the seeds of creeping authoritarianism. Since the constitution's inception, the unchecked powers of the executive have been increasingly deployed to the detriment of Russian democracy. Press freedoms, civil society and electoral competition have all been significantly constrained. Meanwhile, corruption, coercion and incompetence contaminate the public sector. As a result, Russia has evolved into a kind of illiberal democracy.

Moscow reflects these larger developments of Russian politics. The capital has known but one boss since 1992, Yury Luzhkov. The sometimes populist, sometimes nationalist, but always opportunist mayor has built a juggernaut political machine that exemplifies the marriage of power and money in the New Russia. Luzhkov's fiefdom includes a vast army of regulators, tax collectors, prosecutors, litigators, realtors and PR specialists, who make sure that nobody takes a slice of the Moscow pie without paying for it.

TOP FIVE BARGAINS

For the thrifty, a few bargains remain in Moscow. Also see the boxed text, p63.

- **Business lunch** (p120) Three filling courses usually cost around R200.
- **Classical performing arts** (p145) The cheapest tickets are often as little as R100, even at major venues such as the Bolshoi.
- **Moscow Times** (p223) A daily dose of news, plus a weekly entertainment section that's chock full of fun, all for free.
- **Free Internet access** (p221) With purchase of food or drink at the stylish Phlegmatic Dog.
- **Transport** (p214) Ride the metro for a mere R13, or take a taxi across town for R150 or less.

ENVIRONMENT

CLIMATE

Moscow's continental climate enjoys five seasons: spring, summer, autumn, winter – and Russian winter. The deepest, darkest part of winter is undeniably cold, but if you are prepared, it can be an adventure. Furs and vodka keep people warm, and snow-covered landscapes are picturesque. A solid snow pack covers the ground from November to March. The lowest recorded temperature is -42°C, although it's normally more like -10°C for weeks on end. Occasional southerly winds can raise the temperature briefly to a balmy 0°C. Daylight hours during winter are very few.

During the spring thaw – late March and early April – everything turns to mud and slush. Summer comes fast in June, and temperatures are comfortable until well into September. The highest recorded temperature is 39°C, although on a humid August day you'll swear it's hotter than that. July and August are the warmest, wettest months.

GREEN MOSCOW

'Green Moscow' is taken very literally in the Russian capital, where parks, forests and gardens cover almost one third of the area. This translates into 18 sq metres of green space per person – impressive, compared to the average of 7 sq metres in other same-sized capitals.

Moscow's major environmental problem is air and noise pollution from industrial and private sources. The increase in road traffic exacerbates both problems, and air quality also suffers from the widespread use of leaded fuels and uncontrolled emissions by vehicles.

In 1994 Moscow implemented the Ecological Improvement Plan, which included measures such as automobile inspections and industrial regulations. The city administration claims that a steady decrease in air pollution has resulted, although concrete figures are not available. Since 1999, the city has converted 1000 buses and other municipal vehicles to alternative, low-emission energy sources. In 2002 the city introduced a plan for more stringent requirements for petrol and diesel emissions (meeting EU standards by 2010). A related measure is to replace the entire fleet of city vehicles in the next 10 to 15 years. The estimated benefit is a 50% reduction in emissions!

In preparation for its bid for the 2012 Olympics, Moscow added some additional, rather vague plans to its list of environmental priorities. They involved introducing industrial regulations to reduce airborne contaminants and to improve waste management. That the city administration recognises the importance of these measures is encouraging. How this plan will be implemented – in light of the unsuccessful Olympic bid – remains to be seen.

URBAN PLANNING & DEVELOPMENT

Post-Soviet Moscow has been a hotbed of development. Skyscrapers and steeples are changing the city skyline; the metro is expanding in all directions; and office buildings, luxury hotels and shopping centres are going up all over the city. Entire neighbourhoods – once dominated by nondescript Soviet blocks – are now bustling urban centres with their own markets, shops and characters.

The latest target for intensive urban development is the area around Krasnaya Presnya Park and the World Trade Centre (see p84 for details). Mayor Luzhkov has dubbed this neighbourhood 'Moscow City' and slated it as the future location of the city administration. A new mini metro line is in the works, with stops at the World Trade Centre (Mezhdunarodnaya) and in the heart of the new development (Delovoy Tsentr). Developers have followed suit, building shiny glass and metal buildings on either side of the Moscow River and a cool pedestrian bridge connecting them. The skyscrapers are hardly even built, but they are already being claimed by multinational corporations and Russian enterprises for their offices.

Such development is an exciting sign of the city's sense of prosperity and possibility. It is also a source of contention among architects, historians and other critics, who claim that Moscow is losing its architectural heritage.

The nonprofit group, Moscow Architectural Preservation Society (MAPS), estimates that more than 400 buildings have been razed in the past decade, including as many as 60 buildings of historical interest. The latter are supposed to be protected by federal law, but critics claim that the laws are useless in the face of corruption and cash.

Activists go so far as to compare Luzhkov to Stalin, when it comes to development, claiming that the city has lost more buildings during the contemporary period than any time since the 1930s. That the mayor's wife is a prominent developer who has made millions from city contracts only adds fuel to their fire.

Architects and historians are most distressed about the city's tendency to tear down and rebuild, instead of preserve. Many buildings might look old, but they are mere replicas, as for example along ulitsa Arbat (see p87). Or, developers maintain the historic façade, but destroy the building behind it, such as the Rimsky-Korsakov complex where Café Pushkin is located. As one critic observed, 'It is…like the Bolsheviks in the 1920s, but at least they had an ideal for the city.'

TOP FIVE CONTROVERSIAL RECONSTRUCTION PROJECTS

- **Detsky Mir** (p155) Spared in the 1990s, but now slated for 'renovation' in honour of its upcoming jubilee.
- **Hotel Moskva** (p66) Critics wonder why it's necessary to destroy a historic building with architectural quirks to create a brand new building with the same architectural quirks.
- **Krasny Oktyabr** (p112) Soon to become luxury condominiums.
- **Manezh Exhibition Centre** (p65) Recent reconstruction was prompted by a fire – widely believed to be arson.
- **Rimsky-Korsakov complex** (p112) A mere façade of the historic building it once was.

Arts & Architecture ∎

Arts & Architecture

Moscow has always been known for the richness of its culture, ranging from the classic to the progressive. Whether a Tchaikovsky opera or an Ostrovsky drama, the classical performing arts in Moscow are among the best – and cheapest – in the world. The Tretyakov Gallery and Pushkin Fine Arts Museum house internationally famous collections of Russian and impressionist art.

Of course, New Russia comes with new forms of art and entertainment. This bohemian side of Moscow – be it a beatnik band at an underground club, or an avant-garde exhibit at the Museum of Modern Art – provides a glimpse of Russia's future. Sometimes intellectual and inspiring, sometimes debauched and depraved, it is *always* eye-opening.

BALLET

First brought to Russia under Tsar Alexis Mikhailovich in the 17th century, ballet in Russia evolved as an offshoot of French dance combined with Russian folk and peasant dance techniques. Moscow's Bolshoi Theatre (p146) dates from 1776. Under the Soviets ballet was treated as a natural resource. Its highly privileged status allowed ballet companies to perform lavish productions and have no-expense-spared star searches.

At the Bolshoi, Yury Grigorovich emerged in the 1960s as a bright new choreographer, with productions of *Spartacus, Ivan the Terrible* and other successes. Grigorovich directed the company for over 30 years, but not without controversy. In the late 1980s, he came to loggerheads with some of his leading dancers. Stars such as Maya Plisetskaya, Ekaterina Maximova and Vladimir Vasiliev resigned, accusing him of being 'brutal' and 'Stalinist'. With encouragement from President Yeltsin, Grigorovich finally resigned in 1995, prompting his loyal dancers to stage the Bolshoi's first-ever strike.

Under artistic director Vladimir Vasiliev, the Bolshoi commenced a turnaround. During the years of his stewardship, productions included *Swan Lake* and *Giselle*, starring dancers such as Nina Anaiashvili, Sergei Filin and Svetlana Lunkina. Reviews were initially positive, but trouble was brewing. Politics and finances made Vasiliev's task near impossible, and he soon came under fire for mismanagement.

A power struggle ensued, with the ever-present Yury Grigorovich playing a leading role. Finally, in 2004, the rising star Alexey Ratmansky was appointed artistic director. Born in 1968 in Ukraine, Ratmansky is young but accomplished. Of his more than 20 ballets, *Dreams of Japan* was awarded a prestigious Golden Mask award in 1998. Yury Grigorovich continues to play an active role in Moscow's ballet scene. The Bolshoi often performs his classic compositions. In 2005 he was president of the jury for the 10th Annual International Competition of Ballet Artists. The Bolshoi's brightest star is currently Maria Alexandrova.

The Bolshoi is Moscow's most celebrated (and therefore most political) ballet company. But other dance companies in Moscow have equally talented dancers and directors. Both the Moscow Classical Ballet Theatre and the Stanislavsky & Nemirovich-Danchenko Musical Theatre (p147) stage excellent performances of the Russian classics.

The New Ballet (p146), directed by Aida Chernova and Sergei Starukhin, stages a completely different kind of dance. Dubbed 'plastic ballet', it combines dance with pantomime and drama. Productions vary widely, incorporating elements such as folk tales, poetry and improvised jazz. This bizarre, playful performance art is a refreshing addition to Moscow's dance scene.

MUSIC

The classics never go out of style. This is certainly true for music in Moscow, where Mussorgsky, Stravinsky and especially Tchaikovsky still feature in concert halls on an almost-daily basis. The atmosphere in these places is a little stuffy, but the musicianship is first-rate and the compositions are timeless. Music in Moscow takes many forms, however. And these days, Western rock, blues and jazz are also ubiquitous in the capital. Russified versions of these popular genres can be heard in pubs and clubs all over Moscow.

CLASSICAL

As the cultural heart of Russia, Moscow was a natural draw for generations of composers. Its rich cultural life drew talent from throughout Russia, even during the years in which St Petersburg was the Russian capital.

The defining period of Russian classical music was from the 1860s to 1900. As Russian composers (and painters and writers) struggled to find a national identity, several influential schools formed, from which some of Russia's most famous composers and finest music emerged. The so-called Group of Five, which included Modest Mussorgsky (1839–81) and Nikolai Rimsky-Korsakov (1844–1908), believed that a radical departure was necessary, and they looked to *byliny* (folk music) for themes. Mussorgsky penned *Pictures at an Exhibition* and the opera, *Boris Gudunov*; Rimsky-Korsakov is best known for *Scheherazade*.

Pyotr Tchaikovsky (1840–93) also embraced Russian folklore and music, as well as the disciplines of Western European composers. Tchaikovsky is widely regarded as the father of Russian national composers. His output, including the magnificent *1812 Overture;* his concertos and symphonies; the ballets *Swan Lake, Sleeping Beauty* and *The Nutcracker;* and his opera *Yevgeny Onegin* are among the world's most popular classical works. They are certainly the shows that are staged most often at the Bolshoi and other theatres around Moscow (see p145).

Following in Tchaikovsky's romantic footsteps was Sergei Rachmaninov (1873–1943) and the innovative Igor Stravinsky (1882–1971). Both fled Russia after the revolution. Stravinsky's *The Rite of Spring* – which created a furore at its first performance in Paris – and *The Firebird* were influenced by Russian folk music. Sergei Prokofiev (1891–1953), who also left Soviet Russia but returned in 1934, wrote the scores for Eisenstein's films *Alexander Nevsky* and *Ivan the Terrible,* the ballet *Romeo and Juliet,* and *Peter and the Wolf,* so beloved by music teachers of young children. His work, however, was condemned for 'formalism' towards the end of his life.

Similarly, the beliefs of Dmitry Shostakovich (1906–75) led to him being alternately

Performers at an underground club

praised and condemned by the Soviet government. He wrote brooding, bizarrely dissonant works, as well as accessible traditional classical music. After official condemnation by Stalin, Shostakovich's *7th Symphony – the Leningrad* – brought him honour and international standing when it was performed by the Leningrad Philharmonic during the Siege of Leningrad. The authorities changed their minds again and banned his anti-Soviet music in 1948, then 'rehabilitated' him after Stalin's death.

Classical opera was performed regularly during the Soviet period, and continues to be popular. In March 2005 the Bolshoi premiered *Rosenthal's Children,* with music by Leonid Desyatnikov and words by Vladimir Sorokin, its first new opera in 26 years, to a hail of protests over its alleged pornographic plot (see the boxed text, p32). More often, though, Moscow theatres and performance halls (see p145) feature classics from the 19th and 20th centuries that Russians know and love.

ROCK

Russian music is not all about classical composers. Ever since the 'bourgeois' Beatles filtered through in the 1960s, Russians both young and old have been keen to sign up for the pop revolution. Starved of decent equipment and the chance to record or perform to big audiences, Russian rock groups initially developed underground. By the 1970s – the Soviet hippy era – the music had developed a huge following among the disaffected, distrustful youth. Although bands initially imitated their Western counterparts, by the 1980s a home-grown sound was emerging.

Boris Grebenshikov and his band Akvarium (Aquarium) from Yekaterinburg caused a sensation wherever they performed; Grebenshikov's folk rock and introspective lyrics became the emotional cry of a generation. At first, all music was circulated by illegal tapes known as *magizdat,* passed from listener to listener; concerts were held, if at all, in remote halls in city suburbs, and even to attend them could be risky.

The god of Russian rock was Viktor Tsoy, originally from Kazakhstan. His group Kino was the stuff of legends. A few appearances in kung-fu-type flicks helped make Tsoy the 'King of Cool', and his early death in a 1990 car crash ensured the legend a long shelf life. To this day, fans gather on the anniversary of his death (August 15) and play his music.

Many contemporary favourites on the Russian rock scene have been playing together since the early days. One of the most notable Moscow bands is Mumi-Troll, led by the literate, androgynous Ilya Lagushenko. After 25 years, the band continues to produce innovative stuff. Their 2005 album, *Mergers & Acquisitions,* provides a sharp commentary on contemporary Russian culture.

The pseudo-lesbian performance of girl duo Tatu at the 2003 Eurovision Song Contest helped alert international listeners that Russian pop today is as good (or bad, depending on your point of view) as the rest of the world's. Elena Kiper is the songwriter behind some of Tatu's bigger hits, but she has joined Oleg Borshevsky to form the group Nichya. The style is certainly similar, but appeals to a more mature audience.

Gaining worldwide renown is B-2, whose members, Shura and Leva, now reside in Australia. In 2005 this 'post-punk' duo appeared on Red Square alongside the Pet Shop Boys at Live-8 Moscow. The goth rocker Linda, a hometown favourite, also used the international event to show off her sound, which is an eclectic blend of world and dance music.

RUSSKY ROCK *Kathleen Pullum*

Huge stadium shows and colossal festivals have become pillars of Russian rock culture, with the largest rock events of the year enticing fans to relax with a few beers, wreak some havoc and rock out with 50,000 of their closest friends. The most prominent festivals take place in the summer months, mostly due to weather constraints.

Krylya (www.krylya.ru), or 'Wings', is generally held the last weekend of July. This festival gained notoriety when it was targeted by two Chechen female suicide bombers in 2003. (The women were stopped by security but ended up killing a score of people.) After a brief relocation to Luzhniki Stadium, where security could be better monitored, the festival returned to the Tushino airfield outside of Moscow in 2005. The two-day event draws tens of thousands of visitors and several dozen bands from Russia and the Commonwealth of Independent States (CIS). Performers in 2005 included veterans Chaif and Spleen and current stars Zemfira and Umaturman.

The granddaddy of Russian rock festivals, however, is **Nashestviye** (www.nashestvie.nashe.ru), which is hosted by Russian rock radio station Nashe (meaning 'Ours') in the first or second week of August. Nashe broadcasts all over Russia, and is widely considered *the* forum where emerging Russian musicians get their start. Nashestviye is a three-day festival that expands every year. In 2005 the event added more performers and three stages, allowing different subcategories in Russian rock to emerge. Alternative rock, Russian reggae, 'wild music' and others are all grouped together in the concert schedule. Among a list of nearly 100 performers, from old legends to new faces, 2005 highlights included Russian punk-styled, notoriously naughty Leningrad – barred by Moscow's mayor from performing in the capital city – along with B-2, Mumi-Troll, Billy's Band, Two Siberians and many more well-known acts. Nashestviye is held at Emmaus, near Tver, accessible by *elektrichka* (suburban train). Camping on the festival grounds for the duration will cost you just R500.

Kathleen is the editor-in-chief of the magazine, element

Switch on Russian MTV, and you'll see local versions of boy bands and disco divas doing their sometimes desultory, sometimes foot-tapping stuff. Meanwhile, Moscow clubs (p140) are filled with garage bands, new wave, punk, hard rock and many Beatles cover bands.

LITERATURE

Although Russian writers really only got going in the 19th century, they have wasted little time in establishing themselves a prime place in the cannon of world literature, producing renowned classics in the fields of poetry, plays and novels. Most of the big names of the

MOSCOW FICTION

- *Anna Karenina* (Leo Tolstoy) tells of the tragedy of a woman who violates the rigid sexual code of her time, and offers a legitimate alternative for readers who don't have time for *War & Peace*. Tolstoy represents a pinnacle of world literature, and many of his novels are set at least partly in Moscow.
- *Dead Souls* (Nikolai Gogol) is a biting satire that gives a special, cynical insight into 19th-century provincial Russia. Gogol has created some of Russian literature's most memorable characters, and the absurd Pavel Ivanovich Chichikov is no exception. This novel was written – and subsequently thrown into the fire – in Gogol's tiny Moscow flat.
- *A Hero of Our Time* (Mikhail Lermontov) is a short but important novel set in the Caucasus, though the author lived in Moscow. Its cynical antihero, Pechorin, is an indirect comment on the political climate of the times.
- *The Twelve* (Alexander Blok) is pretty much a love letter to Lenin. Ironically, Blok later grew deeply disenchanted with the revolution, consequently fell out of favour and died a sad, lonely poet. In one of his last letters, he wrote, 'She did devour me, lousy, snuffling dear Mother Russia, like a sow devouring her piglet.'
- *The Ordeal* (Alexey Tolstoy) is a trilogy that takes place during the revolution and civil war. Alexey, not to be confused with his more famous ancestor, was one of the few Soviet authors who managed to produce serious literary work without being censored.
- *Dr Zhivago* (Boris Pasternak) recounts the romantic tale of a doctor who is separated from his lover by the events of the revolution. The author was not allowed to accept the Nobel Prize that was awarded to this dramatic novel, which was written at his dacha outside of Moscow.
- *The Master and Margarita* (Mikhail Bulgakov) has the Devil turn up in Moscow to cause all manner of anarchy and make idiots of the system and its lackeys. This darkly comic novel is the most telling fiction to come out of the Soviet Union.
- *Children of the Arbat* (Anatoly Rybakov) is based on the author's own experiences as an idealistic youth on the eve of the Great Purges. This tragic novel paints a vivid portrait of 1930s Russia. It was written in the 1960s, but published only in 1987.
- *Moscow To the End of the Line* (Venedict Erofeev), written in 1970, is a novel that recounts a drunken man's train trip to visit his lover and child on the outskirts of the capital. As the journey progresses, the tale becomes darker and more hallucinogenic. *Moscow Stations* is another bleakly funny novella recounting alcohol-induced adventures.
- *On the Golden Porch* (Tatyana Tolstaya) is a collection of short stories focusing on the domestic life of regular people – big souls in little flats – in 1990s Moscow. Tolstaya, another distant descendent of Leo, was one of the first post-Soviet writers to earn international attention.
- *The Slynx* (Tatyana Tolstaya), the celebrated author's earlier, lesser-known novel, is set in postnuclear-war Moscow that seems strangely similar to Moscow in the 1990s. In this dystopia, an uneducated scribe learns enough history to start his own revolution.
- *Homo Zapiens* (Viktor Pelevin) is the latest novel from this darkly comic author, and tells the tale of a literature student who takes a job as a copyrighter for New Russian gangsters, offering a hilarious commentary on contemporary Russia. Pelevin won the 1993 Russian 'Little Booker' Prize for short stories.
- *Russian Beauty* (Victor Erofeev) tells the tale of a wily beauty from the provinces who sleeps her way to the top of the Moscow social scene. She finds herself pregnant just about the same time she finds God. Caustically funny and overtly bawdy, this bestseller in Russia has been translated into 27 languages.
- *The Winter Queen* (Boris Akunin) is one in the series of popular detective novels featuring the foppish Erast Fandorin as a member of the 19th-century Moscow police force. Several of these are now being made into movies (p33).
- *White on Black* (Ruben Gallego) is an autobiographical account of surviving the bleak, cruel Soviet orphanage system. Gallego's exquisitely written memoir was the 2003 Russian Booker Prize winner.

Golden Age of Russian literature passed through Moscow at one time or another, and you can visit museums dedicated to Alexander Pushkin (p89 and p92), Leo Tolstoy (p95 and p93), Fyodor Dostoevsky (p80) and Mikhail Lermontov (p88) in the capital. For a walk through Moscow's literary heritage, follow the Literary Sojourn on p115.

Spanning from the end of the 19th century up until the early 1930s, the Silver Age of Russian literature produced additional towering talents. This period corresponded with the rise of the symbolist movement, represented in Moscow by poet Alexander Blok (1880–1921). Vladimir Mayakovsky (1893–1930) – practically the revolution's official bard – also has a museum (p75) dedicated to his memory. Both of these poets were praised by the Bolsheviks as examples of established writers who had seen the light, yet both of their lives ended in disillusionment and tragedy.

In 1932 the Communist Party officially demanded socialist realism from art and literature. This meant 'concrete representation of reality in its revolutionary development…in accordance with…ideological training of the workers in the spirit of Socialism'. Henceforth artists and writers had the all but impossible task of conveying the Party's messages, as well as not falling foul of Stalin's notoriously fickle tastes.

The Soviet Union's most celebrated writers – the likes of Boris Pasternak (1890–1960) and Mikhail Bulgakov (1890–1940) – were silenced in their own country, while their works received international acclaim. Many other accounts of Soviet life were printed in *samizdat* (underground) publications, secretly circulated among the literary community. Now famous novels such as Rybakov's *Children of the Arbat* were published in Russia only with the loosening of censorship under *glasnost*.

Recent years have seen a flowering of Russian publishing, and the traditional Russian love of books seems as strong as ever. Just note the number of people reading novels to wile away the minutes on the Moscow metro.

ARCHITECTURE

The Russian capital is an endless source of amusement and amazement for the architecture aficionado. The city streets are a textbook of Russian history, with churches, mansions, theatres and hotels standing as testament to the most definitive periods. Despite the tendency to demolish and rebuild (exhibited both in the past and in the present), Moscow has so far managed to preserve an impressive array of architectural gems.

MEDIEVAL MOSCOW

The earliest Russian architecture – developed in Kyivan Rus – was based on the 'cross in square' church plan borrowed from 9th-century Byzantium. At its simplest, this consisted of three aisles, each with an eastern apse (semicircular end), a dome or 'cupola' over the central aisle next to its apse, and high vaulted roofs forming a crucifix shape centred on the dome. As Russian culture moved north, Novgorod, Pskov and Vladimir-Suzdal developed their own variations on the pattern in the 11th and 12th centuries. Roofs grew steeper to prevent heavy northern snows collecting on them and crushing them, and windows grew narrower to keep the cold out.

Moscow in the 15th century looked to these earlier centres for inspiration in its grand building programme. Though the architects of two of the Moscow Kremlin's three great cathedrals built between 1475 and 1510 (p54) were Italian, they took Vladimir's churches as their models; the third cathedral was by builders from Pskov.

IMPERIAL MOSCOW

Later in the 16th century many of the north Russian wooden church features, such as the *shatyor* (tent roof) and the onion dome on a tall drum, were translated into brick. This change contributed to a new, uniquely Russian architecture, more vertical in effect than the Byzantine shape. St Basil's Cathedral (p63), the Ivan the Great Bell Tower in the Kremlin (p58), and the Ascension Church at Kolomenskoe (p105) are three highlights from this era.

In the 17th century builders in Moscow added tiers of *kokoshniki* (gables), colourful tiles and brick patterning to create jolly, merchant-financed churches, such as St Nicholas of the Weavers (p93) and the Trinity in Nikitniki (p77). In the middle of the century, Patriarch Nikon outlawed such frippery shortly after the construction of the Nativity of the Virgin in Putinki (p82).

Embellishments returned later with the Western-influenced Moscow baroque. This style featured ornate white detailing against red-brick walls, such as at the Epiphany Cathedral in the monastery with the same name (p77) in Kitay Gorod.

In 1714 it all came to a halt. Peter the Great's edict banned stone construction in Moscow and everywhere else in Russia, as all the resources were needed for the new city of St Petersburg. But frequent fires and a general outcry from Moscow's wealthy elite meant that the order was rescinded in 1722.

In the later 18th century, the grandiose Russian Empire style developed under Tsar Alexander. Moscow abounds with Empire-style buildings, since much of the city had to be rebuilt after the fire of 1812. The flamboyant decorations of earlier times were used on the huge new buildings erected to proclaim Russia's importance.

A series of architectural revivals, notably of early Russian styles, began in the late 19th century. The first, a pseudo-Russian phase, produced GUM (State Department Store; p63), the State History Museum (p64) and the Leningradsky vokzal (Leningrad station; p79). The early-20th-century neo-Russian movement produced the extraordinary Kazansky vokzal (Kazan station; p79), which embraces no fewer than seven earlier styles; Style Moderne (Russian Art Nouveau) yielded the bizarre Yaroslavsky vokzal across Komsomolskaya ploshchad (p79).

SOVIET MOSCOW

The revolution gave reign to young constructivist architects, who rejected superficial decoration in favour of buildings whose appearance was a direct function of their uses and materials – a new architecture for a new society. They used lots of glass and concrete in uncompromising geometric forms.

Konstantin Melnikov was probably the most famous constructivist, and his own house (p88) off ulitsa Arbat is one of the most interesting examples of the style. The *Izvestia*

SEVEN SISTERS

The foundations for seven large skyscrapers were laid in 1947 to mark Moscow's 800th anniversary. Stalin had decided that Moscow suffered from a 'skyscraper gap' when compared to the USA, and ordered the construction of these seven behemoths to jump-start the city's skyline.

One of the main architects, Vyacheslav Oltarzhevsky, had worked in New York during the skyscraper boom of the 1930s, and his experience proved essential. (Fortunately he'd been released from a Gulag in time to help.)

With their widely scattered locations, the towers provide a unique visual look and reference for Moscow. Their official name in Russia is *vystony dom* (high-rise) as opposed to *neboskryob* (foreign skyscraper). They have been nicknamed variously 'Seven Sisters', 'wedding cakes', 'Stalin's sisters' and more:

Apartment Block (Map pp248–9; Kudrinskaya pl 1, Barrikadnaya) 1954; 160m high; The Real McCoy (p133) eatery and bar is here.

Apartment Block (Map p255; Kotelnicheskaya nab 17/1, Zayauzie) 1952; the Illuzion cinema (p150) is here.

Transport Ministry (Map p254; ul Sadovaya-Spasskaya, Chistye Prudy) 1953; 133m high; near Krasnye Vorota metro.

Foreign Affairs Ministry (Map pp252–3; Smolenskaya-Sennaya pl 32/34, Arbat District) 1952; 27 floors; near Smolenskaya metro.

Hotel Ukraina (Map pp248–9; Kutuzovsky pr 2/1, Barrikadnaya) 1957; 200m high with 29 floors.

Leningradskaya Hotel (Map p254; Kalanchevskaya ul 21/40, Chistye Prudy) 1954; the smallest of the group.

Moscow State University (Map pp246–7; Universitetskaya pl 1, Outer Moscow) 1953; 236m high with four huge wings and 36 floors.

building (p111) on Pushkinskaya ploshchad is another. In the 1930s, the constructivists were denounced. Another revival, monumental classicism, inspired a 400m-high design for Stalin's pet project, a Palace of Soviets, which (mercifully) never got off the ground.

Stalin favoured neoclassical architecture, which echoed ancient Athens ('the only culture of the past to approach the ideal', according to Anatoly Lunacharsky, the first Soviet Commissar of Education). Stalin also favoured building on a gigantic scale to underline the might of the Soviet state. Often, convict labour was used, with a high death toll, to create enormous structures around the country. They reached their apogee in Stalin's seven skyscrapers – the 'Seven Sisters'. Gothic in effect, the skyscrapers popped up around Moscow soon after WWII (see the boxed text, p29).

In 1955 a schizophrenic decree ordered architects to avoid 'excesses'. A bland International Modern style – constructivism without the spark, you might say – was then often used for prestigious buildings, while drab blocks of cramped flats sprouted seemingly everywhere to house the people. These tower blocks, not unlike those constructed for the masses in other cities around the world, were ugly then and have not improved since.

CONTEMPORARY MOSCOW

Since the end of the Soviet Union, architectural energies and civic funds have mostly gone into the restoration of decayed churches and monasteries, as well as the rebuilding of structures such as the Cathedral of Christ the Saviour (p90).

As far as contemporary commercial and cultural buildings are concerned, post-Soviet architects have not been kind to Moscow. Featuring bright metals and mirrored glass, modern blocks tend to be plopped down in the middle of otherwise unassuming vintage buildings. The trend has sparked a campaign to preserve the city's historic architecture (see p22).

VISUAL ARTS
ICONS

Up until the 17th century religious icons were Russia's key art form, though only in the 20th century did they really come to be seen as 'works of art', as opposed to objects of worship. Originally painted by monks as a spiritual exercise, icons are images intended to aid the veneration of the holy subjects they depict, and are sometimes believed able to grant luck, wishes or even miracles. They're most commonly found on the iconostasis (screen) of a church.

Traditional rules decreed that only Christ, the Virgin, angels, saints and scriptural events could be painted on icons – all of which were supposed to be copies of a limited number of approved prototype images. Christ images include the Pantokrator (All-Ruler) and the Mandilion, the latter called 'not made by hand' because it was supposedly developed from the imprint of Christ's face on St Veronica's handkerchief. Icons were traditionally painted in tempera (inorganic pigment mixed with a binder such as egg yolk) on wood. When they faded, they were often touched up, obscuring the original work.

The beginning of a distinct Russian icon tradition came when artists in Novgorod started to draw on local folk art in their representation of people, producing sharply outlined figures with softer faces and introducing lighter colours, including pale yellows and greens. The earliest outstanding painter was Theophanes the Greek (Feofan Grek in Russian), who lived between 1340 and 1405. Working in Byzantium, Novgorod and Moscow, Theophanes brought a new delicacy and grace to the form. His finest works are in the Annunciation Cathedral of the Moscow Kremlin (p60).

Andrei Rublyov, a monk at Sergiev Posad's Trinity Monastery of St Sergius (p195) and Moscow's Andronikov Monastery (p102) – 20 years younger than Theophanes – was the greatest Russian icon painter. His most famous work is the dreamy *Old Testament Trinity*, in Moscow's Tretyakov Gallery (p100).

The layman Dionysius, the leading late-15th-century icon painter, elongated his figures and refined the use of colour. Sixteenth-century icons grew smaller and more crowded, their figures more realistic and Russian-looking. In 17th-century Moscow, Simon Ushakov moved towards Western religious painting with the use of perspective and architectural backgrounds.

PEREDVIZHNIKI

The major artistic force of the 19th century was the Peredvizhniki (Wanderers) movement, which saw art as a vehicle for promoting national awareness and social change. The movement gained its name from the touring exhibitions with which it widened its audience. These artists were patronised by the industrialists Savva Mamontov – whose Abramtsevo estate (p193) near Moscow became an artists' colony – and by the brothers Pavel and Sergei Tretyakov (after whom the Tretyakov Gallery is named). Artists included Vasily Surikov, who painted vivid Russian historical scenes, Nicholas Ghe (biblical and historical scenes), and Ilya Repin, perhaps the best loved of all Russian artists, whose works ranged from social criticism *(Barge Haulers on the Volga),* to history *(Zaporozhie Cossacks Writing a Letter to the Turkish Sultan)* to portraits. Many Peredvizhniki masterpieces are on display at the Tretyakov Gallery (p100).

Inspired by sparkling Byzantine and Venetian mosaics, the work of late 19th-century genius Mikhail Vrubel showed early traces of Western influence. His panels on the sides of Hotel Metropol are some of his best work (see the boxed text, p166).

FUTURISM

From about 1905 Russian art became a mishmash of groups, styles and 'isms', as it absorbed decades of European change in a few years. It finally gave birth to its own avant-garde futurist movements, which in turn helped Western art go head over heels.

Mikhail Larionov and Natalya Goncharova were at the centre of the Cézanne-influenced Knave of Diamonds group (which Vasily Kandinsky was associated with) before developing neoprimitivism, a movement based on popular arts and primitive icons. Works by all of these artists are on display at the New Tretyakov Gallery (p99), as well as the Moscow Museum of Modern Art (p80).

In 1915 Kazimir Malevich announced the arrival of Suprematism. His utterly abstract geometrical shapes (with the black square representing the ultimate 'zero form') finally freed art from having to depict the material world, and made it a doorway to higher realities. See one of his four *Black Square* paintings at the New Tretyakov. Another famed Futurist, who managed to escape subordinate 'isms', was Vladimir Mayakovsky, who was also a poet.

TOP FIVE ART MUSEUMS

- Museum of Private Collections (p91)
- New Tretyakov Gallery (p99)
- Pushkin Fine Arts Museum (p91)
- Rerikh Gallery (p92)
- Tretyakov Gallery (p100)

SOVIET ERA ART

Futurists turned to the needs of the revolution – education, posters and banners – with enthusiasm. They had a chance to act on their theories of how art shapes society. But at the end of the 1920s, Formalist (abstract) art fell out of favour. The Communist Party wanted socialist realism (see Literature, p28). Images of striving workers, heroic soldiers and inspiring leaders took over, plenty of which are on display at the New Tretyakov Gallery (p99). Two million sculptures of Lenin and Stalin dotted the country – Malevich ended up painting penetrating portraits and doing designs for Red Square parades; Mayakovsky committed suicide.

After Stalin an avant-garde 'conceptualist' underground was allowed to form. Ilya Kabakov painted or sometimes just arranged the debris of everyday life to show the gap between the promises and realities of Soviet existence. Erik Bulatov's 'Sotsart' style pointed to the devaluation of language by ironically reproducing Soviet slogans and depicting words disappearing over the horizon. In 1962 the authorities set up a show of such 'unofficial' art at the Manezh Exhibition Centre; Khrushchev called it 'dogshit' and sent it back underground. In the mid-1970s, it resurfaced in the Moscow suburbs – only to be literally bulldozed back down.

CONTEMPORARY ART

Although many contemporary painters of note have left Russia for the riches of the West, the country is still churning out promising young artists, whose work is on display at a few specialist art galleries (see the boxed text, p158).

One of the most popular painters in Russia today is the religious artist Ilya Glazunov, a staunch defender of the Russian Orthodox cultural tradition. Hundreds of thousands of people visit exhibitions of his work, most recently at his new namesake gallery (p90). More notorious than popular is the artist and architect Zurab Tsereteli, whose monumental buildings and statues (many monumentally ugly) grace Moscow. See the boxed text, p92 for more on Tsereteli, or check out his gallery (p93).

Artists are now freer than ever before to depict all aspects of Russian life, but there have, of late, been several public attacks on modern art (see the boxed texts, below and p78). Somewhat balancing this disturbing trend is the Moscow Biennale of Contemporary Art (see p9).

CINEMA & TV

CINEMA

Russian – or rather Soviet – cinema first flourished shortly after the revolution. Sergei Eisenstein's *Battleship Potemkin* (1925) remains one of the landmarks of world cinema, famous for its Odessa Steps sequence recreated in many other films, most notably Brian de Palma's *The Untouchables*. Charlie Chaplin described *Battleship Potemkin* as 'the best film in the world'. It and scores of other films marked the output of Moscow's film studios, the most active in the country during the 20th century.

During the Communist era, the fate of any movie was decided by the vast bureaucracy of Moscow-based Goskino, which funded films and also distributed them. It was known for its aversion to risks (which during the Stalin era was undoubtedly smart).

During a 1986 congress of Soviet filmmakers held in Moscow, *glasnost* touched the USSR's movie industry. By a large vote, the old and conservative directors were booted out of the leadership and renegades demanding more freedom were put in their place. During the remaining years of communism, over 250 previously banned films were released. For the first time, films began to explore real, contemporary issues.

ART UNDER ATTACK

Since journalists have largely failed (see Media, p18), contemporary Russian artists are now taking on President Putin and the sacred cows of Russia's establishment. At the Russia II exhibition, part of the 2005 Moscow Biennale of Contemporary Art, protest art included works that tackled themes of terrorism, the war in Chechnya and the Russian Orthodox Church. Predictably, a group of Orthodox Christians filed a criminal complaint against the exhibition.

It's not the first time art has provoked such complaints. In 2003 an art exhibit mocking the Russian Orthodox Church at Moscow's Andrei Sakharov Museum and Public Centre was closed following protests (p78). Agitprop artist Avdey Ter Oganyan lives in exile in Berlin because of death threats made against him. Ter Oganyan hit the headlines when he chopped up Christian icons on the street with an axe in the name of art. He was charged with incitement under the federal antihatred law.

In March 2005 the Putin-supporting youth group Moving Together picketed the Bolshoi's staging of *Rosenthal's Children*, a new opera with a libretto by Vladimir Sorokin. His novel *Goluboye Salo (Blue/Gay Lard)*, depicting sex between former Soviet leaders Josef Stalin and Nikita Khrushchev, had already got him into trouble with the authorities in 2002. In a typically Soviet-style knee-jerk reaction, right-wing politicians were quick to denounce the opera as pornographic, vulgar and unfitting of the Bolshoi, despite not having seen the work.

MOSCOW FILMS

- *Irony of Fate* (*Ironiya Sudby ili s Legkim Parom;* 1975), directed by Eldar Ryazanov, is a classic and national favourite screened on TV every New Year's eve. After a mindbending party in Moscow, the protagonist wakes up in St Petersburg, unbeknownst to him. Lo and behold, his key fits into the lock of a building that looks exactly like his at the same address in a different town. Comedy ensues.
- *Little Vera* (1989), Vasily Pichul's groundbreaking film, caused a sensation with its frank portrayal of a family in chaos (exhausted wife, drunken husband, rebellious daughter) and its sexual frankness – mild by Western standards but startling to the Soviet audience.
- *Burnt by the Sun* (1994) tells the story of a loyal apparatchik who becomes a victim of Stalin's purges. Mikhalkov's celebrated film won an Oscar for best foreign film in 1994.
- *Brother* (Brat; 1997) is a gangster drama by Alexei Balabanov that portrays the harshness of post-Soviet Russia. A geeky kid – played by superstar Sergei Brodov – returns from his army service and joins his brother working as a hit man in St Petersburg. The sequel, *Brat 2* (2000), follows the star to the capital; like most sequels, it does not live up to the original.
- *Night Watch* (*Nochnoy Dozor;* 2004) is a Russian mix of *The Matrix* and *Dracula.* Directed by Timur Bekmambetov, the glossy sci-fi fantasy thriller took in box office revenues in excess of US$16 million in Russia alone. In true Hollywood style, there will be a sequel in 2006.
- *You I Love* (*Ya Lyublu Tebya;* 2004), directed by Olga Stolpovskaya and Dmitry Troitsky, is a quirky, independent film that's an offbeat and sometimes charming tale of modern love in Moscow, with not a hammer and sickle in sight!
- *The State Councellor* (*Statsky Sovetnik*), a 2005 blockbuster, is based on a tsarist thriller penned by Boris Akunin (see p27). It is directed by that old warhorse of Russian cinema Nikita Mikhailkov, who co-stars in it along with Oleg Menshikov, heartthrob of a million Russian housewives.

However, by the time Nikita Mikhalkov's *Burnt by the Sun* won the Oscar for the best foreign movie in 1994, Russian film production was suffering as funding disappeared during the economic chaos of the early 1990s, and audiences stayed away from cinemas.

Since the mid-1990s, Moscow's film industry has made a remarkable comeback. Mos-Film – the successor to Goskino – is one of the largest production companies in the world, producing almost all of Russia's film, TV and video programming. Moscow is indeed the Russian Hollywood. Unfortunately, just like its American counterpart, the industry does not leave much room for artsy, independent films that are not likely to be blockbusters.

Fortunately, the Moscow Interfest (International Film Festival; p10) offers a venue for directors of independent films from Russia and abroad to compete for international recognition. In recent years Russian films have won the top prize, although this is not always the case. Boris Khlebnikov and Alexei Pogrebsky won in 2003 for *Koktebel,* their heart-warming tale of a father and son taking a cross-country journey in search of new lives. The 2004 winner was *Harvest Time,* Marina Razbezhkina's nostalgic look at life on a collective farm in the 1950s. In 2005 the award for best film went to *Dreaming of Space,* a film that contrasts the feeling of optimism in the air in 1957 with the bleak reality of life in a northern port city.

TV

Entertainment programming on TV is dominated by crime series, in which shaven-headed veterans of the war in Chechnya pin down conspiring oligarchs and politicians. That said, Russian TV does provide a wide choice of programmes, some of which are modelled on Western formats. The most popular show at the time of research was a reality show called *Dom,* or House. Similar to MTV's *The Real World,* the series brought together disparate personalities – mostly minor Russian celebrities – to live under one roof. The resulting show was filled with shagging and scandal. Viewers were looking forward to more of the same in the follow-up season, cleverly dubbed *Dom Dva (House Two).*

Programmes do include high-quality, educational shows – documentaries shown have been especially good in the last few years. Kultura is an excellent national, noncommercial channel dedicated to arts and culture.

Other unconventional channels have recently emerged, reflecting social trends. Zvezda (Star) belongs to the Defence Ministry and is supposed to encourage young people to serve in the army. Spas TV is designed to summon lost souls under the auspices of the Orthodoxy. And the English-language Russia Today is preparing an onslaught of Kremlin propaganda for Western audiences.

CIRCUS

While Western circuses grow smaller and scarcer, the Russian versions are like those from childhood stories – prancing horses with acrobats on their backs, snarling lions and tigers, heart-stopping high-wire artists and hilarious clowns. No wonder the circus remains highly popular, with around half the population attending a performance once a year.

The Russian circus has its roots in the medieval travelling minstrels *(skomorokhi)*. And circus performers today still have the lifestyle of such travelling minstrels. The Russian State Circus company, RosGosTsirk, assigns its members to a particular circus for a performance season, then rotates them around to other locations. What the members give up in stability, they gain in job security. RosGosTsirk ensures them employment throughout their circus career.

Many circus performers find their calling not by chance, but by ancestry. It is not unusual for generations of one family to practice the same circus skill, be it tightrope walking or lion taming. As one acrobat explained quite matter-of-factly: 'We can't live without the circus. There are very few who leave.'

Moscow is home to several circuses, including the acclaimed Nikulin Circus on Tsvetnoy bulvar (see p149). Its namesake is the beloved clown Yury Nikulin, who is described as 'the honour and conscience of the Russian circus'.

Speaking of honour and conscience, most of the major troupes have cleaned up their act with regard to the treatment of animals. Certainly in Moscow circuses, it is unlikely you will see animals treated cruelly or forced to perform degrading acts.

Clowns performing at the Nikulin Circus (p149)

THEATRE

Drama has long been an important part of the arts scene in Moscow, ever since Konstantin Stanislavsky implemented his innovated approach of method acting and made Anton Chekhov a success in the process (see the boxed text, p147). During the Soviet period, the stage was sometimes used as a forum for social criticism – indeed, the rebellious director of the Taganka Theatre, Yury Lyubimov, was sent into exile as a result of his controversial plays. These days, the capital hosts over 40 theatres, which continue to entertain and provoke audiences. While the most famous venues, such as the MKhT and the Maly Theatre, primarily stick to the classics, many lesser-known venues are staging cutting-edge contemporary drama. For details, see p147.

History

History

THE RECENT PAST
COPS IN THE KREMLIN

In December 1999, Boris Yeltsin delivered his customary televised New Year's greeting to the nation. On this occasion, the burly president shocked his fellow countrymen yet again by announcing his resignation from office and retirement from politics. The once combative Yeltsin had grown weary from a decade full of political adversity and physical infirmity.

Yeltsin turned over the office to his recently appointed prime minister, Vladimir Putin. As an aide to the president, Putin had impressed Yeltsin with his selfless dedication, shrewd mind and principled resolve. It was Yeltsin's plan to spring this holiday surprise on the unprepared political opposition to bolster Putin's chances in the upcoming presidential election. The plan worked. In March 2000, Putin became the second president of the Russian Federation.

Mystery surrounds the cop in the Kremlin: he is a former KGB chief, but an ally of St Petersburg's democratic mayor; well-heeled in European culture, but nostalgic for Soviet patriotism; diminutive in stature, but a black belt in karate.

In his first term, Putin's popular approval ratings shot through the onion domes. He brought calm and stability to Russian politics after more than a decade of crisis and upheaval. The economy finally bottomed out and began to show positive growth. The improved economic situation led to budget surpluses for the first time since the 1980s, and wages and pensions were paid in full and on time.

Putin vowed to restore the authority of the Moscow-based central state, engineering a constitutional reform to reduce the power of regional governors and launching a second war against radical Chechen separatists. His main opponent in the 2000 election, Moscow Mayor Yury Luzhkov, took note and hastily allied his political machine with Putin's new 'Unity' party.

Putin was re-elected in 2004. His second term accelerated the disturbing trend toward a more authoritarian approach to politics. Former police officials were named prime minister and speaker of the parliament. Restraints on mass media, civil society and nongovernmental agencies were further tightened. Russia's big business tycoons were cowed into submission after independent-minded oil magnate Mikhail Khodorkovsky was jailed for tax evasion (see the boxed text, opposite).

Where Russia's young tycoons failed, its senior citizens succeeded. Putin's 2005 attempt to scrap the existing system of subsidised social services was met with unexpected resistance from protesting pensioners. Thousands filled Moscow's streets, denouncing the pension reforms and forcing Putin to back off his plan.

TERROR IN THE CAPITAL

Though the origins of the Russian–Chechen conflict date to the 18th century (see the boxed text, p38), it is only in recent times that Moscow has felt its consequences so close to home. In September 1999, mysterious explosions in the capital left more than 200 people dead. Chechen terrorists were blamed for the bombings, although the evidence was scant. Conspiracy theorists had a field day.

In 2002, Chechen rebels wired with explosives seized a popular Moscow theatre, demanding independence for Chechnya. Nearly 800 theatre employees and patrons were held hostage for three days. Russian troops responded by flooding the theatre with immobilising

TIMELINE	1147	1326
	Founding of Moscow by Yury Dolgoruky; the first low walls are built around the settlement	Moscow becomes the headquarters of the Russian Orthodox Church

THE TAXMAN COMETH   *Jerry Easter*

In October 2003, the cosy world of Moscow millionaires was rocked by the arrest of Russia's richest man, Mikhail Khodorkovsky, for tax evasion. The event marked a turning point in postcommunist politics.

Khodorkovsky was one of Russia's self-proclaimed 'oligarchs', a group of about a dozen big-business tycoons with formidable political clout. These robber barons managed to gain control of the economy's most valued assets in rigged privatisation deals made in the 1990s.

Khodorkovsky, in particular, enjoyed a phenomenal rise to riches. He took advantage of Gorbachev's limited market reforms to try his hand as an entrepreneur, starting up a software company and commercial bank. During the Yeltsin years, Khodorkovsky's business ventures blossomed into a multibillion dollar financial-industrial empire, by adeptly manipulating his access to political patronage. The centrepiece of this empire was the Yukos Oil Company, which he acquired at auction with a US$350 million bid. The company was valued at US$9 billion when it went public only two years later.

Soon after taking office, President Putin summoned the anxious oligarchs to the Kremlin for a chat. Putin clarified his position on their ill-gotten gains: stay out of politics, invest in Russia and you can hold on to your wealth. Khodorkovsky apparently was unimpressed. The brash billionaire actively opposed the government's effort to raise taxes on the energy sector, he financed the electoral campaigns of Putin's political rivals, set up his own nongovernmental organisation and speculated about running for the presidency himself in 2008.

Enough was enough. In October 2003, masked commandos seized Khodorkovsky from his private plane at a Siberian airport. The tycoon languished in jail while prosecutors compiled a long list of allegations. His company, Yukos, was hit with bills for unpaid taxes and fines, covering the years 2000 to 2003, for more than US$15 billion. Khodokorvsky's personal tax debt was US$2 billion.

The Yukos Affair was a showcase of unchecked coercive powers. The combined forces of the secret police, the justice ministry and the tax police were mobilised against the company and its top directors. The legal system provided no protection. The courts followed the prosecutor's recommendations in close step. On one occasion when a Moscow magistrate made a decision in favour of Yukos, she was quickly removed from the case. Due process was ignored. Yukos bank accounts were frozen and its assets seized. Even the state-controlled media piled on, airing a documentary that tied Khodorkovsky to Chechen terrorists and murdered journalists.

In late May 2005, the Yukos Affair finally reached its climax, when Khodorkovsky was sentenced to nine years in prison. Earlier, the state had already begun the process of redistributing the prised pieces of the company.

But the episode had larger implications. The Yukos Affair was roundly denounced by Western governments and business leaders, while Khodorkovsky was recast from villain to victim by Western media. In the meantime, economic investment in the Russian economy dropped off precipitously.

For Putin, however, the political benefits were worth the bad press. As a new election season opened, the president was cheered for his aggressive populism. The president and his party subsequently were big winners.

Furthermore, the Yukos case had a profound effect on the behaviour of big business. Further tax investigations revealed billions of dollars in back taxes owed by other tycoons, who expressed a willingness to settle. Tax rates in the energy sector were increased with the begrudging consent of industry leaders. By concentrating its coercive resources at one highly visible target, the Russian state fundamentally transformed its relationship with big business.

Jerry is an associate professor at Boston College

toxic gas, disabling hostage-takers and hostages alike and preventing the worst-case scenario. The victims' unexpectedly severe reaction to the gas and a lack of available medical facilities resulted in 120 deaths and hundreds of illnesses. The incident refuelled Russia's relentless and ruthless campaign to force the Chechens into capitulation

Chechen terrorists have responded in kind, with smaller scale insurgencies taking place regularly; and Muscovites are all-too-aware of the ongoing conflict. The strike closest to home occurred in February 2004, when a bomb exploded in a metro carriage travelling between Avtozavodskaya and Paveletskaya stations, killing 39 and injuring over 100.

Other incidents have served as unnerving reminders, including a series of attacks that coincided with the horrific school siege in Beslan, which resulted in 331 deaths. A couple

1327	1360
Ivan 'Moneybags' Danilovich establishes Moscow as the capital of the Vladimir-Suzdal principality	A 'White Stone Kremlin' with limestone walls is built on the site of the present-day structure

CONFLICT IN CONTEXT

The 1990s marked the revival of a war that is more than 200 years old. In the late 18th century, Catherine II (the Great) expanded the Russian empire southward into the Caucasus. The Chechens – a fiercely independent, Muslim mountain tribe – refused to recognise Russian rule.

In the 19th century, Russia sought to consolidate its claim on the Caucasus to maintain access to southern sea routes and to thwart British expansion into the region. The tsar ordered General Yermelov, a veteran of the Napoleonic Wars, to pacify the mountain peoples. An intense 30-year conflict ensued between Russians and Chechens, with displays of wanton savagery on both sides. The leader of the Chechen resistance, Imam Shamil, became a larger-than-life folk hero and the inspiration for today's separatist fighters. Chechnya was tenuously incorporated into the empire through deals that Russia struck with the more cooperative of the Chechen clans, but separatist sentiments remained strong.

Under Soviet rule, a Chechen independence revolt broke out during the Nazi invasion, even while thousands of Chechens fought against the Germans. Toward the end of WWII, Stalin wreaked his revenge terrorising villages and deporting nearly 500,000 Chechens to remote areas of Central Asia and Siberia. In 1969 the statue of General Yermelov in the Chechen capital of Grozny was dynamited.

National separatists declared Chechnya independent in the early 1990s. President Yeltsin tried unsuccessfully to cajole, buy off and threaten Chechnya into submission. In 1994 he unleashed a military assault on the renegade republic. By 1996, fighting had subsided as Russian troops were contained to a few pockets of influence, and rebel gangs ruled the mountainous countryside in a condition of de facto independence.

The Russian military recommenced hostilities in 1999, kicking off the 'second' Chechen War. Provoked by the incursion of Chechen rebels into neighbouring Dagestan, attacks in Moscow that were blamed on Chechen terrorists and political pressure, Russian troops descended on war-torn Chechnya with a vengeance.

The fighting continues. Though the Caucasus seems far off, the repercussions of war continue to reach Moscow, as terrorists make their dissatisfaction known in the capital (see p36). Prospects for a negotiated peace appear all but nonexistent.

of days earlier, in late August 2004, two planes that took off from Moscow exploded almost simultaneously in mid-air, killing all 90 passengers, including the suicide bombers on board. Soon after, a suicide bomber failed to enter Rizhskaya metro station, but still managed to kill 10 and injure 50 people on the street.

Meanwhile, Chechens living in Moscow have endured increased harassment, both officially and unofficially. They complain of increasing difficulty obtaining residency permits and constant and unwarranted attention from Moscow police. No less damaging is the growing mistrust between Russians and Chechens, as the racial tension continues to mount.

THE PARTY AFTER THE PARTY

Since 1999, Russia has recorded positive economic growth. With the devaluation of the rouble, domestic producers are more competitive and more profitable. A worldwide shortage of energy resources has heaped benefits on the economy. The Russian oil boom, going strong since 2000, has enabled the government to run budget surpluses, pay off its foreign debt and lower tax rates.

Moscow, in particular, has prospered. The city's congested roadways are replete with luxury driving machines. The new economy has spawned a small group of 'New Russians', who are alternately derided and envied for their garish displays of wealth. According to *Forbes* magazine, the Russian capital boasts the largest contingent of resident billionaires in the world. (Russia ranks second only to the US in total billionaires.) And in 2005, Yelena Baturina, property magnate and wife of Mayor Luzhkov, became Russia's first female billionaire.

Apart from this elite, Russia's transition to the market economy came at enormous social cost. The formerly subsidised sectors of the economy, such as education, science and health-

1380	1382
Dmitry Donskoy defeats the Golden Horde in the Battle of Kulikovo	Moscow is burned to the ground by the Mongols of the vengeful Golden Horde

care, were devastated. For many dedicated professionals, it became close to impossible to eke out a living in their chosen profession. Sadly, many of the older generation – whose hard-earned pensions were reduced to a pittance – paid the price for this transformation. Many have been forced to beg and scrimp on the margins of Moscow's new marketplace.

Following decades of an austere and prudish Soviet regime, Muscovites revelled in their new-found freedom. Liberation, libation, defiance and indulgence were all on open display. Those reared in a simpler time were no doubt shocked by the immodesty of the younger generation.

In the 21st century, the rhythms of the city seem to have steadied. Decadence is still for sale, but it has become more corporate; espresso coffees have replaced five-for-one drink specials. Moscow, however, remains the most freewheeling city in Russia; for the cynics there are no surprises, and for the ambitious there are no limits.

FROM THE BEGINNING

The hilly terrain of the region has supported human inhabitants for at least 5000 years. Its earliest occupants were forest-dwelling hunter-gatherer tribes that lived off the plentiful bounty of the woodlands and waters. More than 2500 years ago, small agricultural settlements started sprouting up along the many rivers and lakes in the region. These first farmers were descendants of the Ugro-Finnic tribes that long ago populated the northern Eurasian forests.

MEDIEVAL MOSCOW

Early Settlement & Founding

Around the 10th century, eastern Slav tribes began to migrate to the region from the Kyivan Rus principality further west, eventually assimilating or displacing the earlier inhabitants. They came to cultivate hardy cereal crops in the abundant arable land and to escape the political volatility of the fractious principality.

The Krivich tribe settled in the north, while the Vyatich tribe relocated to the south. Present-day Moscow grew up on the Vyatich side as a trading post between these two Slav tribes, near the confluence of the Moscow (Moskva) and Yauza Rivers. For a brief time, these outlying communities enjoyed an autonomous existence away from the political and religious powers of the medieval Kyivan Rus state.

Anxious to secure his claim of sovereignty over all the eastern Slavs, Vladimir I, Grand Prince of Kyivan Rus, made his son Yaroslav the regional vicelord, who oversaw the collection of tribute and undertook the conversion of pagans. Upon his death, in 1015, Vladimir's realm was divided among his sons, leading to a protracted and often violent period of family feuds. In this conflict, the descendants of Yaroslav inherited the northeastern territories of the realm, wherein they established the Golden Ring of towns, fortresses and monasteries (see p185).

Political power gradually shifted eastward. Under Vladimir Monomakh, Yaroslav's grandson, the Vladimir-Suzdal principality became a formidable rival in the medieval Russian realm. When Vladimir ascended the throne as Grand Prince, he appointed his youngest son, Yury Dolgoruky, to look after the region.

Legend has it that Prince Yury stopped at Moscow on his way back to Vladimir from Kyiv (Kiev). Believing that Moscow's Prince Kuchka had not paid him sufficient homage, Yury put the impudent *boyar* (high-ranking noble) to death and placed Moscow under his direct rule.

Moscow is first mentioned in the historic chronicles in 1147, when Yury invited his allies to a banquet there: 'Come to me, brother, please come to Moscow.' Moscow's strategic

1475-1516	1480
Grand Prince Ivan III oversees the building of new Kremlin walls and three great cathedrals therein	Ivan III is crowned Ruler of all Russia, earning him the moniker 'Ivan the Great'

importance prompted Yury to construct a moat-ringed wooden palisade on the hilltop and install his personal vassal on site.

With its convenient access to riverways and roads, Moscow soon blossomed into a regional economic centre, attracting traders and artisans to the merchant rows just outside the Kremlin's walls. In the early 13th century, Moscow became the capital of a small independent principality, though it remained a contested prize by successive generations of *boyar* princes.

Mongol Yoke & the Rise of Muscovy

Beginning in 1236, Eastern Europe was overwhelmed by the marauding Golden Horde, a Mongol-led army of nomadic tribesmen, who appeared out of the eastern Eurasian steppes and were led by Chinggis (Genghis) Khaan's grandson, Batu.

The ferocity of the Golden Horde raids was unprecedented, and quickly Russia's ruling princes acknowledged the region's new overlord. The Golden Horde's khan would constrain Russian sovereignty for the next two centuries, demanding tribute and allegiance from the Slavs.

The Mongols introduced themselves to Moscow by razing the city and killing its governor. Their menacing new presence levelled the political playing field in the region, thereby creating an opportunity for a small Muscovite principality.

The years of Mongol domination coincided with the rise of medieval Muscovy in a marriage of power and money. After Novgorod's Alexander Nevsky thwarted a Swedish invasion from the west, Batu Khan appointed him Grand Prince of Rus and moved Nevsky's throne to Vladimir, where he could be watched more closely. Meanwhile, Alexander's brother, Mikhail, was charged with looking after Moscow. The Golden Horde was mainly interested in tribute, and Moscow was more conveniently situated to monitor the river trade and road traffic. With Mongol backing, Muscovite officials soon emerged as the chief tax collectors in the region.

As Moscow prospered economically, its political fortunes rose as well. In the late 13th century, a new dynasty was created in Moscow under Prince Daniil. His son Yury Danilovich won the khan's favour and in the early 14th century, Moscow – for the first time – held the seat of the Grand Prince. Yury's brother, Ivan Danilovich, earned the moniker of Moneybags (Kalita) because of his remarkable revenue-raising abilities.

Ivan Kalita used his good relations with the khan to manoeuvre Moscow into a position of dominance in relation to his rival princes. By the middle of the 14th century, Moscow had absorbed its erstwhile patrons, Vladimir and Suzdal.

Soon Moscow became a nemesis rather than a supplicant to the Mongols. In the 1380 Battle of Kulikovo, Moscow's Grand Prince Dmitry, Kalita's grandson, led a coalition of Slav princes to a rare victory over the Golden Horde on the banks of the Don River. He was thereafter immortalised as Dmitry Donskoy. This feat did not break the Mongols, however, who retaliated by setting Moscow ablaze only two years later. From this time, however, Moscow acted as champion of the Russian cause.

Visitors to Moscow during the early 15th century said it was 'awesome', 'brilliant' and 'dirty', comparable to Prague or Florence, and twice as large. Toward the end of the

The Church of the Trinity in Nikitniki (p77), one of the many churches built in Moscow between the 15th and 17th centuries,

1555-61	1560
Construction of St Basil's Cathedral in honour of the taking of Kazan by Ivan IV	Ivan IV's wife dies provoking a reign of terror and earning him the moniker 'Ivan the Terrible'

15th century, Moscow's ambitions were realised as the once diminutive duchy evolved into an expanding autocratic state. Under the long reign of Grand Prince Ivan III (the Great), the eastern Slav independent principalities were forcibly consolidated into a single territorial entity. The growing influence of the Polish-Lithuanian Commonwealth in the west forced Ivan to take action. In 1478, after a seven-year assault, Ivan's army finally subdued the prosperous merchant principality of Novgorod and evicted the Hansa trading league.

After Novgorod's fall, the 'gathering of the lands' picked up pace as the young Muscovite state annexed Tver, Vyatka, Ryazan, Smolensk and Pskov. In 1480 Poland-Lithuania's King Casimer conspired with the Golden Horde to join forces in an attack on Muscovy from the south. Casimer, however, became preoccupied with other matters, and Ivan's army faced down the Mongols at the Ugra River without a fight. Ivan now refused outright to pay tribute or deference to the Golden Horde and the 200-year Mongol yoke was lifted. A triumphant Ivan had himself crowned 'Ruler of all Russia' in a solemn Byzantine-style ceremony.

Ivan the Terrible

At the time of the death of Ivan the Great, the borders of Muscovy stretched from the Baltic region in the west to the Ural Mountains in the east and the Barents Sea in the north. The south was still the domain of hostile steppe tribes of the Golden Horde.

In the 16th century, however, the Golden Horde fragmented into the Khanates of Crimea, Astrakhan, Kazan and Sibir, from where they controlled vital river networks and continued to raid Russian settlements. At this time, Ivan the Great's grandson, Ivan IV (the Terrible), led the further expansion and consolidation of the upstart Muscovy state. In the 1550s, Muscovy conquered the Kazan and Astrakhan Khanates, thus securing control over the Volga River. Two decades later, a Cossack army commissioned by Ivan defeated the Khan of Sibir, opening up a vast wilderness east of the Urals. Ivan was less successful against the Crimean Tatars, who dominated the southern access routes to the Black Sea.

On the home front, the reign of Ivan IV spelt trouble for Moscow. Ivan came to the throne in 1533 at age three with his mother as regent, though she died only five years later. Upon reaching adulthood, 13 years later, he was crowned 'Tsar of all the Russias'. (The Russian word 'tsar' is derived from the Latin term 'caesar'.) Ivan IV's marriage to Anastasia, a member of the Romanov *boyar* family, was a happy one, unlike the five that followed her early death.

THE RUSSIAN ORTHODOX CHURCH

As Moscow emerged as a political capital, it also took on the role of religious centre. Relations between the Church and the Grand Prince were always closely intertwined. In the 1320s, Metropolitan Pyotr, head of the Russian episcopate, departed from Vladimir and moved into the Kremlin.

In the mid-15th century, a separate Russian Orthodox Church was organised, independent of the Greek Church. In the 1450s, when Constantinople fell to heathen Turks, the Metropolitan declared Moscow to be the 'Third Rome', the rightful heir of Christendom. Ivan the Great vowed to make Moscow a stronghold of spirituality. Under Ivan the Terrible, the city earned the nickname of 'Gold-Domed Moscow' because of the multitude of monastery fortresses and magnificent churches constructed within the city.

In 1547 the city was consumed by fire. The tragedy provoked hysteria when a crowd became convinced that the inferno was the work of Ivan's grandmother, a suspected witch. The mob stormed the Kremlin and killed Ivan's uncle.

The year in which his beloved Anastasia died, 1560, marked a turning point for Ivan. Believing her to have been poisoned, he started a reign of terror against the ever-intriguing and jealous *boyars,* earning himself the sobriquet *grozny* (literally 'dreadfully serious', but in his case translated as 'terrible'). Later, in a fit of rage, he even killed his eldest son and heir to the throne.

1571	1591-1613
Moscow is burned to the ground by Crimean Tatars	The so-called 'Time of Troubles', when Russia is ruled by a string of pretenders to the throne

Ivan suffered from a fused spine and took mercury treatments to ease the intense pain. The cure, however, was worse than the ailment; it gradually made him insane.

The last years of Ivan's reign proved ruinous for Moscow. In 1571 Crimean Tatars torched the city, burning most of it to the ground. Ivan's volatile temperament made matters worse by creating political instability. At one point he vacated the throne and concealed himself in a monastery.

Upon his death, power was passed to his feeble-minded son, Fyodor. For a short time, Fyodor's brother-in-law and able prime minister, Boris Godunov, succeeded in restoring order to the realm. By the beginning of the 17th century, however, Boris was dead, Polish invaders occupied the Kremlin and Russia slipped into a 'Time of Troubles'. Finally, the Cossack soldiers relieved Moscow of its uninvited Polish guests and political stability was achieved with the coronation of Mikhail as tsar, inaugurating the Romanov dynasty.

IMPERIAL MOSCOW
Peter the Great & the Spurned Capital

Peter I, known as 'the Great' for his commanding frame (reaching over 2m) and equally commanding victory over the Swedes, dragged Russia kicking and screaming into modern Europe. Born to Tsar Alexey's second wife in 1672, Peter spent much of his youth in royal residences in the Moscow countryside, organising his playmates in war games. Energetic and inquisitive, he was eager to learn about the outside world. As a boy, he spent hours in Moscow's European district; as a young man, he spent months travelling in the West. In fact, he was Russia's first ruler to venture abroad. Peter briefly shared the throne with his half-brother, before taking sole possession in 1696.

Peter wilfully imposed modernisation on Moscow. He ordered the *boyars* to shave their beards, imported European advisers and craftsmen, and rationalised state administration. He built Moscow's tallest structure, the 90m-high Sukharev Tower, and next to it founded the College of Mathematics and Navigation.

MOSCOW'S DEVELOPMENT – THE EARLY YEARS

Today, the red brick towers and sturdy stone walls of the Kremlin occupy the founding site of Moscow. Perched atop the Borovitsky Hills, the first Kremlin, built in 1147, was a simple wooden fort that overlooked a strategic bend in the Moscow River, at the intersection of a network of waterways feeding the Upper Volga and Oka Rivers.

With the rise of the Muscovy state during the late 14th century, Moscow city underwent its own impressive development. The city's defence structures were upgraded. The Kremlin was refortified and expanded when Dmitry Donskoy replaced the wooden walls with a more durable limestone edifice as the once-small village grew into a prosperous urban centre. By the early 15th century, Moscow was the largest town in the Russian lands, with a population surpassing 50,000 people.

Between 1475 and 1516, Ivan III (the Great) launched a rebuilding effort to celebrate his military successes. He imported a team of Italian artisans and masons for a complete renovation of the fortress. The Kremlin's famous thick brick walls and imposing watchtowers were constructed at this time (see the boxed text, p56). Next to the Kremlin, traders and artisans set up shop in the surrounding Kitay Gorod. After the Crimean Tatars devastated the city in 1571, a stone wall was erected around these commercial quarters. Ivan IV (the Terrible) celebrated the defeat of Kazan with the erection of St Basil's Cathedral on Red Square (Krasnaya ploshchad; see p63).

The city developed in concentric rings outward from this centre. Outside the Kremlin walls, the city's inhabitants were mostly clergy, merchants, artisans and labourers. Moscow was ringed by noble estates, monastery holdings and small farms. A 16km earthen rampart was also built around the city to establish a forward line of defence. The town recovered quickly from fire, famine and fighting; its population topped 100,000 and then 200,000. In the early 17th century, Moscow was the largest city in the world.

1613	1712
Mikhail Romanov is crowned tsar, inaugurating the Romanov dynasty	Peter I (the Great) moves the Russian capital to St Petersburg

Yet, Peter always despised Moscow for its scheming *boyars* and archaic traditions. In 1712 he startled the country by announcing the relocation of the capital to a swampland, recently acquired from Sweden in the Great Northern War. St Petersburg would be Russia's 'Window on the West', and everything that Moscow was not – modern, scientific and cultured. Alexander Pushkin later wrote that 'Peter I had no love for Moscow, where, with every step he took, he ran into remembrances of mutinies and executions, inveterate antiquity and the obstinate resistance of superstition and prejudice.'

The spurned former capital quickly fell into decline. With the aristocratic elite and administrative staff departing for marshier digs, the population fell by more than a quarter by 1725. The city suffered further from severe fires, a situation exacerbated by Peter's mandate to direct all construction materials to St Petersburg.

In the 1770s, Moscow was devastated by an outbreak of bubonic plague, which claimed more than 50,000 lives. It was decreed that the dead had to be buried outside the city limits. Vast cemeteries, including Danilovskoye and Vagankovskoye, were the result. The situation was so desperate that residents went on a riotous looting spree that was violently put down by the army. Empress Catherine II (the Great) responded to the crisis by ordering a new sanitary code to clean up the urban environment and silencing the Kremlin alarm bell that had set off the riots. By 1780, St Petersburg's population surpassed that of Moscow.

By the turn of the 19th century, Moscow had recovered from its gloom. The population climbed back to over 200,000, its previous high point. Peter's exit had not caused a complete rupture. The city retained the title of 'First-Throned Capital' because coronations were held there. When Peter's grandson, Peter III, relieved the nobles of obligatory state service in 1762, many returned to Moscow. Moreover, many of the merchants had never left Moscow and, after the initial shock, their patronage and wealth became visible again throughout the city.

The late 18th century also saw the construction of the first embankments along the Moscow River, which were followed by bridges. In the 1700s, Russia's first university, museum and newspaper were started in Moscow. This new intellectual and literary scene would soon give rise to a nationalist-inspired cultural movement, which would embrace those features of Russia that were distinctly different from the West.

Napoleon & the Battle of Moscow

In 1807 Tsar Alexander I negotiated the Treaty of Tilsit. It left Napoleon in charge as Emperor of the west of Europe and Alexander as Emperor of the east, united (in theory) against England. The alliance lasted until 1810, when Russia resumed trade with England. A furious Napoleon decided to crush the tsar with his Grand Army of 700,000 – the largest force the world had ever seen for a single military operation.

The vastly outnumbered Russian forces retreated across their own countryside throughout the summer of 1812, scorching the earth in an attempt to deny the French sustenance, and fighting some successful rearguard actions.

Napoleon set his sights on Moscow. In September, with the lack of provisions beginning to bite the French, Russian general Mikhail Kutuzov finally decided to turn and fight at Borodino, 130km from Moscow (see p205). The battle was extremely bloody, but inconclusive, with the Russians withdrawing in good order. More than 100,000 soldiers lay dead at the end of a one-day battle.

Before the month was out, Napoleon entered a deserted Moscow. Defiant Muscovites burned down two-thirds of the city rather than see it occupied by the French invaders. Alexander, meanwhile, ignored Napoleon's overtures to negotiate.

With winter coming and supply lines overextended, Napoleon declared victory and retreated. His badly weakened troops stumbled westward out of the city, falling to starvation, disease, the bitter cold and Russian snipers. Only one in 20 made it back to the relative safety of Poland. The tsar's army pursued Napoleon all the way to Paris, which Russian forces briefly occupied in 1814.

1812	1905
Muscovites burn their own city in anticipation of the invasion by Napoleon's Grand Army	War in the Far East provokes general strikes in Moscow and St Petersburg

The 19th Century

Moscow was feverishly rebuilt in just a few years following the war. Monuments were erected to commemorate Russia's hard-fought victory and Alexander's 'proudest moment' – a Triumphal Arch (see p106), inspired by their former French hosts, was placed at the top of Tverskaya ulitsa on the road to St Petersburg. The sculpture of Minin and Pozharsky, who had liberated Moscow from a previous foreign foe, adorned Red Square (see p64). And the immensely grandiose Cathedral of Christ the Saviour, which took almost 50 years to complete, went up along the river embankment outside the Kremlin (see p90).

The building frenzy did not stop with national memorials. In the city centre, engineers diverted the Neglinnaya River to an underground canal and created two new urban spaces: the Alexandrovsky Garden (p61), running alongside the Kremlin's western wall; and Theatre Square (p66), featuring the glittering Bolshoi Theatre and later the opulent Metropol Hotel. The rebuilt Manezh, the 180m-long imperial stables, provided a touch of neoclassical grandeur to the scene (p65).

Meanwhile, the city's two outer defensive rings were replaced with the tree-lined Boulevard Ring and Garden Ring roads. The Garden Ring became an informal social boundary line: on the inside were the abodes and amenities of the merchants, intellectuals, civil servants and foreigners; on the outside were the factories and dosshouses of the toiling, the loitering and the destitute.

A post-war economic boom changed the city forever. The robust recovery was at first led by the big merchants, long the mainstay of the city's economy. In the 1830s, they organised the Moscow Commodity Exchange. By mid-century, industry began to overtake commerce as the city's economic driving force. Moscow became the hub of a network of new railroad construction, connecting the raw materials of the East to the manufacturers of the West. With a steady supply of cotton from Central Asia, Moscow became a leader in the textile industry. By 1890, more than 300 of the city's 660 factories were engaged in cloth production and the city was known as 'Calico Moscow'. While St Petersburg's industrial development was financed largely by foreign capital, Moscow drew upon its own resources. The Moscow Merchant Bank, founded in 1866, was the country's second-largest bank by century's end.

The affluent and self-assured business elite extended its influence over the city. The eclectic tastes of the nouveaux riches were reflected in the multiform architectural styles of their mansions, salons and hotels. The business elite eventually secured direct control over the city government, removing the remnants of the old *boyar* aristocracy. In 1876, Sergei Tretyakov, artful entrepreneur and art patron, started a political trend when he became the first mayor who could not claim noble lineage.

The increase in economic opportunity in the city occurred simultaneously with a decline of agriculture and the emancipation of the serfs. As a result, the city's population surged, mostly driven by an influx of rural job seekers. By 1890, Moscow could claim over one million inhabitants. That number would increase by another 50% in less than 20 years. Moscow still ranked second to St Petersburg in population, but, unlike the capital, Moscow was a thoroughly Russian city – its population was 95% ethnic Russian.

By 1900, more than 50% of the city's inhabitants were first-generation peasant migrants. Some stayed for only short stints in between the planting and harvesting seasons, others adjusted to the unfamiliar rhythm of industrial society and became permanent residents. They settled in the factory tenements outside the Garden Ring and south of the river in the Zamoskvorechie district.

The influx of indigents overwhelmed the city's meagre social services and affordable accommodation. At the beginning of the 20th century, Moscow's teeming slums were a breeding ground for disease and discontent. The disparity of wealth among the population grew to extremes. Lacking a voice, the city's less fortunate turned an ear to the outlawed radicals.

1914-17	1917
Russia suffers immeasurably from losses in WWI	Tsar Nicholas II succumbs to a mob of workers in St Petersburg

RED MOSCOW
Revolutionary Moscow

The tsarist autocracy staggered into the new century. In 1904 the impressionable and irresolute Tsar Nicholas II was talked into declaring war on Japan over some forestland in the Far East. His imperial forces suffered a decisive and embarrassing defeat, touching off a nationwide wave of unrest.

Taking their cue from St Petersburg, Moscow's workers and students staged a series of demonstrations, culminating in the October 1905 general strike, forcing political concessions from a reluctant Nicholas. In December, the attempt by city authorities to arrest leading radicals provoked a new round of confrontation, which ended in a night of bloodshed on hastily erected barricades in the city's Presnya district.

Vladimir Ilych Ulyanov (Lenin) called the failed 1905 Revolution the 'dress rehearsal for 1917', vowing that next time Russia's rulers would not escape the revolutionary scourge. Exhausted by three years of fighting in WWI, the tsarist autocracy meekly succumbed to a mob of St Petersburg workers in February 1917. Unwilling to end the war and unable to restore order, the provisional government was itself overthrown in a bloodless palace coup, orchestrated by Lenin's Bolshevik Party (which was eventually renamed the Communist Party). In Moscow, regime change was not so easy, as a week of street fighting left more than 1000 dead. Radical socialism had come to power in Russia.

Fearing a German assault, Lenin ordered that the capital return to Moscow. In March 1918, Lenin set up shop in the Kremlin and the new Soviet government expropriated the nicer downtown hotels and townhouses to conduct affairs. The move unleashed a steady stream of favour-seeking sycophants on the city. The new communist-run city government authorised the redistribution of housing space, as scores of thousands of workers upgraded to the dispossessed digs of the bourgeoisie.

The revolution and ensuing civil war, however, took its toll on Moscow. Political turmoil fostered an economic crisis. In 1921 the city's factories were operating at only 10% of their prewar levels of production. Food and fuel were in short supply. Hunger and disease stalked

Crowns in the Kremlin Armoury (p61)

1918	1930s
Vladimir Ilych Lenin moves the capital back to Moscow; the Kremlin is closed to visitors	Stalin launches a campaign of modernisation and a reign of terror

the darkened city. The population dropped precipitously from two million in 1917 to just one million in 1920. Wearied workers returned to the villages in search of respite, while the old elite packed up its belongings and moved beyond the reach of a vengeful new regime.

Stalin's Moscow

In May 1922, Lenin suffered the first of a series of paralysing strokes that removed him from effective control of the Party and government. He died, aged 54, in January 1924. His embalmed remains were put on display in Moscow (see p63). St Petersburg was renamed Leningrad in his honour, and a personality cult was built around him – all orchestrated by Josef Stalin.

The most unlikely of successors, Stalin outwitted his rivals and manoeuvred himself into the top post of the Communist Party. Ever paranoid, Stalin later launched a reign of terror against his former Party rivals, which eventually consumed nearly the entire first generation of Soviet officialdom. Hundreds of thousands of Muscovites were systematically executed and secretly interred on the ancient grounds of the old monasteries.

In the early 1930s, Stalin launched Soviet Russia on a hell-bent industrialisation campaign. The campaign cost millions of lives, but by 1939 only the USA and Germany had higher levels of industrial output. Moscow set the pace for this rapid development. Political prisoners became slave labourers. The building of the Moscow-Volga Canal was overseen by the secret police, who forced several hundred thousand 'class enemies' to dig the 125km-long ditch.

The brutal tactics employed by the state to collectivise the countryside created a new wave of peasant immigrants that flooded to Moscow. Around the city, work camps and bare barracks were erected to shelter the huddling hordes who shouldered Stalin's industrial revolution. At the other end, Moscow also became a centre of a heavily subsidised military industry, whose engineers and technicians enjoyed a larger slice of the proletarian pie. The Party elite, meanwhile, moved into new spacious accommodation such as the Dom Naberezhnya (House of the Embankment), across the river from the Kremlin.

Under Stalin, a comprehensive urban plan was devised for Moscow. On paper, it appeared as a neatly organised garden city; unfortunately, it was implemented with a sledge-hammer. Historic cathedrals and bell towers were demolished in the middle of the night. The Kitay Gorod wall was dismantled for being 'a relic of medieval times'. Alexander's Triumphal Arch and Peter's Sukharev Tower likewise became victims of unsympathetic city planners, eager to wrench Moscow into a proletarian future.

New monuments marking the epochal transition to socialism went up in place of the old. The first line of the marble-bedecked metro was completed in 1935. The enormous Cathedral of Christ the Saviour was razed with the expectation of erecting the world's tallest building, upon which would stand an exalted 90m statute of Lenin. This scheme was later abandoned and the foundation hole instead became the world's biggest municipal swimming pool. Broad thoroughfares were created and neo-Gothic skyscrapers girded the city's outer ring.

In the 1930s, Stalin's overtures to enter into an anti-Nazi collective security agreement were rebuffed by England and France. Vowing that the Soviet Union would not be pulling their 'chestnuts out of the fire', Stalin signed a nonaggression pact with Hitler instead.

Thus, when Hitler launched 'Operation Barbarossa' in June 1941, Stalin was caught by surprise and did not emerge from his room for three days.

The ill-prepared Red Army was no match for the Nazi war machine, which advanced on three fronts. By December, the Germans were just outside Moscow, within 30km of the Kremlin. Only an early, severe winter halted the advance. A monument now marks the spot, near the entrance road to Sheremetyevo airport, where the Nazis were stopped in their tracks. Staging a brilliant counteroffensive, Soviet war hero General Zhukov staved off the attack and pushed the invaders back.

1935	1944
Opening of the Sokolniki line of the Moscow metro	The Nazi advance on Moscow is halted by a severe Russian winter

Post-Stalinist Moscow

Stalin died in March 1953. His funeral procession brought out so many gawkers that a riot ensued and scores of mourners were trampled to death. The system he built, however, lived on, with a few changes.

First, Nikita Khrushchev, a former mayor of Moscow, tried a different approach to ruling. He curbed the powers of the secret police, released political prisoners, introduced wide-ranging reforms and promised to improve living conditions. Huge housing estates grew up around the outskirts of Moscow; many of the hastily constructed low-rise projects were nicknamed *khrushchoby,* after *trushchoby* (slums). Khrushchev's populism and unpredictability made the ruling elite a bit too nervous and he was ousted in 1964.

TOP FIVE HISTORY BOOKS

- *Comrade Criminal* (Stephen Handelman) is an in-depth investigation of the Russian mafia, written by the Moscow correspondent for the *Toronto Star.*
- *Lenin's Tomb* (David Remnick) describes the *Washington Post's* Moscow correspondent's entertaining and award-winning first-hand account of the collapse of the Soviet Union.
- *Midnight Diaries* (Boris Yeltsin) is a truly insider perspective on the Yeltsin years, recounting tales of oligarchs and alcohol.
- *Moscow: Governing the Socialist Metropolis* (Timothy Colton) delivers a comprehensive (937-page!) history of modern Moscow.
- *Pushkin's Button* (Serena Vitale) is a fascinating recounting of the duel that killed Russia's most famous poet.

Next came the long, stagnant reign of ageing Leonid Brezhnev. Overlooking Lenin's mausoleum, he presided over the rise of a military superpower. Brezhnev provided long sought-after political stability and material security. Most Russians, even today, say that their living standard was higher in Brezhnev's time.

During these years, the Cold War shaped Moscow's development as the Soviet Union enthusiastically competed with the USA in the arms and space races. The aerospace, radio-electronics and nuclear weapons ministries operated factories, research laboratories and design institutes in and around the capital. By 1980, as much as one-third of the city's industrial production and one-quarter of its labour force were connected to the defence industry. Moscow city officials were not privy to what went on in these secretly managed facilities. As a matter of national security, the KGB discreetly constructed a second subway system, Metro-2, under the city.

Still, the centrally planned economy could not keep pace with rising consumer demands. While the elite lived in privilege, ordinary Muscovites stood in line for goods. For the Communist Party, things became a bit too comfortable. Under Brezhnev, the political elite grew elderly and corrupt, while the economic system slid into a slow, irreversible decline. And the goal of turning Moscow into a showcase socialist city was quietly abandoned.

Nonetheless, Moscow enjoyed a postwar economic boom. The city underwent further expansion, accommodating more and more buildings and residents. Brezhnev showed a penchant for brawny displays of modern architecture. Cavernous concrete-and-glass slabs, such as the now defunct Hotel Rossiya, were constructed to show the world the modern face of the Soviet Union. The cement pouring reached a frenzy in the build-up to the 1980 Summer Olympics. However, Russia's invasion of Afghanistan caused many nations to boycott the Games and the facilities mostly stood empty.

Appreciation for Moscow's past, however, began to creep back into city planning. Most notably, Alexander's Triumphal Arch was reconstructed (see p106), though plans to re-erect Peter's tall Sukharev Tower were not realised. Residential life continued to move further away from the city centre, which was increasingly occupied by the governing elite. Shoddy high-rise apartments went up on the periphery and metro lines were extended outward.

1953	1961
Stalin dies and is entombed next to Lenin on Red Square; he is succeeded by Nikita Khrushchev	Stalin is removed from the mausoleum on Red Square and buried in the Kremlin wall

The attraction for Russians to relocate to Moscow in these years was, and continues to be, very strong. City officials tried desperately to enforce the residency permit system, but to no avail. In 1960 the population topped six million, and, by 1980, it surpassed eight million. The spillover led to the rapid growth of Moscow's suburbs. While industry, especially the military industry, provided the city's economic foundation, many new jobs were created in science, education and public administration. The city became a little more ethnically diverse, particularly with the arrival of petty-market traders from Central Asia and the Caucasus.

TRANSITIONAL MOSCOW
The Communist Collapse

The Soviet leadership showed it was not immune to change. Mikhail Gorbachev came to power in March 1985, with a mandate to revitalise the ailing socialist system. Gorbachev soon launched a multifaceted programme of reform under the catchphrase 'perestroika' (restructuring). Gorbachev recognised that it would take more than bureaucratic reorganisations and stern warnings to reverse economic decline. He believed that the root of the economic crisis was society's alienation from the socialist system. Thus, he sought to break down the barrier between 'us and them'.

His reforms were meant to engage the population and stimulate initiative. Glasnost (openness) gave new voice to both a moribund popular culture and a stifled media. Democratisation introduced multicandidate elections and new deliberative legislative bodies. Cooperatives brought the first experiments in market economics in over 50 years. Gorbachev's plan was to lead a gradual transition to reform socialism, but in practice, events ran ahead of him. Moscow set the pace.

In 1985 Gorbachev promoted Boris Yeltsin from his Urals bailiwick into the central leadership as the new head of Moscow. Yeltsin was given the assignment of cleaning up the corrupt Moscow Party machine and responded by sacking hundreds of officials. His populist touch made him an instant success with Muscovites, who were often startled to encounter him riding public transport or berating a shopkeeper for not displaying his sausage. During Gorbachev's ill-advised antialcohol campaign, Yeltsin saved Moscow's largest brewery from having to close its doors.

More importantly, Yeltsin embraced the more open political atmosphere. He allowed 'informal' groups, unsanctioned by the Communist Party, to organise and express themselves in public. Soon Moscow streets, such as those in the Arbat district, were hosting demonstrations by democrats, nationalists, reds and greens. Yeltsin's renegade style alienated the entire Party leadership, one by one. He was summarily dismissed by Gorbachev in October 1987, though he would later be heard from again.

Gorbachev's political reforms included elections to reformed local assemblies in the spring of 1990. By this time, communism had already fallen in Eastern Europe and events in the Soviet Union were becoming increasingly radical. In their first free election in 88 years, Muscovites turned out in large numbers at the polls and voted a bloc of democratic reformers into office.

The new mayor was economist Gavril Popov, and the vice-mayor was Yury Luzhkov. Popov immediately embarked on the 'decommunisation' of the city, selling off housing and state businesses and restoring prerevolutionary street names. He clashed repeatedly with the Soviet leadership over the management of city affairs. Popov soon acquired a key ally when Yeltsin made a political comeback as the elected head of the new Russian Supreme Soviet.

On 18 August 1991, the city awoke to find a column of tanks in the street and a 'Committee for the State of Emergency' claiming to be in charge. This committee was composed of leaders from the Communist Party, the KGB and the military. They had already detained Gorbachev at his Crimean dacha and issued directives to arrest Yeltsin and the Moscow city leadership.

1964-82	1985
The so-called 'Years of Stagnation' under Leonid Brezhnev	Mikhail Gorbachev implements *perestroika* (restructuring) and *glasnost* (openness)

But the ill-conceived coup quickly went awry and confusion ensued. Yeltsin, Popov and Luzhkov made it to the Russian parliament building, the so-called White House (see p86), to rally opposition. Crowds gathered at the White House, persuaded some of the tank crews to switch sides, and started to build barricades. Yeltsin climbed on a tank to declare the coup illegal and call for a general strike. He dared the snipers to shoot him, and when they didn't, the coup was over.

The following day, huge crowds opposed to the coup gathered in Moscow. Coup leaders lost their nerve, one committed suicide, some fell ill and the others simply got drunk. On 21 August, the tanks withdrew; the coup was foiled. Gorbachev flew back to Moscow to resume command, but his time was up as well. On 23 August, Yeltsin banned the Communist Party in Russia.

Gorbachev embarked on a last-ditch bid to save the Soviet Union with proposals for a looser union of independent states. Yeltsin, however, was steadily transferring control over everything that mattered from Soviet hands into Russian ones. On 8 December, Yeltsin and the leaders of Ukraine and Belarus, after several rounds of vodka toasts, announced that the USSR no longer existed. They proclaimed a new Commonwealth of Independent States (CIS), a vague alliance of fully independent states with no central authority. Gorbachev, a president without a country or authority, formally resigned on 25 December, the day the white, blue and red Russian flag replaced the Soviet red flag over the Kremlin.

Rebirth of Russian Politics

Buoyed by his success over Gorbachev and coup plotters, Yeltsin (now Russia's president) was granted extraordinary powers by the parliament to find a way out of the Soviet wreckage. Yeltsin used these powers, however, to launch radical economic reforms and rapprochement with the West. In so doing, he polarised the political elite. As Yeltsin's team of economic reformers began to dismantle the protected and subsidised command economy, in early 1992, the parliament finally acted to seize power back from the president. A stalemate ensued that lasted for a year and a half.

The executive-legislative conflict at the national level was played out in Moscow politics as well. After the Soviet fall, the democratic bloc that had brought Popov to power came apart. In Moscow, a property boom began, as buildings and land with no real owners changed hands at a dizzying rate with dubious legality. Increasingly, the mayor's office was at odds with the city council, as well as the new federal government. Popov began feuding with Yeltsin, just as he had previously with Gorbachev.

In June 1992, the impulsive Popov resigned his office in a huff. Without pausing to ask him to reconsider, Vice-mayor Yury Luzhkov readily assumed the mayor's seat (see the boxed text, p50). The city council passed a vote of no confidence in Luzhkov and called for new elections, but the new mayor opted simply to ignore the resolution.

Throughout 1993, the conflict between President Yeltsin and the Russian parliament intensified. Eight different constitutional drafts were put forward and rejected. In September 1993, parliament convened with plans to remove many of the president's powers. Before it could act, Yeltsin issued a decree that shut down the parliament and called for new elections.

Events turned violent. Yeltsin sent troops to blockade the White House, ordering the members to leave it by 4 October. Many did, but on 2 and 3 October, a National Salvation Front appeared, in an attempt to stir popular insurrection against the president. They clashed with the troops around the White House and tried to seize Moscow's Ostankino TV centre.

The army, which until this time had sought to remain neutral, intervened on the president's side and blasted the parliament into submission. In all, 145 people were killed and another 700 wounded – the worst such incident of bloodshed in the city since the Bolshevik takeover in 1917. Yeltsin, in conjunction with the newly subjugated parliament, put together

1991

A failed palace coup results in the dissolution of the Soviet Union; Boris Yeltsin is elected president of the new Russian Federation

1993

Yeltsin orders troops to force the parliament out of the White House, provoking the most violent political conflict since 1917

49

THE MAYOR IN THE CAP

Within the Moscow city government, the election of Yury Luzhkov as mayor set the stage for the creation of a big-city boss in the grandest of traditions. Through a web of financial arrangements, ownership deals and real-estate holdings, Luzhkov is as much a CEO as he is mayor. His financial interests range from the media to manufacturing and from five-star hotels to shopping malls.

When Luzhkov was first elected in June 1992, Moscow was exempted from the privatisation process then sweeping the country. This allowed the city government to retain ownership of land and property. In addition, hardly a business venture of any size receives approval from the authorities without the government as a partner. Most of the large Western hotels can boast the Moscow government as an investor, an arrangement that obviously has its advantages when city inspectors come calling. Luzhkov is also seen as the driving force behind myriads of construction (and reconstruction) projects, which have raised the protests of preservationists.

But Luzhkov also plays the role of populist with genuine aplomb, cleaning streets and planting trees. He consistently supports patriotic causes and identifies himself with nationalist themes. He has been generous with the city's money in the restoration of the long-neglected churches and historic monuments. His 'bread and circus' strategy has included hosting spectacular city celebrations, such as 1997's over-the-top 850th anniversary fete. Luzhkov also made crime prevention a priority, a policy appreciated by voters, who put personal safety ahead of concepts such as human rights.

Blessed with the riches of Moscow, the mayor delivers the goods. He won election three times: in 1996 with 95% of the vote, in 1999 with 70%, and in 2003 with 75%.

the 1993 constitution that created a new political system organised around strong central executive power.

Throughout the 1990s, Yeltsin suffered increasingly from heart disease. Come 1996, however, he was not prepared to step down from his 'throne'. Insider deals reached a peak in the 1996 presidential election. Russia's newly rich financiers, who backed Yeltsin's campaign, were rewarded with prized state-owned assets in lucrative, rigged privatisation auctions, and policy-making positions in the government. In a scene reminiscent of the medieval *boyars,* the power grabs of these 'oligarchs' became more brazen during Yeltsin's prolonged illness.

Economic Prosperity

In the New Russia, wealth was concentrated in Moscow. While the rest of Russia struggled to survive the collapse of the command economy, Moscow emerged quickly as an enclave of affluence and dynamism. By the mid-1990s Moscow was replete with all the things Russians had expected capitalism to bring, but which had yet to trickle down to the provinces: banks, shops, restaurants, casinos, BMWs, bright lights and nightlife.

The city provided nearly 25% of all tax revenues collected by the federal government. Commercial banks, commodity exchanges, big businesses and high-end retailers all set up headquarters in the capital. By the late 1990s, Moscow had become one of the most expensive cities in the world.

When the government defaulted on its debts and devalued the currency in 1998, it appeared that the boom had gone bust. But as the panic subsided, it became clear that it was less a crisis and more a correction for a badly overvalued rouble. In the aftermath, Russian firms became more competitive and productive with the new exchange rate. Wages started to be paid again and consumption increased.

Above all else, Moscow remains a centre of power – the seat of the president, government and legislature. While it may be true, in general, that power and wealth tends to find each other, this is especially the case in postcommunist Russia, where politicians have enormous control over the redistribution of economic resources. The hallways of the Duma and the offices of the White House magnetically attract favour seekers and fortune hunters.

1999	2005
Vladimir Putin succeeds Yeltsin as president	Moscow's population estimated to reach 10 million and beyond

Sights

Sights

Moscow is massive, and not only in terms of area. Wide pavements packed with people, busy thoroughfares crowded with cars, neck-wrenching skyscrapers towering above on either side of the street: its big-city appearance and attitude can be more than a little overwhelming. Not to mention the thousands of museums, parks, restaurants and clubs that welcome visitors. Where to start?

For the purposes of this book, we've broken the capital into 12 manageable areas, each defined by geography and also by activities and atmosphere. We start at the heart of it all, where Moscow was born. The Kremlin's ancient walls contain churches and treasures that could keep a visitor occupied for days. Just outside the Kremlin walls, in the area defined as the City Centre, visitors can see Moscow's most famous sights – from St Basil's to the Bolshoi Theatre and Lubyanka Prison.

From the centre, we move out into the surrounding neighbourhoods, again starting with the most ancient. Just east of Red Square, Kitay Gorod was the first settlement outside the Kremlin Walls in the 13th and 14th centuries – an era that is still remembered for its architecture.

Successive neighbourhoods form a circle around the Kremlin, following the Boulevard Ring and the Garden Ring roads (see the boxed text, p76). To the northeast is Chistye Prudy, named after the ponds that sparkle with sunlight on the main boulevard, but dwarfed by chaotic Komsomolskaya ploshchad.

Directly north of the Kremlin is the Petrovsky District, Moscow's swankiest shopping area, named after its main street and historic St Peter's monastery. West of Petrovsky District is the Tverskoy District, named for Tverskaya ulitsa, Moscow's most prominent commercial

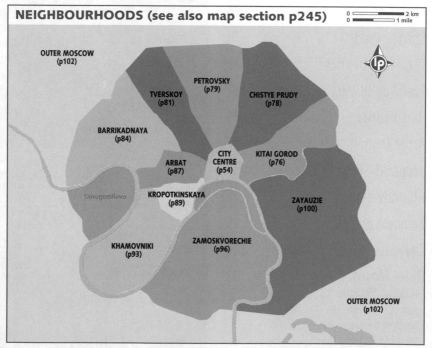

NEIGHBOURHOODS (see also map section p245)

0 ——— 2 km
0 ——— 1 mile

OUTER MOSCOW (p102)

PETROVSKY (p79)

TVERSKOY (p81)

CHISTYE PRUDY (p78)

BARRIKADNAYA (p84)

ARBAT (p87)

CITY CENTRE (p54)

KITAI GOROD (p76)

Dorogomilovo

KROPOTKINSKAYA (p89)

ZAYAUZIE (p100)

KHAMOVNIKI (p93)

ZAMOSKVORECHIE (p96)

OUTER MOSCOW (p102)

district. West of Tverskoy – out past the Garden Ring – is Barrikadnaya, so called for the barricades and street fighting that took place here during the 1905 revolution.

West of the Kremlin is the Arbat District, home to (and namesake of) the famous street that came alive with artists in the 1960s. To the southwest is Kropotkinskaya, surrounding the gargantuan Cathedral of Christ the Saviour; and Khamovniki, site of Novodevichy Convent. Directly south of the Kremlin, Zamoskvorechie is another historic part of Moscow with church-lined streets. Zayauzie sits to the southeast, isolated by rivers and dominated by Taganka ploshchad.

Moscow is greater than these 12 areas, sprawling all the way out to the Outer Ring Road (MKAD; see the boxed text, p76). Sights worth visiting on the city outskirts include the once-country estates that were built by prerevolutionary aristocrats. The only elevation that deserves the name in the whole flat expanse is the Sparrow Hills (Vorobyovy Gory), 6km southwest of the Kremlin, which is topped by the Moscow University skyscraper.

ITINERARIES

One Day

If you have but one day in Moscow, spend it seeing what makes this city famous: St Basil's Cathedral (p63), Lenin's Tomb (p63) and the Kremlin (p54). Allow a few hours in the afternoon to gawk at the gold and gems in the Armoury (p61). For dinner, indulge in a historic feast at Café Pushkin (p129).

Three Days

Spend a day running around Red Square, as described above.

Art lovers should spend the second day at either the Pushkin Fine Arts Museum (p91) or the Tretyakov Gallery (p100), two world-class art museums. After lunch, follow a walking tour in the surrounding neighbourhood; the Architecture Amble (see p108) admires the grand houses in the Arbat District and Kropotkinskaya, near the Pushkin; the Church Walk (see p113) is an opportunity to see the highlights of Zamoskvorechie, near the Tretyakov.

Plan a night out on the town. Get tickets to *Swan Lake* at the Stanislavsky-Nemirovsky Musical Theatre (p147), or to perhaps something more daring at the New Ballet (p146). If you prefer to participate rather than spectate, head to Karma Bar (p141) to tear up the dance floor.

On the third day, hit the ATM and head to the Izmaylovo (Vernisazh) Market (p162) near Izmaylovsky Park for some serious souvenir shopping. Recuperate in the park on the grounds of the Izmaylovo Royal Estate (p104). In the evening, go out for some Caucasian food. Try Karetny Dvor (p133) or Tiflis (p136) for Georgian wine and shashlyk.

One Week

Take in all of the activities suggested in the three-day itinerary. Then, plan an overnight excursion to Vladimir and Suzdal (see p187 and p190), the highlights of the Golden Ring. Use your remaining days to visit Novodevichy Convent (p95), the All-Russia Exhibition Centre (p103) or Arkhangelskoe (p205).

FOR CHILDREN

Got kids with you in Moscow? They might not appreciate an age-old icon or a Soviet hero, but Moscow has plenty to offer the little ones.

Alexandrovsky Garden (p61) **& Patriarch's Ponds** (p84) Both have small playground areas and plenty of room for the kids to run around.

All-Russia Exhibition Centre (p103) Amusement park rides and video games in a socialist-realist setting.

Central Museum of the Armed Forces (p103) Let the kids climb around on army tanks, as opposed to monkey bars.

Gorky Park (p99) Thrilling rides in summer and ice skating in winter make it the ultimate Russian experience.

Matryoshka Museum (p84) Dolls and more dolls.

Moscow Zoo (p85) Big cats for little kids.

Sculpture Park (p100) See all the Soviet heroes and climb around on them, too.

ORGANISED TOURS

CAPITAL TOURS Map pp248-9
☎ 232 2442; www.capitaltours.ru; Gostinny Dvor, ul Ilyinka 4; Ⓜ Kitay Gorod
This spin-off of Dom Patriarshy Tours offers a twice-daily Kremlin/Armoury tour (adult/child US$37/20; Ⓨ 10.30am & 3pm Fri-Wed) and Moscow city tour (adult/child US$20/10; Ⓨ 11am & 2.30pm). Tours depart from Gostinny Dvor.

DOM PATRIARSHY TOURS Map pp248-9
☎ /fax 795 0927; http://russiatravel-pdtours.netfirms.com; Vspolny per 6, Moscow school No 1239; Ⓜ Barrikadnaya
Provides unique English-language tours on just about any specialised subject; some provide access to otherwise closed museums. Day tours range from US$16 to US$40 per person. Look for the monthly schedule at upmarket hotels and restaurants, or online.

CITY CENTRE

Eating p123; Shopping p155; Sleeping p165
The Kremlin – synonymous with politics and power – is the geographic centre and political heart of the capital. In 1147 Yury Dolgoruky summoned his allies to this very spot, thus marking Moscow's beginnings. Ever since, the Kremlin has served as the symbol of the state. From here Ivan the Terrible unleashed his terror, Napoleon watched Moscow burn, Lenin fashioned the dictatorship of the proletariat, Gorbachev orchestrated *perestroika* and Yeltsin concocted the New Russia.

In the early days, all the residents lived within the low wall that surrounded the fortress. These days, nobody lives in the City Centre. Official buildings, historic museums, grand theatres, luxury hotels and shopping centres line the streets. The wide boulevards and ceremonial squares are best suited for parades, rallies, concerts and other pomp and circumstance.

This is the domain of officialdom, which visitors will perceive immediately. The police presence is very visible, directing cars and pedestrians in an orderly fashion. Official events often cause the closure of Red Square, if not the surrounding streets. Even under normal circumstances, when Lenin's Tomb is open to the public, pedestrians are strictly controlled by surly men in uniform. They usher visitors in one side and out the other and prohibit casual strollers. The atmosphere is befitting Russia's authoritarian image. The powerful Kremlin walls, the stately buildings and the proliferation of police emphasise the idea that this regime takes itself seriously (as have all regimes that have ruled from their roost in the Kremlin).

Nonetheless, the City Centre is the area where visitors to Moscow spend most of their time, and rightly so. The historical significance and architectural magnificence of this 1-sq-km space is truly awe-inspiring.

Orientation

The Kremlin is a north-pointing triangle with 750m sides, occupying a spot of land on little Borovitsky Hill. Red Square lies outside its eastern wall, while Alexandrovsky Garden flanks the western wall. The Moscow (Moskva) River flows to the south, so the best views of the Kremlin are from Sofiyskaya naberezhnaya, across the river. North of the Kremlin, above the apex, is Manezhnaya ploshchad, named after the royal stables that once occupied this spot.

The City Centre lies in the arc around the Kremlin bound by Mokhovaya ulitsa, Okhotny ryad, Teatralny proezd and Lubyansky proezd. The arc is punctuated by three squares – Manezhnaya ploshchad, Teatralnaya ploshchad and Lubyanskaya ploshchad. Parts of Kitay Gorod are also contained within this arc. But for the purposes of this book, Kitay Gorod is treated as a separate neighbourhood.

KREMLIN

The apex of Russian political power, the Kremlin (☎ 202 3776; www.kremlin.museum.ru; adult/student & child R300/150, pho-

---

TRANSPORT

With the exception of Red Square, each of the squares in the arc of the City Centre has its own metro stop (or stops, as the case may be): Lubyanka at Lubyanskaya ploshchad; Teatralnaya at Teatralnaya ploshchad; and Okhotny Ryad at Manezhnaya ploshchad. To access Red Square, use Okhotny Ryad or Ploshchad Revolyutsii. The entrance to the Kremlin is on the west side of the complex, so it is closest to metro stations Alexandrovsky Sad and Biblioteka imeni Lenina.

All of these stations are within walking distance of each other (although the trek around the outside of the Kremlin is longer than it appears)

TOP FIVE CITY CENTRE SIGHTS

- **Armoury** (p61) Museum of royal treasures.
- **Assumption Cathedral** (p57) Golden domes glistening in the sun.
- **Lenin's Tomb** (p63) Pay your respects to the Communist leader.
- **State History Museum** (p64) Exhibits from the Stone Age to the present.
- **St Basil's Cathedral** (p63) Famous onion domes and spires

tography permit R50; ☯ 9.30am-4pm Fri-Wed; Ⓜ Alexandrovsky Sad, Borovitskaya or Biblioteka imeni Lenina) is not only the kernel of Moscow, but also the whole country. A kremlin – or fortified stronghold – has existed on this site since Moscow's earliest years. When Moscow became the capital of medieval Rus in the 1320s, the Kremlin served as the headquarters of the Russian Orthodox Church and the seat of the prince. The 'White Stone Kremlin' – which had limestone walls – was built shortly thereafter.

However, most of the present-day buildings, walls and towers date from the 15th and 16th centuries. After his marriage to the Byzantine princess Sofia Paleologue, the ambition of Ivan III (the Great) was to build a capital that would equal the fallen Constantinople in grandeur, political power, achievements and architecture. In an effort to build the 'Third Rome', Ivan brought stonemasons and architects from Italy, who built new walls, three great cathedrals, and other structures, most of which are still standing.

Although Peter I (the Great) shifted the capital to St Petersburg, the tsars still showed up here for coronations and other celebrations. Over the years, the biggest threat to the Kremlin was Napoleon, who blew up parts of it before making his retreat in 1812. Fortunately, the timely arrival of Russian troops prevented total destruction. The citadel wouldn't be breached again until the Bolsheviks stormed the place in November 1917.

The Kremlin remained closed to the public until 1955. It was Stalin who, in 1935, had the imperial double-headed eagles removed from the wall's five tallest towers, replacing them with the distinctive red-glass stars still there today.

Before entering the Kremlin, deposit all bags at the **left luggage office** (per bag R60; ☯ 9am-6.30pm), under the Kutafya Tower, near the main ticket office. The main ticket office is in the Alexandrovsky Garden, just off Manezhnaya ploshchad. The ticket covers entry to all buildings except the Armoury and Diamond Fund Exhibition; it also does not include the special exhibits that are sometimes held inside the Ivan the Great Bell Tower.

In any case, you can and should buy tickets for the Armoury here, to avoid queuing up once inside. Arrive early before tickets sell out. There's also an entrance at the southern Borovitskaya Gate, mainly used by those heading straight to the Armoury or the Diamond Fund Exhibition.

Inside the Kremlin, the police will keep you from straying into the out-of-bounds areas. Visitors wearing shorts will be refused entry.

Visiting the Kremlin buildings and the Armoury is at least a half-day affair. If you intend to visit the Diamond Fund or other special exhibits, plan on spending most of the day here.

ENTRANCE TOWERS Map p258

The **Kutafya Tower** (Kutafya bashnya), which forms the main visitors' entrance today, stands apart from the Kremlin's west wall, at the end of a ramp over the Alexandrovsky Garden. The ramp was once a bridge over the Neglinnaya River and used to be part of the Kremlin's defences; this river has been diverted underground, beneath the Alexandrovsky Garden, since the early 19th century. The Kutafya Tower is the last of a number of outer bridge towers that once stood on this side of the Kremlin.

From the Kutafya Tower, walk up the ramp and pass through the Kremlin walls beneath the 1495 **Trinity Gate Tower** (Troitskaya bashnya), the tallest of the Kremlin's towers. Right below your feet were the cells for prisoners in the 16th century. On your way to Sobornaya ploshchad you pass the buildings described following, that are closed to visitors.

GOVERNMENT BUILDINGS Map p258

The lane to the right (south), immediately inside the Trinity Gate Tower, passes the 17th-century **Poteshny Palace** (Poteshny dvorets), which Stalin decided to move into. The yellow Poteshny Palace was built by Tsar Alexey Mikhailovich and housed the first Russian theatre. Here Tsar Alexey enjoyed various comedic performances. In keeping with conservative Russian Orthodox tradition, however, after the shows he would go to the *banya* (Russian bathhouse), then attend a church service to repent his sins.

The bombastic marble, glass and concrete **State Kremlin Palace** (Gosudarstvenny Kremlyovsky dvorets), built between 1960 and 1961 for Communist Party congresses, is also a concert and ballet auditorium that holds 6000 people. North of the State Kremlin Palace is the 18th-century **Arsenal**, commissioned by Peter the Great to house

TOWERS OF POWER

The present Kremlin walls were built between 1485 and 1495, replacing the limestone walls from the 14th century. The walls are 6m to 17m tall, depending on the landscape, and 2m to 5m thick. They stretch for 2235m. Originally, a 32m-wide moat encircled the northern end of the Kremlin, connecting the Moscow and Neglinnaya Rivers.

The 20 distinctive towers were built mostly between 1485 and 1500, with tent roofs added in the 17th century. Originally, the towers had lookout posts and were equipped for heavy fighting. Most were designed by Italian masons. The more interesting towers are on the eastern and southern sides. Starting at the northern corner and going clockwise:

Corner Arsenal Tower (Arsenalnaya bashnya) The stronghold of the Kremlin with walls 4m thick. A well built into the basement to provide water during sieges still survives today.

St Nicholas Tower (Nikolskaya bashnya) Previously a gated defensive tower on the northeastern flank. Through this gate, Dmitry Pozharsky and Kozma Minin (as depicted in the statue in front of St Basil's Cathedral) led a civilian army and drove out the Polish occupiers.

Senate Tower (Senatskaya bashnya) Originally a nameless, gateless tower, and finally named after the construction of the Senate in the 18th century.

Saviour Gate Tower (Spasskaya bashnya) The Kremlin's 'official' exit onto Red Square. This gate – considered sacred – was used for processions in tsarist times. The two white-stone plaques above the gate commemorate the tower's construction. Between the tower's double walls, a staircase links five of its 10 levels. The current clock was installed in this gate tower in the 1850s. Hauling 3m hands and weighing 25 tonnes, the clock takes up three of the tower's levels. Its melodic chime sounds every 15 minutes across Red Square and across the country (on the radio).

Tsar Tower (Tsarskaya bashnya) A later addition (1680), which sits on top of the Kremlin wall. Legend has it that Ivan the Terrible watched executions and other Red Square activities from the old wooden tower that previously stood on this site.

Alarm Tower (Nabatnaya bashnya) Housed the Spassky Alarm Bell, which was used to warn of enemy attacks and to spur popular uprisings. After quashing one uprising, Catherine the Great was so outraged that she had the clapper removed from the bell, so it could sound no more. The bell remained mute in the tower for 30 years before it was finally removed.

Konstantin & Yelena Tower (Konstantino-Yeleninskaya bashnya) Built to protect the settlements outside the city, it is complete with firing platforms and a drawbridge over the moat. During the 17th century this tower was used as a prison, earning it the nickname 'torture tower'.

Moskvoretskaya Tower The round tower at the southeastern corner.

Petrovskaya Tower

First & Second Nameless Towers Both destroyed in 1771 because they interfered with the construction of the Kremlin Palace, but rebuilt after its completion.

Secret Tower (Taynitskaya bashnya) The first tower built (1485), it is named after a secret passageway leading down to the river.

Annunciation Tower (Blagoveshchenskaya bashnya) Named for the miracle-working icon on the façade. In 1633 the so-called Laundry Gate was constructed nearby for Kremlin washerwomen to go down to the Moscow River, but it was later bricked up.

Water Tower (Vodovzvodnaya bashnya) A circular tower erected at the confluence of the Moscow and Neglinnaya Rivers. From 1633 a water lift in the tower pumped water to a reservoir and supplied a system of underground piping for the Kremlin.

workshops and depots for guns and weaponry. An unrealised plan at the end of the 19th century was to open a museum of the Napoleonic Wars in the Arsenal. Now housing the Kremlin Guard, the building is ringed with 800 captured Napoleonic cannons.

The offices of the president of Russia, the ultimate seat of power in the modern Kremlin, are in the yellow, triangular former **Senate** building, a fine 18th-century neoclassical edifice, east of the Arsenal. Built in 1785 by architect Matvei Kazakov, it was noted for its huge cupola. In the 16th and 17th centuries this area was where the *boyars* (high-ranking Russian nobles) lived. Next to the Senate is the 1930s **Supreme Soviet** (Verkhovny Soviet) building.

PATRIARCH'S PALACE Map p258
Patriarshy dvorets
This palace was mostly built in the mid-17th century for Patriarch Nikon, whose reforms sparked the break with the Old Believers (p101). The palace contains an exhibit of 17th-century household items, including jewellery, hunting equipment and furniture. From here you can access the five-domed **Church of the Twelve Apostles**, which has a gilded wooden iconostasis and a collection of icons by the leading 17th-century icon painters.

The highlight is perhaps the ceremonial **Cross Hall** (Krestovaya palata), where feasts for the tsars and ambassadors were held. From the 18th century the room was used to produce *miro* (a holy oil used during church services, which contains over 30 herbal components); the oven and huge pans from the production process are on display.

Now quiet, the palace in its heyday was a busy place. Apart from the Patriarch's living quarters, it had huge kitchens, warehouses and cellars stocked with food, workshops, a school for high-born children, offices for scribes, dormitories for those waiting to be baptised, stables and carriage houses.

ASSUMPTION CATHEDRAL Map p258
Uspensky sobor
On the northern side of Sobornaya ploshchad, with five golden helmet domes and four semicircular gables facing the square, the Assumption Cathedral was the focal church of prerevolutionary Russia, and the burial place of most of the heads of the Russian Orthodox Church from the 1320s to

1700. A striking 1660s fresco of the Virgin Mary faces Sobornaya ploshchad, above the door once used for royal processions. If you have limited time in the Kremlin, come straight here. The visitors' entrance is at the western end.

In 1470 Russian architects Krivtsov and Myshkin were commissioned by Ivan the Great to replace the old dilapidated cathedral, which dated from 1326. As soon as the ceiling was put up, one of the walls collapsed. During Soviet times, history books said this calamity was the result of bad workmanship, but today revisionist history indicates that a bad earthquake caused the collapse. Either way, Krivtsov and Myshkin lost their jobs, and Italian architect Aristotle Fioravanti was given a crack at it. After the foundation was completed, Aristotle toured Novgorod, Suzdal and Vladimir to acquaint himself with Russian architecture. His design is a more spacious version of the Assumption Cathedral at Vladimir, with a Renaissance twist.

In 1812 French troops used the cathedral as a stable; they looted 295kg of gold and over five tonnes of silver from here, but much of it was recovered. The church closed in 1918. According to some accounts, in 1941, when the Nazis were on the outskirts of Moscow, Stalin secretly ordered a service in the Assumption Cathedral to protect the city from the enemy. The cathedral was officially returned to the Church in 1989, but it operates as a museum.

The interior of the Assumption Cathedral is unusually bright and spacious, full of warm golds, reds and blues. The west wall features a scene of the Apocalypse, a favourite theme of the Russian Church in the Middle Ages. The pillars have pictures of martyrs on them, as martyrs are considered to be the pillars of faith. Above the southern gates there are frescoes of Yelena and Constantine, who brought Christianity to Greece and the south of Russia. The space above the northern gate depicts Olga and Vladimir, who brought Christianity to the north.

Most of the existing murals on the cathedral walls were painted on a gilt base in the 1640s, with the exception of three grouped together on the south wall: *The Apocalypse (Apokalipsis), The Life of Metropolitan Pyotr (Zhitie Mitropolita Petra)* and *All Creatures Rejoice in Thee (O tebe raduetsya)*. These are attributed to Dionysius and his followers, the cathedral's original 15th-century mural painters. The tombs of many leaders of the Russian Church (metropolitans up to 1590, patriarchs from 1590 to 1700) are against the north, west and south walls.

Near the south wall is a tent-roofed wooden throne made in 1551 for Ivan the Terrible, known as the **Throne of Monomakh**. Its carved scenes highlight the career of 12th-century Grand Prince Vladimir Monomakh of Kiev. Near the west wall there is a shrine with holy relics of Patriarch Hermogen, who was starved to death during the Time of Troubles in 1612.

The **iconostasis** dates from 1652, but its lowest level contains some older icons. The 1340s *Spas yaroe oko (Saviour with the Angry Eye)* is second from the right. On the left of the central door is the *Vladimir-skaya Bogomater (Virgin of Vladimir)*, an early-15th-century Rublyov school copy of Russia's most revered image: the *Vladimir-skaya Ikona Bogomateri (Vladimir Icon of the Mother of God)*. The 12th-century origi-nal, now in the Tretyakov Gallery (p100), stood in the Assumption Cathedral from the 1480s to 1930. One of the oldest Rus-sian icons, the 12th-century red-clothed *Svyatoy Georgy (St George)* from Novgorod, is by the north wall.

The original icons of the lower, local tier are symbols of victory brought from Vladimir, Smolensk, Veliky Ustiug and other places. The south door was brought from the Nativity of the Virgin Cathedral in Suzdal (see p191).

CHURCH OF THE DEPOSITION OF THE ROBE Map p258
Tserkov Rizpolozhenia

This delicate single-domed church, beside the west door of the Assumption Cathe-dral, was built between 1484 and 1486 in exclusively Russian style. It was the private chapel of the heads of the Church, who tended to be highly suspicious of such people as Italian architects.

Originally an open gallery or porch sur-rounded the church; it was later removed and the church was connected with the palace for the convenience of the tsars. The interior walls, ceilings and pillars are cov-ered with 17th-century frescoes. It houses an exhibition of 15th- to 17th-century woodcarvings.

IVAN THE GREAT BELL TOWER Map p258
Kolokolnya Ivana Velikogo; special exhibits adult/ student & child R100/50

With its two golden domes rising above the eastern side of Sobornaya ploshchad, the Ivan the Great Bell Tower is the Kremlin's tallest structure – a landmark visible from 30km away. Before the 20th century it was forbidden to build any higher than this tower in Moscow.

Its history dates back to the Church of Ioann Lestvichnik Under the Bells, built on this site in 1329 by Ivan I. In 1505 the Italian Marco Bono designed a new belfry, origi-nally with only two octagonal tiers beneath a drum and a dome. In 1600 Boris Godunov raised it to 81m, a public works project de-signed to employ the thousands of people who had come to Moscow during a famine.

The building's central section, with a guilded single dome and a 65-tonne bell, dates from between 1532 and 1542. The tent-roofed annexe, next to the belfry, was commissioned by Patriarch Filaret in 1642 and bears his name. Exhibitions from the Kremlin collections are shown on the ground level.

TSAR CANNON & BELL Map p258
Tsar Pushka & Kolokol

North of the bell tower is the 40-tonne Tsar Cannon. It was cast in 1586 by the black-smith Ivan Chokhov for Fyodor I, whose portrait is on the barrel. Shot has never sullied its 89cm bore and certainly not the cannonballs beside it, which are too big even for this elephantine firearm.

Beside (not inside) the bell tower stands the world's biggest bell, a 202-tonne mon-ster that has never rung. An earlier version, weighing 130 tonnes, fell from its belfry during a fire in 1701 and shattered. Using these remains, the current Tsar Bell was cast in the 1730s for Empress Anna Ivanovna. The bell was cooling off in the foundry casting pit in 1737 when it came into con-tact with water, causing an 11-tonne chunk to break off. One hundred years later, the architect Monferrand took the damaged bell out of the pit and put it on a pedestal. The bas-reliefs of Empress Anna and Tsar Alexey, as well as some icons, were etched on its sides.

South of the bell, the pleasant park of Ivanovskaya ploshchad offers spectacular views south over Moscow.

ARCHANGEL CATHEDRAL Map p258
Arkhangelsky sobor

The Archangel Cathedral at the southeastern corner of Sobornaya ploshchad was for centuries the coronation, wedding and burial church of tsars. It was built by Ivan Kalita in 1333 to commemorate the end of the great famine, and dedicated to Archangel Michael, guardian of the Moscow princes. By the turn of the 16th century it had fallen into disrepair and was rebuilt between 1505 and 1508 by the Italian architect Alevisio Novi. Like the Assumption Cathedral, it is five-domed and essentially Byzantine-Russian in style. However, the exterior has many Venetian Renaissance features – notably the distinctive scallop shell gables and porticoes.

The tombs of all Muscovy's rulers from the 1320s to the 1690s are here, bar one (the absentee is Boris Godunov, whose body was taken out of the grave on the order of a False Dmitry and buried at Sergiev Posad in 1606). The bodies are buried underground, beneath the 17th-century sarcophagi and 19th-century copper covers. Tsarevich Dmitry (a son of Ivan the Terrible), who died mysteriously in 1591, lies beneath a painted stone canopy.

It was Dmitry's death that sparked the appearance of a string of impersonators, known as False Dmitrys, during the Time of Troubles. Ivan's own tomb is out of sight behind the iconostasis, along with those of his other sons: Ivan (whom he killed) and Fyodor I (who succeeded him). From Peter the Great onwards, emperors and empresses were buried in St Petersburg; the exception being Peter II, who died in Moscow and is here. Some 17th-century murals were uncovered during restorations in the 1950s. The south wall depicts many of those buried here; on the pillars are some of their predecessors, including Andrey Bogolyubsky, Prince Daniil and Alexander Nevsky.

HALL OF FACETS Map p258
Granovitaya palata

Named for its Italian Renaissance stone facing, the Hall of Facets was designed and built by Marco Ruffo and Pietro Solario between 1487 and 1491, during the reign of Ivan the Great. Its upper floor housed the tsars' throne room, scene of banquets and ceremonies. Access to the Hall of Facets was via an outside staircase from the square below. During the Streltsky Rebellion of 1682, several of Peter the Great's relatives were tossed down the exterior **Red Staircase**, so called because it ran red with their blood. (It's no wonder that Peter hated Moscow and decided to start afresh with a new capital in St Petersburg.) Stalin destroyed the staircase, but it was rebuilt in 1994.

The hall is 500 sq metres with a supporting pillar in the centre. The walls are decorated with gorgeous murals of biblical and historical themes, although none is original. Alas, the building is closed to the public.

TEREM PALACE Map p258
Teremnoy dvorets

The 16th- and 17th-century Terem Palace is the most splendid of the Kremlin palaces.

Tsar Cannon (p58), Kremlin

Made of stone and built by Vasily III, the palace's living quarters include a dining room, living room, study, bedroom and small chapel. Unfortunately, the palace is closed to the public, but you can glimpse its cluster of 11 golden domes and chequered roof behind and above the Church of the Deposition of the Robe.

ANNUNCIATION CATHEDRAL Map p258
Blagoveshchensky sobor

The Annunciation Cathedral, at the southwest corner of Sobornaya ploshchad, contains the celebrated icons of master painter Theophanes the Greek (Feofan Grek in Russian). They have a timeless beauty that appeals even to those usually left cold by icons.

Vasily I built the first wooden church on this site in 1397. Between 1484 and 1489, Ivan the Great had the Annunciation Cathedral rebuilt to serve as the royal family's private chapel. Originally the cathedral had just three domes and an open gallery around three sides. Ivan the Terrible, whose tastes were more elaborate, added six more domes and chapels at each corner, enclosed the gallery and gilded the roof.

Under Orthodox law, Ivan's fourth marriage disqualified him from entering the church proper, so he had the southern arm of the gallery converted into the **Archangel Gabriel Chapel** (Pridel Arkhangela Gavriila), from which he could watch services through a grille. The chapel has a colourful iconostasis, dating from its consecration in 1564, and an exhibition of icons.

Many murals in the gallery date from the 1560s. Among them are the *Capture of Jericho* in the porch, *Jonah and the Whale* in the northern arm of the gallery, and the *Tree of Jesus* on its ceiling. Other murals feature ancient philosophers, such as Aristotle, Plutarch, Plato and Socrates, holding scrolls with their own wise words. Socrates' scroll reads: 'No harm will ever come to a good man. Our soul is immortal. After death the good shall be rewarded and the evil punished.' Plato's says: 'We must hope God shall send us a heavenly Teacher and a Guide.'

The small central part of the cathedral has a lovely jasper floor. The 16th-century frescoes include Russian princes on the north pillar and Byzantine emperors on the south, both with Apocalypse scenes above them. But the cathedral's real treasure is the iconostasis, where in the 1920s restorers uncovered early-15th-century icons by three of the greatest medieval Russian artists.

Theophanes most likely painted the six icons at the right-hand end of the biggest row of the six tiers of the iconostasis. From left to right, these are the Virgin Mary, Christ Enthroned, St John the Baptist, the Archangel Gabriel, the Apostle Paul and St John Chrysostom. Theophanes was a master of portraying pathos in the facial expressions of his subjects, setting these icons apart from most others.

The third icon from the left, Archangel Michael, is ascribed to Andrei Rublyov, who may also have painted the adjacent St Peter. Rublyov is also reckoned to be the artist of the first, second, sixth, seventh and probably the third and fifth icons from the left of the festival row, above the deesis row. The seven icons at the right-hand end are attributed to Prokhor of Gorodets.

The basement – a remnant of the previous 14th-century cathedral on this site – contains a fascinating exhibit on the **Archaeology of the Kremlin**. The artefacts date from the 12th to 14th centuries, showing the growth of Moscow during this period.

GREAT KREMLIN PALACE Map p258
Bolshoy Kremlyovsky dvorets

Housing the Armoury and much more, the 700-room Great Kremlin Palace was built between 1838 and 1849 by architect Konstantin Thon as an imperial residence for Nicholas I. It is now an official residence of the Russian president, used for state visits and receptions. However, unlike Russian tsars, the president doesn't have living quarters here.

The huge palace incorporates some of the earlier buildings such as the Hall of Facets, Terem Palace and several chapels. Although vast, the building has never received great praise, being criticised as 'barrack-like' and 'pretentious'. Several ceremonial halls are named after saints, including St George, St Vladimir, St Andrew, St Catherine and St Alexander. St George's Hall is mainly used for state awards ceremonies, while major international treaties are signed in St Vladimir's Hall. To save you the trouble, the Great Kremlin Palace (apart from the Armoury – see following) is closed to tourists, except those on an official state visit. From time to time, Dom Patriarshy Tours (p54) brings tourists here.

ARMOURY Map p258

Oruzheynaya palata; adult/student & child
R300/175; ⏲ 10am, noon, 2.30pm & 4.30pm
The Armoury dates back to 1511, when it
was founded under Vasily III to manufacture
and store weapons, imperial arms and regalia for the royal court. Later it also produced
jewellery, icon frames and embroidery.

During the reign of Peter the Great all
craftsmen, goldsmiths and silversmiths
were sent to St Petersburg, and the armoury
became a mere museum storing the royal
treasures. A fire in 1737 destroyed many of
the items. In the early 19th century, new
premises were built for the collection. Much
of it, however, never made it back from
Nizhny Novgorod, where it was sent for safe-
keeping during Napoleon's invasion in 1812.

Another building to house the collection
was completed in 1851, but it was later
demolished to make way for the Palace of
Congresses, now the State Kremlin Palace
(see Government Buildings, p56). So the
Armoury is now housed in the Great Kremlin Palace. Despite the disasters that have
befallen this collection throughout the
centuries, the Armoury still contains plenty
of treasures for ogling, and remains a highlight of any visit to the Kremlin.

The exhibit starts upstairs; your ticket
will specify a time for entry. Here's what
you'll find:

Room 1 Stuffed to the gills with various gold and silver
objects. Don't overdose, as there is plenty more to come.

Room 2 Houses the renowned Easter eggs made from
precious metals and jewels by St Petersburg jeweller,
Fabergé. The tsar and tsarina traditionally exchanged these
gifts each year at Easter. Most famous is the Grand Siberian
Railway egg, with gold train, platinum locomotive and
ruby headlamp, created to commemorate the completion
of the Moscow-Vladivostok line.

Rooms 3 & 4 Armour, weapons and more armour and
more weapons.

Room 5 Here you will find all those gifts proffered by
visiting ambassadors over the years. Each piece of gold or
silver is yet another reason why the average peasant trying
to coax some life out of a mouldy seed might get a little
miffed. Ignoring the plight of the masses, you can enjoy
the skill of the craftspeople who made these items.

Room 6 Coronation dresses of 18th-century empresses
(Empress Elizabeth, we're told, had 15,000 other dresses).

Room 7 Contains the joint coronation throne of boy-tsars
Peter the Great and his half-brother, Ivan V (with a secret
compartment from which Regent Sofia prompted them), as
well as the 800-diamond throne of Tsar Alexey, Peter's father.

The gold Cap of Monomakh – jewel-studded and sable-
trimmed – was used for two centuries at coronations.

Room 8 Only the best royal harnesses and equestrian gear.

Room 9 Centuries worth of royal carriages and sledges
line the aisles in this huge room, one of which surely could
have kept a village of potential revolutionaries fed for
several years. The once-glittering gold leafing has faded
and the wood has shrunk revealing gaps in the decoration.
Look for the sleigh in which Elizabeth rode from St Petersburg to Moscow for her coronation, pulled by 23 horses at
a time – about 800 in all for the trip.

DIAMOND FUND EXHIBITION Map p258

Vystavka almaznogo fonda; ☎ 229 2036; adult/
student R350/175; ⏲ 10am-noon, 2-5pm Fri-Wed
If the Armoury hasn't sated your lust for
diamonds, there are more in the separate
Diamond Fund Exhibition in the same
building. The collection, mainly precious
stones and jewellery garnered by tsars and
empresses, includes such weighty beasts
as the 190-carat diamond given to Catherine the Great by her lover Grigory Orlov.
The displays of unmounted diamonds are
stunning, revealing the real beauty of these
gems.

There are almost no signs – even in Russian – as the locals are only allowed in as
part of a guided tour. No tours are offered
in other languages, which is to your advantage, since you do not have to wait as the
Russian visitors do.

ALEXANDROVSKY GARDEN Map p258

Alexandrovsky sad; Ⓜ Alexandrovsky Sad or
Biblioteka imeni Lenina
The first public park in Moscow, Alexandrovsky Garden sits along the Kremlin's
western wall. Colourful flower beds and
impressive Kremlin views make it a favourite strolling spot for Muscovites and tourists
alike. Back in the 17th century, the Neglinnaya River ran through the present gardens, with dams and mills along its banks.
When the river was diverted underground,
the garden was founded by architect Osip
Bove, in 1821. Enter through the original
gates at the northern end.

The **Tomb of the Unknown Soldier** (Mogila
neizvestnogo soldata) at its north end is
a kind of national pilgrimage spot, where
newlyweds bring flowers and have their
pictures taken. The tomb contains the
remains of one soldier who died in December 1941 at Km 41 of Leningradskoe
shosse – the nearest the Nazis came to

Moscow. The inscription reads: 'Your name is unknown, your deeds immortal.' There's an eternal flame, and other inscriptions listing the Soviet hero cities of WWII and honouring 'those who fell for the motherland' between 1941 and 1945. South of the tomb, a row of red urns contains the earth from the 'hero cities': cities that withstood the heaviest fighting during WWII. The changing of the guard happens every hour.

Further south, the obelisk was originally a monument to commemorate the House of Romanovs. In 1918 it had a dramatic change in mission when it was redesignated the **Monument to Revolutionary Thinkers**, in honour of those responsible for the spread of communism in Russia.

RED SQUARE

Immediately outside the Kremlin's northeastern wall is the infamous Red Square, or Krasnaya ploshchad. Commanding the square from the southern end is the building that, more than any other, says 'Russia': St Basil's Cathedral.

Red Square used to be a market square adjoining the merchants' area in Kitay Gorod. It has always been a place where occupants of the Kremlin chose to congregate, celebrate and castigate for all the people to see. Here, Ivan the Terrible publicly confessed his misdeeds in 1547, built St Basil's to commemorate his victories in the 1550s, and later had numerous perceived enemies executed. Red Square also saw the dismembering of the Cossack rebel Stepan Razin in 1671, as well as the en masse execution in 1698 of 2000 members of the Streltsy (Peter the Great's mutinous palace guard).

Soviet rulers chose Red Square for their military parades, perhaps most poignantly on 7 November 1941, when tanks rolled straight off to the front line outside Moscow; and during the Cold War, when lines of ICBMs (intercontinental ballistic missile) rumbled across the square to remind the West of Soviet military might.

Incidentally, the Russian name of Krasnaya ploshchad has nothing to do with communism or the blood that flowed here: *krasny* in old Russian meant 'beautiful' and only in the 20th century did it come to mean 'red', too.

Red Square is closed to traffic, except for the limousines that whiz in and out of the Kremlin's Saviour Gate from time to time. Most people here are sightseers, but that doesn't reduce the thrill of walking on this 400m by 150m area of cobbles, so central to Russian history. It's particularly atmospheric when floodlit at night.

The best way to enter Red Square is through the **Resurrection Gate**. Rebuilt in 1995, it's an exact copy of the original completed on this site in 1680, with its twin red towers topped by green tent spires. The first gateway was destroyed because Stalin thought it an impediment to the parades and demonstrations held in Red Square. Through the gateway is the bright **Chapel of the Iverian Virgin**, originally built in the late 18th century to house the icon of the same name.

The Kremlin (p54) as seen from a pedestrian bridge

GUM Map p258

☎ 921 5763; Red Square (Krasnaya pl) 3;
🕙 10am-10pm; Ⓜ Ploshchad Revolyutsii

The elaborate 19th-century façade on the northeastern side of Red Square is the Gosudarstvenny Universalny Magazin (State Department Store). GUM once symbolised all that was bad about Soviet shopping: long queues and shelves empty of all but a few drab goods. A remarkable transformation has taken place since *perestroika,* and today GUM is a bright, bustling place with over 1000 fancy shops (p155).

KAZAN CATHEDRAL Map p258

Nikolskaya ul 3; admission free; 🕙 8am-7pm, evening service 8pm Mon; Ⓜ Ploshchad Revolyutsii

The tiny Kazan Cathedral, opposite the northern end of GUM, is a 1993 replica. The original was founded in 1636 in thanks for the 1612 expulsion of Polish invaders (for two centuries it housed the *Virgin of Kazan* icon, which supposedly helped to rout the Poles). Three hundred years later, the cathedral was completely demolished, allegedly because it impeded the flow of celebrating workers in May Day and Revolution Day parades.

LENIN'S TOMB Map p258

☎ 923 5527; Red Square (Krasnaya pl); admission free; 🕙 10am-1pm Tue-Thu, Sat & Sun; Ⓜ Ploshchad Revolyutsii

The granite tomb of Lenin, standing at the foot of the Kremlin wall, is another of Red Square's must-sees, especially since (if some people get their way) the former leader may eventually end up beside his mum in St Petersburg. For now, the embalmed leader remains as he has been since 1924 (apart from a retreat to Siberia during WWII). See boxed text, p64, to learn how he keeps his waxy demeanour.

From 1953 to 1961, Lenin shared the tomb with Stalin. In 1961, during the 22nd Party Congress, the esteemed and by then ancient Bolshevik, Madame Spiridonova, announced that Vladimir Ilych had appeared to her in a dream, insisting that he did not like spending eternity with his successor. With that, Stalin was removed and given a place of honour immediately behind the mausoleum.

Before joining the queue at the northwestern corner of Red Square, drop your camera at the left-luggage office in the State History Museum, as you will not be allowed to take it with you. Humourless guards ensure that visitors remain respectful.

After trouping past the embalmed figure, emerge from the mausoleum and inspect the Kremlin wall, where Stalin, Brezhnev and other Communist heavy-hitters are buried. Besides these two, some of the worthies given the honour of burial here:

Felix Dzerzhinsky The founder of the Cheka (forerunner of the KGB).

Yakov Sverdlov A key organiser of the revolution and the first official head of the Soviet State.

Andrei Zhdanov Stalin's cultural chief, and the second most powerful man in the USSR immediately after WWII.

Mikhail Frunze The Red Army leader who secured Central Asia for the Soviet Union in the 1920s.

Inessa Armand Lenin's rumoured lover. She was a respected Bolshevik who was the director of Zhenotdel, an organisation fighting for equality for women within the Communist Party.

John Reed The American author of *Ten Days that Shook the World,* a first-hand account of the revolution.

ST BASIL'S CATHEDRAL Map p258

Intercessional Cathedral; ☎ 298 3304; Red Square (Krasnaya pl); adult/student & child R100/50; 🕙 11am-5pm Wed-Mon; Ⓜ Ploshchad Revolyutsii

No picture can prepare you for the crazy confusion of colours and shapes that is St Basil's Cathedral. This ultimate symbol of Russia was created between 1555 and 1561 (replacing an existing church on the site) to celebrate Ivan the Terrible's capture of the Tatar stronghold, Kazan. The capture took place on 1 October 1552, the feast of the Intercession which gives the cathedral its official name, Intercession Cathedral by

Sights

CITY CENTRE

TOP FIVE FREEBIES

- **Cathedral of Christ the Saviour** (p90) Glitter and gold on a huge scale.
- **Kolomenskoe Museum-Reserve** (p104) Pay to enter the museum, but seeing the beautiful grounds and churches will cost you nothing.
- **Gorky House-Museum** (p84) Tribute to a literary mastermind, housed inside an Art Nouveau masterpiece.
- **Lenin's Tomb** (left) Pay your respects to the founder of the Soviet state.
- **Sakharov Museum** (p77) Political and artistic exhibits, as well as information about the life and times of the dissident.

the Moat (Pokrovsky sobor). Its design is the culmination of a wholly Russian style that had been developed building wooden churches; legend has it that Ivan had the cathedral's architect blinded so that he could never build anything comparable.

The cathedral's apparent anarchy of shapes hides a comprehensible plan of nine main chapels: the tall, tent-roofed one in the centre; four big, octagonal-towered ones, topped with the four biggest domes; and four smaller ones in between.

The misnomer St Basil's actually refers only to the extra northeastern chapel, which was added later. It was built over the grave of the barefoot holy fool Vasily (Basil) the Blessed, who predicted Ivan's damnation and added correctly, as the army left for Kazan, that Ivan would murder a son. Vasily, who died while Kazan was under siege, was buried beside the church that St Basil's soon replaced. He was later canonised.

Only in the 1670s were the domes patterned, giving St Basil's its multicoloured appearance. Between 1772 and 1784 the cathedral received a metal roof and a whitewashing; its domes were gold-leafed in keeping with the fashion of the time. Although Napoleon ordered it to be destroyed in 1812, his troops did not have enough time to complete the task. In 1817 the cathedral returned to its present colourful appearance, the cemetery was closed and the houses and moat surrounding the cathedral were removed.

The interior is open to visitors. Besides a small exhibition on the cathedral itself, it contains lovely frescoed walls and loads of nooks and crannies to explore. A collective ticket (adult/student R230/115) with the State History Museum (below) is available.

Out front of St Basil's is the **statue of Kuzma Minin and Dmitry Pozharsky**, one a butcher and the other a prince, who together raised and led the army that ejected occupying Poles from the Kremlin in 1612. Up the slope is the round, walled **Place of Skulls**, where Ivan the Terrible made his public confession and Peter the Great executed the Streltsy.

STATE HISTORY MUSEUM Map p258

☎ 292 4019; www.shm.ru; Red Square (Krasnaya pl); adult/student & child R150/75; ☺ 11am-7pm Wed-Mon; Ⓜ Ploshchad Revolyutsii

At the northern end of the square, the State History Museum has an enormous collection covering the whole Russian empire from the Stone Age on. The building, dating from the late 19th century, is itself an attraction – each room is in the style of a different period or region, some with highly decorated walls echoing old Russian churches. Reopened in 1997, each year sees

LENIN UNDER GLASS

Red Square is home to the world's most famous mummy, that of Vladimir Ilych Lenin. When he died of a massive stroke (on 22 January 1924, aged 53), a long line of mourners patiently gathered in the depths of winter for weeks to glimpse the body as it lay in state. Inspired by the spectacle, Stalin proposed that the father of Soviet communism should continue to serve the cause as a holy relic. So the decision was made to preserve Lenin's corpse for perpetuity, against the vehement protests of his widow, as well as Lenin's own expressed desire to be buried next to his mother in St Petersburg.

Boris Zbarsky, a biochemist, and Vladimir Voribov, an anatomist, were issued a political order to put a stop to the natural decomposition of the body. The pair worked frantically in a secret laboratory in search of a long-term chemical solution. In the meantime, the body's dark spots were bleached, and lips and eyes sewn tight. The brain was removed and taken to another secret laboratory, to be sliced and diced by scientists for the next 40 years in the hope of uncovering its hidden genius.

In July 1924, the scientists hit upon a formula to successfully arrest the decaying process, a closely guarded state secret. This necrotic craft was passed on to Zbarsky's son, who ran the Kremlin's covert embalming lab for decades. After the fall of communism, Zbarsky came clean: the body is wiped down every few days, and then, every 18 months, thoroughly examined and submerged in a tub of chemicals, including paraffin wax. The institute has now gone commercial, offering its services and secrets to wannabe immortals for a mere million dollars.

In the early 1990s, Boris Yeltsin expressed his intention to heed Lenin's request and bury him in St Petersburg, setting off a furore from the political left as well as more muted objections from Moscow tour operators. It seems that the mausoleum, the most sacred shrine of Soviet Communism, and the mummy, the literal embodiment of the Russian Revolution, will remain in place for at least several more years.

the addition of a few more galleries. A joint ticket (adult/student R230/115) allowing access to the museum and St Basil's Cathedral is available at either spot.

MANEZHNAYA PLOSHCHAD

At the north end of Red Square, through the Resurrection Gate, is Manezhnaya ploshchad (Manezh Square), named after the Kremlin's stables which once occupied this area. The Soviet Union's most successful WWII commander, Marshall Zhukov, presides over this square, mounted on his horse and appearing much like he did at the Victory Day Parade in Red Square on 24 June 1945.

In the last decade, Manezhnaya ploshchad has been transformed with the vast underground Okhotny Ryad shopping mall. From the square, it appears as a series of half-domes and balustrades, and a network of fountains and sculptures. (See p156 for details on shopping here.)

Once dominated by huge hotels, the square's character has changed with the demolition of the Intourist Hotel and Hotel Moskva. The intersection is going decidedly upmarket, as Le Royal Meridien National hotel, which still dominates the corner, is to be joined by the Ritz Carlton Moscow on the site of the Intourist, and the new Hotel Moskva (p66) on the site of the old one.

The fine old edifices to the southwest of the square are: the Russian State Library (p221), including the classical Passkov House dating from 1787; the old Moscow State University building, built in 1793 and named after the celebrated scientist Mikhail Lomonosov; and the historic Hotel National, now known as Le Meridien Royal National (p166).

ARCHAEOLOGICAL MUSEUM
Map pp248-9
☎ 292 4171; Manezhnaya pl 1; admission R100; ⏱ 10am-5.30pm Tue-Sun; Ⓜ Ploshchad Revolyutsii or Okhotny Ryad

An excavation of Voskresensky most (Voskresensky Bridge) – which used to span the Neglinnaya River and commence the road to Tver – uncovered coins, clothing and other artefacts from old Moscow. The museum displaying these treasures is situated in a 7m-deep underground pavilion that was formed during the excavation itself. The entrance is at the base of the once and future Hotel Moskva.

CENTRAL LENIN MUSEUM Map pp248-9
pl Revolyutsii 2; Ⓜ Ploshchad Revolyutsii

The former Central Lenin Museum was once the big daddy of all the Lenin museums, but was closed in 1993 after the White House shoot-out. It is sometimes used for special exhibits, but more often, communist rabblerousers congregate here.

HOUSE OF UNIONS & STATE DUMA
Map pp248-9
Okhotny ryad; Ⓜ Okhotny Ryad or Teatralnaya

The green-columned House of Unions dates from the 1780s. Its ballroom – called the Hall of Columns – is the famous location of one of Stalin's most grotesque show trials, that of Nikolai Bukharin, a leading Communist Party theorist who had been a close associate of Lenin. Next door is the seat of the Russian parliament, the **State Duma**. This glowering building was erected in the 1930s for Gosplan (Soviet State Planning Department), source of the USSR's Five-Year Plans. Both buildings are closed to the public.

MANEZH EXHIBITION CENTRE
Map pp248-9
☎ 292 4459; Manezhnaya ul; ⏱ 11am-8pm Tue-Sun; Ⓜ Alexandrovsky Sad, Borovitskaya or Biblioteka imeni Lenina

The long, low building on the southwestern side of the square is the Manezh, housing art

St Basil's Cathedral (p63)

exhibitions. This neoclassical landmark was badly damaged by a fire in 2004 – sparking much speculation that it was not an accident. It is newly renovated and reopened, and now with the underground parking garage that may have 'sparked' the fire.

TEATRALNAYA PLOSHCHAD

The aptly named Teatralnaya ploshchad, or Theatre Square, opens out on both sides of Okhotny ryad, 200m northeast of Manezhnaya ploshchad. In the early 18th century, the Neglinnaya River ran through here and powered water mills where Hotel Metropol is now. Only in the early 19th century did the square receive its grand appearance, with the construction of the theatres. The 1835 fountain by Vitali – partially blocked by the statue of Karl Marx (Map pp248–9) marks the centre of the square.

BOLSHOI THEATRE Map pp248-9

☎ 292 0050; www.bolshoi.ru; Teatralnaya pl 1; Ⓜ Teatralnaya

While the northern half of the square is surrounded by theatres, its centrepiece is the celebrated Bolshoi, built in 1856. This historic theatre saw the premier of Tchaikovsky's *Swan Lake* in 1877 and *The Nutcracker* in 1919. These days, the main stage is closed for much-needed and long-awaited renovations (until 2008), but the New Stage continues to put on performances (see p146 for details).

Across and down ulitsa Petrovka from the 'Big' Bolshoi is the 'Small' **Maly Theatre**,

THE ONCE & FUTURE HOTEL MOSKVA

After years of rumours, the infamous 1930s-era Moskva hotel on Manezhnaya ploshchad was finally demolished in 2003; one in a long list of Soviet-era institutions to bite the dust. A new luxury hotel is expected to appear in its place in 2006. The story goes that Stalin was shown two possible designs for the original hotel and – not realising they were alternatives – approved both. The builders did not dare to point out his error, and so built half the hotel in constructivist style and half in Stalinist style. The incongruous result became such a familiar feature of the Moscow landscape that the new, high-class hotel being constructed on the site is expected to re-create its predecessor's architectural quirks.

a drama theatre (see p148). On the west side of the square is the National Youth Theatre.

HOTEL METROPOL Map pp248-9

☎ 927 6000; www.metropol-moscow.ru; Teatralny proezd 1/4; Ⓜ Teatralnaya

Sculpted stone, tiled mosaic and wrought iron distinguish the fantastic façade of this luxury hotel – one of Moscow's finest examples of Art Nouveau architecture. The mosaic on the western side, the *Princess of Dreams*, is a masterpiece by Mikhail Vrubel depicting a Russian fairy tale (see boxed text, p166). The interior is no less exquisite, and tourists are usually not discouraged from going inside. Don't miss the spectacular stained-glass ceiling in the restaurant.

OLD FIELDS Map pp248-9

Starye Polya; Teatralny proezd; Ⓜ Lubyanka or Teatralnaya

Along Teatralny proezd, archaeologists uncovered the 16th-century fortified wall that used to surround Kitay Gorod, as well as the foundations of the 1493 Trinity Church. Coins, jewellery and tombstones were also excavated here. Besides the remains of the wall and the church, you can now see a statue of Ivan Fyodorov, the 16th-century printer responsible for Russia's first book.

The gated walkway of **Tretyakovsky proezd** leads into Kitay Gorod. The archway, built in the 1870s, was apparently financed by the Tretyakov brothers, founders of their namesake gallery (see p100). Apparently, the construction of the medieval-style gate and the opening of the passageway was an attempt to relieve traffic on Nikolskaya ulitsa. Since its reopening in 2000, Tretyakovsky proezd is lined with exclusive shops, including Mercury, which financed much of the restoration.

LUBYANSKAYA PLOSHCHAD

For decades, the broad square at the east end of Teatralny proezd (called Lubyanskaya ploshchad, or Lubyanka Square) was a chilling symbol of the KGB, or Komitet Gosudarstvennoy Bezopasnosti (Committee for State Security). From 1926 to 1990, it was called ploshchad Dzerzhinskogo, after

(Continued on page 75)

1 Live entertainment at Chinese Pilot Dzhao-da (p143), Kitay Gorod **2** Strolling down stylish Stoleshnikov pereulok (p155), Petrovsky District **3** Devushky (young women) at the Hermitage Gardens (p141), Petrovsky District **4** Spectators at a festival at Hermitage Gardens (p141), Petrovsky District

1

3

2

4

1 *The imposing Great Kremlin Palace (p60), Kremlin* **2** *Colour and light adorn the Archangel Cathedral (p59), Kremlin* **3** *Golden domes glisten on the Assumption Cathedral (p57), Kremlin* **4** *The huge clock on the Saviour Gate Tower (p56), Kremlin*

1 *Imperial standard at the Armoury (p61), Kremlin* 2 *The broken 202-tonne Tsar Bell (p58), Kremlin* 3 *The Kremlin (p54) and the Moscow River* 4 *Stalin-era red star atop a tower, Kremlin (p54)*

1 *Statue of Peter the Great (p92), Zamoskvorechie* 2 *The reconstructed Resurrection Gate (p62), Red Square* 3 *The iconic domes and spires of St Basil's Cathedral (p63), Red Square*

1 *The Triumphal Arch (p106) commemorating Russia's victory over Napoleon* **2** *Mosaic at the Resurrection Gate (p62), Red Square* **3** *Framed view of Lenin's Tomb (p63), Red Square* **4** *One of the domes of St Basil's Cathedral (p63), Red Square*

1 *GUM department store building (p63), Red Square* **2** *People strolling along the cobblestones, Red Square (p62)* **3** *Peaceful Upper St Peter Monastery (p81), Petrovsky District* **4** *Detail from the Tsaritsino Palace (p105)*

1 *Night scene at Tretyakovsky proezd (p66), City Centre*
2 *Moscow State University (p106), one of Stalin's Seven Sisters*
3 *Soviet-era mosaic at Le Royal Meridien National (p166), City Centre* **4** *Exterior of the East-West Hotel (p168), Tverskoy District*

1 Muscovites enjoying the sunshine in Victory Park (p106)
2 Park-bench scene in Alexandrovsky Garden (p61), City Centre
3 Flower bed in the Alexandrovsky Garden (p61), City Centre
4 Landscape artist at Kolomenskoe Museum-Reserve (p104)

(Continued from page 66)

Felix Dzerzhinsky, who founded the Cheka, the KGB's forerunner. A tall statue of Dzerzhinsky dominated the square.

When the 1991 coup collapsed, the statue was memorably removed by angry crowds, with the assistance of a couple of cranes. Now you can see the statue in all its (somewhat reduced) glory in the Sculpture Park, where it stands among others fallen from grace (see p100). There was a movement – reputedly backed by Mayor Luzhkov, strangely enough – to resurrect 'Iron Felix' and return him to his place of honour.

KGB MUSEUM Map pp248-9
ul Bolshaya Lubyanka 12/1; M Lubyanka
This four-room museum is devoted to the history, propaganda and paraphernalia of the Soviet intelligence services. The museum is not open to casual callers, but Dom Patriarshy Tours (see p54) occasionally takes groups there (and provides a translator). Security is super tight: an FSB (Federal Security Service; the KGB's successor) agent leads a small group, room by room, recounting Cold War–era espionage anecdotes. Exhibits include a few fun spy tools, but nothing to really impress a technologically advanced audience. It's predictable, but entertaining.

LUBYANKA PRISON Map pp248-9
Lubyanskaya pl; M Lubyanka
In the 1930s, Lubyanka Prison was the feared destination of thousands of innocent victims of Stalin's purges. Today the grey

building looming on the northeastern side of the square is no longer a prison, but is the headquarters of the FSB. The FSB keeps a pretty good eye on domestic goings-on. The building is not open to the public.

The much humbler **Memorial to the Victims of Totalitarianism** stands in the little garden on the southeastern side of the square. This single stone slab comes from the territory of an infamous 1930s labour camp situated on the Solovetsky Islands in the White Sea.

MAYAKOVSKY MUSEUM Map pp248-9
☎ 921 9387; www.museum.ru/majakovskiy; Lubyansky proezd 3/6; admission R60; ⏱ 1-9pm Thu, 10am-5pm Fri-Tue; M Lubyanka
The startling post-modern entrance on this prerevolutionary mansion is appropriate for a museum dedicated to the revolutionary, futurist poet Vladimir Mayakovsky. The building is actually where Mayakovsky lived in a communal apartment during the last years of his life. The room where he worked – and shot himself in 1930 – has been preserved. Run by the poet's granddaughter, the museum contains an eclectic collection of his manuscripts and sketches, as well as the requisite personal items and family photographs.

MOSCOW CITY HISTORY MUSEUM
Map pp248-9
☎ 924 8490, 924 8058; Novaya pl 12; admission R50; ⏱ 11am-5.30pm Tue-Sun; M Lubyanka
This elaborate Russian Empire–style building dates from 1825. Formerly the John the Baptist Church, it now houses a small

Lubyanka Prison (above)

history museum, demonstrating how the city has spread from its starting point at the Kremlin. Exhibits are heavy on artefacts from the 13th and 14th centuries, especially household items and weapons and other representations of medieval Moscow.

POLYTECHNICAL MUSEUM Map pp248-9

☎ 923 0756; Novaya pl 3/4; adult/student R150/75; ◷ 10am-5pm Tue-Sun; Ⓜ Lubyanka
Occupying the entire block of Novaya ploshchad, this giant museum covers the history of Russian science, technology and industry. Indeed, the museum claims to be the largest science museum in the world. The permanent exhibits cover just about every aspect of Soviet scientific achievement, from a model of Lomonosov's laboratory to Mendeleev's development of the periodic table to Popov's first radio receiver.

While the museum's focus is scientific, the building is also architecturally interesting and visually appealing. Three different parts of the structure were built at different times and in different styles: the oldest, central section (1877) represents the Russian Byzantium era; the eastern section (1896) is inspired by 17th-century Russian styles; and the western section (1907) is Art Nouveau.

KITAY GOROD

Eating p124; Shopping p156
The narrow old streets east of Red Square are among the oldest in Moscow, estab-
lished in the 13th century as an early trade and financial centre. Kitay Gorod means – literally – 'Chinatown', but actually has nothing to do with China. The name derives from *kita*, which means 'wattle', after the palisades that reinforced the earthen ramp erected around this early Kremlin suburb. The area's ancient, bustling streets and exquisite, tiny churches make it an ideal place for an enjoyable stroll (see p114 for details).

Orientation

Kitay Gorod is bound, quite definitively, by Red Square in the west and by the Moscow River in the south. The northern border is ulitsa Pokrovka (called ulitsa Maroseika closer to the Kremlin). This portion of the Boulevard Ring is called – appropriately enough – Pokrovsky bulvar. The streets contained therein are a confusing maze of windy one-ways and narrow no-throughways, packed with churches and monasteries.

A significant piece of Kitay Gorod, just east of Red Square, is inside the area bound by Lubyansky proezd. Sights in this area are listed under Kitay Gorod, not City Centre, for the sake of consistency.

For the purposes of this book, Kitay Gorod also includes sights that are east of the Boulevard Ring, including those around the section of the Garden Ring, called Zemlyanoy val. Just off this road is busy Kursky vokzal (Kursk station; see p216 for train services). A constant bustle

RINGS AROUND MOSCOW

Picture Moscow as five ring roads that spread out from the centre:

- **Inner Ring Road** About 300m north of the Kremlin, it's formed by the streets Mokhovaya ulitsa, Okhotny ryad, Teatralny proezd and the squares of Novaya ploshchad and Staraya ploshchad. Three other important squares – Manezhnaya ploshchad, Teatralnaya ploshchad and Lubyanskaya ploshchad – punctuate this ring.
- **Boulevard Ring** (Bulvarnoe Koltso) About 1km from the Kremlin. It's mostly dual carriageway, with a park strip down the middle. Each section has a different name, always ending in 'bulvar'. The Boulevard Ring ends as it approaches the Moscow River in the southwest and southeast.
- **Garden Ring** (Sadovoe Koltso) About 2km out. Most of this ring's northern sections are called Sadovaya-something (Garden-something) ulitsa; some of its southern sections are called ulitsa-something-val, recalling its origins as a rampart *(val)*. And the difference between the Garden and Boulevard rings? The Garden Ring is the one *without* any gardens.
- **'Third' Ring** (Tretoe Koltso) Located about 4.5km from the Kremlin, it's a new, eight-lane, high-speed motorway, recently built to absorb some of the traffic from Moscow streets. The motorway provides motorists with a speedy route across (or rather, around) town.
- **Outer Ring Road** (Moskovskaya Koltsovaya Avtomobilnaya Doroga; MKAD) Some 15km to 20km from the Kremlin, it forms the city limits.

surrounds Moscow's biggest train station, due in part to the Atrium shopping centre nearby (p156).

CHORAL SYNAGOGUE Map p254

☎ 924 0472; Bolshoy Spasoglinishchevsky per 10; ☼ 9am-6pm; Ⓜ Kitay Gorod

Moscow's oldest synagogue was built in 1891 by the businessman Polyakov, who made his fortune in the sugar industry. It was the only synagogue that continued to operate throughout the Soviet period, in spite of Bolshevik demands to convert it into a workers' club. The interior is quite exquisite.

CHURCH OF THE TRINITY IN NIKITNIKI Map pp248-9

Ipatyevsky per; Ⓜ Kitay Gorod

This little gem of a church, built in the 1630s, is an exquisite example of Russian baroque. Its onion domes and tiers of red and white spade gables rise from a square tower. Its interior – only partially open due to renovation – is covered with 1650s' gospel frescoes by Simon Ushakov and others. A carved doorway leads into St Nikita the Martyr's Chapel, above the vault of the Nikitnikov merchant family, one of the patrons who financed the construction of the church.

ENGLISH HOUSE Map pp248-9

☎ 298 3952; ul Varvarka 4A; admission R20; ☼ 11am-6pm Tue-Sun; Ⓜ Kitay Gorod

This reconstructed 16th-century house, white with peaked wooden roofs, was the residence of England's first emissaries to Russia (sent by Elizabeth I to Ivan the Terrible). It also served as the base for English merchants, who were allowed to trade duty free in exchange for providing military supplies to Ivan. Ironically, this museum has no signs or descriptions in English.

MONASTERY OF THE EPIPHANY

Map pp248-9

Bogoyavlensky per 2; Ⓜ Ploshchad Revolyutsii

This monastery, the second-oldest in Moscow, was founded in 1296 by Prince Daniil, son of Alexander Nevsky. One of the first abbots of the monastery was Stefan, the brother of Sergei Radonezhsky (patron saint of Russia and founder of the Trinity Monastery of St Sergius). The current **Epiphany Cathedral** was constructed in the 1690s in the Moscow baroque style.

ROMANOV CHAMBERS IN ZARYADIE

Map pp248-9

☎ 924 4529; ul Varvarka 10; admission R150; ☼ 10am-5pm Thu-Mon, 11am-6pm Wed; Ⓜ Kitay Gorod

This small but interesting museum is devoted to the lives of the Romanov family, who were mere *boyars* (nobles) before they became tsars. The house was built by Nikita Romanov, whose grandson Mikhail later became the first tsar of the 300-year Romanov dynasty. Exhibits (with descriptions in English) show the house as it might have been when the Romanovs lived here in the 16th century. Some of the artistic detail, such as the woodwork in the women's quarters, is amazing. Enter from the rear of the building.

SYNOD PRINTING HOUSE Map pp248-9

Nikolskaya ul 15; Ⓜ Ploshchad Revolyutsii

This is where Ivan Fyodorov reputedly produced Russia's first printed book, *The Apostle,* in 1563. (You can see the man himself at Old Fields, p66). In 1703 the first Russian newspaper *Vedomosti* was also printed here. Up until the early 19th century, Kitay Gorod was something of a printing centre, home to 26 of Moscow's 31 bookshops at the time.

SAKHAROV MUSEUM Map p254

☎ 923 4115; www.wdn.com/asf; ul Zemlyanoy val 57; admission free; ☼ 11am-7pm Tue-Sun; Ⓜ Chkalovskaya

South of Kursky vokzal by the Yauza River is a two-storey house in a small park containing the Andrei Sakharov Museum. Its displays cover the life of Sakharov, the nuclear-physicist-turned-human-rights advocate, detailing the years of repression in Russia and providing a history of the courage shown by the dissident movement. Temporary expositions cover current human-rights issues (see boxed text, below, for one example). There are signs in English and audio guides are planned. Look out for a piece of genuine Berlin Wall in front of the building.

ZAIKONOSPASSKY MONASTERY
Map pp248-9
Nikolskaya ul 7-9; (M) Ploshchad Revolyutsii
This monastery was founded by Boris Godunov in 1600, although the church was built in 1660. The name means 'Behind the Icon Stall', a reference to the busy icon trade that once took place here. On the orders of Tsar Alexey, the Likhud brothers, scholars of Greek, opened the Slavonic Greek and Latin Academy on the monastery premises in 1866. (Mikhail Lomonosov was a student here.) The academy later became a divinity school, and was transferred to the Trinity Monastery of St Sergius (see p195) in 1814.

CHISTYE PRUDY
Eating p125; Shopping p157; Sleeping p166

Chistye Prudy, or 'Clean Ponds', refers to the lovely little pond that graces the Boulevard Ring at its intersection with ul Pokrovka. The Boulevard Ring is always a prime location for strolling, but the addition of the quaint pond makes this a desirable address indeed. Paddleboats in summer and ice skating in winter are essential parts of the ambiance. Pick a café and (depending on the season) sip a beer or a coffee while watching boaters or skaters go by.

This area was not always so swank. Back in the 17th century, it was the home of Moscow's meat markets and slaughterhouses. In fact, Myasnitskaya ulitsa means 'butcher street'. Peter the Great gifted the land to the merchant Alexander Menshikov, who cleaned up the area. As a part of this effort, Alexander renamed it Chistye Prudy. Besides the pond itself and the lovely architecture in the surrounding streets, the area is home to Moscow's first post office,

---

CAUTION: CENSORSHIP

In January 2003 Yury Samodurov, director of the Sakharov Museum in Moscow, premiered a contemporary-art exhibit entitled 'Caution: Religion'. The exhibit cast a critical eye on the clash between the nascent Orthodox revival and the emerging mass-consumer culture in Russia. It depicted, among others, the image of Jesus on a Coke can and the Seven Deadly Sins being committed by an average Russian family in daily life. The message: despite the sharp increase in citizens who identify themselves as Orthodox Christian, it is the values and identities of mass-consumer culture that dominate post-communist society.

The exhibit elicited a shrill reaction from the Russian Orthodox Church, nationalist politicians and some patriotic hooligans, who were so offended by it that they vandalised the museum. The uproar attracted the attention of the state prosecutor.

The episode is revealing of the way in which Russia's long tradition of dissent has evolved in postcommunist times. Throughout the Soviet period, dissent most often took political forms, correcting the lies of the regime and exposing its brutalities. As a prime example, the museum's inspiration and namesake, Andrei Sakharov, spent nearly six years under house arrest in Nizhny Novgorod for criticising Soviet policy. When communism collapsed, some wondered if Russia's long tradition of dissent would fade away with the commissars. As evidenced by 'Caution: Religion', dissent in post-Soviet Russia has not disappeared, but it is taking on new cultural forms.

The case against heretical artists also highlights another side of postcommunist Russia. Under the administration of thin-skinned President Putin, free expression has been curtailed, independent media has been intimidated and human-rights advocates have been silenced. The regime that espoused liberal political values has come to reflect an embattled Russian nationalism.

The charges brought against the museum included inciting ethnic hatred and offending true believers. The prosecutor demanded – in the name of religious sensibility – that the exhibit should be destroyed and museum officials should be punished. In March 2005, a Moscow court handed down the verdict. Museum director Samudorov and his deputy were found guilty and ordered to pay a fine of R100,000 each. Outside the courthouse, angry Christians were not appeased. 'These kind of people should be beaten in the face', one true believer railed.

Samudorov said that he would appeal the court's finding, taking the case, if necessary, all the way to the European Court of Human Rights in Strasbourg. The communist dictatorship may have fallen, but the ghost of Andrei Sakharov still haunts the Kremlin.

TRANSPORT

The area immediately around Chistye Prudy is easily accessible by the metro stop of the same name, as well as its connected station, Turgenevskaya. Komsomolskaya, on the Ring line, serves Komsomolskaya ploshchad. An intermediary stop near the Garden Ring is Krasnye Vorota.

founded in 1783 in one of the houses of the former Menshikov estate.

Northeast of here, the atmosphere changes radically at Komsomolskaya ploshchad. The three main train stations surrounding the square – and the diverse and dubious crowds that frequent them – make this one of Moscow's hairiest places.

This one square captures not only Moscow's social diversity, but also its architectural diversity. Kazansky vokzal (Kazan station; see p216 for services), on the south side of the square, was built between 1912 and 1926 and is a retrospective of seven building styles that date back to a 16th-century Tatar tower in Kazan. The style of architect Alexey Shchusev changed over the years, and his later work includes Lenin's tomb.

Leningradsky vokzal (Leningrad station; see p216), with the tall clock tower on the northern side of the square, is Moscow's oldest, built in 1851. It is very similar to its counterpart at the far end of the line, the Moscow station in St Petersburg. Yaroslavsky vokzal (Yaroslavl station; see p217) is a 1902–04 Art Nouveau fantasy by Fyodor Shekhtel.

The 26-storey 'wedding cake' west on Komsomolskaya ploshchad is Hotel Leningradskaya. One of Stalin's 'Seven Sisters' (see boxed text, p29), it is now home to the Agriculture Ministry, 600m south on the Garden Ring.

Orientation

From Lubyanskaya ploshchad, Myastnitskaya ulitsa heads northeast to the Boulevard Ring (here, Chistoprudny bulvar). This intersection is the location of the Chistye Prudy metro stop, although the pond itself is a little further south along the boulevard. Chistye Prudy encompasses the streets surrounding this area, stretching as far west as ulitsa Bolshaya Lubyanka and south to ulitsa

Pokrovka. From Chistye Prudy metro station, prospekt Akademika Sakharova goes further northeast to Komsomolskaya ploshchad, Moscow's transport hub.

MENSHIKOV TOWER Map p254
Arkhangelsky per; M Chistye Prudy
Hidden behind the post office, this famous tower was built between 1704 and 1706 on the order of Menshikov from his newly founded estate. The tower – one of Moscow's first baroque buildings – was originally 3m taller than the Ivan the Great Bell Tower. A thunderstorm in 1723 saw it hit by lightning and seriously damaged by fire. Trouble plagued the owner as well. Menshikov fell from grace after the death of Peter the Great, and he was exiled to Siberia. The tower was neglected for several decades. When finally repaired in the 1780s, it lost much of its height and elegance. Today, it houses the working **Church of Archangel Gabriel**.

YELOKHOVSKY CATHEDRAL
Map pp246-7
Church of the Epiphany in Yelokhovo; www.mospat .ru; Spartakovskaya ul 15; M Baumanskaya
Spartakovskaya ulitsa is the unlikely address of Moscow's senior Orthodox cathedral. This role was given to the Church of the Epiphany in Yelokhovo in 1943. (The Patriarch had been evicted from the Kremlin's Assumption Cathedral in 1918.) The Patriarch leads important services here today.

Built between 1837 and 1845 with five domes in a Russian eclectic style, the cathedral is full of gilt and icons. Not to mention old women kneeling, polishing, lighting candles, crossing themselves and kissing the floor. In the northern part of the cathedral is the tomb of St Nicholas the Miracle Worker (Svyatoy Nikolay Ugodnik). A shrine in front of the right side of the iconostasis contains the remains of St Alexey, a 14th-century metropolitan.

PETROVSKY DISTRICT
Eating p126; Shopping p157; Sleeping p167
Now restored to its fashionable prerevolutionary status, the Petrovsky District constitutes Moscow's glossiest central shopping area. Petrovsky Passage was one of the earliest converts to the consumer culture,

Sights

when it was transformed into a light- and fountain-filled shopping centre, bursting with upscale shops. The Central Department Store (TsUM), once a source of drab Soviet products, is now Moscow's finest department store, selling top-of-the-line name brands at out-of-this-world prices. The luxurious Marriott Royal Aurora hotel dominates the corner around Stoleshnikov pereulok. This cobblestone side street – closed to road traffic – is one of Moscow's sleekest streets, home to the most exclusive (and expensive) boutiques. Southeast of here, Kuznetsky most is lined with restaurants and shops that are more populist, but no less popular. If you don't come to shop, come to watch the shoppers. This is the place to see the gaudy and the glamour of Moscow's New Russians.

Just to prove that New Russia is not without culture or conviction, the Petrovsky District is home to the funky and fanciful Moscow Museum of Modern Art. Across the street, the age-old Upper St Peter Monastery offers a poignant contrast. The magnificent New Opera stands amid the splendour of the Hermitage Gardens (containing Penthouse No 1 and Cabaret – two of Moscow's most exclusive clubs – see p143).

Sadly, the downside of this gentrification is that people no longer live in these neighbourhoods. In the area around Kuznetsky most, for example, the population has dropped from 20,000 to less than 1000 in the past decade. Only a few old-style residential buildings remain.

Orientation

From Teatralnaya ploshchad, ulitsa Petrovka runs almost directly north to the Garden Ring. The southern stretch is particularly vibrant, boasting upscale department stores, shopping malls and the richer-than-thou pedestrian strip, Stoleshnikov pereulok. Ulitsa Petrovka culminates at its intersection with the Boulevard Ring (here, Petrovsky bulvar). This busy corner is home to a few ultra trendy restaurants and bars, a cutting-edge contemporary-art museum and the centuries-old Upper St Peter Monastery.

North of the Boulevard Ring, ulitsa Petrovka changes name to Karetny ryad, but it is no less inviting. This northern stretch is dominated by the lovely Hermitage Gardens, flanked by the New Opera, and more restaurants, shops and galleries. While ulitsa Petrovka is the hub of this area, surrounding streets are equally attractive. Kuznetsky most runs parallel to Teatralny proezd.

For our purposes, the Petrovsky District is bound by ulitsa Bolshaya Lubyanka in the east and ulitsa Bolshaya Dimitrovka in the west. It stretches north to the Garden Ring and beyond.

DOSTOEVSKY HOUSE-MUSEUM

Map pp248-9

☎ 281 1085; ul Dostoevskogo 2; admission R50; ◷ 2-8pm Wed & Fri, 11am-6pm Thu, Sat & Sun; Ⓜ Novoslobodskaya

While this renowned Russian author is more closely associated with St Petersburg, Fyodor Dostoevsky was actually born in Moscow, and his family lived in a tiny apartment on the grounds of Marinsky Hospital. He lived here until the age of 16, when he went to St Petersburg to enter a military academy. The family's Moscow flat has been recreated according to Dostoevsky's own descriptions and childhood journals. The overwhelming impression is one of extreme poverty and tumultuous family relations, which characterised the writer's youth and – indeed – defined the themes of his work. Visitors can also see the family's library, toys and many other personal items, including his quill pen and an original autograph.

MOSCOW MUSEUM OF MODERN ART Map pp248-9

☎ 231 4408; ul Petrovka 25; adult/student R150/75; ◷ noon-8pm Wed-Fri, noon-7pm Sat-Mon; Ⓜ Chekhovskaya

A pet-project of the ubiquitous Zurab Tsereteli (see the boxed text, p93), this newish museum is housed In a classical 18th-century merchant's home, originally designed by Matvei Kazanov (architect of the Arsenal in the Kremlin). It is the perfect light-filled setting for an impressive collection of 20th-century paintings, sculptures and graphics, which includes both Russian and foreign artists. The highlight is the collection of avant-garde art, with works by Chagall, Kandinsky and Malevich. Unique to this museum is its exhibit of 'nonconformist' artists from the 1950s and '60s – those whose work was not acceptable to the Soviet regime. The gallery also hosts temporary exhibits that often feature contemporary artists. Be sure not to bypass the whimsical sculpture garden in the courtyard.

MUSEUM OF DECORATIVE & FOLK ART Map pp248-9

☎ 923 7725; Delegatskaya ul 3 & 5; admission R50; ⊙ 10am-5pm Sat-Thu; Ⓜ Tsvetnoy Bulvar

Just beyond the Garden Ring, this museum showcases the centuries-old arts and crafts traditions from all around Russia and the former Soviet republics. It includes all the goodies you might find in souvenir shops or at the Izmaylovo Market (see p162), but these antique pieces represent the crafts at their most traditional and their most authentic. Of the 40,000 pieces in the collection, you might see painted Khokhloma woodwork from Nizhny Novgorod, including wooden toys and *matryoshka* dolls; baskets and other household items made from birch bark, a traditional technique from Siberia; intricate embroidery and lacework from the north, as well as the ubiquitous Pavlov scarves; and playful Dymkovo pottery and Gzhel porcelain. Look also for the so-called 'propaganda porcelain' – fine china decorated with revolutionary themes.

The museum is known for its impressive collection of Palekh – black lacquer boxes and trays painted with detailed scenes from Russian fairytales. The collection fills two rooms. It features, among others, pieces by Ivan Golikov and Ivan Markichev, often considered the originators of the Palekh style.

UPPER ST PETER MONASTERY

Map pp248-9

cnr ul Petrovka & Petrovsky bul; admission free; ⊙ 8am-8pm; Ⓜ Chekhovskaya

The Upper St Peter Monastery (Petrovsky monastyr) was founded in the 1380s as part of an early defensive ring around Moscow. The grounds are pleasant in a peaceful, near-deserted way. The main onion-domed **Virgin of Bogolyubovo Church** dates from the late 17th century. The loveliest structure is the brick **Cathedral of Metropolitan Pyotr**, restored with a shingle roof. (When Peter the Great ousted the Regent Sofia in 1690, his mother was so pleased she built him this church.)

TVERSKOY DISTRICT

Eating p129; Shopping p159; Sleeping p168

Moscow's main drag is Tverskaya ulitsa – the start of the road to Tver and on to St Petersburg. It is a wide highway, crowded with cars whizzing by (or creeping, as the case may be). The pavements are crowded with shoppers, and the selection of stores is vast.

This busy street lacks the personality of some of Moscow's other districts, due in part to the soulless reconstruction in the 1930s. Residents also claim that recent development has driven out local shops that used to cater to the community. Today, Tverskaya ulitsa is lined with restaurants, bars, theatres and shops, giving it a modern bright-lights, big-city atmosphere.

The first of the prominent squares along this main road is known, appropriately, as Tverskaya ploshchad. Yury Dolgoruky, traditionally considered Moscow's founder, presides over the square. So does Mayor Luzhkov, as the buffed-up five-storey building opposite is the mayor's office.

Exterior of Upper St Peter Monastery (left)

Sights **TVERSKOY DISTRICT**

TRANSPORT

The metro's green Zamoskvoretskaya line follows
Tverskaya ulitsa north from Manezhnaya ploshchad
past Belorussky vokzal (Belarus station). Stops include
Teatralnaya (connecting with Okhotny Ryad and
Ploshchad Revolyutsii), Tverskaya (connecting with
Pushkinskaya and Chekhovskaya), Mayakovskaya and
Belorusskaya. Alternatively, Trolleybus Nos 12 and 20
run up and down Tverskaya ulitsa as far as Belorussky
vokzal. For sights around ploshchad Nikitskie Vorota,
Arbatskaya metro station is also useful.

Heading north, each busy intersection has its own unique personality, crowded shopping centres, metro stop and traffic jams. From the square that bears his name, a statue of Alexander Pushkin surveys his domain. Pushkin Cinema, Café Pushkin and Pushkinskaya metro station are all within sight; apparently Pushkin has taken the place of Lenin in New Russian ideology.

If the hustle and bustle of Tverskaya ulitsa wears you out, sneak away from the main drag for a breather. Many churches are tucked into these streets, including the 17th-century Church of SS Cosma and Damian, behind Tverskaya ploshchad. West of here, through the arch across Bryusov pereulok, is the unexpected gold-domed Church of the Resurrection, which is full of fine icons rescued from churches torn down during the Soviet era.

The pedestrian strip on Kamergersky pereulok is a prime people-watching spot. The trendy cafés and restaurants that line this side street provide perfect vantage points for Moscow's most beautiful people to don their shades and check each other out. Tverskoy bulvar – peaceful, pleasant and blooming with trees – is possibly the loveliest stretch of the Boulevard Ring; see the walking tour on p110 for more details.

Patriarch's Ponds, by the Garden Ring, hearkens back to Soviet days, when the parks were populated with children and babushkas. In the back streets around Bolshaya Nikitskaya ulitsa many old mansions have survived, some renovated, others dilapidated. Most of those inside the Boulevard Ring were built by the 18th-century aristocracy, outside, by rising 19th-century industrialists. With little traffic, Bolshaya Nikitskaya ulitsa is excellent for a quiet ramble (see p115).

Orientation

The bottom of Tverskaya ulitsa – at Manezhnaya ploshchad (see p65) – is the city's hub. From here, the busy street heads northwest, past the trendy pedestrian side street Kamergersky pereulok and the city's Central Telegraph office. The prominent Pushkinskaya ploshchad (Pushkin Square), marks the intersection of Tverskaya ulitsa with the Boulevard Ring (here, Tverskoy bulvar). Further northwest, Tverskaya ulitsa intersects with the Garden Ring at Triumfalnaya ploshchad. The metro stop still bears the square's former moniker, Mayakovskaya, named after the poet whose statue dominates the square. Just west of here is Patriarch's Ponds, flanked by one of Moscow's most exciting streets to eat out in, Spiridonovka pereulok (see p120).

Tverskaya ulitsa changes name to 1-ya Tverskaya Yamskaya ulitsa and continues northwest to Belorussky vokzal (Belarus station). For our purposes, the Tverskoy District encompasses the area that surrounds Tverskaya ulitsa, from ulitsa Bolshaya Dmitrovka in the east to Bolshaya Nikitskaya ulitsa in the south.

Bolshaya Nikitskaya ulitsa runs almost parallel to Tverskaya – from the Moscow State University building, on Mokhovaya ulitsa, to the Garden Ring. Ploshchad Nikitskie Vorota, where Bolshaya Nikitskaya ulitsa crosses the Boulevard Ring, is named after the Nikitsky Gates in the old city walls, which the ring has replaced.

CHURCH OF THE NATIVITY OF THE VIRGIN IN PUTINKI Map pp248-9
ul Malaya Dmitrovka 4; Ⓜ Pushkinskaya or Tverskaya
When this church was completed in 1652, the Patriarch Nikon responded by banning tent roofs like those featured here. Apparently, he considered such architecture too Russian, too secular and too far from the Church's Byzantine roots. Fortunately, the Church of the Nativity has survived to grace this corner near Pushkinskaya ploshchad.

CHURCHES OF THE GRAND & SMALL ASCENSION Map pp248-9
Bolshaya Nikitskaya ul; Ⓜ Arbatskaya
In 1831 the poet Alexander Pushkin married Natalya Goncharova in the elegant Church of the Grand Ascension, on the western

side of ploshchad Nikitskie Vorota. Six years later he died in St Petersburg, defending her honour in a duel. Such passion, such romance… The church is frequently closed, but the celebrated couple is featured in the Rotunda Fountain, erected in 1999 to commemorate the poet's 100th birthday.

Down the street, the festive **Church of the Small Ascension** sits on the corner of Voznesensky pereulok. Built in the early 17th century, it features whitewashed walls and stone embellishments carved in a primitive style.

CONTEMPORARY HISTORY MUSEUM
Map pp248-9

☎ 299 6724; www.sovr.ru; Tverskaya ul 21; admission R50; ☯ 10am-6pm Tue-Sun; Ⓜ Pushkinskaya or Tverskaya

Formerly known as the Revolution Museum, this retro exhibit traces Soviet history from the 1905 and 1917 revolutions up to the 1980s. The highlight is the extensive collection of propaganda posters, in addition to all the Bolshevik paraphernalia. Look for the picture of the giant Palace of Soviets

(Dvorets Sovietov) that Stalin was going to build on the site of the blown-up – and now rebuilt – Cathedral of Christ the Saviour. English-language tours are available with advance notice.

GLINKA MUSEUM OF MUSICAL CULTURE Map pp248-9

☎ 972 3237; ul Fadeeva 4; admission R50; ☯ noon-7pm Tue-Sun; Ⓜ Mayakovskaya

Musicologists will be amazed by this massive collection of musical instruments from all over the world. The museum boasts over 3000 instruments – handcrafted works of art – from the Caucasus to the Far East. Russia is very well represented – a 13th-century *gusli* (traditional instrument similar to a dulcimer) from Novgorod, skin drums from Yakutia, a *balalaika* (triangular, three-stringed instrument) by the master Semyon Nalimov – but you can also see such classic pieces as a violin made by Antoni Stradivari. Recordings accompany many of the rarer instruments, allowing visitors to experience what they sound like.

HOW MATRYOSHKA GOT HER START

Rare is the tourist that leaves Russia without a *matryoshka* – one of the most Russian of all souvenirs. The hand-painted wooden nesting doll which so symbolises Russia is not, as you might imagine, an ancient handcraft developed and perfected by generations of peasant families. Rather, the concept was adapted from a traditional Japanese toy.

In the 19th century, Russian artists were eager to embrace cultural styles that would unite traditional and modern elements, and contribute to the growing sense of national identity at that time. Savva Mamontov, a celebrated patron of the arts, established art studios at his Abramtsevo estate (p193) where artists could do just that. Toys were considered a particularly creative form of folk art, and Savva's brother, Anatoly, set up a workshop to revive and develop folk-peasant toys. In this workshop, Mamontov had a collection of toys from around the world, including a Japanese nesting doll depicting the Buddhist sage Fukuruma. Inspired by this prototype, the toy maker Vassily Zviozdochkin and the artist Sergei Maliutin created the earliest Russian nesting dolls, identifiable by their Slavic features and peasant dress.

During this time, Matryona and Matryosha were popular female names. Derived from the word for 'mother', the names conjured up images of a healthy, plump woman with plenty of children. Thus the diminutive of the name was applied to the nesting dolls, symbolic of motherhood, fertility and Mother Russia.

At the beginning of the 20th century, large-scale production of the Russian *matryoshka* began at the toy centre at Sergiev Posad. Here, artists developed a unique, realistic style of painting the dolls, depicting colourful scenes of village life, patriotic historical figures and beloved literary characters.

The Bolshevik regime began cracking down on this creative outlet as early as 1923. The exhibition and sale of any *matryoshki* not consistent with the regime's artistic or ideological goals were banned. The ban also included the depiction of such controversial figures as tailors, bakers and any entrepreneurial types; Gypsies (Roma), Jews and other ethnic groups; fantastical figures such as mermaids and goblins; and so on. Eventually, the *matryoshka's* diversity and creativity diminished, and she adopted one standard female image. Factory production began in the 1930s, and this 'art' was nearly lost.

The 1990s saw a revival of the more original *matryoshka*, designed and painted by individuals. Production returned to artists and craftsmen, who are free to paint whom and how they wish. As a result, modern-day *matryoshki* take on every imaginable character and style.

Once again (this time due to market forces), artists often get inspiration for this Russian handcraft from foreign sources. From Warner Brothers to the Bush brothers, from the Red Sox to the Red Wings, from the *Simpsons* to *Star Wars*, many Western popular cultural images are depicted on the dolls these days.

This incredible collection started with a few instruments that were donated by the Moscow Tchaikovsky Conservatory at the end of the 19th century. The collection grew exponentially during the Soviet period. It was named after Mikhail Glinka in 1945, in honour of the nationalist composer's 150th birthday.

GORKY HOUSE-MUSEUM Map pp248-9

☎ 290 5130; Malaya Nikitskaya ul 6/2; admission free, photographs R100; ⏲ 11am-6pm Wed-Sun; Ⓜ Pushkinskaya or Tverskaya

This fascinating 1906 Art Nouveau mansion was designed by Fyodor Shekhtel and gifted to celebrated author Maxim Gorky in 1931. The house is a visual fantasy with sculpted doorways, ceiling murals, stained glass, a carved stone staircase and exterior tile work. Besides the fantastic décor, it contains many of Gorky's personal items, including his extensive library. A small room in the cupola houses random, rotating exhibits of contemporary or quixotic artwork.

LYUBAVICHESKAYA SYNAGOGUE

Map pp248-9

Bolshaya Bronnaya ul 6; Ⓜ Pushkinskaya or Tverskaya

Converted to a theatre in the 1930s, this building was still used for gatherings by the Jewish community throughout the Soviet period. The rug on the altar hides a trapdoor leading to a small cell where Jews used to hide from the communists. Today the building serves as a working synagogue, as well as a social centre for the small but growing Jewish community in Moscow (see p13).

MATRYOSHKA MUSEUM Map pp248-9

☎ 291 9645; Leontevsky per 7; admission free; ⏲ 10am-6pm Mon-Thu, 10am-5pm Fri; Ⓜ Pushkinskaya or Tverskaya

On a quiet side street, the Matryoshka Museum – formerly the Museum of Folk Art – is a two-room museum showcasing designer *matryoshka* dolls and different painting techniques. The centrepiece is a 1m-high *matryoshka* with 50 dolls inside. The exhibit demonstrates the history of this favourite Russian souvenir. Don't come looking for modern-day pop-culture inspired dolls because the museum takes a traditionalist tact.

PATRIARCH'S PONDS Map pp248-9

Bolshoy Patriarshy per; Ⓜ Mayakovskaya

Once this area contained several ponds that kept fish for the Patriarch's court (hence the name). Patriarch's Pond was immortalised by writer Mikhail Bulgakov, who had the devil appear here in *The Master and Margarita*. The initial paragraph of the novel describes the area to the north of the pond, where the devil enters the scene and predicts the rapid death of Berlioz.

Bulgakov's flat, where he wrote the novel and lived up until his death, is around the corner on the Garden Ring. Although the empty flat used to be a hang-out for dissidents and hooligans, it now has tight security appropriate to this high rent district.

The small park west of the Patriarch's Ponds, however, is still free for all. It's a popular spot for babushkas pushing strollers, lovers kissing on park benches and kids renting ice skates. It has a huge statue of 19th-century Russian writer Ivan Krylov, known to Russian children for his didactic tales.

BARRIKADNAYA

Eating p132; Shopping p159; Sleeping p168

Bolshaya Nikitskaya ulitsa intersects the Garden Ring at Kudrinskaya ploshchad, and the surrounding neighbourhood is known as Barrikadnaya, so called because it saw heavy street fighting and barricades during the 1905 and 1917 uprisings.

Just south of here, along the Moscow River, is the site of one of Moscow's largest ongoing urban projects, known as Moscow-City (see p22). Indeed, the development plan includes the construction of a new mini metro line. Mayor Luzhkov has grand plans to move much of the city administration to this new urban centre.

The area seems, perhaps, an unlikely locale for a new town hall. But the World

TRANSPORT

Conjoined metro stops Barrikadnaya and Krasnopresnenskaya serve this area. Another station called Ulitsa 1905 Goda is further west. A mini metro line now branches off from Kievskaya to serve the new Moscow-City development, including the new station at Delovoy Tsentr and the coming-soon station at Mezhdunarodnaya.

Trade Centre (WTC) and the exhibition centres, and Krasnaya Presnya Park have made this neighbourhood a hotbed of business activity. Ulitsa 1905 goda, which heads north from the WTC, may not look hip-hop happening, but these staid Stalinist structures are home to some of Moscow's most innovative restaurants (see p120).

The neighbourhood is well and truly up-and-coming, with an emphasis on 'up'. Skyscrapers of glass and steel tower 20 stories over the rest of the city, shining like beacons to Moscow's wheelers, dealers and fortune seekers. Amid all the construction, the Stalinist Hotel Ukraina still stands on the opposite side of the river, almost a tribute to times gone by.

Orientation

Barrikadnaya centres around Kudrinskaya ploshchad, where Bolshaya Nikitskaya ulitsa and Povarskaya ulitsa intersect with the Garden Ring. This wide and noisy stretch of the Garden Ring (here, Novinsky bulvar) makes it easy to believe the story that the ring's widening and tree felling in the 1930s were done to enable warplanes to land. The skyscraper at Kudrinskaya ploshchad is one of the Stalinist neo-Gothic 'Seven Sisters' (see the boxed text, p29) – an apt landmark for this busy urban intersection.

The main road heading west out of the square is Barrikadnaya ulitsa, but it changes name to ulitsa Krasnaya Presnya, and then to Zvenigorodskoe shosse when it intersects with busy ulitsa 1905 goda.

South of here, the Moscow River loops up from the south. The northern bank of the river is marked by the impressive façades of the White House and the WTC, with more tall glass and steel structures on the way. West of the WTC, a new pedestrian bridge connects two shiny skyscrapers on either side of the river.

CHEKHOV HOUSE-MUSEUM
Map pp248-9

☎ 291 6154; ul Sadovaya-Kudrinskaya 6; admission R30; ⊙ 11am-5pm Tue-Sun; Ⓜ Barrikadnaya

'The colour of the house is liberal, ie red', Anton Chekhov wrote of his house on the Garden Ring, where he lived from 1886 to 1890. The red house now contains the Chekhov House-Museum, with bedrooms, drawing room and study all intact. The overall impression is one of a peaceful and cultured family life. The walls are decorated with paintings that were given to Chekhov by Levitan (painter) and Shekhtel (Art Nouveau architect), who often visited him here. Photographs depict the playwright with literary greats Leo Tolstoy and Maxim Gorky. One room is dedicated to Chekhov's time in Melikhovo (see p207), showing photographs and manuscripts from his country estate.

MOSCOW ZOO Map pp248-9

☎ 253 6367; www.zoo.ru/moscow; cnr Barrikadnaya & Bolshaya Gruzinskaya uls; adult/child R80/free; ⊙ 9am-8pm Tue-Sun Apr-Sep, 9am-5pm Tue-Sun Oct-Mar; Ⓜ Barrikadnaya or Krasnopresnenskaya

Popular with families, this big zoo is surprisingly well maintained and populated with lots of wildlife, though enclosures are often too close for animal comfort. The highlight is the big cats exhibit, starring several Siberian tigers. Huge flocks of feathered

Children at the Moscow Zoo (above)

friends populate the central pond, making for a pleasant stroll for bird-watchers. For a new perspective on Moscow's nightlife, check out the nocturnal animal exhibit. This interior space is artificially lit by night, so that the animals remain awake. The black lighting allows visitors to see them prowling around as they would during the darkest hours.

For more four-legged fun, follow the footbridge across Barrikadnaya ulitsa to see the exhibits featuring animals from each continent.

SHALYAPIN HOUSE-MUSEUM

Map pp248-9

☎ 205 6326; Novinsky bul 25; admission R30; ✸ 10am-5pm Tue & Sat, 11.30am-6pm Wed & Thu, 10am-3.30pm Sun; Ⓜ Barrikadnaya

The world-famous opera singer, Fyodor Shalyapin (also spelt Chaliapin), lived in this quaint cottage from 1910 to 1920, with his Italian wife and five children. In Russian cultural life, the eminent bass stands alongside icons such as Konstantin Stanislavsky and Maxim Gorky. Indeed, his stature is evident from the museum exhibit, which features photographs of the singer in such

admirable company, as well as gifts and correspondence that they exchanged. More interesting for theatre buffs are the posters featuring Shalyapin's most celebrated performances, as well as original stage costumes. Occasional concerts are held in the museum's white room.

WHITE HOUSE Map pp248-9

Krasnopresnenskaya nab 2; Ⓜ Krasnopresnenskaya or Barrikadnaya

Moscow's White House, scene of two crucial episodes in recent Russian history, stands just north of Novoarbatsky most. It was here that Boris Yeltsin rallied the opposition that confounded the 1991 hardline coup, then two years later sent in tanks and troops to blast out conservative rivals – some of them the same people who backed him in 1991. The images of Yeltsin climbing on a tank in front of the White House in 1991, and of the same building ablaze after the 1993 assault, are among the most unforgettable from those tumultuous years.

The White House – officially called the House of Government of the Russian Federation (Dom pravitelstva Rossiyskoy federatsii) – fronts a stately bend in the Moscow River, with the Stalinist Hotel Ukraina rising

THE LAST OF MODERNISM IN MOSCOW Clementine Cecil

Russia's seminal contributions to international modernist architecture are sparse, elegant buildings that stand out among Moscow's grand Stalinist parades and colourful Orthodox churches. But most of these buildings have gone without even basic maintenance since they were constructed in the late 1920s and early '30s, and now they are on the edge of extinction.

Narkomfin (Novinsky bul 25; Ⓜ Barrikadnaya or Krasnopresnenskaya), the model for Le Corbusier's *Unité D'Habitation,* is set slightly back from the Garden Ring, wedged between the US embassy and Novinsky Passage shopping centre. On the World Monuments Fund Watch List since 2002, this building is an early experiment in semicommunal living, and a prototype for contemporary apartment blocks. Narkomfin was designed and built between 1928 and 1930 by Moisei Ginzburg and Ignatii Milinis for members of the National Finance Ministry. There was room for 50 families in duplex apartments. Communal space was maximised and individual space was minimised. Apartments had minute kitchens and people were encouraged to eat in the communal dining room in the neighbouring utilities block.

Narkomfin was built strictly on Corbusian principles: pillar supports, supporting frames, wall-screens, horizontal windows, open planning and flat, functional roofs. Yet it predated Le Corbusier's vertical city. The story goes that the young architect asked Ginzburg for copies of the layouts of the duplex apartments, which he took back to Paris and developed into his own revolutionary designs.

Despite its iconic status, Narkomfin is on the edge of collapse. Few Muscovites know of its existence, and so dilapidated is its façade that most who pass think it is an abandoned ruin. Half of its apartments are still inhabited but its roof is leaking and the walls are at the point of falling away due to water damage. The building is scheduled for demolition due to advanced deterioration, which has been speeded along by the recent construction of a shopping centre next door. Mayor Luzhkov has spoken openly against constructivist buildings, calling them 'flat-faced.' Moscow's chief architect, Alexander Kuzmin, grimly joked that the buildings are doomed, as 'they do not convert easily into casinos'.

Clementine is the cofounder of the Moscow Architecture Preservations Society (www.maps-moscow.com)

on the far bank. This corner of Moscow is particularly appealing when these buildings and Novoarbatsky most are lit up at night.

ARBAT DISTRICT

Eating p134; Shopping p160; Sleeping p169

Moscow's most famous street, ulitsa Arbat, is something of an art market, complete with instant portrait painters, soapbox poets, jugglers and buskers (as well as some pickpockets). It is undeniable that the Arbat today has been taken over by souvenir stands and pavement cafés. Nonetheless, it still evokes a free-thinking artistic spirit.

Near ulitsa Arbat's eastern end, the Wall of Peace is composed of hundreds of individually painted tiles on a theme of international friendship.

Just off the well-worn cobblestones of the Arbat lie the quiet lanes of old Moscow, a city once inhabited by writers and their heroes, old nobles and the nouveau riche. The era and its people are long gone, but you can still sense them in the grand houses they left behind. See p108 for details a walking tour that includes some of these grand houses.

Until the 1960s, ulitsa Arbat was Moscow's main westward artery. Then a swathe was bulldozed through the streets to its north, taking out the old Arbatskaya ploshchad, a monastery and half a dozen churches. The result was present-day ulitsa Novy Arbat – wide, fast and filled with traffic.

TRANSPORT

Two large squares – each with their own metro station – anchor the opposite ends of ulitsa Arbat. In the west, Smolenskaya metro is at Smolenskaya-Sennaya ploshchad; and in the east, Arbatskaya metro is at Arbatskaya ploshchad.

Note that both Smolenskaya and Arbatskaya are stops on the light-blue Filyovskaya line as well as the dark blue Arbatsko-Pokrovksaya line, which can be confusing. The really tricky part is that you cannot change lines between these stations, so make sure you go in the entrance serving the line that you need. The exception is the Arbatskaya stop on the Arbatsko-Pokrovskaya line, which is linked to other lines via Biblioteka imeni Lenina, Borovitskaya or Alexandrovsky Sad.

Orientation

The Arbat District centres on Arbatskaya ploshchad, the square formed at the intersection of Vozdvizhenka ulitsa (which runs west from the Kremlin), Novy Arbat ulitsa (which continues west to become the road to Smolensk) and the Boulevard Ring (here, Nikitsky bulvar). Wide, busy Novy Arbat slices the district almost in half.

Just south of the square, ulitsa Arbat (sometimes called 'stary Arbat', or 'old Arbat') is a 1.3km pedestrian mall that stretches to Smolenskaya-Sennaya ploshchad on the Garden Ring. On this square is one of Stalin's 'Seven Sisters', the Foreign Affairs Ministry. 'Stary' ulitsa Arbat defines the character of the neighbourhood. But it is sadly isolated by the busyness and traffic around Smolenskaya-Sennaya ploshchad and Arbatskaya ploshchad.

North of here (as far as Bolshaya Nikitskaya ulitsa), evocative names identify the area as an old settlement of court attendants: Khlebny (bread), Skatertny (tablecloth), Serebryany (silver) and Plotnikov (carpenters). Aristocrats and artists eventually displaced the original residents, and the mansions that line the streets reflect that change. These days, many of these buildings are occupied by embassies and cultural institutions.

For the purposes of this book, the Arbat district extends over the Borodinsky most and the Novoarbatsky most to include the area known as Dorogomilovo, which is south of the Moscow River and around Kievsky vokzal (Kyiv or Kiev station).

BULAT OKUDZHAVA STATUE

Map pp248-9

ul Arbat; Ⓜ Smolenskaya

The statue at the corner of Plotnikov pereulok is of Bulat Okudzhava, a 1960s cult poet, singer and songwriter, much of whose work was dedicated to the Arbat (he lived at No 43; see boxed text, p88).

GOGOL MEMORIAL ROOMS

Map pp248-9

☎ 291 1224; Nikitsky bul 7; admission free; ☿ reading room noon-7pm Mon-Fri, memorial rooms noon-7pm Mon & Wed-Fri, noon-5pm Sat & Sun; Ⓜ Arbatskaya

The 19th-century writer Nikolai Gogol spent his final tortured months here. The rooms – now a small but captivating museum – are arranged as they were when Gogol lived

ARBAT, MY ARBAT

> Arbat, my Arbat, You are my calling.
> You are my happiness and my misfortune.
>
> Bulat Okudzhava

For Moscow's beloved bard Bulat Okudzhava, the Arbat was not only his home, it was his inspiration. Although he spent his university years in Georgia dabbling in harmless verse, it was only upon his return to Moscow – and to his cherished Arbat – that his poetry adopted the freethinking character for which it is known.

He gradually made the transition from poet to songwriter, stating that, 'Once I had the desire to accompany one of my satirical verses with music. I only knew three chords; now, 27 years later, I know seven chords, then I knew three.' While Bulat and his friends enjoyed his songs, the composers, singers and guitarists did not. The ill-feeling subsided when a well-known poet announced that '...these are not songs. This is just another way of presenting poetry.'

And so a new form of art was born. The 1960s were heady times – in Moscow as elsewhere – and Okudzhava inspired a whole movement of liberal-thinking poets to take their ideas to the streets. Vladimir Vysotsky and others – some political, others not – all followed in Okudzhava's footsteps, their iconoclastic lyrics and simple melodies drawing enthusiastic crowds all around Moscow.

The Arbat today – crowded with tacky souvenir stands and overpriced cafés – bears little resemblance to the hallowed haunt of Okudzhava's youth. But its memory lives on in the bards and buskers, painters and poets who still perform for strolling crowds on summer evenings.

here. You can even see the fireplace where he infamously threw his manuscript of *Dead Souls*. An additional 'reading room' contains a library of Gogol's work and other reference materials about the author. The quiet courtyard contains a statue of the emaciated, sad author, surrounded by some of his better-known characters in bas-relief.

HOUSE OF FRIENDSHIP WITH PEOPLES OF FOREIGN COUNTRIES
Map pp248-9
Vozdvizhenka ul 16; Ⓜ **Arbatskaya**
The 'Moorish Castle' studded with seashells was built in 1899 for an eccentric merchant, Arseny Morozov, who was inspired by a real one in Spain. The inside is sumptuous and equally over the top. Morozov's mother, who lived next door, apparently declared of her son's home, 'Until now, only I knew you were mad; now everyone will.' This place is not normally open to the public, but sometimes exhibitions are held here.

LERMONTOV HOUSE-MUSEUM
Map pp248-9
☎ 291 5298; ul Malaya Molchanovka 2; adult/student/child R30/25/20; ☽ 2-5pm Wed & Fri, 11am-4pm Thu, Sat & Sun; Ⓜ Arbatskaya
'While I live I swear, dear friends, not to cease to love Moscow.' So wrote the 19th-

century poet Mikhail Lermontov about his hometown. The celebrated author of *A Hero of Our Time* lived in this little pink house on a small lane off Novy Arbat ulitsa. Here, he was raised by his grandmother, and wrote poetry and prose in the primitive office in the attic. Today, the cosy bungalow evokes the family's everyday life, displaying the poet's books, artwork and hobbies.

MELNIKOV HOUSE Map pp248-9
Krivoarbatsky per 10; Ⓜ **Smolenskaya**
This concoction of brick, plaster and diamond-shaped windows was built between 1927 and 1929 by Konstantin Melnikov – the great constructivist architect who was denounced in the 1930s. Melnikov continued to live in the house, one of the few privately owned homes in the USSR, until his death in 1974. The house is still owned by the architect's family and it is not usually open to the public, although Dom Patriarshy Tours occasionally brings groups here (see p54). For more details on the house, see the boxed text, opposite.

MUSEUM OF ORIENTAL ART
Map pp248-9
☎ 202 4555; Nikitsky bul 12A; admission R100; ☽ 11am-8pm Tue-Sun; Ⓜ Arbatskaya
For the sake of accuracy, this impressive museum on the Boulevard Ring should

probably be called the Museum of Asian and African Art, as the collection of tens of thousands of pieces represents both continents. The collection covers an equally vast time period, from ancient times to the 20th century, including painting, sculpture and folk art. The exhibit also includes an interesting feature on Nikolay Rerikh (see p92), the Russian artist and explorer who spent several years travelling and painting in Asia.

PUSHKIN HOUSE-MUSEUM

Map pp248-9

☎ 241 4212; ul Arbat 53; admission R40; ⏱ 10am-5pm Wed-Sun; Ⓜ Smolenskaya

After Alexander Pushkin married Natalya Goncharova at the nearby Church of the Grand Ascension (see p82), they moved to this charming blue house on the old Arbat. The museum provides some insight into the couple's home life – a source of much Russian romanticism. (The lovebirds are also featured in a statue across the street.)

Literary buffs will appreciate the poetry readings and other performances that take place here, this place should not be confused with the Pushkin Literary Museum (p92), which focuses on the poet's literary influences.

KROPOTKINSKAYA

Eating p135; Sleeping p170

The obvious and inevitable centrepiece of Kropotkinskaya is the spectacular Cathedral of Christ the Saviour. Its sheer size and splendour guarantee its role as a love-it-or-hate-it landmark and controversy spark. It is amazingly opulent, garishly grandiose and truly historic. It is, no doubt purposefully, the defining feature of the neighbourhood.

It is not, however, the highlight of Kropotkinskaya. This graceful neighbourhood is a 'museum' of classical mansions, especially along ulitsas Prechestinka and Ostozhenka (see the walking tour, p108).

CONSTRUCTIVISM: ARCHITECTURE FOR A NEW MAN *Clementine Cecil*

Constructivism was part of the Russian avant-garde movement that followed the revolution, and lasted until Stalin's reactionary regime became entrenched in the early 1930s. The term first appeared in the early '20s, and has increasingly been associated only with architecture; the most visible of the arts. The new movement identified with the new political and social order; it represented the culture of the future. During this brief period, architects devised new forms of living for a 'New Man': the Soviet citizen.

It was a time of great experimentation in form, building materials and technology. Much of the building technology utilised in Constructivism came from the Bauhaus school. In the depression following WWI, foreign architects came to Russia to practice. However, this very internationalism led to the official rejection of constructivism. Under Stalin, contact with the West was deemed 'antirevolutionary', thus discrediting the buildings.

Constructivist buildings are light, transparent, full of windows, and stand on pillars. Stalin, with his iron fist, wanted a grander style proclaiming the might of the Soviet Empire as it entered a phase of economic prosperity. Architects were ordered to return to the classical model, so buildings were brought back down to earth from their pillar supports, and decoration began to dominate over function.

The **Melnikov House**, dating from 1927–29, was the only private house built under Communism. The plot of land was granted thanks to a rare moment of cultural vision on behalf of the authorities. The architect Melnikov created his new home from two interlocking cylinders.

The house was experimental also in its designation of living space. The whole family slept in one room, painted a golden yellow and divided by narrow wall screens. Melnikov softened the corners in the room, even those on the hexagonal windows, to create a soothing environment for peaceful sleep.

This house, an icon of the Russian avant-garde, is still intact and is inhabited by the architect's son, Viktor Melnikov, now in his nineties. Although blind, Viktor is a tireless guide and carrier of his father's vision. He has tried to keep the house exactly as it was when his father lived there, down to the tubes of paint scattered across his desk. Viktor sometimes shows around visitors who ring the bell, but due to his age and blindness, a tour is not always guaranteed.

This seminal work of architecture underwent restoration in the 1990s. However, the work was poorly executed and the house has been suffering from the after-effects ever since. The Moscow Architectural Preservation Society (MAPS) nominated this structure to the 2006 World Monuments Fund (WMF) Watch List. The organisation is presently raising money with the WMF for emergency repairs, while Viktor is trying to persuade the Culture Ministry to make the house-studio into a museum in his father's honour, and to undo the harm of previous preservation work.

Sights

KROPOTKINSKAYA

Furthermore, these streets are also home to a slew of world-class museums and art galleries, making Kropotkinskaya one of Moscow's most vibrant art districts. The Pushkin Fine Arts Museum and the neighbouring Museum of Private Collections are long-standing attractions for art lovers, housing unexpected but impressive collections. In recent years, the area has also seen a flourishing of smaller galleries.

Renovating and resurrecting some of the neighbourhood's incredible architecture, celebrated contemporary artists Zurab Tsereteli and Ilya Glazunov have both opened galleries. The Russian Academy of Art and the Moscow House of Photography exhibit varied work by up-and-coming artists. These new additions complement and add value to the Rerikh Museum, an often-overlooked gem featuring work by the mystical artist. Indeed, the grand cathedrals aside, Kropotkinskaya is a veritable goldmine for art lovers, who could easily spend several days appreciating all of its riches.

Orientation

Ulitsa Volkhonka branches out from the southwest corner of the Kremlin to the Boulevard Ring (here, Gogolevsky bulvar). This intersection is dominated by the massive Christ the Saviour Cathedral and the classical edifice of the Pushkin Fine Arts Museum. An incongruous Fredrick Engels oversees the activity from a corner of the square.

From here, ulitsa Prechistenka continues southwest to the Garden Ring. The equally grand ulitsa Ostozhenka heads more directly south, running somewhat parallel to the Moscow River. Ulitsa Ostozhenka intersects with the Garden Ring (here, Zubovsky bulvar) as the latter heads east to cross the Moscow River.

This neighbourhood borders the Arbat District in the north, with a rough boundary at pereulok Sivtsev Vrazhek. It is bounded in the west by the Garden Ring and in the south by the Moscow River.

CATHEDRAL OF CHRIST THE SAVIOUR
Map pp252-3

☎ 201 2847; www.xxc.ru; ul Volkhonka 15; admission free, guided tours R330; ⏰ 10am-5pm daily, tours 2pm Sat & Sun; Ⓜ Kropotkinskaya

This gargantuan cathedral now dominates the skyline along the Moscow River. It sits on the site of an earlier and similar church of the same name, built between 1839 and 1883 to commemorate Russia's victory over Napoleon. The original was destroyed during Stalin's orgy of explosive secularism. Stalin planned to replace the church with a 315m-high 'Palace of Soviets' (including a 100m statue of Lenin), but the project never got off the ground – literally. Instead, for 50 years the site served an important purpose: the world's largest swimming pool.

This time around, the church was completed in a mere two years and at an estimated cost of US$350 million, in time for Moscow's 850th birthday in 1997. Much of the work was done by mayor Luzhkov's favourite architect Zurab Tsereteli (see the boxed text, p92), and it has aroused a range of reactions from Muscovites, from pious devotion to abject horror. Muscovites should at least be grateful they can admire the shiny domes of a church instead of the shiny dome of Lenin's head.

GLAZUNOV GALLERY Map pp252-3

☎ 291 6949; ul Volkhonka 13; adult/student R150/100; ⏰ 11am-6pm Tue-Sun; Ⓜ Kropotkinskaya

This elaborate Russian empire–style mansion, opposite the Pushkin Fine Arts Museum, houses a new gallery dedicated to the work of Soviet and post-Soviet artist Ilya Glazunov. Apparently this gallery was a long time coming, due primarily to the artist's own insistence on moulded ceilings, marble staircases and crystal chandeliers. But now it is open and the interior is impressive: three floors filled with fanciful illustrations of historic events and biblical scenes.

Glazunov is famous for his huge, colourful paintings that depict hundreds of people, places and events from Russian history in one monumental scene. His most famous work is *Eternal Russia (Bechnaya Rossiya),* while more recent examples are *Mystery of the 20th Century* and the *Market of our Democracy.* Such social commentary is a rather recent development, of course; the artist's earlier work tended to focus on medieval and fairy-tale themes.

MOSCOW HOUSE OF PHOTOGRAPHY Map pp252-3

☎ 231 3325; www.mdf.ru; ul Ostozhenka 16; admission free; ☷ 11am-6pm; Ⓜ Kropotkinskaya
In addition to the exciting and innovative photography exhibits that are held on site, this gallery also organises the annual International Photography Festival, usually held in conjunction with a foreign partner. The result is widely acclaimed, cutting-edge contemporary photography, exhibited at venues around the city. Exhibits have also featured works from the archives of some prominent photographers from the Soviet period.

MUSEUM OF PRIVATE COLLECTIONS

Map pp252-3

☎ 203 1546; ul Volkhonka 14; admission R40; ☷ noon-7pm Wed-Sun; Ⓜ Kropotkinskaya
Next door to the Pushkin Fine Arts Museum, this smaller museum shows off art collections donated by private individuals, many of whom amassed the works during the Soviet era. Exhibits are organised around the collections, each as a whole, and the details of collectors and donors are displayed alongside the art. The centrepiece, perhaps, is the collection of the museum's founder, Ilya Silberstein, an accomplished historian of Russian literature and art. Other highlights include a collection of Old Believer icons from the 16th to 20th centuries, the Lemkul room exhibiting fantastic glassworks, and impressive exhibits of 20th-century artists such as Alexander Rodchenko and Barbara Stepanova.

TOP FIVE KROPOTKINSKAYA SIGHTS

- **Cathedral of Christ the Saviour** (opposite) This massive creation evokes a range of reactions.
- **Glazunov Gallery** (opposite) Huge colourful paintings in an impressive mansion.
- **Pushkin Fine Arts Museum** (right) Fabulous museum of foreign art.
- **Rerikh Museum** (p92) The place for lovers of fantastical art.
- **Tolstoy Literary Museum** (p93) Study the great man's literary influences.

PUSHKIN FINE ARTS MUSEUM

Map pp252-3

☎ 203 7998; www.museum.ru/gmii; ul Volkhonka 12; adult/student R300/150, audio guide R250; ☷ 10am-6pm Tue-Sun; Ⓜ Kropotkinskaya
This is Moscow's premier foreign-art museum. It is famous for its impressionist and postimpressionist paintings, but also has a broad selection of European works from the Renaissance onwards, mostly appropriated from private collections after the revolution. There is also an amazing (read: mind-numbing) array of statues through the ages.

Keep an eye open for any special exhibitions at the Pushkin. In recent years it has revealed some fabulous art hoards that were kept secret since seizure by the Red Army from Germany at the end of WWII. The museum is also making an effort to mount some ambitious temporary exhibitions from its vast legitimate holdings.

On display are many of the most famous paintings by Matisse, such as *Goldfish*; some lesser-known pieces by Picasso; a few exquisite primitive paintings by Rousseau; and works by Miro, Kandinsky and Chagall. The museum also contains several pieces by Van Gogh, including the scorching *Red Vineyards* and the tragic *Prison Courtyard*, painted in the last year of his life.

The extensive collection of French impressionist works is based on the collection of two well-known Moscow art patrons, Sergei Shchukin and Ivan Morozov. It includes representative paintings by Manet, Monet and Renoir, and sculptures from Rodin's *Gates of Hell* and *Monument to the Townspeople of Calais*. The rich collection of 20th-century art continues to grow, with recent additions by Arp and others.

The highlight of the Pushkin's permanent display is the four incredible rooms of impressionist and postimpressionist paintings and sculpture. But don't neglect the 17th-century Dutch and Flemish paintings, including the dramatic Rembrandts, especially his moving *Portrait of an Old Woman*.

The Ancient Civilisation exhibits contain a surprisingly excellent collection, complete with ancient Egyptian weaponry, jewellery, ritual items and tombstones. Most of the items were excavated from burial sites, including two haunting mummies. Another room houses the impressive exhibit *Treasures of Troy*, which is actually from the

Sights

KROPOTKINSKAYA

excavation of a settlement dating to 2500 BC. A German archaeologist donated the collection to the city of Berlin, from where it was appropriated by the Soviets in 1945.

PUSHKIN LITERARY MUSEUM

Map pp252-3

☎ 202 8531; ul Prechistenka 12; admission R40; ☺ 10am-5.30pm Tue-Sun; Ⓜ Kropotkinskaya

Housed in a beautiful empire-style mansion dating from 1816, this museum is devoted to Russia's favourite poet's life and work. Personal effects, family portraits, (mostly) reproductions of notes and handwritten poetry provide insight into the work of the beloved bard.

The elegant interior recreates a fancy 19th-century atmosphere, especially the grand ballroom which is decorated with mirrors, sconces, chandeliers and heavy drapes. Several rooms are dedicated to Pushkin's specific works, demonstrating the links between his personal life and the poetry he produced. Perhaps the most interesting exhibit is 'Pushkin & His Time', which puts the poet in a historical context, demonstrating the influence of the Napoleonic Wars, the Decembrists' revolt and other historic events. This literary museum provides much more in-depth insights than the Pushkin House-Museum on ulitsa Arbat (p89).

RERIKH MUSEUM Map pp252-3

☎ 203 6419; Maly Znamensky per 3/5; adult/ student R150/75; ☺ 11am-6pm Wed-Sun; Ⓜ Kropotkinskaya

Nikolay Rerikh (known internationally as Nicholas Roerich) was a Russian artist from the late 19th and early 20th centuries, whose fantastical artwork is characterised by rich, bold colours, primitive style and mystical themes. This museum, founded by the artist's son, Sergei, includes work by father and son, as well as other family heirlooms and personal items. The artwork is intriguing: Rerikh spent a lot of time in the Altay Mountains of Siberia, Central Asia and India, so his paintings feature distinctive landscapes and mythological scenes. The building – the 17th-century Lopukhin manor – is a grand setting to admire the artwork.

RUSSIAN ACADEMY OF ART

Map pp252-3

☎ 201 4150; ul Prechistenka 21; R40; ☺ noon-7pm Tue-Sun; Ⓜ Kropotkinskaya

Next door to the Tsereteli Gallery, the Russian Academy of Art hosts rotating exhibits in the historic 19th-century mansion of the Morozov estate. Despite the institutional-sounding name, this is part of the Tsereteli empire. But it still puts on inspired and varied shows featuring mostly contemporary Russian and foreign artists.

LEAVING A MARK ON MOSCOW

Zurab Tsereteli is nothing if not controversial. As the chief architect of the Okhotny Ryad shopping mall and the massive Cathedral of Christ the Saviour, he has been criticised for being too ostentatious, too gaudy, too overbearing and just plain too much.

The most despised of Tsereteli's masterpieces is the gargantuan statue of Peter the Great, which now stands in front of the Krasny Oktyabr chocolate factory on the Moscow River. At 94.5m (that's twice the size of the *Statue of Liberty* without her pedestal), Peter towers over the city. Questions of taste aside, Muscovites were sceptical of the whole idea: why pay tribute to Peter the Great, who loathed Moscow, and even moved the capital to St Petersburg? Some radicals even attempted – unsuccessfully – to blow the thing up. After that incident, a 24-hour guard had to stand watch.

Mixed reactions are nothing new to Zurab Tsereteli. An earlier sculpture of Christopher Columbus has been rejected by five North American cities for reasons of cost, size and aesthetics. Some believe that the Peter the Great statue is actually a reincarnation of homeless Chris. Despite his critics, who launched a 'Stop Tsereteli' website, this favourite artist of Moscow Mayor Yury Luzhkov does not stop.

He launched the Moscow Museum of Modern Art, and took over the Russian Academy of Art. He recently opened the aptly named Tsereteli Gallery, which houses room after room of the artist's primitive paintings and elaborate sculptures.

Rumour has it that Tsereteli's next project is a theme park in a northwest Moscow suburb. Apparently, a 350-hectare plot has already been designated for the so-called 'Park of Wonders', which will be based on Russian fairy tales. As one Moscow journalist observed, 'For the sake of the children, let's hope Tsereteli's fairy tale heroes are not as scary as his Peter the Great.'

TOLSTOY LITERARY MUSEUM

Map pp252-3

☎ 202 2190; www.tolstoymuseum.ru;
ul Prechistenka 11; adult/student R100/30;
🕑 11am-6pm Tue-Sun; Ⓜ Kropotkinskaya

Opposite the Pushkin Literary Museum is the Tolstoy Literary Museum, supposedly the oldest literary memorial museum in the world (founded in 1911). In addition to its impressive reference library, the museum contains exhibits of manuscripts, letters and artwork focusing on Leo Tolstoy's literary influences and output. Family photographs, personal correspondence and artwork from the author's era all provide insight into his work. This museum undoubtedly contains the largest collection of portraits of the great Russian novelist. Entire exhibits are dedicated to his major novels such as *Anna Karenina* and *War & Peace*. The museum does not contain so much memorabilia from Tolstoy's personal life, which is on display at the estate-museum in Khamovniki (p96).

TSERETELI GALLERY Map pp252-3

☎ 201 4150; ul Prechistenka 19; R150;
🕑 noon-6pm Tue-Sun; Ⓜ Kropotkinskaya

Housed in the 18th-century Dolgoruky mansion, this is the latest endeavour of the tireless Zurab Tsereteli. The gallery shows how prolific this guy is. The rooms are filled with his often over-the-top sculpture and primitive paintings. If you don't want to spend the time or money exploring the gallery, just pop into the Artist's Gallery café (see p135), which is an exhibit in itself.

KHAMOVNIKI

Eating p136; Sleeping p170

Set on a sort of peninsula formed by the Moscow River, Khamovniki feels a bit isolated. South of the Garden Ring, its streets are not so clogged with cars; its pavements are nearly empty; there is not a crane or wrecking ball in sight. Peaceful parks – Skver Devichego Polya (Maiden's Field) and Mandelshtam Park – offer respite to passers-by, but they are not as busy as the parks closer to the centre.

The Tolstoy Estate-Museum also maintains an air of an artist's retreat on the edge of town. At the southern end of ulitsa Lva Tolstogo is the beautiful Church of St Nicholas of the Weavers.

TRANSPORT

The red Sokolnicheskaya metro line runs from the city centre at Teatralnaya and Biblioteka imeni Lenina, via Kropotkinskaya, out to the district of Khamovniki. The stops here are Park Kultury (also on the Ring line), Frunzenskaya and Sportivnaya. If you prefer to travel above ground, you might consider taking trolleybus No 5 or 15, both of which run down ulitsas Prechistenka and Bolshaya Pirogovskaya from Kropotkinskaya metro station.

The district's outstanding attraction is the Novodevichy Convent and Cemetery. A cluster of sparkling domes behind turreted walls on the river, the convent is rich in history. The name 'Novodevichy' (New Maidens) probably originates from a market, once held in the locality, where Tatars bought Russian girls to sell to Muslim harems.

The huge Luzhniki sports complex (p151) occupies the area within the wide river bend southwest of the Novodevichy. Luzhniki – meaning 'marshes', which is what this area used to be – was the main venue for the 1980 Olympics. It is always a hive of activity. Across the river is Sparrow Hills and the vibrant area surrounding the Moscow State University (p106), which offers a remarkable contrast to sleepy Khamovniki.

Orientation

This region is surrounded on three sides by the Moscow River, as it dips down south and loops back up to the north. Its northern boundary is the Garden Ring. At its intersection with Bolshaya Pirogovskaya ulitsa (the extension of ulitsa Prechistenka), a brooding statue of Tolstoy sits in the park, Skver Devichego Polya. The Tolstoy Estate-Museum is just south of here on ulitsa Lva Tolstogo, while the Novodevichy Convent and Cemetery are about 1.6km further southwest.

CHURCH OF ST NICHOLAS OF THE WEAVERS Map pp252-3

Tserkov Nikoli v Khamovnikakh; ul Lva Totstogo;
Ⓜ Park Kultury

This church, commissioned by the weavers' guild in 1676, vies with St Basil's Cathedral for the most colourful in Moscow. The ornate green-and-orange-tapestry exterior houses an equally exquisite interior, rich in frescoes and icons.

NOVODEVICHY CEMETERY Map pp252-3

Luzhnetsky proezd; admission R30; ⊗ **9am-6pm;**
Ⓜ **Sportivnaya**

Adjacent to the Novodevichy Convent, the Novodevichy Cemetery is one of Moscow's most prestigious resting places – a veritable 'who's who' of Russian politics and culture. Here you will find the tombs of Chekhov, Gogol, Mayakovsky, Prokofiev, Stanislavsky, Eisenstein and Gromyko,

among many other Russian and Soviet notables.

In Soviet times Novodevichy Cemetery was used for eminent people, whom the authorities judged unsuitable for the Kremlin wall, most notably, Khrushchev. The intertwined white-and-black blocks round Krushchev's bust were intended by sculptor Ernst Neizvestny to represent Khrushchev's good and bad sides.

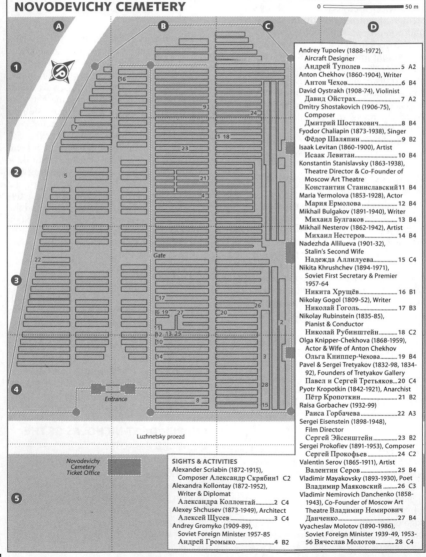

NOVODEVICHY CEMETERY

Andrey Tupolev (1888-1972), Aircraft Designer
  Андрей Туполев 5 A2
Anton Chekhov (1860-1904), Writer
  Антон Чехов 6 B4
David Oystrakh (1908-74), Violinist
  Давид Ойстрах 7 A2
Dmitry Shostakovich (1906-75), Composer
  Дмитрий Шостакович 8 B4
Fyodor Chaliapin (1873-1938), Singer
  Фёдор Шаляпин 9 B2
Isaak Levitan (1860-1900), Artist
  Исаак Левитан 10 B4
Konstantin Stanislavsky (1863-1938), Theatre Director & Co-Founder of Moscow Art Theatre
  Константин Станиславский 11 B4
Maria Yermolova (1853-1928), Actor
  Мария Ермолова 12 B4
Mikhail Bulgakov (1891-1940), Writer
  Михаил Булгаков 13 B4
Mikhail Nesterov (1862-1942), Artist
  Михаил Нестеров 14 B4
Nadezhda Allilueva (1901-32), Stalin's Second Wife
  Надежда Аллилуева 15 C4
Nikita Khrushchev (1894-1971), Soviet First Secretary & Premier 1957-64
  Никита Хрущёв 16 B1
Nikolay Gogol (1809-52), Writer
  Николай Гоголь 17 B3
Nikolay Rubinstein (1835-85), Pianist & Conductor
  Николай Рубинштейн 18 C2
Olga Knipper-Chekhova (1868-1959), Actor & Wife of Anton Chekhov
  Ольга Книппер-Чехова 19 B4
Pavel & Sergei Tretyakov (1832-98, 1834-92), Founders of Tretyakov Gallery
  Павел и Сергей Третьяков ... 20 C4
Pyotr Kropotkin (1842-1921), Anarchist
  Пётр Кропоткин 21 B2
Raisa Gorbachev (1932-99)
  Раиса Горбачева 22 A3
Sergei Eisenstein (1898-1948), Film Director
  Сергей Эйзенштейн 23 B2
Sergei Prokofiev (1891-1953), Composer
  Сергей Прокофьев 24 C2
Valentin Serov (1865-1911), Artist
  Валентин Серов 25 B4
Vladimir Mayakovsky (1893-1930), Poet
  Владимир Маяковский 26 C3
Vladimir Nemirovich Danchenko (1858-1943), Co-Founder of Moscow Art Theatre Владимир Немирович
  Данченко 27 B4
Vyacheslav Molotov (1890-1986), Soviet Foreign Minister 1939-49, 1953-56 Вячеслав Молотов 28 C4

SIGHTS & ACTIVITIES
Alexander Scriabin (1872-1915),
  Composer Александр Скрябин1 C2
Alexandra Kollontay (1872-1952), Writer & Diplomat
  Александра Коллонтай...........2 C4
Alexey Shchusev (1873-1949), Architect
  Алексей Щусев 3 C4
Andrey Gromyko (1909-89), Soviet Foreign Minister 1957-85
  Андрей Громыко.....................4 B2

The tombstone of Nadezhda Alliluyeva, Stalin's second wife, is surrounded by unbreakable glass to prevent vandalism. A recent addition is Raisa Gorbachev, the sophisticated wife of the last Soviet premier, who died of leukaemia in 1999.

If you want to investigate this place in depth, buy the Russian map (on sale at the kiosk), which pinpoints nearly 200 graves.

NOVODEVICHY CONVENT Map pp252-3
☎ 246 8526; Luzhnetsky proezd; adult/student R150/75, photo permit R60; ☼ grounds 8am-8pm daily, museums 10am-5pm Wed-Mon; Ⓜ Sportivnaya
The Novodevichy Convent was founded in 1524 to celebrate the taking of Smolensk from Lithuania, an important step in Moscow's conquest of the old Kyivan Rus

lands. From early on, noblewomen would retire to the convent, some more willingly than others. Novodevichy was rebuilt by Peter the Great's half-sister, Sofia, who used it as a second residence when she ruled Russia as regent in the 1680s. By this time the convent was a major landowner: it had 36 villages and about 10,000 serfs around Russia.

When Peter was 17, he deposed Sofia and confined her to Novodevichy; in 1698 she was imprisoned here for life after being implicated in the Streltsy rebellion. (Legend has it that Peter had some of her supporters hanged outside her window to remind her not to meddle.) Sofia was joined in her enforced retirement by Yevdokia Lopukhina, Peter's first wife, whom he considered a nag.

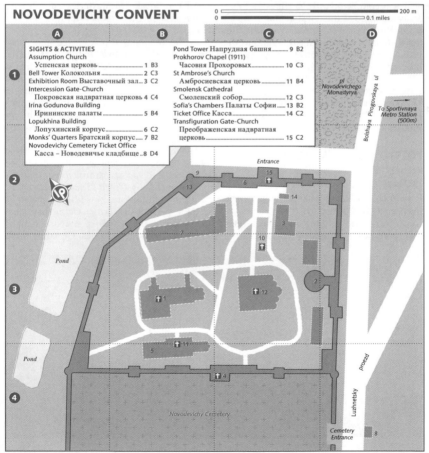

NOVODEVICHY CONVENT

0 — 200 m
0 — 0.1 miles

SIGHTS & ACTIVITIES
Assumption Church
  Успенская церковь 1 B3
Bell Tower Колокольня 2 C3
Exhibition Room Выставочный зал... 3 C2
Intercession Gate-Church
  Покровская надвратная церковь 4 C4
Irina Godunova Building
  Иринінские палаты 5 B4
Lopukhina Building
  Лопухинский корпус.................... 6 C2
Monks' Quarters Братский корпус.... 7 B2
Novodevichy Cemetery Ticket Office
  Касса – Новодевичье кладбище ..8 D4

Pond Tower Напрудная башня........... 9 B2
Prokhorov Chapel (1911)
  Часовня Прохоровых..................... 10 C3
St Ambrose's Church
  Амбросиевская церковь 11 B4
Smolensk Cathedral
  Смоленский собор........................ 12 C3
Sofia's Chambers Палаты Софии...... 13 B2
Ticket Office Касса.........................14 C2
Transfiguration Gate-Church
  Преображенская надвратная
  церковь 15 C2

pl Novodevichego Monastyrya

Bolshaya Pirogovskaya ul

To Sportivnaya Metro Station (500m)

Entrance

Pond

Pond

Luzhnetsky proezd

Novodevichy Cemetery

proezd

Cemetery Entrance

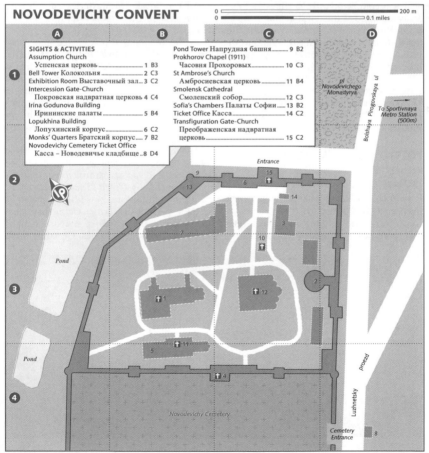

You enter the convent through the red and white Moscow baroque **Transfiguration Gate-Church**, built in the north wall between 1687 and 1689. The first building on the left, after the ticket office, contains a room for temporary exhibitions. Yevdokia Lopukhina lived in the **Lopukhin Building** against the north wall, while Sofia probably lived in the chambers adjoining the **Pond Tower**.

The oldest and most dominant building in the grounds is the white **Smolensk Cathedral**, modelled in 1524–25 on the Kremlin's Assumption Cathedral. It was closed at the time of research, but the sumptuous interior is covered in 16th-century frescoes. The huge iconostasis – donated by Sofia – has some more icons from the time of Boris Godunov. The **tombs** of Sofia, a couple of her sisters and Yevdokia Lopukhina are in the south nave.

The **bell tower**, against the convent's east wall, was completed in 1690 and is generally regarded as the finest in Moscow. Other churches on the grounds include the red-and-white **Assumption Church**, dating from 1685 to 1687, and the 16th-century **St Ambrose's Church**.

Boris Godunov's sister, Irina, lived in the building adjoining the latter church. Today, **Irina's Chambers** hold a permanent exhibit of 16th- and 17th-century religious artwork such as icons and embroidery.

TOLSTOY ESTATE-MUSEUM
Map pp252-3
☎ 246 9444; www.tolstoymuseum.ru; ul Lva Tolstogo 21; adult/student R100/30; ☻ 10am-5pm Wed-Sun; Ⓜ Park Kultury
Leo Tolstoy's winter home during the 1880s and 1890s now houses an interesting mu-

seum dedicated to the writer's home life. While it's not particularly opulent or large, the building is fitting for junior nobility – which Tolstoy was. Exhibits here demonstrate how Tolstoy lived, as opposed to his literary influences, which are explored at the Tolstoy Literary Museum (see p93). See the salon where Rachmaninov and Rimsky-Korsakov played piano, and the study where Tolstoy himself wove his epic tales.

ZAMOSKVORECHIE
Eating p137; Shopping p161; Sleeping p170
Zamoskvorechie ('Beyond Moscow River') stretches south from opposite the Kremlin, inside a big loop in the river. South was the direction from which Tatars used to attack, so Moscow's defensive forces were stationed in Zamoskvorechie (Donskoy and Danilovsky Monasteries), along with quarters devoted to servicing the royal court.

After the Tatar threat abated, more and more merchants moved to the area from the noisy and crowded Kitay Gorod. Zamoskvorechie once boasted Moscow's greatest number of churches, built by merchants in the 17th and 18th centuries to secure luck in business. Only at the end of the 18th century were merchants joined by nobles, and later by factory owners and their workers. Playwright Alexander Ostrovsky, who lived here in the 19th century, often described the secluded life of Zamoskvorechie in his plays, including *Groza (The Storm)*.

Although this area was little damaged by Stalin, present-day critics claim that it has suffered at the hands of mayor Luzhkov and his developer-cronies. Certainly, con-

The Novodevichy Convent (p95) at dusk

TRANSPORT

Tretyakovskaya and Novokuznetskaya metro stations serve the northern tip of Zamoskvorechie, near the Tretyakov Gallery. The northern part of this district is also accessible by walking over the Bolshoy Moskvoretsky most from the Kremlin, a route that traverses the island.

Oktyabrskaya metro station serves the square by the same name. Polyanka station lies in a sort of Zamoskvorechie no-man's land to the north of here. Gorky Park and the New Tretyakov are midway between Oktyabrskaya and Park Kultury stations – a 1km walk in either direction. At the eastern end of this district, Paveletskaya ploshchad has its own metro station by the same name.

struction marks every corner, each site representing another battle between local residents and municipal developers. The most controversial project is the planned development of the island between the Moscow River and the Vodootvodnoy Canal, which includes the conversion of the Krasny Oktyabr factory into luxury condominiums. Nonetheless, Zamoskvorechie is still a varied, intriguing area, which you can explore by following the walking tour described on p113.

Zamoskvorechie is also a thriving art district, thanks to the proliferation of galleries at the Central House of Artists (p161), not to mention both branches of the Tretyakov Gallery. From almost any vantage point in Zamoskvorechie you can see the giant sculpture of Peter the Great, product of the tireless Zurab Tsereteli (see the boxed text, p92).

Orientation

Directly south of the Kremlin, Zamoskvorechie is surrounded by the Moscow River on three sides. The Vodootvodny (Drainage) Canal slices across the top of this district, preventing spring floods in the city centre and creating a sliver of an island opposite the Kremlin.

The main roads, ulitsas Bolshaya Yakimanka, Bolshaya Ordynka and Pyatnitskaya run roughly parallel to each other, heading southward from the canal. Ulitsa Bolshaya Yakimanka terminates at busy Oktyabrskaya ploshchad, recently voted by Muscovites as the ugliest square in the city.

West of Oktyabrskaya ploshchad, along the Moscow River, is Gorky Park, the Sculpture Park and the massive New Tretyakov Gallery. East of Oktyabrskaya ploshchad, along the Garden Ring (here, ulitsa Zatsepsky val), busy Paveletsky vokzal (Paveletsky station) dominates the square of the same name.

BAKHRUSHIN THEATRE MUSEUM
Map p255

☎ 953 4470; ul Bakhrushina 31/12; admission R100; ☽ noon-6pm Wed-Mon; Ⓜ Paveletskaya
Russia's foremost stage museum, founded in 1894, is in the neo-Gothic mansion on the north side of Paveletskaya ploshchad. The museum exhibits all things theatrical – stage sets, costumes, scripts and personal items belonging to some of Russia's stage greats. The exhibits are not limited only to drama, but also trace the development of opera, ballet and puppetry. Highlights include the costumes and stage set from *Boris Godunov* (starring the famous bass, Fyodor Shalyapin) and the ballet shoes worn by Vaslav Nijinsky.

CHURCH OF ST JOHN THE WARRIOR
Map pp252-3

ul Bolshaya Yakimanka; Ⓜ Oktyabrskaya
The finest of all Zamoskvorechie's churches mixes Moscow and European baroque styles, resulting in a melange of shapes and colours. It was commissioned by Peter the Great in thanks for his 1709 victory over Sweden at Poltava. Although it's a working church, it is often locked; the 17th-century iconostasis is reputedly a masterpiece.

TOP FIVE ZAMOSKVORECHIE SIGHTS

- **Danilovsky Monastery** (p98) The Orthodox Church's spiritual and administrative centre.
- **Gorky Park** (p99) Festive refuge from the hustle and bustle.
- **New Tretyakov Gallery** (p99) Showcase of 20th-century Russian art.
- **Sculpture Park** (p100) See the fallen heroes of the Soviet era.
- **Tretyakov Gallery** (p100) Superb Russian icons and other prerevolutionary art.

DANILOVSKY MONASTERY Map pp246-7

☎ 955 6757; Danilovsky val; admission free;
🕑 7am-7pm; Ⓜ Tulskaya

The headquarters of the Russian Orthodox Church stand behind white fortress walls. The Danilovsky Monastery was built in the late 13th century by Daniil, the first Prince of Moscow, as an outer city defence. It was repeatedly altered over the next several hundred years, and served as a factory and a detention centre during the Soviet period.

It was restored in time to replace Sergiev Posad as the Church's spiritual and administrative centre, and the official residence of the Patriarch during the Russian Orthodoxy's millennium celebrations in 1988. Today, it radiates an air of purpose befitting the Church's role in modern Russia.

On holy days this place seethes with worshippers murmuring prayers, lighting candles and ladling holy water into jugs at the tiny chapel inside the gates. Enter beneath the pink **St Simeon Stylite Gate-Church** on the north wall.

The monastery's oldest and busiest church is the **Church of the Holy Fathers of the Seven Ecumenical Councils**, where worship is held continuously from 10am to 5pm daily. Founded in the 17th century and rebuilt repeatedly, the church contains several chapels on two floors: the main one upstairs is flanked by side chapels to St Daniil (on the northern side) and SS Boris and Gleb (south). On the ground level, the small main chapel is dedicated to the Protecting Veil, and the northern one to the prophet Daniil. The yellow and neoclassical **Trinity Cathedral**, built in the 1830s, is an austere counterpart to the other buildings.

West of the cathedral are the patriarchate's External Affairs Department and, at the far end of the grounds, the **Patriarch's Official Residence**. Against the north wall, to the east of the residence, there's a 13th-century Armenian carved-stone cross or *khachkar,* a gift from the Armenian Church. The church guesthouse, in the southern part of the monastery grounds, has been turned into the elegant Hotel Danilovskaya (p179).

DONSKOY MONASTERY Map pp246-7

☎ 952 1646; Donskaya ul; admission free;
🕑 7am-7pm; Ⓜ Shabolovskaya

The youngest of Moscow's fortified monasteries, it was founded in 1591 and built

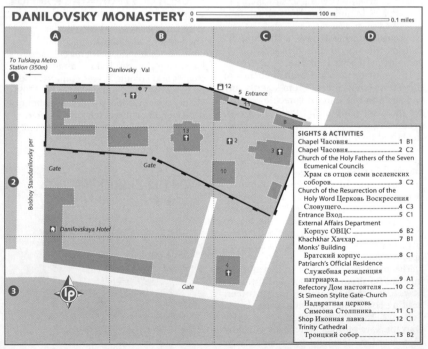

DANILOVSKY MONASTERY

0 — 100 m
0 — 0.1 miles

To Tulskaya Metro Station (350m)

Danilovsky Val

Danilovsky Hotel

Entrance

SIGHTS & ACTIVITIES		
Chapel Часовня	1	B1
Chapel Часовня	2	C2
Church of the Holy Fathers of the Seven Ecumenical Councils Храм св отцов семи вселенских соборов	3	C2
Church of the Resurrection of the Holy Word Церковь Воскресения Словущего	4	C3
Entrance Вход	5	C2
External Affairs Department Корпус ОВЦС	6	B2
Khachkhar Хачхар	7	B1
Monks' Building Братский корпус	8	C1
Patriarch's Official Residence Служебная резиденция патриарха	9	A1
Refectory Дом настоятеля	10	C2
St Simeon Stylite Gate-Church Надвратная церковь Симеона Столпника	11	C1
Shop Иконная лавка	12	C1
Trinity Cathedral Троицкий собор	13	B2

to house the *Virgin of the Don* icon (now in the Tretyakov Gallery). This revered icon is credited with the victory in the 1380 battle of Kulikovo; it's also said that in 1591, the Tatar Khan Giri retreated without a fight after the icon showered him with burning arrows in a dream.

Most of the monastery, surrounded by a brick wall with 12 towers, was built between 1684 and 1733 under Regent Sofia and Peter the Great. From 1918 to 1927 it was the Russian Orthodox Church headquarters; later it was closed as a monastery, falling into neglect despite being used as an architecture museum. Restored in 1990 and 1991, it's now back in Church hands.

The **Virgin of Tikhvin Church** over the north gate, built in 1713 and 1714, is one of the last examples of Moscow baroque. In the centre of the grounds is the large brick **New Cathedral**, built between 1684 and 1693; just to its south is the smaller **Old Cathedral**, dating from 1591 to 1593.

When burials in central Moscow were banned after the 1771 plague, the Donskoy Monastery became a graveyard for the nobility, and it is littered with elaborate tombs and chapels.

The Donskoy Monastery is a five-minute walk from Shabolovskaya metro. Go south along ulitsa Shabolovka, then take the first street west, 1-y Donskoy proezd.

GORKY PARK Map pp252-3
☎ 237 1266; ul Krymsky val; adult/child R50/15; ◷ 10am-10pm; Ⓜ Park Kultury or Oktyabrskaya
Part ornamental park, part funfair, Gorky Park is one of Moscow's most festive places to escape the hubbub of the city. Officially the Park of Culture, it's named after Maxim Gorky, and stretches almost 3km along the river upstream of Krymsky most. You can't miss the showy entrance, marked by colourful flags waving in the wind and the happy sounds of an old-fashioned carousel.

Inside, Gorky Park has a small Western-style amusement park with two roller coasters and almost a dozen other terror-inducing attractions (aside from the view of the Peter the Great statue). Space buffs can shed a tear for the *Buran,* the Soviet space shuttle that never carried anyone into space. Most of the rides cost R30 to R60.

In winter, the ponds are flooded for skating and tracks are made for cross-country skiing. Skis/skates are available for rental for R50/80 per hour.

LENIN FUNERAL TRAIN Map p255
Traurny proezd V I Lenina, Paveletsky vokzal; admission free; ◷ 10am-6pm Mon-Fri; Ⓜ Paveletskaya
The wide square on the Garden Ring is dominated by the Paveletsky vokzal (Pavelets station). The finest loco in the neighbourhood, however, stands idle in an air-conditioned pavilion just east of the station. It is the funeral train that brought Lenin's body to Moscow from Gorki Leninskie, where he died, in January 1924. The old steam engine is in beautiful condition, but does not attract many visitors these days. From Kozhevnichenskaya ulitsa, cut behind the row of kiosks and through the overgrown park to the pavilion in the back.

NEW TRETYAKOV GALLERY
Map pp252-3
☎ 238 1378; www.tretyakov.ru; ul Krymsky val; adult/student & child R225/130; ◷ 10am-6.30pm Tue-Sun; Ⓜ Park Kultury or Oktyabrskaya
The premier venue for 20th-century Russian art is this branch of the State Tretyakov Gallery, better known as the New Tretyakov. This place has much more than the typical socialist realist images of muscle-bound men wielding scythes and busty women milking cows (although there's that too). The exhibits showcase avant-garde artists such as Malevich, Kandinsky, Chagall, Goncharova and Popova.

In the same building as the Tretyakov, the **Central House of Artists** (see p161) is a huge exhibit space used for contemporary-art shows.

Tretyakov Gallery (p100)

OSTROVSKY ESTATE-MUSEUM

Map pp252-3

☎ 951 1140; ul Malaya Ordynka 9; admission R30;
🕐 noon-5.30pm Wed-Sun; Ⓜ Tretyakovskaya
Alexander Ostrovsky is the 19th-century
playwright who is often considered the
greatest Russian realist writer. This museum
is devoted to his life and work for the
Maly Theatre, which he founded, and to
Zamoskvorechie, where he lived and loved.
Some of the writer's personal effects are on
display here. More intriguing are the paintings and engravings of old Moscow, which
featured so prominently in Ostrovsky's
work.

SCULPTURE PARK Map pp252-3

☎ 290 0667; Krimsky val 10; admission R50;
🕐 9am-9pm; Ⓜ Park Kultury or Oktyabrskaya
The wonderful, moody Sculpture Park, behind and beside the New Tretyakov, is Moscow's most atmospheric spot to indulge in
some Soviet nostalgia. Formerly called the
Park of the Fallen Heroes, it started as a collection of Soviet statues (Stalin, Dzerzhinsky, a selection of Lenins and Brezhnevs)
put out to pasture after they were ripped
from their pedestals in the post-1991 wave
of anti-Soviet feeling. These discredited
icons have now been joined by contemporary work, including an eerie bust of Stalin
surrounded by heads representing the
millions of purge victims.

TRETYAKOV GALLERY Map pp252-3

☎ 951 1362, 953 5223; www.tretyakov.ru;
Lavrushinsky per 10; adult/student R225/130,
audio tour R120 extra; 🕐 10am-6pm Tue-Sun;
Ⓜ Tretyakovskaya
Nothing short of spectacular, this branch
of the State Tretyakov Gallery holds the
world's best collection of Russian icons and
an outstanding collection of other prerevolutionary Russian art, particularly the 19th-
century Peredvizhniki, or Wanderers.

The original part of the building is a
likeness of an old boyar castle, designed by
Viktor Vasnetsov between 1900 and 1905.
The collection is based on that of the 19th-
century industrialist brothers Pavel and
Sergei Tretyakov (Pavel was a patron of the
Peredvizhniki).

Within the museum grounds is the Church
of St Nicholas in Tolmachi where Pavel Tretyakov
regularly attended services. It was transferred to this site and restored in 1997, and
now functions as exhibit hall and working
church. The exquisite five-tiered iconostasis
dates back to the 17th century. The centrepiece is the revered 12th-century Vladimir
Icon of the Mother of God, protector of all
Russia.

The Tretyakov's 62 rooms are numbered
and progress in chronological order from
rooms 1 to 54, followed by eight rooms
containing icons and jewellery. In rooms 20
to 30, the art of the most prominent Peredvizhniki artists occupies its own rooms.
Look for Repin's realist work, including the
tragic Ivan the Terrible and his Son Ivan, in
rooms 29 and 30. A selection of Levitan's landscapes is in room 37. Vrubel's masterpieces,
including Demon Seated (1890), are in rooms
32 and 33.

Icons are found on the ground floor in
rooms 56 to 62. Rublyov's Holy Trinity (1420s)
from Sergiev Posad, widely regarded as
Russia's greatest icon, is in room 60.

Show up early to beat the queues. The
entrance to the gallery is through a lovely
courtyard; the Engineer's Building (Lavrushinsky
per 12) next door is reserved for special exhibits. Thanks to a lavish renovation during
the early 1990s, the gallery has wheelchair
access.

ZAYAUZIE

Taganskaya ploshchad on the Garden Ring
is the monster intersection – loud, dusty
and crowded – that is the hub of Zayauzie,
the area south of the little Yauza River. The
district was originally developed in the 16th
and 17th centuries as the territory of the
blacksmith guild. Around the square, which
was built up in the 1970s and 1980s, little
remains from this early period, but traces
of the past are still found in the streets that
radiate from it.

TRANSPORT

Ploshchady Taganskaya and Ilycha have their own
namesake metro stops. Taganskaya, which is on both
the Ring line and the purple Tagansko Krasnopresnenskaya line, is also cojoined with Marksistskaya,
on the yellow Kalininskaya line.

Another station further south is Proletarskaya (and
cojoined Krestlanskaya Zastava station), which is the
closest access point to the Novospassky Monastery

Wandering north on Goncharnaya ulitsa reveals a few unexpected architectural gems: several impressive classical mansions, an industrialist's manor house now known as Batashyov Palace and the charming church of St Nikita just beyond the Yauza. The whole area, however, is dwarfed by the Kotelnicheskaya Apartment, one of Stalin's Seven Sisters (see the boxed text, p29).

Zayauzie is dotted with 16th-century monasteries that also served as the outer ring of Moscow's defence system, including Novospasskaya and Andronikov. An Old Believers' Community still thrives east of here, as it has for hundreds of years. These historic monasteries somehow seem out of place amid the wide highways and mammoth apartment blocks that dominate the area. The flashing lights and traffic jams on Taganskaya ploshchad certainly represent another world.

This chaotic square is something of an entertainment district, boasting the renowned Taganka Theatre (p148), two legitimate jazz and blues clubs (p145) and a huge new casino. The impressive new Moscow International House of Music (p145) is just across the Moscow River.

Orientation

Zayauzie is a triangular-shaped area, southeast of the Kremlin. It is defined in the north by the little Yauza River, and in the west by the Moscow River. The heart of Zayauzie is Taganskaya ploshchad, which forms at the intersection of the Garden Ring (here, Narodnaya ulitsa and Zemlyanoy val) and several major roads. From the square, Taganskaya ulitsa shoots off to the east, Marksistskaya ulitsa heads on a diagonal to the southeast, and Bolshoy Komenshchiki ulitsa – which becomes Novospassky proezd – heads south toward the monastery of the same name. The Andronikov Monastery towers over the Yauza River to the northeast.

About 4km east of Taganskaya is another busy square, ploshchad Ilycha, formed at the intersection of Rogozsky val and shosse Entusiastov.

ECCLESIASTICAL RESIDENCE Map p255

Krutitskoe Podvorye; 1-y Krutitsky per; admission free; 🕑 **10am-6pm Wed-Mon;** Ⓜ **Proletarskaya**
Across the road south of Novospassky Monastery is the sumptuous Ecclesiastic

Residence. It was the home of the Moscow metropolitans after the founding of the Russian patriarchate in the 16th century, when they lost their place in the Kremlin.

NOVOSPASSKY MONASTERY Map p255

☎ **276 9570; Verkhny Novospassky proezd; admission free;** 🕑 **7am-7pm Mon-Sat, 8am-7pm Sun;** Ⓜ **Proletarskaya**
Another 15th-century fort-monastery is 1km south of Taganskaya ploshchad: the New Monastery of the Saviour, or Novospassky Monastery.

The centrepiece, the **Transfiguration Cathedral**, was built by the imperial Romanov family in the 1640s in imitation of the Kremlin's Assumption Cathedral. Frescoes depict the history of Christianity in Russia; the Romanov family tree, which goes as far back as the Viking Prince Rurik, climbs one wall. The other church is the 1675 **Intercession Church**.

Under the river bank, beneath one of the monastery towers, is the site of a mass grave for thousands of Stalin's victims. At the northern end of the grounds are the brick **Assumption Cathedral** and an extraordinary Moscow-baroque **gate tower**.

OLD BELIEVERS' COMMUNITY

Map pp246-7
Staroobryadcheskaya Obshchina; admission free; 🕑 **9am-6pm Tue-Sun;** Ⓜ **Ploshchad Ilycha**
One of Russia's most atmospheric religious centres is the Old Believers' Community, located at Rogozhskoe, 3km east of Taganskaya ploshchad. The Old Believers split from the main Russian Orthodox Church in 1653, when they refused to accept certain reforms. They have maintained old forms of worship and customs ever since. In the late 18th century, during a brief period free of persecution, rich Old Believer merchants founded this community, among the most important in the country.

The yellow classical-style **Intercession Church** contains one of Moscow's finest collections of icons, all dating from before 1653, with the oldest being the 14th-century *Saviour with the Angry Eye (Spas yaroe oko)*, protected under glass near the south door. The icons in the deesis row (the biggest row) of the iconostasis are supposedly by the Rublyov school, while the seventh, *The Saviour*, is attributed to Rublyov himself. North of the church is the **Rogozhskoe Cemetery**.

Visitors are welcome at the church, but women should take care to wear long skirts (no trousers) and headscarves. The community is a 30-minute walk from ploshchad Ilycha. Otherwise, take trolleybus No 16 or 26, or bus No 51, east from Taganskaya ploshchad; get off after crossing a railway. Rogozhskoe's tall, green-domed 20th-century bell tower is clearly visible to the north.

RUBLYOV MUSEUM OF EARLY RUSSIAN CULTURE & ART Map p254

☎ 278 1467; Andronyevskaya pl 10; adult/student R85/40; ⏱ 11am-6pm Thu-Tue; Ⓜ Ploshchad Ilycha
On the grounds of the former Andronikov Monastery, the Rublyov Museum exhibits icons from days of yore and from the present. Unfortunately, it does not include any work by its acclaimed namesake artist. It is still worthwhile visiting, not least for its romantic location. Andrei Rublyov, the master of icon painting, was a monk here in the 15th century; he's buried in the grounds, but no-one knows quite where.

In the centre of the monastery grounds is the compact Saviour's Cathedral, built in 1427, the oldest stone building in Moscow. The cluster of *kokoshniki*, or gables of colourful tiles and brick patterns, is typical of Russian architecture from the era. To the left is the combined rectory and 17th-century Moscow-baroque Church of the Archangel Michael; to the right, the old monks' quarters house the museum.

OUTER MOSCOW

Eating p138; Shopping p161; Sleeping p179

Moscow extends all the way to the Outer Ring Road, a multilane highway known as MKAD (p76). And the city continues to sprawl, especially as large international stores, shopping centres and movie theatres spring up on the outskirts. Retailers are real-ising that Muscovites – who now own cars – are willing to drive to places that offer lower prices and larger selections. Furthermore, there are few space constraints on the outskirts, meaning cheaper real estate and bigger stores.

By the same token, people are moving to the outskirts. The Russian version of suburban sprawl comes in two forms: gated communities containing the mansions of Moscow's nouveaux riches, who choose not to live in the busy centre; and massive Soviet-style blocks housing Muscovites who can't afford to live any closer to the centre.

Outer Moscow offers a few sights to lure the traveller out of the centre, not to mention a vast array of accommodation options that are more affordable than those in the centre.

Orientation

The main roads heading north out of the centre are: Leningradsky prospekt (also called Leningradskoe shosse further north), which is the continuation of Tverskaya and Tverskaya-Yamskaya ulitsas; and prospekt Mira, which is the continuation of ulitsas Sretenka and Bolshaya Lubyanka. The former heads toward Sheremetyevo airport, while the latter is where you will find Rizhsky Market and the All-Russia Exhibition Centre.

West of the centre, Kutuzovsky prospekt leads to the Borodino Panorama, Victory Park and beyond. The neighbourhood known as Fili is just north of here.

In the southwest, Moscow State University dominates the neighbourhoods around Sparrow Hills. Both prospekts Vernadskogo and Leninsky head out of the centre through the neighbourhood known as Yugo-Zapadnaya, or 'southwest'. Varshavskoe shosse comes directly south out of the centre through Zamoskvorechie to the Donskoy and Danilovsky Monasteries and beyond. Prospekt Andropova leads from Taganskaya ploshchad to the Kolomenskoe Museum-Reserve.

Heading east, Shchyolkovskoe shosse leads to the long-distance bus station, passing just north of Izmaylovsky Park. Shosse Entuziastov passes just south of Izmaylovsky Park. Ryazansky prospekt runs further south, passing Kuskovo Park.

TRANSPORT

No less than 14 branches of the metro extend out from central Moscow. More often than not, there is a stop near your destination, which is specified in the listings below. If additional transport is required, such as a bus or trolley from the metro stop, this information is provided in the review.

NORTH OF THE CENTRE
ALL-RUSSIA EXHIBITION CENTRE
Map pp246-7

Vserossiysky Vystavochny Tsentr (VVTs); ☎ 544 3400; www.vvcentre.ru; ☒ pavilions 10am-6pm, grounds 9am-7pm; Ⓜ VDNKh

No other place sums up the rise and fall of the great Soviet dream quite as well as the All-Russia Exhibition Centre. The old initials by which it's still commonly known, VDNKh, tell half the story – they stand for Vystavka Dostizheny Narodnogo Khozyaystva SSSR (USSR Economic Achievements Exhibition).

Originally created in the 1930s, the VDNKh was expanded in the 1950s and '60s to impress upon one and all the success of the Soviet economic system. Two kilometres long and 1km wide, it is composed of wide pedestrian avenues and grandiose pavilions, glorifying every aspect of socialist construction from education and health to agriculture, technology and science. The pavilions represent a huge variety of architectural styles, symbolic of the contributions from diverse ethnic and artistic movements to the common goal. Here you will find the kitschiest socialist realism, the most inspiring of socialist optimism and, now, the tackiest of capitalist consumerism.

VDNKh was an early casualty when those in power finally admitted that the Soviet economy was in dire straits – funds were cut off by 1990. Today, as the VVTs, it's a commercial centre, with its pavilions given over to sales of the very imported goods that were supposed to be inferior; much of the merchandise on sale is low-priced clothing and the like from China. The domed Kosmos (Space) pavilion towards the far end became a wholesaler for TV sets and VCRs, and Lenin's slogan 'Socialism is Soviet power plus electrification' still adorns the electrification pavilion to its right. Although you may not want to do your shopping here, VVTs does host international trade exhibitions.

For tourists, it's a fascinating visit to see the remnants of socialism's achievements. Muscovites are not so easily amused, however. Fortunately the new VVTs also offers other distractions, including an amusement park, paint ball, a stocked fish pond and an open-air circus.

CENTRAL MUSEUM OF THE ARMED FORCES Map pp246-7
☎ 681 6303; ul Sovietskoy Armii 2; admission R30, English-language guided tour R650; ☒ 10am-4.30pm Wed-Sun; Ⓜ Novoslobodskaya

Covering the history of Soviet and Russian military since 1917, this massive museum occupies 24 exhibit halls, plus open-air exhibits. Over 800,000 military items, including uniforms, medals and weapons, are on display. Among the highlights are remainders of the American U2 spy plane (brought down in the Urals in 1960), and the victory flag raised over Berlin's Reichstag in 1945. Take trolleybus No 69 (or walk) 1.3km east from the Novoslobodskaya metro.

COSMONAUTICS MUSEUM Map pp246-7
☎ 283 7914; adult/child R40/20, English audio guide R100; ☒ 10am-7pm Tue-Sun; Ⓜ VDNKh

The soaring 100m titanium obelisk outside the All-Russia Exhibition Centre is a monument 'To the Conquerors of Space', built in 1964 to commemorate the launch of Sputnik. In its base is the Cosmonautics Museum, a high-concept series of displays from the glory days of the Soviet space program. Exhibits rely heavily on cool space paraphernalia – Yury Gagarin's space suit, the first Soviet rocket engine, and lots of charts and diagrams of various expeditions. The highlight is the awe-inspiring video footage from various orbit missions. Sadly there is no gift shop selling freeze-dried astronaut food.

OSTANKINO PALACE & TOWER
Map pp246-7
☎ 286 6288; admission R40; ☒ 10am-6pm Wed-Sun mid-May–Sep; Ⓜ VDNKh

The pink-and-white Ostankino Palace, a wooden mansion with a stucco exterior made to resemble stone, was built in the 1790s as the summer pad of Count Nikolai Sheremetev, probably Russia's richest aristocrat of the time. Its lavish interior, with hand-painted wallpaper and intricate parquet floors, houses the count's art treasures. The centrepiece is the oval theatre-ballroom built for the Sheremetev troupe of 250 serf actors, who also played in Kuskovo Park (see p104). In 1801 Count Nikolai married one of the troupe, Praskovia Zhemchugova, and the two retired to Ostankino to avoid court gossip.

Only the Italian Pavilion is open for visits. The hours are limited, and it's closed on days when it rains or when humidity is over 80%.

After a fire in 2000, the 540m **Ostankino TV Tower** closed to the public, although it still provides a distinctive landmark for the area. Apparently, the tower has been repaired – complete with an observation platform and a sky-high café – and is expected to reopen soon.

To reach Ostankino Palace, walk west from VDNKh metro, across the car parks, to pick up tram No 7 or 11, or trolleybus No 13, 36, 69 or 73 west along ulitsa Akademika Korolyova.

EAST OF THE CENTRE

IZMAYLOVO PARK & ROYAL ESTATE

Map pp246-7

☎ 166 5881; Izmaylovskoe sh; admission free; ☼ 11.30am-5pm Wed-Sun; Ⓜ Partizanskaya

Izmaylovo is best known for its extensive **arts and crafts market** (see p162), held every weekend beside the royal estate. After shopping, Izmaylovsky Park and the crumbling royal estate are nice for a picnic or more serious outdoor activity.

A former royal hunting reserve 10km east of the Kremlin, **Izmaylovsky Park** is the nearest large tract of undeveloped land to central Moscow. Its 15 sq km contain a recreation park at the western end, and a much larger expanse of **woodland** (Izmaylovsky Lesopark) east of Glavnaya alleya, the road that cuts north–south across the park. Trails wind around this park, making it a good place to escape the city for hiking or biking. To get there, head south (away from the giant Hotel Izmaylovo complex) from Partizanskaya metro.

The **royal estate** is on a small, moated island to the northwest of the park. Tsar Alexey had an experimental farm here in the 17th century, where Western farming methods and cottage industries were sampled. It was on the farm ponds that his son Peter learnt to sail in a little boat; he came to be called the Grandfather of the Russian Navy.

Past an extensive 18th-century barracks (now partly occupied by the police) is the beautiful five-domed 1679 **Intercession Cathedral**, an early example of Moscow baroque. The nearby triple-arched, tent-roofed

Ceremonial Gates (1682) and the squat brick **bridge tower** (1671) are the only other original buildings remaining. The latter contains an exhibition hall.

KUSKOVO PARK & MANSION Map pp246-7

☎ 370 0160; ul Yunosti 2; admission per exhibit R50-150; ☼ 10am-4pm Wed-Sun Nov-Mar, to 6pm Wed-Sun Apr-Oct; Ⓜ Ryazansky Prospekt

When Count Pyotr Sheremetev married Varvara Cherkasskava in 1743, their joint property amounted to 1200 villages and 200,000 serfs. They turned their country estate at Kuskovo, 12km east of the Kremlin, into a mini-Versailles, with elegant buildings scattered around formal gardens, as well as an informal park. It's a pleasant trip out from central Moscow.

The main wooden mansion, **Kuskovo Mansion**, overlooks a lake where the count staged mock sea battles to entertain Moscow society. Across the lake to the south is the informal park. North of the mansion in the formal grounds are an **orangery**, now housing an exhibition of 18th- to 20th-century Russian ceramics; an **open-air theatre**, where the Sheremetev troupe of serf actors performed twice weekly; a pondside grotto with exotic 'sea caverns'; a **Dutch house**, glazed inside with Delft tiles; an **Italian villa**; a **hermitage** for private parties; and a **church** with a wooden bell tower.

The buildings are closed when humidity exceeds 80% or when it's very cold, counting out much of the winter.

Bus Nos 133 and 208 go from Ryazansky Prospekt metro to the park.

SOUTH OF THE CENTRE

KOLOMENSKOE MUSEUM-RESERVE

Map pp246-7

☎ 115 2768; admission grounds free; ☼ grounds 10am-9pm, museum & cabin 10am-5pm; Ⓜ Kolomenskaya

Set amid 4 sq km of parkland, on a bluff above a bend in the Moscow River, the Kolomenskoe Museum-Reserve is an ancient royal country seat and Unesco World Heritage Site. Many festivals are held here during the year, so check if anything is happening during your visit.

From Bolshaya ulitsa, enter at the rear of the grounds through the 17th-century **Saviour Gate** to the whitewashed **Our Lady of Kazan Church**, both built in the time of Tsar Alexey.

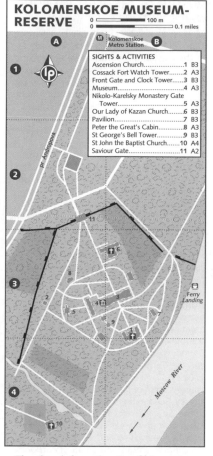

KOLOMENSKOE MUSEUM-RESERVE

0		100 m
0		0.1 miles

Kolomenskoe Metro Station

SIGHTS & ACTIVITIES
Ascension Church......................1 B3
Cossack Fort Watch Tower........2 A3
Front Gate and Clock Tower......3 B3
Museum...................................4 A3
Nikolo-Karelsky Monastery Gate
    Tower...................................5 A3
Our Lady of Kazan Church.........6 B3
Pavilion...................................7 B3
Peter the Great's Cabin............8 A3
St George's Bell Tower..............9 B3
St John the Baptist Church.......10 A4
Saviour Gate.........................11 A2

Ferry Landing

Moscow River

1532 for Grand Prince Vasily III, it probably celebrated the birth of his heir, Ivan the Terrible. It is actually an important development in Russian architecture, reproducing the shapes of wooden churches in brick for the first time, and paving the way for St Basil's 25 years later. Immediately west of it are the round 16th-century **St George's Bell Tower** and another 17th-century tower.

About 300m further southwest across a gully, the white **St John the Baptist Church** was built for Ivan the Terrible in the 1540s or 1550s. It has four corner chapels that make it a stylistic 'quarter-way house' between the Ascension Church and St Basil's.

Among the old wooden buildings on the grounds, is **Peter the Great's cabin** (adult/child R200/100), where he lived while supervising ship and fort building at Arkhangelsk.

TSARITSINO PALACE Map pp246-7

☎ 921 0139; admission R100; ☯ 11am-5pm Wed-Fri, 10am-6pm Sat & Sun; Ⓜ Orekhovo or Tsaritsino

On a wooded hill in far southeast Moscow, Tsaritsino Palace is the eerie shell of the exotic summer home that Catherine the Great began in 1775 but never finished. She allowed architect Vasily Bazhenov to work on it for 10 years before sacking him; apparently he had included a twin palace for her out-of-favour son, Paul. She hired another architect, Matvey Kazakov, but eventually gave up altogether as money was diverted to wars against Turkey. What stands now is mostly Bazhenov's fantasy combination of old Russian, Gothic, classical and Arabic styles.

The **Great Palace** is merely a shell of a building, nonetheless impressive for all its arches and towers. Rebuilding is often talked about, but long in coming. The palace is surrounded by equally enticing outbuildings: the **Opera House**, a near-perfect venue for concerts; the ornate **kitchen** (khlebny dom); and the light-filled **Small Palace**, which sometimes houses exhibits. The Patterned Bridge, which you are likely to pass under en route to/from the metro, is so called for the ornate Gothic designs adorning the pink brick.

The English-style wooded park stretches all the way south to the **Upper Tsaritsinsky Pond**, which has rowing boats available for hire in summer, and west to the Tsaritsino Palace complex.

The church faces the site of his great wooden palace, which was demolished in 1768 by Catherine the Great. Ahead, the white, tent-roofed 17th-century **front gate and clock tower** mark the edge of the old inner palace precinct. The golden double-headed eagle that tops the gate is the symbol of the Romanov dynasty.

The adjacent buildings house an interesting **museum** (adult/child R300/100) with a bit of everything: a model of Alexey's wooden palace, material on rebellions associated with Kolomenskoe, and Russian handcrafts from clocks and tiles to woodcarving and metalwork.

Outside the front gate, overlooking the river, rises Kolomenskoe's loveliest structure, the quintessentially Russian **Ascension Church**. Built between 1530 and

WEST OF THE CENTRE

BORODINO PANORAMA Map pp246-7

☎ 148 1967; Kutuzovsky pr 38; adult/student R50/30; ☯ 10am-5pm Sat-Thu; Ⓜ Park Pobedy or Kutuzovskaya

Following the vicious but inconclusive battle at Borodino (see p205) in August 1812, Moscow's defenders retreated along what are now Kutuzovsky prospekt and ulitsa Arbat, pursued by Napoleon's Grand Army. Today, about 3km west of Novoarbatsky most and Hotel Ukraina (where Russian commander Mikhail Kutuzov stopped for a war council) is the Borodino Panorama, a pavilion with a giant 360° painting of the Borodino battle. Standing inside this tableau of bloodshed – complete with sound effects – is a powerful way to visualise the event.

The Triumphal Arch, further out, celebrates Napoleon's eventual defeat. It was demolished at its original site in front of the Belorusskaya metro station during the 1930s and reconstructed here in a fit of post-WWII public spirit.

About 1.5km north of the Borodino Panorama in the neighbourhood of Fili, you will discover the 1690s Church of the Intercession, a beautiful red-brick Moscow baroque confection.

MEMORIAL SYNAGOGUE AT POKLONNAYA HILL Map pp246-7

☎ 148 1907; Minskaya ul; admission free; ☯ 10am-6pm Tue-Thu, noon-7pm Sun; Ⓜ Park Pobedy

This synagogue opened in 1998 as a part of the complex at Victory Park (see following). It is a memorial to Holocaust victims, as well as a museum of the Russian Jewry. Admission is with a guide only, so you must make arrangements in advance, especially if you want a tour in English. Otherwise, you might be able to join an existing group.

MUSEUM OF THE GREAT PATRIOTIC WAR & VICTORY PARK Map pp246-7

☎ 142 4185; ul Bratiev Fonchenko 10; admission R30; ☯ 10am-5pm Tue-Sun; Ⓜ Park Pobedy

To the west of the Borodino Panorama, Victory Park is a huge memorial complex celebrating the Great Patriotic War. The park includes endless fountains and monuments, the Memorial Synagogue at Poklonnaya Hill (see left) and the memorial Church of St George. The dominant monument is a 142m obelisk (every 10cm represents a day of the war).

The Museum of the Great Patriotic War, located within the park, has a diorama of every major WWII battle the Russians fought in. Exhibits highlight the many heroes of the Soviet Union, and also show weapons, photographs, documentary films, letters and many other authentic wartime memorabilia.

SPARROW HILLS Map pp246-7

Universitetskaya ploshchad; Ⓜ Vorobyovy Gory

The best view over Moscow is from Universitetskaya ploshchad on the Sparrow Hills. From here, most of the city spreads out before you. It is also an excellent vantage point to see Luzhniki, the huge stadium complex built across the river for the 1980 Olympics, as well as Novodevichy Convent and the Cathedral of Christ the Saviour.

Behind Universitetskaya ploshchad is the Stalinist spire of Moscow State University (Moskovsky Gosdarstvenny Universitet), one of the 'Seven Sisters'. The building, is the result of four years of hard labour by convicts between 1949 and 1953. It boasts an amazing 36 stories and 33km of corridors. The shining star that sits atop the spire is supposed to weigh 12 tonnes. Among other socialist realist frills on the façade, look for the eager students looking forward to communism. The building is not open to the public, which is a shame, because the lobby is equally elaborate, featuring bronze statues of distinguished Soviet scientists.

Walking Tours ■

Walking Tours

Moscow is a city for walking, which is evident from the hordes of people crowding the pavements. Of course it is too huge to walk everywhere, which is why there is the metro. Much of the city was built during a time when cars were a rarity (or nonexistent for that matter), so despite the proliferation of road traffic on the streets today, most of the city is accessible by public transport and a strong pair of legs.

The following walking tours provide some suggested routes by which to see the city under your own steam. The Underground Odyssey (p117) is a tour of the artistic highlights of Moscow's metro system.

ARCHITECTURE AMBLE

Just off the well-worn cobblestones of touristy ulitsa Arbat lie the quiet lanes of old Arbat, a district once inhabited by writers and their heroes, old nobles and the nouveaux riches.

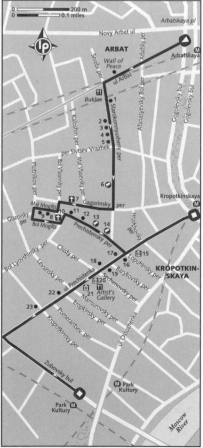

Its people are long gone, but you can still sense them in the grand houses they left behind.

The tour starts at the eastern end of the Arbat. Walk southwest on ulitsa Arbat and turn south into Starokonyusheny pereulok. The **green wooden house 1** at No 38 looks exquisite after some recent renovations. On the western side of the street, the architecture reads like a text book of Art Nouveau: the fine tile work of **No 41 2**, the somewhat disproportionate sculptures supporting the balconies of **No 39 3**, the imitation rough stone of **No 37 4** and the neo-Empire style of **No 35 5**. These are the so-called *dokhodnye doma*: flats built for rich professionals who couldn't afford their own house, but were wealthy enough to afford the luxury of a spacious and stylish apartment. In the next block, on the right, and dating from the late 19th century, No 23 is now the **Canadian Embassy 6** (p220).

At Gagarinsky pereulok, turn right and head west. Hidden in the yard at No 20 is the **Church of the Martyr Vlasy 7**. The church itself dates from the 17th century, and the refectory and bell tower are from the 19th century.

AMBLE FACTS

Start Arbatskaya ploshchad (Ⓜ Arbatskaya)
End Zubovsky bulvar (Ⓜ Park Kultury)
Distance 4km
Duration Three hours
Pit Stops Artists' Gallery (p135); Bukloe (p134)

Turn south into Bolshoy Vlasevsky pereulok, then turn west and proceed along Maly Mogiltsovsky pereulok. Notice the stucco decorations of No **4A 8** in subdued shades of green.

Turn south on Plotnikov pereulok once you reach the end of the side street. The building at No 4, erected in 1907 by the architect Zherikhov, is said to have housed a **brothel 9** popular with Moscow's political and intellectual elite. Its frieze has frivolous full-sized reliefs of Tolstoy, Pushkin, Gogol and others, all enjoying the company of Greek gods.

Turn left and walk east along Bolshoy Mogiltsovsky pereulok. At No 2/2 you'll find the run-down 18th-century **Church of Assumption in Mogiltsy 10**. According to Leo Tolstoy, this is the church Natasha Rostova attended in *War & Peace*.

Walk around the church in a counterclockwise direction till you reach Prechistenky pereulok. Turn right and proceed eastward along the lane. The building at No 12 was the **home of the writer Nikolai Ostrovsky 11** (not to be confused with the playwright Alexander Ostrovsky). Nikolai lived here between 1930 and 1932, when he wrote *How the Steel was Tempered*. Back in the day, this novel about the birth of the Soviet Union was required reading.

The elegant **Art Nouveau mansion 12** at No 10 was recently renovated for a private residence. Nearby, No 8, now housing the **Moroccan Embassy 13**, was built by the architect Valcott, who also designed the Hotel Metropol. The affluent mansion at the corner of Starokonyushenny pereulok is the **Austrian Embassy 14**.

Proceed along the side street till you reach the intersection. Now you are at your main destination, ulitsa Prechistenka. Catch your breath as you prepare to see a dozen of the loveliest buildings from the 17th to the early 20th centuries clustered along one street. Turn southwest on ulitsa Prechistenka.

On the east side at No 11, the former Lopukhin mansion now houses the **Tolstoy Literary Museum 15** (p93). A member of the Fabergé family lived in one of the **luxurious apartments 16** at No 13. In 1917 he fled Russia in a hurry, leaving behind all his belongings, which gave rise to rumours that there were treasures hidden in the walls of the apartment. And, in fact, there were. In the late 1970s a cache of silver was found during planned repairs.

Opulent **No 20 17** once belonged to the 1812 Napoleon war hero General Yermolov. Later, the millionaire Ushkov purchased the house and completely rebuilt it according to the tastes of his wife, the finicky prima ballerina Alexandra Balashovaya. No 22 dates back to the 18th century, but is best known as the **first Moscow fire station 18**, which was founded here in 1835.

No 17, on the east side, once belonged to Denis Davydov, another hero of the Napoleonic Wars. It now houses the city's **Building Maintenance Committee 19**.

The next building, a masterpiece by architect Lev Kekushev, is now the home of the **Tsereteli Gallery 20** (p93) and the funky café, Artists' Gallery (p135). At No 21, the Morozov mansion houses the **Russian Academy of Art 21** (p92). The industrialist Morozov, a great lover of impressionist art, rebuilt this mansion to accommodate his famous collection. Both the collection and the mansion now belong to the Academy.

At No 28, the early-20th-century **Dokhodny dom 22**, again by Kekushev, is generously decorated with sculptures, stucco, iron grilles and other detailing. The building at No 32 used to house the private **Polivanov Men's School 23**. The famed school's students included the poet Bryusov, the artist Golovin, and the first Russian world champion chess master, Alexin.

To reach the nearest metro station, continue down ulitsa Prechistenka to the Garden Ring (Zubovsky bulvar) and turn left. Park Kultury is 400m southeast. Alternatively, stroll back up ulitsa Prechistenka to Kropotkinskaya.

Tolstoy's writing case in the Tolstoy Literary Museum (p93)

AROUND THE RING

The Boulevard Ring was created in the late 18th and early 19th centuries, replacing Moscow's old defensive walls with a dual-carriage ring road. The new boulevard circling the city centre was lined with stately mansions and theatres. And the shady path between the two carriageways became the place for Moscow residents to promenade.

Today the Boulevard Ring has lots more cars than carriages. But the strip of green down the middle is still a pleasant place to walk and is Moscow's oddest-shaped park. Eight kilometres long by 20m wide, it forms a near-complete circle around the centre, from the banks of the Yauza River southeast of the Kremlin to the banks of the Moscow River in the southwest. This walking tour takes you most of the way around the ring.

A stroll around the ring is a pleasant way to explore some of Moscow's most enticing neighbourhoods, often boasting elegant pre-Revolutionary architecture. The path is lined with flowerbeds and studded with

WALK FACTS

Start Chistoprudny bulvar (Ⓜ Chistye Prudy)
End Christ the Saviour Cathedral
(Ⓜ Kropotkinskaya)
Distance 5km
Duration Four hours
Pit Stops Tent (p126); Bar 30/7 (p141)

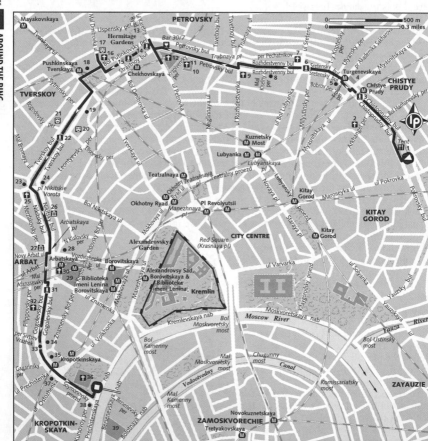

statues of past Russian cultural greats. Street artists and mobile phone users are also on hand injecting a flavour of present-day Russian culture.

The Boulevard Ring changes its name at every major intersection, but it is usually 'something-bulvar', and it is always recognizable by the green strip down the centre. If you are not up for the walk, you can do most of this tour by trolleybus: Nos 15 and 31 run both ways along the ring between Trubnaya ploshchad (Ⓜ Tsvetnoy bulvar) and ulitsa Prechistenka (Ⓜ Kropotkinskaya).

Start east of the centre on Chistoprudny bulvar. **Chistye Prudy 1**, or 'Clean Ponds', refers to the lovely pond that graces the Boulevard Ring at its intersection with ulitsa Pokrovka. The surrounding area was largely developed by the merchant Alexander Menshikov in the 18th century. As you head north along Chistoprudny bulvar, you will see the golden cross that tops **Menshikov Tower 2** (p79) to your left.

At the centre of the boulevard, near the Chistye Prudy metro, stands a statue in honour of **Alexander Griboyedov 3**, a 19th-century playwright and diplomat. His comedy *Woe from Wit*, a brilliant satire on Moscow aristocratic life, is one of Russia's most often-staged plays. Note the aristocratic characters from the play sculpted into the base of the memorial.

Cross the busy intersection at Myasnitskaya ulitsa, where the Boulevard becomes Sretensky bulvar. At No 11, the **Lukoil Skyscraper 4** stands shiny, modern and out of place. But when viewed from across the square, the reflective façade offers a lovely image of the baroque building across the street at **No 6 5**.

At the opposite end of Sretensky bulvar stands a monument to **Nadezhda Krupskaya 6** – revolutionary, writer and wife of Vladimir Ilych Lenin. Krupskaya is widely recognised as Lenin's top advisor and confidante, and an active Bolshevik in her own right.

Cross ulitsa Sretenka, signalling the start of Rozhdestvenny bulvar. On the corner, the pretty whitewashed **Church of the Assumption of the Virgin 7** is a working church and usually open for a look around its candle-lit interior. The 18th-century building at No 14 is a baroque beauty. In the 1830s this building served as a **Centre for Writers 8**, hosting readings and meetings attended by the likes of Mikhail Lermontov and Alex Gertsen (Herzen).

At the end of the block on the left-hand side, duck into the **Nativity Monastery 9** (Rozhdestvensky monastir), for which this section of the boulevard is named. Founded in 1380, it is one of Moscow's oldest monasteries, and it looks it. The walled grounds contain a 16th-century church and a grand bell tower. Some of the frescoes in the church have been restored, but otherwise this place has an air of dilapidated grace.

Continue straight on the Boulevard Ring along Petrovsky bulvar (don't get confused by Tsvetnoy bulvar, another dual-carriageway road that goes off to the north). The left-hand side of this strip is dotted with architectural and religious landmarks. Look for the Art Nouveau **apartment complex 10** *(ansambl zhilikh domov)* at No 4 Krapivensky pereulok. Designed by the architect Rodionov, the façade is characterised by its quite extraordinary tortoise-shell brick pattern, which extends all the way around the horseshoe-shaped building. The complex nearly hides the equally decorative **Church of Sergei in Krapivnika 11**, which is visible from the side street.

The corner of Petrovsky bulvar and ulitsa Petrovka is dominated by its namesake **Upper St Peter Monastery 12** (Petrovsky monastir; p81). The entrance is on ulitsa Petrovka.

Cross ulitsa Petrovka and continue on to Strastnoy bulvar. Weather permitting, this section of the Boulevard Ring is dotted with summer cafés *(letny kafe)*, as are the pleasant **Hermitage Gardens 13** just north of here. Sculptures along the way commemorate two celebrated musicians: **Vladimir Vyssotsky 14**, bard and social revolutionary from the 1960s; and **Sergei Rachmaninov 15**, the celebrated turn-of-the-century pianist and composer.

Cross Bolshoy Putinkovsky pereulok to the north side, so you can admire the tent roofs on the **Church of the Nativity of the Virgin in Putinki 16** (p82) and the impressive façade of the **Lenkom Theatre 17** (p147).

You are now entering busy Pushkinskaya ploshchad, so named for the gallant poet whose statue commands the square. This square is the nearest thing to a Russian Fleet St. On the northern side, east of Tverskaya ulitsa, squat the offices of **Izvestia 18**, formerly the newspaper of the USSR Supreme Soviet, now a bland daily.

Make your way across Tverskaya ulitsa via the underground *perekhod* (crosswalk). Continue southwest along the path that runs between the two lanes of traffic on Tverskoy bulvar. On the left, Café Pushkin (p129) is part of the **Rimsky Korsakov Quarter 19**, named after Catherine the Great's paramour, who owned the buildings. Although the complex dates from the 18th and 19th centuries, most of it was destroyed during renovation, leaving only the original façade that fronts Tverskoy bulvar.

The huge brown block at No 22 is the newly renovated building of the **Gorky Moscow Art Theatre 20** (p144). Previously on this site stood the house of Praskova Yurevna, a socialite fond of hosting extravagant balls and operas. At one of these infamous events, Alexander Pushkin supposedly met his future wife, Natalya Goncharova.

Hidden behind other buildings on the north side is the 17th-century Church of Ioann Chrysostom, which was commissioned by Mikhail Romanov to house the *Icon of Ioanna Bogoslova*. The church was taken over by the **Pushkin Drama Theatre 21** (p148) during the Soviet period, and the fate of the icon is unknown.

In the middle of the boulevard is a **statue of Sergei Yesenin 22**, an early-20th-century poet who was in and out of favour throughout the Soviet era. Writing about love and landscapes earned him the nickname 'the peasant poet'. His short, stormy life was torn apart by no less than five marriages and violent bouts with alcoholism. He finally took his life in 1925 at the age of 30.

At the bottom of the street is one of the most beautiful squares in Moscow. Nikitskie Gates (Nikitskie Vorota) takes its name from the gates that stood here from the 15th to the 18th centuries. At the corner of the square, the **Rotunda Fountain 23**, by Zurab Tsereteli, hides a statue of Pushkin and Goncharova, erected in 1999 to celebrate the poet's birthday.

On the square's eastern side is the headquarters of the Russian news agency **Itar-Tass 24**. Its windows are full of fantastic photos of the events of the week. South of the square, the beautiful **Church of Feodor Studit 25** is all that remains of a 17th-century monastery founded by the Patriarch Filaret. The enchanting white bell tower is a 1990s' replica of the original.

Continue south on the Boulevard Ring, now called Nikitsky bulvar. The classical building at No 12A now houses the **Museum of Oriental Art 26** (p88), but it was built for the musical Lunin family. The moulded lyre on the front of this elegant house is a reminder of the many musical evenings that took place here. The quiet courtyard at No 7 contains a gloomy statue of Nikolai Gogol and the **Gogol Memorial Rooms 27** (p87), where the writer spent his final, tortured months.

Nikitsky bulvar ends at busy Arbatskaya ploshchad. Take a moment or two to gawk at the exotic, **Moorish House of Friendship with Peoples of Foreign Countries 28** (p88) at the corner of Vozdvizhenka ulitsa.

South of the square, the hulking **Ministry of Defence 29** occupies much of the block. It leaves just a corner of space for the sweet **SS Boris & Gleb Chapel 30**, which seems out of place amid the whizzing cars and hordes of people. Built in 1997, the chapel commemorates a 1483 church of the same name that was destroyed in the 1930s.

Continuing south, the **statue of Nikolai Gogol 31** marks the start of Gogolevsky bulvar, another peaceful stretch of the Boulevard Ring. The golden domes of the 17th-century **Church of the Apostle Philip 32** rise above the baroque buildings on the west side of the street. Further down the street, artists set up **stalls 33** to hawk their paintings, often featuring the eye-catching Christ the Saviour Cathedral, which is visible from here.

On the east side, the ostentatious, multicolumned **mansion at No 10 34** served as a meeting place for the Decembrists. This group of liberal-minded nobility rallied for reform in the early 19th century – and were promptly exiled to Siberia. The building at No 6 was part of the **Tretyakov estate 35**, and in fact housed the Tretyakov collection at the end of the 19th century.

The boulevard ends at its intersection with ulitsa Prechistenka, at the base of the mammoth **Cathedral of Christ the Saviour 36** (p90). **Fredrick Engels 37** surveys the square from its western side.

Walk along the Cathedral's wide marble terrace to the back, where it overlooks the Moscow River. From here, you have a fantastic view of the amazing Art Nouveau masterpiece at **No 1 Kursovoy pereulok 38**. Ornate brickwork and detailed tile mosaics adorn the exterior – a product of the architect Zhukov and the artist Malyutin. Built in 1886, it now houses administrative services for the diplomatic corps.

Across the river, **Krasny Oktyabr Confectionary 39**, Moscow's most beloved sweet maker, and **Peter the Great 40**, Moscow's most hated landmark, are in plain view. This little island is the subject of a fierce debate; developers intend to convert the sweet factory into luxury condominiums.

The iron bridge leads to the opposite bank, where there is talk of establishing an art district by filling the old warehouses with studios and galleries. In the meantime, it is something of a bridge to nowhere, but the views of the Kremlin and the Cathedral are breathtaking.

CHURCH WALK

The atmosphere of 19th-century Moscow lives on in the low buildings, old courtyards and clusters of onion domes along narrow ulitsa Bolshaya Ordynka, which runs 2km down the middle of Zamoskvorechie to Serpukhovskaya ploshchad; Pyatnitskaya ulitsa is roughly parallel, 200m to the east. The many churches located in the area make up a wonderful scrapbook of Muscovite architectural styles. Take the tour now, as developers are quickly changing the landscape of this graceful neighbourhood.

The name 'Ordynka' comes from *orda* (horde); until the 16th century this was the start of the road to the Golden Horde's capital on the Volga, where the Tatar ambassadors lived. Other sources maintain that the street received its name from the *'ordyntsy'*, who lived in this area in the 15th century. *'Ordyntsy'* were the people taken hostage by Tatars then bought by wealthy Russians to work as servants.

Start at Pyatnitskaya ulitsa, at the intersection of Klimentovsky pereulok. At No 26, the **St Clement's Church 1** commands the corner. Built in the 1740s, this is a rare example of true baroque architecture in Moscow.

Head up Pyatnitskaya ulitsa toward the Vodootvodny Canal, and turn left on Chernigovsky pereulok. The small, white **SS Mikhail and Fyodor Church 2**, dating from the late 17th century, has two rows of spade gables and five domes on a thin tower. The larger **St John the Baptist Church 3**, from the same period, houses an exhibition of Russian glassware. St John's Bell Tower, the Zamoskvorechie landmark that fronts Pyatnitskaya ulitsa, was added in 1753.

Continue to the end of Chernigovsky pereulok and cross busy ulitsa Bolshaya Ordynka to peek down the narrow Kadashevsky 2-y pereulok. The tall **Resurrection Church in Kadashi 4** – which houses a restoration centre for some other churches – is under restoration itself. Its rich late-17th-century decoration is a fine example of Moscow baroque. The tall and elegant belfry earned the nickname 'the candle'.

Turn left on Kadashevsky 1-y pereulok and left again on Kadashevsky 3-y pereulok to see some of Zamoskvorechie's small back alleys, before heading back to ulitsa Bolshaya Ordynka. Turn right, and walk south to the busy intersection with Klimentovsky pereulok. You can't miss the empress-style **Virgin of Consolation of All Sorrows Church 5** at No 20, which dates mostly from between 1828 and 1833.

Continue south. At No 27A, the blue-and-white **Church of St Nicholas in Pyzhi 6** is a typical five-domed, mid-17th-century church, with

WALK FACTS

Start Klimentovsky pereulok (Ⓜ Novokuznetskaya)
End Oktyabrskaya ploshchad (Ⓜ Oktyabrskaya)
Distance 2km
Duration One hour
Pit Stops Garden (p137); Coffee Bean (p121); Pancho Villa (p138)

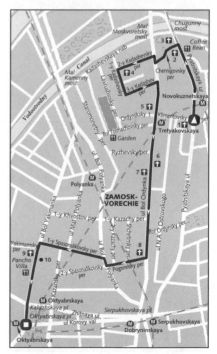

spade gables and thin onion domes. It is a working church, so it is likely to be open for a peek inside. Opposite, the new-Russian **SS Martha and Mary Convent 7** at No 34A was built between 1908 and 1912. Its pretty single-domed Intercession Church contains impressive, colourful frescoes, although the church is normally open only for services. At the beginning of the 20th century, the convent was famous for its charitable work.

Further south at No 60/2, **St Catherine Church 8** was built in 1767 to celebrate the enthronement of Catherine II (the Great). The ceiling has fragments of murals by 18th-century artist Dmitry Levitsky.

From here, turn right on Pogorelsky pereulok and continue on 1-y Spasonalikovsky pereulok all the way to ulitsa Bolshaya Yakimanka. Your eyes will immediately alight on the finest of all the Zamoskvorechie churches, **Church of St John the Warrior 9** (p97). This bold blend of Russian and European baroque produces delightful results. Opposite, the **residence of the French Ambassador 10** is equally striking.

Continue south to Oktyabrskaya ploshchad, where you can cool off with a margarita at Pancho Villa (p138) or hop on the metro.

KITAY GOROD TOUR

This walking tour winds its way through Kitay Gorod, which – settled in the 13th century – is one of the oldest parts of Moscow. It became an active trade and financial centre: records from the 17th century show that this area contained 72 rows of trading arcades. Street names such as Khrustalny pereulok (Crystal Lane) and Vetoshny pereulok (Carpet Lane) remain from that era. Even more intriguing are remnants of the old city wall and the tiny, colourful churches, which pepper the narrow streets of Kitay Gorod.

Start at the Hotel Metropol, southeast of Teatralnaya metro, and walk east down Teatralny proezd to the stately gate. This historical and architectural complex is **Old Fields 1** (p66), which includes excavations of the 16th-century fortified wall that used to surround Kitay Gorod, and the foundations of the 1493 Trinity Church. Beside the remains of the wall and the church stands the memorial statue of Ivan Fedorov, reputedly responsible for producing Russia's first printed book in 1563. The gated walkway of Tretyakovsky proezd leads into Kitay Gorod.

Walk down Tretyakovsky proezd and turn right to head west along Nikolskaya ulitsa, Kitay Gorod's busiest street. It also used to be the main road to Vladimir.

The ornate building at No 17 was formerly a hotel known as **Slavyansky Bazaar 2.** Here, in 1897, directors Stanislavsky and Nemirovich held their celebrated and very extended meeting, during which they founded the Moscow Art Theatre (MKhT), now named Chekhov Moscow Art Theatre (see the boxed text, p147). The famous hotel is also featured in the Chekhov short story *The Lady with a Lapdog,* as the hotel where Gurov's lover stays when she comes to Moscow.

The green-and-white building, with the lion and unicorn above its entrance at No 15, is the **Synod Printing House 3** (p77), where Ivan Fyodorov printed that first book. Up until the early 19th century, Kitay Gorod

WALK FACTS

Start Teatralnaya ploshchad (Theatre Square; M Teatralnaya)
End Staraya Ploshchad (M Kitay Gorod)
Distance 1.5km
Duration Two hours
Pit Stop Loft Café (p124); Che (p124)

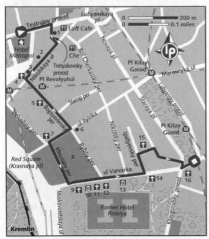

was something of a printing centre, and home to 26 of Moscow's 31 bookshops at the time. The **Zaikonospassky Monastery 4** ('Behind the Icon Stall' Monastery; p78) at Nos 7-9 refers to the busy icon trade that also took place here.

Turn left on Bogoyavlensky pereulok and head south; look out for the Moscow baroque Epiphany Cathedral on the right-hand side. The church was built in the 1690s, but the **Monastery of the Epiphany 5** (p77) dates to the 13th century. If you are lucky, you might catch a concert (or rehearsal) performed in the bell tower.

When you reach the corner of ulitsa Ilynka, notice the exquisite details on the buildings on the south side of the street. Ulitsa Ilyinka was Moscow's financial heart in the 18th and 19th centuries. The old **Stock Exchange 6** is on the corner at No 6. Built in the 1870s, it now houses the Chamber of Commerce and Industry.

Turn right on ulitsa Ilynka and head back toward Red Square. At No 3, the tiny **Cathedral of St Ilyn the Prophet of God 7** is undergoing renovation, but the interior is open. The exposed brick and eroding walls give an air of antiquity to this 1519 church, among the oldest in Moscow.

Turn left and walk down Khrustalny pereulok. The Old Merchants' Court, or **Gostinny Dvor 8**, occupies the block between ulitsas Ilyinka and Varvarka. It is now completely renovated and filled with shops, including some excellent stops for souvenir hunters (see p156).

Take another left and head east on ulitsa Varvarka, which is crowded with tiny churches, old homes and what remains of the giant former Hotel Rossiya. The pink-and-white **St Barbara's Church 9**, now government offices, dates from 1795 to 1804. Like its predecessor on this site, it was a merchants' church, built with funds donated by the rich traders who lived in the nearby Zaryadie neighbourhood. The reconstructed 16th-century **English House 10** (p77), white with peaked wooden roofs, was the residence of England's first emissaries to Russia.

Built in 1698, the **Church of St Maxim the Blessed 11** at No 4 is now a folk-art exhibition hall. Next to it is the pointed bell tower of the 17th-century **Monastery of the Sign 12**, incorporating the monks' building and a golden-domed cathedral.

Tucked in between the street and the former Hotel Rossiya is the small but interesting **Romanov Chambers in Zaryadie 13** (p77), devoted to the lives of the high-ranking Romanov *boyars* (nobles). The colourful **St George's Church 14** at No 12 dates from 1658.

Cross ulitsa Varvarka and walk up Ipatyevsky pereulok. The enchanting 1630s **Church of the Trinity in Nikitniki 15** (p77) is an exquisite example of Russian baroque hidden amid the overbearing façades of the surrounding buildings. At the time of research, only the church's basement was open, but the interior frescoes are fantastic.

Head east from Ipatevsky pereulok out to Staraya ploshchad. At the southern end of this square is **All Saints Cathedral on the Kulishka 16**, which was built in 1687. In 1380 Dmitry Donskoy built the original wooden church on this site to commemorate those who died in the battle of Kulikovo. Some remains of the old city wall can be seen in the underground passage at the corner of ulitsa Varvarka and Staraya ploshchad. This *perekhod* (cross walk) is also the entrance to the Kitay Gorod metro stop.

LITERARY SOJOURN

A walk around Moscow offers a chance to see some original settings from Russian literature, as well as the environs where various authors and poets lived and worked. Start at busy Arbatskaya ploshchad, at the southern end of Nikitsky bulvar. The quiet courtyard at No 7 contains a gloomy statue of Nikolai Gogol and the **Gogol Memorial Rooms 1** (p87), where the writer threw his manuscript for *Dead Souls* into the fireplace.

Across the street at **No 8A 2** is an 18th-century mansion that was home to Colonel Kiselyov, a literature fanatic and friend of Pushkin. Apparently, Pushkin and Goncharova attended a ball at the colonel's home the day after their wedding in 1831. During the Soviet period, this building became the House of the Press, and writers such as Yesenin, Blok and Maya-kovsky all presented their work here. In 1925, just two months after Yesenin recited his poem *Flowers* here, his fans returned to pay him their last respects.

Head west on ulitsa Novy Arbat ulitsa. After one block, turn right in front of the 17th-century **Church of St Simeon the Stylite 3**, which was Gogol's regular parish church. Head north-west along Povarskaya ulitsa and take the first left on ulitsa Malaya Molchanovka. The pink house at No 2 was the home of Mikhail Lermontov, author of *A Hero of Our Time*. It now houses the **Lermontov House-Museum 4** (p88).

Return to Povarskaya ulitsa and turn left, heading northwest. Povarskaya ulitsa (Cooks' Street) was once inhabited by the royal court's cooks. The names of the lanes in this area still evoke the tsars' kitchen: Stolovy (Dining Room), Skatertny (Tablecloth), Khlebny (Bread) and Nozhovy (Cutlery). Turn right on Nozhovy pereulok and head north. Cross Bolshaya Nikitskaya ulitsa. The graceful **Church of the Grand Ascension 5** (p82) was built between 1798 and 1816 by Vasily Bazhenov and Matvei Kazakov. Here Pushkin married Goncharova in 1831; the happy couple grace the **Rotunda Fountain 6**, east of the church.

A statue of the lesser-known Tolstoy (and distant relative of Leo) **Alexei Tolstoy 7** stands in the small park across the lane from the church. Also a writer, Alexei Tolstoy is known primarily for his 20th-century novels about the civil war and the revolution, the most famous being the trilogy *The Ordeal*.

Continue north on Nozhovy pereulok until it ends at Malaya Nikitskaya ulitsa. Opposite the church on Malaya Nikitskaya ulitsa is an Art Nouveau masterpiece at No 6/2 that once was the house of the wealthy merchant Stepan Ryabushinksy. Designed by Fyodor Shekhtel, with mosaics by Mikhail Vrubel, the house was later gifted to writer Maxim Gorky, who often complained about the extravagant décor. The building still houses the **Gorky House-Museum 8** (p84). Behind the Gorky House-Museum is **Alexei Tolstoy's flat 9**.

From Malaya Nikitskaya ulitsa, take an immediate right and head north on ulitsa Spiridonovka. The statue of another early-20th-century poet, **Alexander Blok 10**, stands a bit further up this street. The revolutionary Blok believed that individualism had caused a decline in society's ethics, a situation that would only be rectified by a communist revolution.

Head back to Malaya Nikitskaya ulitsa and turn right. This quiet, shady area is lined with some lovely examples of Russia's prerevolutionary architecture. The 18th-century classical estate at **No 12 11** once belonged to the wealthy Bobrinsky family. It was the model for the Larins' house in Pushkin's poem *Yevgeny Onegin*.

At the end of Malaya Nikitskaya ulitsa, turn right onto the Garden Ring. Popular 19th-century writer Anton Chekhov lived and worked here at No 6 ulitsa Sadovaya-Kudrinskaya. Now called the **Chekhov House-Museum 12** (p85), this is where he wrote such masterpieces as *Three Sisters* and *The Seagull*. Chekhov described his style: 'All I wanted was to say honestly to people: have a look at yourselves and see how bad and dreary your lives are! The important thing is that people should realise that, for when they do, they will most certainly create another and better life for themselves.'

Head back on Malaya Nikitskaya ulitsa. Take the first left and walk north on Vspolny pereulok. At the intersection with ulitsa Spiridonovka, the name changes to Yermolayevsky. Proceed another 200m to

SOJOURN FACTS

Start Arbatskaya ploshchad (Ⓜ Arbatskaya)
Finish Triumfalnaya ploshchad (Ⓜ Mayakovskaya)
Distance 3km
Duration Three hours
Pit Stops Café Margarita (p131); Coffee Mania (p121); Starlite Diner (p131)

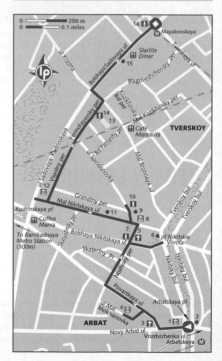

reach the **Patriarch's Ponds** 13 (p84), infamous as the opening scene of *The Master and Margarita*, by Mikhail Bulgakov. The huge statue west of the pond is the 19th-century Russian writer **Ivan Krylov** 14, known to every Russian child for his didactic tales. Scenes from his stories are depicted around the statue of the writer.

Turn left on Malaya Krasina ulitsa and head out to the Garden Ring. Turn right and walk one block north. The otherwise nondescript building along at No 10 used to house **Bulgakov's flat** 15, where he wrote *The Master and Margarita* and lived up until his death. The empty flat used to be a hang-out for dissidents and hooligans, but now the building has tight security appropriate for this high-rent district.

Up ahead is Triumfalnaya ploshchad, previously named for the poet and playwright Vladimir Mayakovsky, whose **statue** 16 stands in its centre. A favourite of the Bolshevik regime, Mayakovsky sought to demystify poetry, adopting crude language and ignoring traditional poetic techniques.

From here you can break for lunch at the Starlite Diner (p131), or hop on the metro.

UNDERGROUND ODYSSEY

The Moscow metro is a marvel of urban design. Every day, as many as nine million people use the metro system – that's more than in New York and London combined. What's more, this transport system combines function and form. Many of Moscow's metro stations are marble-faced, frescoed, gilded works of art. So while you are waiting for that train, stroll around and admire the frescoed ceilings, mosaic tiles and crystal chandeliers. Note that diversity of theme is not a strength here: it does not go too far beyond revolutionary heroism, unity between the workers and peasants, and friendship between the Soviet peoples. But the craftsmanship is nonetheless extraordinary. Not exactly a walking tour, this odyssey is an opportunity to explore the most magnificent of Moscow's metro stations.

These days, the metro has implemented a sort of public-relations campaign. You will notice posters decorated with pretty, smiling young ladies in uniform promising 'Good weather, any time of year.' These *devushky* (young women) bear little resemblance to the babushkas sitting at the bottom of the escalators, but let's not mull over a technicality.

When Stalin announced plans for *Metrostroy* (construction of the metro), loyal communists turned out in droves to contribute their time and energy to this project. Thousands of people toiled around the clock in dire conditions, but it was all worth it when the first metro line opened in 1935, travelling from Park Kultury in the south to Sokolniki in the north (known as the Sokolnicheskaya, or Sokolniki line). Apparently, the first stations are very deep because they were designed to double as bomb shelters.

Start at **Komsomolskaya** 1, the station where the Sokolnicheskaya line intersects with the Koltsevaya line, or Ring line. The station is named for the youth workers who helped to construct the first stations. At the Komsomolskaya (Sokolnicheskaya line) station, you will see the Komsomol emblem at the top of the limestone pillars. The Komsomolskaya (Koltsevaya line) station has a huge stuccoed hall, the ceiling featuring mosaics of past Russian military heroes including Peter the Great, Dmitry Donskoy and Alexander Suvorov.

From Komsomolskaya, proceed around the ring, getting off at each stop along the way. When you are through admiring the underground artwork, hop back on the train (heading in the same direction) and go to the next station.

Next stop, **Prospekt Mira** 2 is decorated in elegant gold-trimmed white porcelain. The bas-reliefs feature productive farmers picking fruit, children reading books and other happy socialists.

The stained-glass panels at **Novoslobodskaya** 3 envelop this station in Art Nouveau artistry. Besides the usual cast of workers and farmers, you might recognise Vladimir Ilych Lenin.

The ceilings at **Belorusskaya** 4 station are festooned with mosaics. Once again, the models were joyful, productive workers and farmers – this time from Belarus, as you can tell from the traditional dress.

Done in dramatic red-and-white marble, **Krasnopresnenskaya** 5 has bas-reliefs depicting the fateful events of 1905 and 1917. This neighbourhood was the scene of some of the terrible battles from those years. Not to mention the fateful events of 1991 and 1993 (see p48), which also took place nearby.

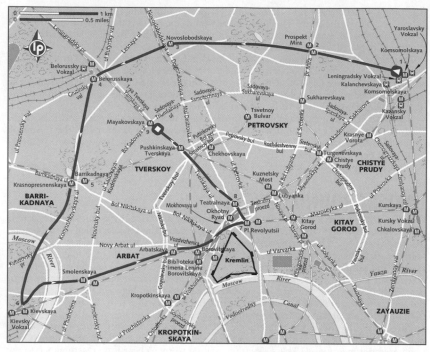

ODYSSEY FACTS

Start Komsomolskaya ploshchad
(Ⓜ Komsomolskaya)
Finish Triumfalnaya ploshchad (Ⓜ Mayakovskaya)
Distance 3km
Duration Three hours
Pit Stops Café Margarita (p131); Coffee Mania (p121);
Starlite Diner (p131)

At **Kievskaya 6** you don't have to break your neck looking at the ceiling, as the mosaics adorn the walls. The themes are predicably Ukrainian, or more accurately, Russo-Ukrainian. Look for Pushkin among the Ukrainian folk singers and also the friendship between Russian and Ukrainian farmers. Other scenes are from Ukrainian history, such as the *Battle of Poltava*, 1709. At Kievskaya, switch over to the Arbatsko-Pokrovskaya line, which is dark blue. The hall of this station continues the theme, with panels depicting 300 years of Russian-Ukrainian cooperation. The colourful frescoes stand out against the elegant marble columns and granite floor.

From here, take the train to **Ploshchad Revolyutsii 7**, one of the most dramatic stations. The life-size bronze statues in the main hall and beside the escalators illustrate the idealised roles of ordinary Russians. Heading up the escalators, the themes are: carrying out and protecting the revolution, industry, agriculture, hunting, education, sport and child-rearing.

Switch to **Teatralnaya 8**, on the Zamoskvoretskaya line (green). This station was formerly called 'Ploshchad Sverdlova' in honour of Lenin's right-hand man, whose bust is in the hall. The labradorite and marble that adorn this hall are apparently from the original Church of Christ the Saviour.

Take the Zamoskvoretskaya line to **Mayakovskaya 9**, the *piece de resistance* of the Moscow metro. This grand-prize winner at the 1938 World's Fair in New York has an Art Deco central hall that's all stainless steel and pink rhodonite. This is also one of the deepest stations (33m), which allowed it to serve as an air-raid shelter during WWII.

Eating

Eating

In the past decade, Moscow has blossomed into a culinary capital. Foodies will be thrilled by the plethora of dining options, from old-fashioned *haute russe* to contemporary fusion. Young chefs are breaking down Soviet stereotypes and showing the world how creative they can be. They're importing exotic ingredients, rediscovering ancient cooking techniques and inventing new ones. And Moscow diners are eating it up. Literally. Restaurants are packed with patrons eager to sample world cuisines, sip expensive wines, share small plates, eat raw fish, taste exotic fruits and smoke hookahs.

So when you tire of borscht (beetroot soup) and beef stroganoff, you'll be able to find excellent European, American and Asian cuisine. Many of these restaurants have foreign-trained chefs, foreign management and standards, and foreign prices to match. Cuisine from the former Soviet republics – such as Georgia and Armenia, Uzbekistan and Ukraine – is also ubiquitous and delicious (see the boxed text, p13, for more on Russian food).

Because of the explosion of eateries in Moscow, restaurateurs are desperate to entice diners. Themed restaurants are all the rage, so your dinner experience might include picking out produce at an Asian market (see p127), sharing company with farm animals (p133) or watching a belly dancer shake her thang (p125). The effect is sometimes classy, sometimes comical, but always interesting.

The good news is that the best restaurants still manage to keep their focus on the food, producing ever more innovative cuisine for an ever more informed clientele (see the boxed text, p131).

TOP FIVE EAT STREETS
- **Kamergersky pereulok** (p129), Tverskoy District. Trendy and pedestrian-friendly.
- **Tverskaya ulitsa** (p129), Tverskoy District. Main street Moscow offers plenty of options for a feast.
- **Ulitsa Petrovka** (p126), Petrovsky District. Shopping and spending works up quite an appetite.
- **Spiridonevsky pereulok** (p131), Tverskoy District. Exceptional eating on a tiny strip near Patriarch's Ponds.
- **Ulitsa 1905 goda** (p132), Barrikadnaya. Moscow's most over-the-top themed dining.

Opening Hours

Many eateries are open from noon to midnight daily, often with later hours on Friday and Saturday. For this book, hours are listed only when they vary from this standard.

Discounts of up to 25% are often available for dining before 4pm or 5pm. Alternatively, many places offer a fixed price 'business lunch' during this time. This is a great way to sample some of the pricier restaurants around town.

How Much?

Sudden wallet-thinning shock is common at many Moscow restaurants, where prices are geared to free-spending New Russians and flush expats rather than the average person. The situation is improving, though. Muscovites are eating out in droves, and restaurants, cafés and kiosks are opening up left and right to cater to them.

While diners with deep pockets might spend upwards of R2000 at upmarket Moscow restaurants, most visitors can expect to pay about R600 to R1000 per person for a meal in the capital. 'Business lunch' specials are usually R200 to R500, offering excellent value for a midday meal (usually three courses). Frequent the places listed under 'Cheap Eats' for meals that cost R200 or less.

Some restaurants set their menu prices in *uslovie yedenitsiy* (often abbreviated as y.e.), or standard units, which is equivalent to euros or US dollars (although you will have to pay in roubles calculated at the exchange rate of the day). Prices in this chapter are quoted in roubles, regardless of the currency quoted on the menu. Credit cards are widely accepted, especially at upmarket restaurants.

COFFEE MANIA

Moscow's temperatures occasionally call for a warming drink, so it's nice to know you are never far from a freshly brewed cup o' joe. With bohemian coffee houses seemingly opening on every corner, Moscow might be called the Russian Seattle; and what, you ask, might be the Russian Starbucks?

You could claim that **Coffee Bean** started the coffee thing off in Moscow, as the original outlet on Tverskaya ulitsa has been around for years. It's still the coolest café in the city, with high ceilings, fantastic architectural details and large windows looking out on to the main drag. Coffee drinks cost around R100; it's one of the rare places that does not allow smoking. Not quite as bohemian as Coffee Bean (and who can be surprised with a name like this?), **Coffee Mania** is a trendy spot, and the menu includes tasty soups, salads and sandwiches as well as coffees. The Bolshaya Nikitskaya branch in the Arbat district has a delightful outdoor seating area in front of the Moscow Tchaikovsky Conservatory.

A French café that feels more European than its counterparts, **Le Gateau** has dark leather furniture and richly coloured walls. The attempt to bring Paris to Moscow carries over to the menu, which features dark coffee and fresh croissants. This is a charming place for breakfast (R85 to R135), lunch (R165 to R180) or a dose of caffeine, any time of day.

Formerly Zen Coffee, **Montana Coffee** offers breakfast and a business lunch, besides the double espresso decaf cappuccinos. It is physically impossible to do a serious stroll of the trendy pedestrian strip on Kamergersky pereulok without stopping to sip a drink at this outlet. Those with a sweet tooth will not be able to resist **Shokolodnitsa** for coffee and desserts; it's also popular among night owls.

Kitay Gorod & Chistye Prudy

Coffee Bean (Map pp248–9; ☎ 207 4043; ul Sretenka 22/1, Chistye Prudy; ⏰ 8am-10pm; Ⓜ Sukharevskaya)

Coffee Bean (Map p254; ☎ 923 9793; ul Pokrovka 18, Kitay Gorod; ⏰ 8am-10pm; Ⓜ Chistye Prudy)

Shokolodnitsa (Map p254; ☎ 924 2843; ul Myasnitskaya 24/7, Chistye Prudy; ⏰ 24hr; Ⓜ Chistye Prudy)

Petrovsky District

Coffee Mania (Map pp248–9; ☎ 924 0075; Pushechnaya ul; ⏰ 8am-11pm; Ⓜ Kuznetsky Most)

Le Gateau (Map pp248–9; ☎ 725 6876; Sadovaya Samotechnaya ul 24/27; ⏰ 8am-1am; Ⓜ Tsvetnoy Bulvar)

Shokolodnitsa (Map pp248–9; ☎ 937 4639; Pushechnaya ul 7/5; ⏰ 24hr; Ⓜ Kuznetsky Most)

Tverskoy District

Coffee Bean (Map pp248–9; ☎ 788 6357; Tverskaya ul 10; ⏰ 8am-11pm; Ⓜ Pushkinskaya)

Le Gateau (Map pp248–9; ☎ 937 5678; Tverskaya ul 23; ⏰ 24hr; Ⓜ Pushkinskaya)

Montana Coffee (Map pp248–9; ☎ 234 1784; Lesnaya ul 1/2; ⏰ 8am-midnight Sun-Tue, 24hr Wed-Sat; Ⓜ Belorusskaya)

Montana Coffee (Map pp248–9; ☎ 292 5114; Kamergersky per 6; ⏰ 9am-11pm; Ⓜ Teatralnaya)

Barrikadnaya & Arbat Districts

Coffee Mania (Map pp248–9; ☎ 290 0141; Kudrinskaya pl 46/54, Barrikadnaya; ⏰ 8am-midnight; Ⓜ Barrikadnaya)

Coffee Mania (Map pp248–9; ☎ 775 4310; Bolshaya Nikitskaya ul 13, Moscow Tchaikovsky Conservatory, Arbat District; ⏰ 8am-1am; Ⓜ Aleksandrovsky Sad)

Le Gateau (Map pp248–9; ☎ 981 4940; Novinsky bul 31, Barrikadnaya; ⏰ 10am-10pm; Ⓜ Krasnopresnenskaya)

Shokolodnitsa (Map pp248–9; ☎ 241 0620; ul Arbat 29, Arbat District; ⏰ 8am-11pm; Ⓜ Arbatskaya)

Zamoskvorechie

Coffee Bean (Map pp252–3; ☎ 953 6726; Pyatnitskaya ul 5; ⏰ 8am-10pm; Ⓜ Tretyakovskaya)

Le Gateau (Map pp252–3; ☎ 937 0532; Paveletskaya pl 2; ⏰ 8am-1am; Ⓜ Paveletskaya)

Montana Coffee (Map pp252–3; ☎ 235 5282; Paveletskaya pl 1; ⏰ 8am-11pm Mon-Fri, 9am-10pm Sat & Sun; Ⓜ Paveletskaya)

Shokolodnitsa (Map pp252–3; ☎ 238 2734; ul Bolshaya Yakimanka 58/2; ⏰ 24hr; Ⓜ Oktyabrskaya)

Booking Tables

Most of the fancier places require booking in advance for dinner, as well as for lunch or brunch on weekends.

Tipping

The standard for tipping in Moscow is 10%, while a slightly lesser percentage is acceptable at more casual restaurants. The service charge is occasionally included in the bill, in which case an additional tip isn't necessary.

Self-Catering

If you want to eat like an old-time Muscovite, you'll buy your own food and cook it at home. Even if cooking in Moscow isn't feasible, the local exotic food and drinks are among the most interesting and affordable items by which to remember Russia. Most characteristic are vodka and caviar, the *za-*

Blackboard inside Coffee Bean café (p121)

kuski (appetisers) of the tsar's court and the Soviet politburo. High-quality vodka is packaged in a wide variety of decorative bottles, some with historical or regional themes. Vodka connoisseurs admire the design and shape of the bottles almost as much as the fiery brew itself.

The Russian sweet tooth is notorious (a fact that's evident from the profusion of gold teeth). Russians adore confections and chocolate, and without fail prefer locally produced treats over any old Belgian or Swiss chocolate. Never mind that the major Russian confectionaries are largely owned by Cadbury or Nestle, eating Russian chocolate is a matter of national pride. (Keep this in mind when buying chocolate for Russian friends.) Many companies produce beautiful pieces with fancy wrapping and colourful boxes in honour of local events, holidays or historical places. The Krasny Oktyabr factory on the banks of the Moscow River is widely considered the best confectioner around. Sample some of its wares at **Confael Chocolate** (p160).

FARMERS' MARKETS

The Russian market *(rinok)* is a busy, bustling place, full of activity and colour. Even if you're not shopping, it's entertaining to peruse the tables piled high with multicoloured produce: homemade cheese and jam; golden honey straight from the hive; vibrantly coloured spices pouring out of plastic bags; slippery silver fish posing on beds of ice; and huge slabs of meat hanging from the ceiling. Many vendors bring their products up from the Caucasus to sell them in the capital. Prices are lower and the quality of product is often higher than in the supermarkets. Bring your own bag and don't be afraid to haggle.

The **Dorogomilovsky market** (Map pp252–3; ul Mozhaysky val 10, Khamovniki; Ⓨ 10am-8pm; Ⓜ Kievskaya) is among Moscow's largest, with overflow spreading along Kievskaya ulitsa to Kievsky vokzal (Kyiv station). Other centrally located farmers' markets include **Danilovsky Market** (Map pp246–7; Mytnaya ul 74, Zamoskvorechie; Ⓜ Tulskaya) and **Rizhsky Market** (Map pp246–7; pr Mira 94-96; Ⓜ Rizhskaya).

SUPERMARKETS

Gone are the days when shopping for food required waiting in a different line for each item. These days, Moscow boasts several Western-style supermarkets, complete with prepackaged foods, Western brands and shopping carts. The selection is impressive, compared to what stocked the shelves in the early 1990s. Unless you stick to Russian brands, prices tend to be as high as – if not higher than – prices in the West.

Once a Scandinavian haven in Moscow, **Kalinka Stockmann** (Map pp248–9; ☎ 785 2500; Smolensky Passage, Karmanitsky pr, Arbat District; Ⓨ 10am-10pm; Ⓜ Smolenskaya) has a pricey foreign-goods supermarket in the basement. The **ABCs of Taste** (Map pp248–9; Sadovaya-Triumfalnaya ul 22/31, Tverskoy District; ⏰24hr; Ⓜ Mayakovskaya) is a Russian chain of deluxe markets, selling premium quality (mostly imported) goods.

The Turkish-owned **Ramstore** (www.ramstore.ru; ⏰24hr) includes eight shopping malls, as well as a number of supermarkets in and around Moscow. 'Club card' (membership R25) holders are eligible for discounts of R20 to R30 on some products. The selection available is impressive, but these places can be overwhelming due to their size and the number of shoppers they attract. Of the many Ramstore outlets around the city, these are the most convenient:

Barrikadnaya (Map pp248–9; ☎ 255 5412; Krasnaya Presnya 23; Ⓜ Ulitsa 1905 Goda)

Chistye Prudy (Map p254; ☎ 207 3165; Komsomolskaya pl 6, Moskovsky Univermag; Ⓜ Komsomolskaya)

Khamovniki (Map pp252–3; ul Usachyova 35; Ⓜ Sportivnaya)

The well-stocked **Seventh Continent supermarkets** (☎777 779; ⏰24hr) are the most convenient and reasonable places to stock up on foodstuffs. You can grab a cart and peruse the aisles just like at home. Products available are Russian and imported – it's still expensive, but not prohibitively so. Branches around the city:

Arbat District (Map pp248–9; ul Arbat 54/2; Ⓜ Smolenskaya)

Kitay Gorod (Map pp248–9; ul Bolshaya Lubyanka 12/1; Ⓜ Lubyanka)

Kropotkinskaya (Map pp252–3; ul Serafimovicha 2; Ⓜ Kropotkinskaya)

SPECIALITY SHOPS

Peek inside the **Yeliseev Grocery Store** (Map pp248–9; Tverskaya ul 14, Tverskoy District; ⏰8am-9pm Mon-Sat, 10am-6pm Sun; Ⓜ Pushkinskaya or Tverskaya) for a glimpse of prerevolutionary grandeur, as the store is set in the former mansion of the successful merchant Yeliseev. It now houses a market selling caviar and other delicacies.

For all things from India, from nan to curry to basmati rice, visit **India Spices** (Map pp248–9; ☎ 207 1621; ul Sretenka 36/2, Chistye Prudy; ⏰9am-9pm; Ⓜ Sukharevskaya).

CITY CENTRE

You might wonder where all the government officials eat, considering the shortage of restaurants in the city centre. (Head over to GlavPivTorg, on Lubyanskaya ploshchad, and you might just get your answer.)

Moscow has come a long way in developing a consumer culture, but the dining options in the city centre suggest the capital still has a way to go. The area where the vast majority of tourists spend the majority of their time is markedly void of eateries. Pack a picnic on the day you visit the Kremlin – otherwise, you can check out the few places around Lubyanskaya ploshchad (Lubyanka Square).

RED SQUARE

ONE RED SQUARE Map p258   Russian
☎ 292 1196; www.redsquare.ru; Red Square (Krasnaya pl) 1; business lunch R360-480, meals R800-1000; Ⓜ Teatralnaya
This place is located in the State History Museum. Appropriately, chef Alexander Filin is something of a historian, and he successfully re-creates the cuisine that was enjoyed in the days of yore, complete with old-fashioned ingredients and some old-fashioned names. For real culinary history buffs, check out the schedule of historic dinners, re-creating specific meals in history, such as Nicholas II's Easter dinner in 1900. The only drawback is the dark basement setting – a drab venue for an otherwise exciting eating experience.

TOP FIVE MEALS WITH A VIEW

- **Loft Café** (p124), City Centre. Lofty views of Lubyanskaya ploshchad (Lubyanka Square).
- **Panorama** at the Golden Ring Hotel (p169), Arbat District. A 360° panorama from 80m up.
- **Pavilion** (p132), Tverskoy District. Picture windows facing Patriarch's Ponds.
- **Red Bar** (p133), Barrikadnaya. See the city skyline from the top of this new skyscraper.
- **Tent** (p126), Chistye Prudy. Watch the sun set over the Chistye Prudy.

www.lonelyplanet.com

Eating

CITY CENTRE

123

LUBYANSKAYA PLOSHCHAD

GLAVPIVTORG Map pp248-9   Russian

☎ 928 2591; ul Bolshaya Lubyanka 5; business lunch R125-195, meals R600-1000; Ⓜ Lubyanka
At the 'central beer restaurant No 5', every effort is made to re-create an upmarket apparatchik dining experience. The Soviet fare is authentic, but not too authentic. So you might get a side dish of peas, but the peas will be fresh and sweet. Add three varieties of tasty beer brewed on site, and you've got a restaurant to suit any ideology.

LOFT CAFÉ Map pp248-9   Fusion

☎ 933 7713; Nikolskaya ul 25; meals R800-1000; ☽ 9am-midnight; Ⓜ Lubyanka
On the top floor of the Nautilus shopping centre, next door to the luxury spa, you'll find this tiny, trendy café. An even tinier terrace gives a fantastic view of Lubyanskaya ploshchad. Innovative dishes fuse the best of Russian cuisine with Western and Asian influences – for example, grilled salmon with spinach, pine nuts and caviar sauce.

SHIELD & SWORD Map pp248-9   Russian

☎ 222 4446; ul Bolshaya Lubyanka 13/16; meals R400-800; Ⓜ Lubyanka
In an all-too-appropriate location opposite the former Lubyanka prison, this novelty place is also known as the 'KGB bar'. You can't miss it, with the emblem of the former security service hanging prominently in the windows. Inside, the Soviet paraphernalia continues: the centrepiece in the dining room is a replica of the Felix Dzerzhinsky statue that once graced Lubyanskaya ploshchad. The menu features Soviet specials – mains such as chicken Kiev and *pelmeni* (dumplings), served more often than not with 100g of vodka. The place is total kitsch, but it actually attracts real-deal old-timers, perhaps longing for yesteryear.

SUSHI VESLA Map pp248-9   Japanese

☎ 937 0521; Nikolskaya ul 25; sushi R100-200 each, meals R600-800; ☽ noon-1am Sun-Thu, noon-3am Fri & Sat; Ⓜ Lubyanka
Sushi is all the rage in Moscow these days. To get in on it, head to this hip Japanese café in the basement of the Nautilus centre (enter from Teatralnaya proezd). Dishes are colour-coded to specify price; at the end of the meal the server clears the empty plates and uses them to calculate the bill.

KITAY GOROD

Although the streets immediately east of Red Square do not contain many eateries, Kitay Gorod boasts its fair share of culinary choices. Head into the less explored area on the east side of Staraya ploshchad. It is a refined residential area with dining to match the clientele, plus a few extravagant, themed restaurants just for fun.

CHE Map pp248-9   Tex Mex

☎ 921 8117; Nikolskaya ul 10/2; meals R800-1000; ☽ 24hr; Ⓜ Lubyanka
The revolution lives on at this popular, divey bar. The walls are covered with revolutionary graffiti and photos of the iconic hero. Patrons get their groove on the dance floor to salsa and meringue music. The cuisine is obviously more Tex-Mex than Cuban, but nobody is complaining about the huge plates of nachos and the spicy chilli. Bartenders also mix a mean *mojito* (rum drink with lime, sugar and mint) with Havana Club rum.

CHEESE HOLE Map p254   European

☎ 917 1676; Pokrovsky bul 6/20; meals R600-900; Ⓜ Kitay Gorod
Fondue, fromage plates, and other cheesy specialities are the highlights of the menu at this hole-in-the-wall. Besides the warm basement with windows looking on to the Boulevard Ring, there is also a summer terrace out the back. Both are perfectly delightful settings for a romantic date or even a solo meal. The place is Swiss-owned, which means French, Italian and German fare all show up on the menu.

EXPEDITION Map p254   Russian

☎ 775 6075; www.expedicia.ru; ul Solyanka 11/6; meals R1000-1500; Ⓜ Kitay Gorod
This outrageous themed restaurant takes diners on an expedition to the great white north, capturing the adventure and excitement of Siberia. You can imagine you arrived by helicopter, as the vehicle is the centrepiece of the dining room. Feast on typical 'northern cuisine' – famous Baikal fish soup *(ukha)*; *pelmeni* stuffed with wild boar or Komchatka crab; and venison

stroganoff. There is also an expensive but authentic Siberian *banya* on the premises (see p150).

KHODZHA NASREDDIN IN KHIVA
Map p254   Uzbek
☎ 917 0444; ul Pokrovka 10; meals R1000-1500; Ⓜ Kitay Gorod

Khodzha Nasreddin is an Uzbek literary folk hero who epitomises the exoticism and eroticism of the mystical East. The restaurant attempts to do the same, providing a sensory experience that overwhelms. For the full effect, dine upstairs, where you will be invited to remove your shoes and recline on plush pillows around low tables. The showcase of the evening entertainment is, of course, belly dancers. The house specialty is undoubtedly the *plov* (pilaf rice with diced mutton and vegetables), the traditional dish of rice and lamb, subtly spiced with cumin and sprinkled with raisins.

MAHARAJA Map p254   Indian
☎ 921 7758; ul Pokrovka 2/1; meals R600-1000; Ⓨ 12.30-11pm; Ⓜ Kitay Gorod

Moscow's oldest Indian restaurant features lots of spicy Tandoori specialties, including several variations of kebabs and rotis hot from the tandoori oven. Vegetarians have no shortage of options. The décor of the lower-level restaurant is understated – a welcome change from the over-the-top theme restaurants that dominate Moscow's dining scene.

NOAH'S ARK Map p254   Armenian
☎ 917 0717; Maly Ivanovsky per 9; meals R800-1000; Ⓜ Kitay Gorod

This Armenian grill features many varieties of shashlyk, many more varieties of cognac and an Armenian orchestra every night. The dining hall is aromatic and atmospheric, thanks to the meat roasting over charcoal in the central brazier.

CHISTYE PRUDY

Pondside dining is certainly an option in this neighbourhood known as 'Clean Ponds'. Choose the plush French affair for a special occasion, or the crazy, crowded Annyushka tram restaurant for a kick. In summer, take 'pondside' to a new level at the trendy Tent. Other options in the area are diverse, including one of the capital's few vegetarian-only restaurants.

ANNYUSHKA Map p254   Russian
Chistoprudny bul; cover R20, mains R150-200; Ⓨ 2pm-midnight; Ⓜ Chistye Prudy

Annyushka is actually a tram that circles the Chistye Prudy. Patrons can get on at several stops along the way, the easiest being at the island at the intersection of Chistoprudny bulvar and Myasnitskaya ulitsa. The food is simple fare – obviously, the cooks prepare it on a tram – but the bar is fully stocked. It's a fun concept, but karaoke is uncalled-for in such close quarters.

AVOCADO Map p254   Vegetarian
☎ 921 7719; Chistoprudny bul 12/2; breakfast R35-65, business lunch R140, meals R200-400; Ⓨ 10am-11pm; Ⓜ Chistye Prudy

Less atmospheric than Jagannath (see p127), Avocado has a more diverse menu, drawing on dishes from cuisines from around the world. Meatless versions of soups and salads, pasta and *pelmeni* are all featured. Grab a seat near the window to watch the passers-by on the boulevard, because the place is otherwise rather austere.

CIBO E VINO Map p254   Italian
☎ 924 0377; ul Pokrovka 21; meals R600-800; Ⓨ 10am-midnight; Ⓜ Chistye Prudy

Italian for 'food and wine', Cibo e Vino is a classy but unpretentious restaurant and wine bar. The menu is brief and selective – a few modern dishes accompanied by a modest selection of French and Italian reds and whites. The understated dining room is intimate enough to bring a date, but comfortable enough to dine alone (especially considering the free wi-fi access). After dinner, slip downstairs to the exotic chill-out room to sip an after-dinner drink or smoke a hookah.

LA CASA Map pp248-9   Italian
☎ 923 6687; Ul Sretenka 4/1; meals R1600-2000; Ⓜ Chistye Prudy or Lubyanka

This airy, elegant trattoria serves high-class (and high-priced) Italian fare – fresh pasta with homemade sauces, grilled seafood and steaks – with a wine list to match. The place is lovely: neutral tones, tiled floors and plush couches create a sophisticated Mediterranean setting. However, you might

Eating **CHISTYE PRUDY**

TOP FIVE KIDS MEALS

- **American Bar & Grill** (p130), Tverskoy District. The playroom is open daily, while a clown engages kids with games between 3pm to 8pm on Saturday and Sunday.
- **Il Patio** (p136), Kropotkinskaya. Have fun with crayons, cartoons and pizza cut into crazy shapes. Kids can also learn how to make their own pizza!
- **Khodzha Nasredin in Khiva** (p125), Kitay Gorod. Kids of all ages get to kick off their shoes and sit on the floor. There are clowns, cartoons and puppet shows from 1pm to 7pm Saturday and Sunday.
- **Parizhsk** (p137), Khamovniki. Parents can dine in peace while their kids stay busy playing computer games. The spacious interior allows young 'uns room to play. There's a kids' party between noon and 5pm Saturday and Sunday.
- **Tinkoff** (p135), Arbat District. Offers a children's menu and cartoons. A clown supervises a kids' playroom from 2pm to 8pm Saturday and Sunday.

get some attitude from the staff if they feel you don't complement the décor.

MODEST CHARMS OF THE BOURGEOISIE Map pp248-9   International
☎ 923 0848; ul Bolshaya Lubyanka 24; meals R400-600; Ⓜ Chistye Prudy or Lubyanka
The main draw of the 'Bourgeoisie' is the cool, casual setting. It's an attractive space, with its arched ceiling, tiled floor and sun motif – ideal for settling into the comfy couches and reading the newspapers that are left lying about. The menu is reasonably priced and wide-ranging, from pizza to sushi and nice fresh salads, but don't expect gourmet fare.

NOSTALGIE ART CLUB Map p254   French
☎ 916 9478; Chistoprudny bul 12A; business lunch R600, meals R1500-2000; Ⓜ Chistye Prudy
One of Moscow's most beloved mafia hangouts. You will recognise it from the plush velvet interior, the decadent menu and the row of big black cars out front. Despite its 'New Russian' reputation, this place knows food and wine, as evidenced by the on-site sommelier school. Nostalgie also publishes *Vino*, Russia's first magazine for oenophiles.

SIMPLE PLEASURES
Map pp248-9   International
☎ 207 4043; ul Sretenka 22; meals R800-1000; Ⓜ Sukharevskaya
The chef is American, but the menu is wide-ranging, including dishes from Italy, Spain and the American South. The common denominators are fresh ingredients and simple cooking techniques, an ideal match for this comfortable, uncluttered space.

SIRENA Map p254   Seafood
☎ 208 1412; www.sirena.su; Bolshaya Spasskaya ul 15; meals R2000-2800; Ⓜ Sukharevskaya
Restaurant emperor Arkady Novikov strikes again, this time serving the freshest of seafood in a seafaring setting. The décor features large fish tanks, filled with colourful fish, peacefully swimming to and fro. The fish on the plates are not so happy, but they are equally lovely – prepared to perfection. The chef incorporates plenty of fresh, seasonal vegetables, calling on Asian and Mediterranean influences to provide a delectable seafood experience. By the way, the menu does feature a few items such as stuffed rabbit and rack of lamb for the landlubbers.

TENT Map p254   International
☎ 916 9486; Chistoprudny bul 12A; meals R600-800; ☻ 24hr; Ⓜ Chistye Prudy
Step into this tent-like structure, and step inside a Bedouin camp, right on the shores of Chistye Prudy. Lounge on comfy cushions and feast on grilled meats, à la the *Thousand and One Nights*. This place is surprisingly democratic (in terms of prices and face control), but still manages to retain its supercool status. It's open in season, approximately May to September.

PETROVSKY DISTRICT
Who could be surprised by the plethora of dining options in this smart shopping district? The range of prices, cuisines and themes is vast. Food in Moscow does not come much simpler or cheaper than at Pelmeshka, while Gallery represents the other end of the scale. Happily, Petrovsky District includes just about everything in between, as well as some interesting and innovating

themed restaurants. So if window-shopping and people-watching works up your appetite, you'll find a restaurant to sate it.

BEIGE CAFE Map pp248-9 — European
☎ 925 6990; ul Rozhdestvenka 12/1; meals R600-800; ⏰ 11am-midnight; Ⓜ Kuznetsky Most
Beige might sound boring, but subtle lines and soft colours render this romantic café anything but. The sensual setting is due in part to the circular room, arched doorways and rounded ceilings. The lack of sharp angles is cosy and comfortable, but still sophisticated. Dine on grilled fish and steaks, pasta, soup and salad, with an emphasis on fresh vegetables – this place is a great find for the health-conscious.

CHEESE Map pp248-9 — Italian
☎ 209 7770; Sadovaya-Samotechnaya ul 16/2; meals R1200-1500; Ⓜ Tsvetnoy Bulvar
Not to be confused with its French neighbour, Cheese Hole (see following), this place also has an interior resembling a block of cheese. The décor might seem silly, but the pizzas, pastas and other Italian dishes are expertly prepared. The salad buffet is hard to resist, overflowing with vegetables, olives, cured meats and cheeses – all the elements of antipasto. If the mouse's perspective doesn't sound atmospheric, request a table on the patio, shaded by umbrellas (yellow, of course) and flanked by potted plants.

CHEESE HOLE Map pp248-9 — European
☎ 209 1007; ul Bolshaya Dmitrovka 32; meals R600-900; Ⓜ Chekhovskaya
Where the original in Kitay Gorod is quintessentially quaint, this newer, second location is self-consciously stylish. The avocado and indigo colour scheme is bold, contrasting with the pale yellow walls and arched ceilings that evoke the inside of a cheese hole. This outlet is meant to be French, as opposed to Swiss, but that does not result in a dramatically different menu. It still features deliciously aromatic fromage in all its forms, including fondue, quiche, sandwiches and cheese plates.

GALLERY Map pp248-9 — Café
☎ 937 4544; ul Petrovka 27; meals R800-1500; ⏰ 24hr; Ⓜ Chekhovskaya
An ultrahip place to see and be seen. Besides the cool music and hot clientele, this elegant café offers an eclectic menu, from the classic chicken cutlet to more sophisticated items such as Chilean sea bass and leg of lamb. The service is surprisingly friendly – sometimes an anomaly at the capital's hotspots.

JAGGANATH Map pp248-9 — Vegetarian
☎ 928 3580, Kuznetsky most 11; meals R300-500; ⏰ 10am-11pm; Ⓜ Kuznetsky Most
If you are in need of vitamins, this is a funky, vegetarian café, restaurant and shop. Its Indian-themed décor is more new-agey than ethnic. Service is slow but sublime, and the food is worth the wait.

KITEZH Map pp248-9 — Russian
☎ 209 6685, fax 924 8448; ul Petrovka 23/10; meals R600-800; Ⓜ Chekhovskaya
The Kitezh is named after a legendary town which – as a defence mechanism – could magically disappear from the sight of an enemy at the sound of a bell. This welcoming eatery re-creates a 17th-century interior in the basement of a building near the Upper St Peter Monastery. The Russian standards are tasty and reasonably priced.

MARKET Map pp248-9 — Seafood
☎ 200 2905; Sadovaya-Samotechnaya ul 18; meals R1200-1500; Ⓜ Tsvetnoy Bulvar
This innovative restaurant evokes a market in Southeast Asia – you're invited to take

Table set for dinner at Market restaurant (p127)

your wicker basket and shop among the displays of colourful produce and fresh fish, choosing the ingredients of your meal. The chef will then cook it up according to your instructions. Or, if you don't trust your culinary instincts, choose from the à la carte menu, which fuses contemporary European and Asian elements to show off the same ingredients. The brains behind this unique place is Arkady Novikov – a restaurant mogul in Moscow.

PANAME Map pp248-9   French
☎ 229 2412; per Stoleshnikov 7/2; meals R800-1200; M Chekhovskaya
Warm lighting and a wide, wooden bar set the stage for classic French fare: this convivial brasserie feels like Paris. The Art Deco painted ceiling and the crooner tinkling the ivories in the corner only enhance the ambience. The menu features traditional dishes from the French regions, as well as specialities such as salmon tartare (R450) and foie gras (R700). A cheaper 'bistro' menu is available, offering favourites such as quiche Lorraine (R250) and croque monsieur (ham-and-cheese sandwich, R210). Enter from the courtyard.

TARAS BULBA Map pp248-9   Ukranian
☎ 200 6082; ul Petrovka 30/7; meals R400-600; M Chekhovskaya
Servers here dress up in traditional embroidered outfits, while Ukrainian tapestries and wood floors provide a homey atmosphere. There's no salad bar, but specialities such as pork stuffed with vegetables and spicy smoked beef are tender and tasty. Other branches include one at **Zamoskvorechie** (Map pp252–3; ☎ 951 3760; Pyatnitskaya ul 14; M Tretyakovskaya).

WHITE SUN OF THE DESERT
Map pp248-9   Uzbek
☎ 209 7525; Neglinnaya ul 29/14; meals R1500-1800; ☺ noon-3am; M Tsvetnoy Bulvar
Based on a Soviet cult film of the same name, this place lends a comic touch to traditional Uzbek fare. The dancing sturgeon and Kalashnikov-toting mannequin are all featured in the film, in case you are confused by the incongruous décor. This is one of Moscow's oldest Uzbek restaurants, tribute to its extensive salad bar and delectable plov.

YAKITORIA Map pp248-9   Japanese
☎ 921 2591; ul Petrovka 16; meals R400-800; ☺ 11am-6am; M Chekhovskaya
In recent years, this chain of sushi restaurants has expanded rapidly throughout the capital (and beyond), drawing rave reviews for efficient service and excellent, fresh fish. This branch features an actual sushi bar, which is ideal for solo diners, who can entertain themselves watching the chefs prepare their meal. Otherwise, the woody dining room is slick and modern, with a more upmarket atmosphere than the other branches.

Cheap Eats
PELMESHKA Map pp248-9   Russian
☎ 292 8392; Kuznetsky most 4/3; breakfast R60, lunch R125, meals R150-200; ☺ 11am-midnight; M Teatralnaya
Pelmeshka is a clean, post-Soviet stolovaya (cafeteria), serving many different kinds of pelmeni, the most filling of Russian favourites. This place is packed with patrons at lunchtime, a sign that the food is tasty as well as cheap.

PIROGI Map pp248-9   Café
☎ 951 7596; Bolshaya Dmitrovka ul 12/1; meals R150-300; ☺ 24hr; M Teatralnaya
This low-key, bohemian place, serves coffee, beers, nibbles and even books, which you can buy, or just peruse while you have a drink. The air is smoky and service is slow, which somehow adds to the intellectual appeal.

YOLKI-PALKI Map pp248-9   Russian
☎ 928 5525; Neglinnaya ul 8/10; meals R200-400; ☺ 11am-midnight; M Kuznetsky Most
This excellent Russian chain is beloved for its country cottage décor and its well-stocked salad bar. Outlets all over the city specialise in traditional dishes and cheap beer. This particular location boasts an outdoor seating area that is often packed at lunchtime. Locations of the other branches of Yolki-Palki include: **Arbat District** (Map pp248–9; ☎ 291 6888; Novy Arbat ul 11; M Arbatskaya); **Zamoskvorechie** (Map pp252–3; ☎ 953 9130; Klimentovsky per 14; M Tretyakovskaya); and **Zayauzie** (Map p255; ☎ 912 9187; Taganskaya pl 2; M Taganskaya).

TVERSKOY DISTRICT

The Tverskoy District – like the hustling, bustling street for which it is named – offers something for everyone. This district covers a large area, and it contains a vast array of eating options. We have divided the district into smaller geographic units: Lower Tverskaya ulitsa, including Kamergersky pereulok; Pushkinskaya ploshchad; Triumfalnaya ploshchad; Patriarch's Ponds, including Spiridonevsky pereulok; and Around Belorussky vokzal.

LOWER TVERSKAYA ULITSA
CAFÉ DES ARTISTES
Map pp248-9   European
☎ 292 4042; www.artistico.ru; Kamergersky per 5/6; business lunch R500, meals R1000-1500; ☺ 11am-1am; Ⓜ Teatralnaya
A restaurant and art gallery in one, this Swiss-owned establishment is an interesting and elegant place to enjoy a meal. The glitzy interior has rich red tapestries, marble walls and a frescoed ceiling. Even better, the leafy summer café is possibly Kamergersky pereulok's loveliest outdoor setting. The menu is full of delicious options, but the specialities of the house include cream of spinach soup and fresh oysters. Art exhibitions held here range from traditional crafts to contemporary photography.

DROVA Map pp248-9   Russian
☎ 229 3227; Bolshaya Dmitrovka ul 7; meals R200-400, buffet R350; ☺ 24hr; Ⓜ Teatralnaya
The self-serve buffet ranges from solyanka (salty soup) to sushi to sweet-and-sour pork. It's not the best place to sample any of these items, but the price is right. Hungry student types really take advantage of the 'all-you-can-eat' option, and the sight is not always pretty. There are additional outlets at Chistye Prudy (Map p254; ☎ 925 2725; Myasnitskaya ul 24; Ⓜ Chistye Prudy) and in the Arbat District (Map pp248–9; ☎ 202 7570; Nikitsky bul 8A; Ⓜ Arbatskaya).

PINOCCHIO Map pp248-9   Italian
☎ 229 7361; Kamergersky per 5/7; meals R600-1000; Ⓜ Teatralnaya
This little pizza café evokes the hospitality and conviviality of the Mediterranean, complete with free-flowing wine and crispy pies

topped with fresh ingredients. One of the highlights of this spot is the konditerskaya, or dessert bar, with an irresistible selection of sweets and pastries. The pizzeria is a small version of the larger (and pricier) restaurant on Kutuzovsky prospekt (see p135).

TIBET Map pp248-9   Asian
☎ 923 2422; Kamergersky per 5/6; mains R400-600; Ⓜ Teatralnaya
On one of the trendiest streets in Moscow, this place will whisk you away to Lhasa. The Dalai Lama surveys the cosy basement, which is otherwise decorated with traditional arts and crafts. Tibetan food comes in ample portions for reasonable prices, with loads of options for vegetarians.

PUSHKINSKAYA PLOSHCHAD
CAFÉ PUSHKIN Map pp248-9   Russian
☎ 229 5590; Tverskoy bul 26A; business lunch R525, meals R1500-2000; ☺ 1st fl 24hr, ☺ 2nd fl noon-midnight; Ⓜ Pushkinskaya or Tverskaya
This is the tsarina of haute-russe dining, with an exquisite blend of Russian and French cuisine. Service and food are done to perfection. The lovely 19th-century building has created a different atmosphere on each floor, including a richly decorated library and a sunny rooftop café.

MAKI CAFÉ Map pp248-9   International
☎ 292 9731; Glinishchevsky per 3; meals R400-600; Ⓜ Pushkinskaya or Tverskaya
With a menu ranging from its namesake maki rolls to fresh green salads to Italian soft drinks, the theme at the Maki Café is diverse. The café is complemented by its minimalist, industrial décor – clunky light fixtures, lots of brick and metal. It appeals to a hip, urban crowd, who appreciate the unusually reasonable prices. The service is efficient but you still may have to wait for a table in the evening.

MEETING PLACE Map pp248-9   European
☎ 229 2373; Maly Gnezdnikovsky per 9/8/7; business lunch R300, meals R600-800; ☺ noon-5am; Ⓜ Pushkinskaya or Tverskaya
The name aptly describes this restaurant-club, which attracts a constant stream of regulars. The food gets mixed reviews, but it's filling and affordable; the many varieties of pelmeni are particularly popular. Most

people come for the friendly atmosphere, summertime garden café and free wi-fi access.

PEKING DUCK Map pp248-9 Chinese
☎ 755 8401; Tverskaya ul 24; meals R500-700; Ⓜ Pushkinskaya or Tverskaya
The décor is simple, modern, even nondescript. That's because the focus is on the food. The namesake house special (R555 for two people) is served the traditional way – with paper-thin pancakes, scallions and plum sauce. It is a delectable experience. Alternatively, a wide selection of vegetarian and other mains is available for about R300.

SCANDINAVIA Map pp248-9 European
☎ 200 4986; Maly Palashevsky per 7; business lunch R490, meals R1500-2800; Ⓜ Pushkinskaya or Tverskaya
There is no better place to indulge in *Shvedsky stol,* or 'Swedish table', than a place called Scandinavia. The cold cut buffet (R600), however, is just the tip of the iceberg at this expat favourite. A delightful summer café features sandwiches, salads and treats from the grill. Inside, the dining room offers a sophisticated menu of modern European delights.

TRIUMFALNAYA PLOSHCHAD
AMERICAN BAR & GRILL
Map pp248-9 American
☎ 250 9525; 1-ya Tverskaya-Yamsakaya ul 2/1; meals R600-800; ⏱ 24hr; Ⓜ Mayakovskaya
One of Moscow's oldest expat hang-outs, this place has lost some of its lustre over the years. With classic fare such as big burgers and spicy chicken wings, it does not draw the crowds it once did. Nonetheless, it's always a pleasant place for cold beers, and you're bound to meet some other *innostrantsy* (foreigners) who are quaffing them, too. The branch at **Zayauzie** (Map p255; ☎ 912 3615; ul Zemlyanoy val 59; ⏱ noon-2am; Ⓜ Taganskaya) still has a great outdoor terrace.

CITY GRILL Map pp248-9 International
☎ 299 0953; Sadovaya-Triumfalnaya ul 2/30; meals R500-700; ⏱ noon-2am; Ⓜ Makakovskaya
Loud music and large-screen TVs don't make for the most atmospheric restaurant

in the capital, but this long-standing bar and grill still has fans. Its appeal is old-fashioned – reliably good and filling food. With food items ranging from the classic Caesar salad to more unusual dishes such as wild boar and pad Thai, there is something for everyone on this menu.

GINGER Map pp248-9 Asian
☎ 250 0029; 1-ya Tverskaya-Yamskaya ul 16; meals R1000-1200; Ⓜ Mayakovskaya
Seafood is the speciality here, and the Asian influence is what makes it special. Ginger's blending of sweet and savoury is an art form, perfected in dishes such as spicy coconut soup, succulent sea bass with caramel sauce, and the famous crab-stuffed orange. Ginger's exotic interior – red walls, gold ceiling – is the perfect venue for such decadence.

GORKY Map pp248-9 European
☎ 775 2456; 1-ya Tverskaya-Yamskaya 3; meals R1500-2000; Ⓜ Mayakovskaya
Gorky – referring to 'hills', not to the writer – is a grandiose space, filled with heavy wooden furniture, plush chairs and marble columns. The stylish setting is perfect for the even-more-stylish guests, who look nothing less than fabulous while nibbling fresh pasta and other contemporary cuisine. The menu is primarily Italian, but the clientele is just about all-Russian.

Dessert at White Sun of the Desert (p128)

RUSSIAN FUSION *Kathleen Pullum*

'Fusion' is a word you'll hear often in Moscow dining circles. The word may refer to a café with a sushi menu in addition to its normal Italian fare or, in the case of many of Moscow's newest and best eateries, it refers to a highly evolved assortment of dishes conceived with several national cuisines in play and integrating the best qualities of each.

With a menu consisting of original dishes with European, Chinese, Russian and other international influences, **Pavilion** (p132) became an immediate hit when it opened in spring 2005. Centrally located on Patriarch's Ponds, the café is housed in a gorgeously restored 19th-century boathouse standing guard at the head of the pond. Large bay windows looking on to the water and plush couches lend the aura of dining in your living room with the neighbours.

Among Russian standards such as *salat olivye*, *pelmeni*, and grilled salmon, the menu boasts innovative dishes such as the heavenly cream of white root soup, served in a hollowed loaf of black bread (R180). A range of Chinese-influenced selections incorporate noodles freshly made on the premises; and the café's delectable bakery items are all homemade.

Olya, Pavilion's PR manager, lovingly explains that the initial concept for the establishment is to serve delicious, healthy food in a tasteful, modern setting for reasonable prices – in short, to raise the bar for Moscow dining.

Pavilion's popularity among young couples and families demonstrates how the next generation quickly picks up new trends. Now that Pavilion has helped open the gate – and others like it have begun to follow – it will be interesting to observe how Russian cooking is reclaimed and how it evolves in the near future.

Kathleen is the editor of element magazine

MON CAFÉ Map pp248-9 — European
☎ 250 8800; 1-ya Tverskaya-Yamskaya ul 4; meals R800-1200; ☺ 24hr; Ⓜ Mayakovskaya
The hot-to-trot clientele is the décor at this otherwise minimalist French café north of the Mayakovskaya metro. Otherwise, the vaguely European fare is tasty, if over-priced. Don your short skirts or black shirts and take a seat on the upper level for the best view of the activity below.

STARLITE DINER Map pp248-9 — American
☎ 290 9638; Bolshaya Sadovaya ul 16; meals 500-700; ☺ 24hr; Ⓜ Mayakovskaya
The outdoor seating and classic diner décor make this a long-time favourite of Moscow expats. The extensive brunch menu includes all kinds of omelettes, French toast and freshly squeezed juice. Otherwise, you can't go wrong with its burgers and milkshakes, any time of day or night. A second location in Zamoskvorechie (Map pp252–3; ☎ 959 8919; ul Korovy val 9, stroyeniye A; Ⓜ Oktyabrskaya) lacks the outdoor seating.

TANDOOR Map pp248-9 — Indian
☎ 299 4593; Tverskaya ul 30/2; meals R500-700; ☺ noon-11pm; Ⓜ Mayakovskaya
The interior features colourful carpets and exotic sculptures, creating an enticing atmosphere. The food is authentic, spicy and delicious, with lots of vegetarian options. It offers a business lunch.

PATRIARCH'S PONDS

CAFÉ MARGARITA Map pp248-9 — Russian
☎ 299 6534; Malaya Bronnaya ul 28; meals R400-600; Ⓜ Mayakovskaya
With walls lined with bookshelves and a location opposite Patriarch's Ponds, this off-beat café is popular with a well-read young crowd. These bookworms are pretty quiet during the day, but the place livens up in the evening, when it often hosts live music.

DELIS Map pp248-9 — Café
☎ 730 5200; Spiridonyevsky per 12/9; meals R300-500; ☺ 8am-8pm; Ⓜ Mayakovskaya
You might go inside this café just to get a cup of coffee; and who could blame you, as it is rich, dark and addictive. But once your eyes light on the display window filled with salads and pastries, you're likely to stay for lunch. Besides the items you can see, the menu features a few simple mains – grilled salmon, tiger shrimp in garlic and lemon sauce etc. Fresh ingredients guarantee delicious results, as promised by the name.

DONNA KLARA Map pp248-9 — Café
☎ 290 6974; Malaya Bronnaya ul 21/13; meals R300-500; ☺ 10am-midnight; Ⓜ Mayakovskaya
Specialising in flaky pastries and dark coffee, this little café is a regular stop for the French community that lives in this area. Homemade soups, sandwiches and quiches make it an ideal lunch spot after strolling around Patriarch's Ponds.

FISH Map pp248-9 Seafood

☎ 209 4410; Bolshoy Kozikhinsky per 12/2; meals R1500-2000; Ⓜ Mayakovskaya

'Finish your Fish!' reads the restaurant's menu. The more difficult task is not finishing the fish, but ordering it. You choose from the vast selection of slippery, silvery creatures, posing on ice at the back of the dining room; decide how you'd like it prepared – grilled, fried, baked, steamed or smoked; then pick from one of many accompanying sweet or savoury sauces. The result will delight any seafood lover. The whole experience takes place in a sophisticated, shimmery setting, featuring large picture windows overlooking Spiridonyevsky pereulok.

PAVILION Map pp248-9 Café

☎ 203 5110; Bolshoy Patriarshy per; meals R600-1000; Ⓧ 24hr; Ⓜ Mayakovskaya

With a prime location overlooking Patriarch's Ponds, this new place promises to be prominent on Moscow's thriving café scene. While the pavilion dates from the 19th century, the interior is chic and contemporary. See the boxed text, p131 for more information.

SAFFRON Map pp248-9 Lebanese

☎ 737 9500; Spiridonyevsky per 12/9; meze R100-300, meals R600-800; Ⓜ Mayakovskaya

While ethnic restaurants in Moscow tend to be overdone, Saffron is understated and sophisticated. Strewn with colourful pillows, it is otherwise simply decorated. Arabic music wafts through the air, but does not obstruct conversation. The menu includes a wide range of hot and cold meze (small plates), as well as a selection of kebabs, all expertly prepared and perfect for sharing.

BELORUSSKY VOKZAL AREA

EAST BUFFET Map pp248-9 Chinese

☎ 937 1350; Novoslobodskaya ul 16; meals R600-700; Ⓜ Novoslobodskaya

The key word here is 'buffet', as in unlimited. For R450 (R550 after 6pm), you are invited to help yourself to all-you-can-eat sweet-and-sour pork, cashew chicken and shrimp tempura. Then you are invited to go back and do it again. The selection is vast, including enough greenery to sate vegetarians.

SILK Map pp248-9 Chinese

☎ 251 4134; 1-ya Tverskaya-Yamskaya ul 29/1; meals R600-800; Ⓧ 11am-5am; Ⓜ Belorusskaya

Not too expensive, but still stylish, Silk is popular for authentic Chinese fare. Connoisseurs credit this to fresh ingredients and bold spices, not to mention the chefs hired straight from China. 'Bamboo Fire' comes highly recommended for those with a tough palate.

SOUP Map pp248-9 Café

☎ 251 1383; Brestskaya 1-ya ul 62; soups R70-100, meals R250; Ⓧ 24hr; Ⓜ Belorusskaya

This aptly named restaurant takes the most appetising element of Russian food to new heights, offering 12 hot and six cold varieties on any given day. The atmosphere is loungey: dim lights, modern furniture and DJs spinning house music from 9pm.

VREMYA YEST Map pp248-9 Russian

☎ 250 9764; Lesnaya ul 1/2; meals R300-600; Ⓧ noon-5am; Ⓜ Belorusskaya

It specialises in cold beer and unusual cocktails. If you can't decide, try the 'pivovar', which mixes vodka with beer. This place is deservedly popular, considering the free-flowing drinks and reasonably priced food. During dinner hour, expect to wait for a table – an excellent excuse to sidle up to the bar and check out that cocktail menu.

YAKITORIA Map pp248-9 Japanese

☎ 250 5385; 1-ya Tverskaya-Yamskaya ul 29/1; meals R400-800; Ⓧ 11am-6am; Ⓜ Belorusskaya

This is the first of 10 branches around Moscow serving sushi and other Japanese fare. Big windows look out to busy Tverskaya-Yamskaya ulitsa; the focal point of the interior is the fresh fish, as it is sliced and diced by sushi chefs in the open kitchen. If raw fish is not for you, try the namesake dish, yakitori (R230 to R345), which is shashlyk from chicken breast, liver and heart.

BARRIKADNAYA

Loud, crowded Kudrinskaya ploshchad might seem an unlikely spot for a pleasant dining experience, but you will be surprised. The shiny new shopping centre, Novinsky Passage, is home to several touted eateries; elegant houses on the quiet streets east of the Garden Ring offer an exquisite atmosphere for sharing a meal; and the World Trade Centre, further south, has its own strip of extravagant themed restaurants featuring excellent cooking. All this, plus it has one of Moscow's favourite expat hang-outs.

CORREA'S Map pp248-9 — European
☎ 933 4684; Bolshaya Gruzinskaya 32; brunch R400-600, sandwiches R200-300, meals R600-1000; ✆ 8am-midnight; Ⓜ Barrikadnaya

It's hard to characterise a place so simple. Correa's is a tiny space – only seven tables. Large windows and an open kitchen guarantee that it does not feel cramped, just cosy. The menu – sandwiches, pizza and grills – features nothing too fancy, but everything is prepared with the freshest ingredients and the utmost care. There's also a Correa's in Zamoskvorechie (see p137).

GOODMAN STEAKHOUSE
Map pp248-9 — American
☎ 981 4941; Novinsky bul 31; business lunch R360, meals R900-1500; Ⓜ Krasnopresnenskaya

Inside the Novinsky Passage shopping centre, this classic American steakhouse is done up in leather and wood, with black-and-white photos on the walls and old movies running on the big screen. It gets rave reviews for filet mignon and rack of lamb. Also Goodman's claims Moscow's best burger for the bargain price of R360.

KARETNY DVOR Map pp248-9 — Caucasian
☎ 291 6376; Povarskaya ul 52; meals R600-800; Ⓜ Barrikadnaya

Moscow's most popular Caucasian place has a simple, relaxed interior and a green, leafy courtyard – both welcoming. Go for classic Azeri fare such as dolmas in grape leaves and lamb kebabs, accompanied by a bottle of Mukuzani (red wine).

LE DUC Map pp248-9 — European
☎ 255 0390; www.leduc.ru; ul 1905 goda 2; meals R2000-2400; Ⓜ Ulitsa 1905 Goda

Le Duc is one in a row of fancy themed restaurants along a stretch of ulitsa 1905 goda. This one re-creates the interior of a medieval castle, while serving diners exquisite French food and wine. Vaulted ceilings, stained-glass windows and staff in costume lend this restaurant a Disney-esque air;

but, fear not, this place takes cuisine very seriously. You won't be disappointed.

REAL MCCOY Map pp248-9 — International
☎ 255 4144; Kudrinskaya pl 1; business lunch R180, meals R500-1000; ✆ 24hr; Ⓜ Barrikadnaya

The main features of this 'bootlegger's bar' are walls plastered in old newspapers and a dining room crowded with expats. The menu is not too memorable, except it includes BBQ ribs and seafood curry and everything in between. Nonetheless, this is a popular spot for drinking, especially the two-for-one happy hour specials (5pm to 8pm).

RED BAR Map pp248-9 — Fusion
☎ 730 0808; 22-24 Kutuzovsky pr; beers R175, meals R1400-1750; ✆ noon-3am; Ⓜ Kievskaya

On the 27th floor of a skyscraper overlooking the Moscow River, Red Bar features funky décor and a fabulous view. The name refers to its colour, not its politics: the whole place is draped in swanky red, except the glistening white piano. The menu is mostly small plates – overpriced, but tasty. The real draws are the floor-to-ceiling windows and views of the city skyline. Come for a sundown drink before heading out to paint the rest of the town red.

SHINOOK Map pp248-9 — Ukranian
☎ 255 0204; ul 1905 goda 2; meals R800-1200; ✆ 24hr; Ⓜ Ulitsa 1905 Goda

In case you didn't think Moscow's themed dining was over the top, this restaurant has re-created a Ukrainian peasant farm in central Moscow. Servers wear colourfully embroidered shirts and speak with Ukrainian accents (probably lost on most tourists). The house speciality is *vareniki* (the Ukrainian version of *pelmeni*). As you dine, you can look out the window at a cheerful babushka while she tends the farmyard animals (very well taken care of, we're assured).

TSDL Map pp248-9 — Russian
☎ 291 1515; Povarskaya ul 50; meals R1500-2000; Ⓜ Barrikadnaya

The acronym stands for Tsentralny Dom Literatov, or Central House of Writers, which is the historic building that houses this fancy restaurant. A glittery chandelier above, plush carpets underfoot and rich oak panelling all around create a sumptuous setting for an old-fashioned Russian feast.

ARBAT DISTRICT

Ulitsa Arbat practically introduced the pavement café to Moscow. Considering that, the selection of restaurants in the Arbat today is mildly disappointing (although there is no shortage of cafés). That said, strollers and shoppers have options to ease their hunger, whether on ulitsa Arbat itself or tucked into the surrounding streets. Novy Arbat ulitsa, to the north, is lined with decent Russian chain restaurants that offer dependably tasty and hearty food.

BUKLOE Map pp248-9   Café
☎ 291 6538; ul Arbat 27/47; meals R200-400;
Ⓜ Arbatskaya

This little light-filled shop is something of a boutique café, selling trendy clothes alongside soup and sandwiches. The fare is varied, but the menu has a Georgian twist, including favourites such as *khachapuri* (cheese bread or cheese pie), *kharcho* (mutton with garlic) and dolmas. Unlike most Caucasian restaurants, this place keeps it light, so you still just might squeeze into that miniskirt on the mannequin.

DIOSKURIYA Map pp248-9   Georgian
☎ 290 6908; Merzlyakovsky per 2; meals R400-600; Ⓜ Arbatskaya

This little house just off Novy Arbat ulitsa is famous for its delicious *khachapuri*, but all the food is highly regarded, especially for the price. The music – a trio of a cappella vocalists – outclasses the standard Georgian restaurant band.

EASTERN QUARTER Map pp248-9   Uzbek
☎ 241 3803; ul Arbat 42/24; meals R400-600;
Ⓜ Smolenskaya

Uzbeks cooking in the open kitchen and more Uzbeks filling up the dining room are the signs that this Central Asian eatery is serving some of Moscow's best ethnic cuisine. The speciality: tasty, filling rice *plov*.

HARD ROCK CAFE Map pp248-9   American
☎ 244 8970; ul Arbat 44; sandwiches R250-300, meals R600-800; ☾ 24hr; Ⓜ Smolenskaya

At long last, those souvenir T-shirts reading 'Hard Rock Cafe Moscow' actually mean something. This is the real deal, complete with framed guitars, chicken wings and a gift shop. The rock'n'roll memorabilia does not include enough representation from Russian rock stars, but there are a few notable exceptions. There's live music on weekends.

JEAN-JACQUES Map pp248-9   French
☎ 290 3886; Nikitsky bul 12; breakfast R50-150, meals R200-600; ☾ 24hr; Ⓜ Arbatskaya

In a prime location on the Boulevard Ring, this friendly wine bar welcomes everybody wanting a glass of wine, a bite to eat, a few songs and a few smiles. The basement setting is cosy but not dark, making it an ideal spot to share a bottle of Bordeaux and nibble on brie. Bottles of wine start at R350, although most are priced around R1000 – still refreshingly reasonable in this town where wine is usually ridiculously overpriced.

Patrons dining at Café des Artistes (p129)

KISHMISH Map pp248-9 — Uzbek
☎ 290 0703; Novy Arbat ul 28; meals R300-500;
☺ 11am-1am; Ⓜ Arbatskaya

It serves simple spicy standards such as shashlyk and *plov* at the cheapest prices you will find. The *dastarkhan,* or salad bar (R200), is chock-full of veggies and salads to fill up the herbivores. This place is decked out like an Uzbek *chaikhana,* or teahouse, complete with plush Oriental carpets, staff in national costume and painted ceramic place settings. Everything was imported from Tashkent (except the staff, presumably). There's another outlet near **Barrikadnaya** (Map pp248–9; ☎ 202 1083; Barrikadnaya ul 8/9; ☺ 11am-midnight; Ⓜ Barrikadnaya).

MEKHANA BANSKO
Map pp248-9 — Bulgarian
☎ 241 3132; Smolenskaya pl 9/1; business lunch R280, meals R600-800; ☺ noon-11pm Sun-Thu, noon-2am Fri & Sat; Ⓜ Smolenskaya

Mekhana Bansko – named for a town in Bulgaria – evokes the atmosphere of a holiday festival in the countryside: colourful table settings, loud folk music, and free-flowing drinks, all set around a big old stone fireplace. The lengthy wine list features many Bulgarian brands, including the restaurant's own label.

PINOCCHIO Map pp248-9 — Italian
☎ 243 6588; Kutuzovsky pr 4/2; meals R1000-2000; Ⓜ Kievskaya

This classy trattoria evokes 1930s Italy, with its black-and-white tiled floors, comfy leather armchairs and sky-high ceilings. Music from the era imbues the neoclassical dining room, creating a luxury setting to sip wine and feast on pasta and grills.

SHESH-BESH Map pp248-9 — Caucasian
☎ 290 1922; Novy Arbat ul 24; meals R400-600; Ⓜ Smolenskaya

Following the newest trend in restaurants – rhyming names – Shesh-Besh is a chain offering hearty Azeri fare. The thick soup is easily a meal in itself, as is the extensive salad bar. The place is not overly atmospheric – this being the TGI Friday's of Azeri cuisine – but the food is still spicy and prices are affordable. Caution: don't confuse Shesh-Besh with nearby Kishmish, which is Uzbek. There are additional rhyming restaurants in **Zamoskvorechie** (Map pp252–3; ☎ 959 5862;

Pyatnitskaya ul 24/1; Ⓜ Novokuznetskaya) and **Zayauzie** (Map p255; ☎ 911 6655; Tovarishchesky per 1; Ⓜ Marksistskaya).

TINKOFF Map pp248-9 — European
☎ 777 3300; Protochny per 11; 500ml beer R129, meals R600-800; ☺ noon-2am; Ⓜ Smolenskaya

Moscow's branch of this nationwide microbrewery features sports on the big screen, lagers and pilsners on draught, and a metre-long sausage on the menu (yikes). The modern interior and excellent food attract a slightly older, upmarket crowd, who come for the impressive line-up of international DJs and bands. It's a classy place for a beer.

Cheap Eats

MOO-MOO Map pp248-9 — Russian
☎ 241 1364; ul Arbat 45/23; meals R100-200; ☺ 9am-11pm; Ⓜ Smolenskaya

You'll recognise this place by its black-and-white Holstein-print décor. This chain of clean, cow-themed cafeterias is spreading rapidly throughout the capital. The self-service offers an easy approach to all the Russian favourites. There are additional outlets at **Lubyanskaya ploshchad** (Map pp248–9; ☎ 923 4503; Myasnitskaya ul 14; Ⓜ Lubyanka) and **Khamovniki** (Map pp252–3; ☎ 245 7820; 26 Komsomolsky pr; ☺ 10am-11pm; Ⓜ Frunsenskaya).

KROPOTKINSKAYA

This neighbourhood – crowded with art galleries and dominated by the massive cathedral – has an eclectic array of eateries. The restaurants complement their surroundings: the whimsical Artist's Gallery inside the Tsereteli Gallery; extravagant Vanilla, opposite the Cathedral of Christ the Saviour, which fits the same description; and Tiflis, one of Moscow's top Georgian restaurants, housed in a gorgeous Georgian manor house.

ARTISTS' GALLERY Map pp252-3 — European
☎ 201 2866; ul Prechistenka 19; business lunch R240, meals R600-1000; Ⓜ Kropotkinskaya

This fantastical restaurant inside the Tsereteli Gallery is everything that you would expect from this over-the-top artist. The five rooms follow different themes, all equally elaborate; it culminates in a huge, light-filled atrium that is wallpapered with stained glass and primitive paintings. The place certainly lives up to its name. The menu is a fusion of European and Asian influences. While secondary to the art, the food is well prepared and artistically presented.

FIVE SPICES Map pp248-9   Chinese
☎ 203 1283; Sivtsev Vrazhek 3/18; meals R500-700; Ⓜ Kropotinskaya

It's a long-time favourite for spicy Chinese food. Five Spices is not the fanciest place in town, but the fanciest place does not serve such consistently tasty sesame chicken and shrimp fried rice for such reasonable prices. The menu is like a Russian novel and includes lots of vegetarian options, including a delectable crispy spring roll.

IL PATIO Map pp252-3   Italian
☎ 298 2530; ul Volkhonka 13A; business lunch R190-280, meals R400-500; Ⓜ Kropotkinskaya

Patio Pizza has gone upmarket, with a new, more Italian name, and a new, more stylish look. Wood-oven pizzas and fresh salad bars are still the highlights of the menu, and fortunately it still has a slew of outlets, each one depicting a different Italian city. The outlet inside the Novinsky Passage at Barrikadnaya (Map pp248–9; ☎ 785 6553; Novinsky bul 31; Ⓜ Barrikadnaya) is a great place to bring your kids, who can watch cartoons or even learn how to make their own pizza. There's another branch in Zayauzie (Map p255; ☎ 230 6662; Taganskaya ul 1/2; ☽ 8am-11pm; Ⓜ Taganskaya).

MONKS & NUNS Map pp248-9   European
☎ 203 6841; per Sivtsev Vrazhek 3; meals R500-700; ☽ noon-midnight; Ⓜ Kropotinskaya

In case you can't tell from the staff, looking mildly embarrassed in their habits and cassocks, this 'beer cellar' aims to re-create a medieval monastery. Don't let the monastic atmosphere derail you from indulging in the huge choice of Trappist ales and beers.

TIFLIS Map pp252-3   Caucasian
☎ 290 2897; ul Ostozhenka 32; meals with wine R1000-1500; Ⓜ Kropotinskaya

The name comes from the Russian word for the Georgian capital, Tblisi, and when you enter this restaurant, you might think you are there. Its airy balconies and interior courtyards recall a 19th-century Georgian

mansion – a romantic and atmospheric setting. Tiflis takes Caucasian cuisine upmarket. All the menu items are particularly delectable when accompanied by the house wine, produced by the restaurateur's winery in Georgia. According to Moscow foodies, Tiflis counts among its regular customers the Russian Minister of Foreign Affairs, Igor Ivanov, who happens to be of Georgian descent.

VANILLA Map pp252-3   Asian
☎ 202 3341; ul Ostozhenka 1; meals R1200-3000; Ⓜ Kropotinskaya

It's hard to say which is more grandiose: the glitzy interior of this ultrafancy establishment; or the Christ the Saviour Cathedral across the street. Actually the views of the cathedral through the restaurant's picture windows are a perfect complement to the crystal chandelier and giant gold-framed mirror in the dining room. The modern Asian menu features sushi and other seafood dishes – all prepared with delightful innovations. The service is top-notch. Don't be put off by the row of Mercedes parked out the front; you will be treated well here, even if you show up on foot.

KHAMOVNIKI

Mama Nina and Mama Zoya are Moscow institutions, famed for filling up poor students and tight-fisted expats with spicy Georgian specialties. The newest Khamovniki addition, Parizhsk, is also affordable. These good-value eating options are representative of this quiet district that is a little way from the centre. These places are worth the trip if you are hungry or broke (or – especially – both).

TOP FIVE SUNDAY BRUNCHES

- **Baltchug Kempinski** (p179), Zamoskvorechie. Splurge on a buffet breakfast.
- **Correa's** (p133), Barrikadnaya. Think fresh fruit and homemade omelettes.
- **Nostalgie** (p126), Chistye Prudy. Brunch with blue notes.
- **Simple Pleasures** (p126), Chistye Prudy. The name says it all.
- **Starlite Diner** (p131), Tverskoy District. Classic Amerikansky breakfast fare.

Staff at Vanilla restaurant (p136)

MAMA NINA Map pp252-3   Caucasian
☎ 201 7743; Sechenovsky per 8; meals R200-400;
Ⓜ Park Kultury

Formerly Mama Zoya, this dark and divey place has changed its name but little else. This Moscow institution serves up tasty, filling Georgian food – possibly the cheapest in town. It's famed for slow service and bad music, which is all part of the charm.

MAMA ZOYA Map pp252-3   Caucasian
☎ 242 8550; Frunzenskaya nab 16; meals R200-400; Ⓜ Park Kultury

See the review for Mama Nina. These two Mamas have been serving cheap shashlyk and other Georgian favourites for years. This place is on a floating platform on the Moscow River, opposite Gorky Park.

PARIZHSK Map pp252-3   French
☎ 247 0912; Zubovsky bul 13, bldg 2; business lunch R180, meals R400-800; ☷ 24hr, happy hr 4-7pm Mon-Fri; Ⓜ Park Kultury

Targeting Muscovites who are nostalgic for Paris, this quaint café draws them in with old-fashioned ad posters and worn wooden furniture, as well as cold beers and hot onion soup. New in 2005, some early reports complained of slow service, but we hope the staff has improved with practice. Otherwise, the friendly café is ideal for solo diners, who can play computer games or watch the running video footage, as well as for groups, who can take advantage of two-for-one happy hour specials. Live music from Thursday to Saturday guarantees Parizhsk will be a popular nightspot, too.

ZAMOSKVORECHIE

The cafés and restaurants in this charming area are outnumbered only by the churches. While Zamoskvorechie is less developed and offers fewer eating options than the districts north of the Kremlin, this situation is rapidly changing: new eateries are opening on a regular basis (which is not the case with the churches).

CORREA'S Map pp252-3   European
☎ 725 6035; ul Bolshaya Ordynka 40/2; brunch R400-600, sandwiches R200-300, meals R600-1000; ☷ 8am-midnight; Ⓜ Tretyakovskaya

This new outlet in Zamoskvorechie offers the same fresh ingredients and straight-forward fare that regular customers have come to love from the namesake restaurant near Barrikadnaya (p133). The distinguishing feature here is its roomy bar area – a nice contrast to the cramped quarters at the original restaurant. Making a reservation is still recommended for Sunday brunch.

GARDEN Map pp252-3   Café
☎ 239 9115; Bolshoy Tolmachyovsky per; breakfast R60-100, meals R500-800; ☷ 24hr; Ⓜ Tretyakovskaya

This appropriately named café is set in the midst of flowering trees in the courtyard opposite the Tretyakov Gallery, drawing a bohemian, artsy crowd. The wooden floors and antique furniture contrast with the modern, jazzy music and contemporary cuisine.

LOS BANDIDOS Map pp252-3   Spanish

☎ 953 0466; ul Bolshaya Ordynka 7; tapas R350-800, meals R1000-1500; Ⓜ Tretyakovskaya
Widely planked floors and dark-stained wood – not to mention the *jamon* (ham) suspended from the ceiling – create the romantic atmosphere associated with Andalusía. The menu does not disappoint, offering a wide array of Spanish red wines and lots of traditional tapas. The paella (R800), chock-full of spicy shellfish, can feed two.

PANCHO VILLA Map pp252-3   Mexican

☎ 238 7913; ul Bolshaya Yakimanka 52; business lunch R120, meals R300-600; ☽ 24hr; Ⓜ Oktyabrskaya
In a new location near Oktyabrskaya ploshchad, this is still Moscow's top choice for Meksikansky food. If the fajitas and margaritas aren't enough of a draw, come for breakfast burritos, happy hour specials (Monday to Thursday) or live Latin music nightly (from 9pm).

OUTER MOSCOW

These days, excellent restaurants are found all over Moscow, not just in the areas surrounding the city centre. Most eateries in outer Moscow cater to the residents of their immediate neighbourhoods, but some are worth a special trip. If you are craving some spicy world cuisines, some of the best options for Indian, Georgian and Korean are here.

NORTH & EAST OF THE CENTRE

PRISONER OF THE CAUCASUS

Map p254   Caucasian

☎ 280 5111; pr Mira 36; meals R800-1200; Ⓜ Prospekt Mira
Moscow's favourite Georgian restaurant is this joint, named after a popular Soviet film. Feast on *lavash* (flat bread) straight from the oven, cheeses from the restaurant's own dairy, and shashlyk from seemingly every animal (R700). Come with a group and enjoy the classically cheesy Georgian music.

VAPIANO Map p254   Italian

☎ 937 8809; pr Mira 26; meals R600-800; Ⓜ Prospekt Mira
Crispy, thin-crust pizzas and 'zillions' of kinds of homemade pasta are ample reward for any diner making the trek out to Vapiano. This place is stylish, but not snobby; comfortable, but not crass. The highlight of the interior is the open kitchen, where patrons can watch the pasta being made. The atmosphere is enhanced by stressed wood furniture, subdued colours, and jar upon jar of uncooked pasta. The latter is also available for purchase by the half-kilo, for those who wish to play Italian chef at home.

YAR Map pp246-7   Russian

☎ 960 2004; Leningradsky pr 32/2; meals R1200-1500; ☽ 10am till last guest; Ⓜ Dinamo
The 90-year-old restaurant was once a favourite among Moscow's elite, including the opera singer Fyodor Shaliapin and the merchant Savva Morozov. These days, an evening at Yar means dining on gourmet fare and taking in a glittering cabaret, complete with showgirls. Even if you don't stay for dinner, stop by this historic spot for a peek at the gilded, chandelier-strewn dining room inside the Sovietsky Hotel (see p180).

SOUTH & WEST OF THE CENTRE

DARBAR Map pp246-7   Indian

☎ 938 8228; 38 Leninsky pr; dinner without alcohol R600; ☽ noon-midnight; Ⓜ Leninsky Prospekt
The Darbar is filled with Indian families enjoying spicy Indian cuisine, so you can tell it's on the mark. The samosas, curries, and dhal all get raves. Our only complaint was a loud Indian orchestra. Darbar is off the lobby of Hotel Sputnik (see p182).

WOORI GARDEN Map pp246-7   Asian

☎ 939 8864; ul Kosygina 15; meals R300; Ⓜ Leninsky Prospekt
This is one of several Korean restaurants in Hotel Orlyonok (see p182), which might also be called Little Korea. The place is out of the way, but good value for a unique, authentic food experience.

Entertainment

Entertainment

With its lively club scene, atmospheric cafés and crowded cultural calendar, this cosmopolitan city offers highbrow, lowbrow and everything in between.

Information

The key to finding out what's on in Moscow is the entertainment weekly *element* (www .element.ru, in Russian), as well as the *Moscow Times* weekly entertainment supplement, called *Context* (www.context.themoscowtimes.com). The *Moscow Times* also puts out a monthly magazine, *Go!* (www.go-magazine.ru), which focuses on restaurant reviews and club news. For a laugh, you can also try the *Exile*, which deals specifically with listings in the lowbrow category, to say the least.

All of these English-language publications are distributed (free!) throughout the city – check at centrally located hotels and popular expat eating and drinking establishments.

DRINKING & CLUBBING

There is not one area of Moscow where bars and pubs are clustered; indeed, the whole city is now littered with such establishments, with more opening every day. Traditionally, ulitsa Arbat is a prime spot for the café scene, especially as it is closed to automobile traffic. Likewise, the newer and trendier Kamergersky pereulok is pedestrian-only, which makes it a hot spot for strollers and drinkers. In summer, these walkways are crowded with guests who clamour for a seat at the sidewalk cafés.

These days, Moscow nightlife is much about being elite. The trendiest spots are guarded by bouncers who take their job a little too seriously. They use 'face control' to keep out potential patrons who won't enhance the atmosphere at their establishment by looking fabulous and spending money. (For more information, see the boxed text, opposite.)

Fortunately, plenty of drinking establishments offer a more welcoming ambiance, for those who don't look fabulous and spend wads of money. Most clubs and bars offer food as well as drinks – whether trendy small plates, traditional pub grub or ever-popular sushi.

12 VOLTS Map pp248-9

☎ 200 1506; Tverskaya ul 12; meals R400-600;
🕙 10pm-7am; Ⓜ Pushkinskaya or Tverskaya
The founders of Moscow's gay and lesbian movement opened this welcoming café-cum-social club, tucked in behind the Bun-

ker club (enter from the courtyard). Besides good food and cheap drinks, the place offers a consultation service for discussing homosexual issues. This is one of the few hangouts that attract lesbians as well as gays.

911 Map pp248-9

☎ 292 2911; Glinishchevsky per 3; admission free;
🕙 noon-2am; Ⓜ Pushkinskaya or Tverskaya
This used to be a straight bar with a gay night, but it has grown into a gay bar with some straight guests – 'gay expansion', as one local in the know describes it. Although the place has a small dance floor and a drag show on Saturday night, it is more of a café scene. Look for the entrance down from Studio Casino.

A PRIORI Map pp248-9

☎ 291 7783; Bolshaya Molchanovka ul 12; cover from R400; 🕙 midnight-10am Fri & Sat;
Ⓜ Arbatskaya
To strut your stuff on the dance floor, head to this progressive house club. It has a huge bi-level dance hall, as well as an exclusive 'sofa zone'. Resident and visiting DJs host dance parties at weekends. It's a new experience every time, as the interior is redesigned every few weeks. There's strict face control, so dress your best.

B2 Map pp248-9

☎ 209 9918; Bolshaya Sadovaya ul 8; admission free; 🕙 24hr; Ⓜ Pushkinskaya or Tverskaya
This huge, four-storey complex has long rated among Moscow's favourite nightlife

TOP FIVE TIPS FOR GETTING PAST FACE CONTROL

- If possible, book a table.
- Dress up: think Barbie doll for women, black for men.
- Arrive by car. The bigger the better.
- Arrive in a small group, preferably with more women than men. If you're alone, imply that you're meeting somebody, even if you're not.
- Speak English. Foreigners are not as special as they used to be, but they're still pretty special. And they still (supposedly) have money.

hot spots, probably because it offers something for everyone. Take your pick from several dance floors, a 'chill-out room', an airy courtyard, billiards, karaoke and more. The place holds over 1500 people, which makes it an excellent venue for top music acts. This is a branch of the original club, Bunker (see p143), on Tverskaya ulitsa.

BAR 30/7 Map pp248-9

☎ 209 5951; ul Petrovka 30/7; admission free;
🕑 24hr; Ⓜ Chekhovskaya or Tsvetnoy Bulvar

This slick new bar on the Boulevard Ring is the latest place to see and be seen in Moscow. If you can snag a seat in the attached 'sun room' seating area, you will enjoy a lovely view of the boulevard promenade. Good luck, as it gets packed at weekends. This place does not have much of a food menu, so plan on dining elsewhere.

BODY & SOUL (CHANCE) Map pp246-7

☎ 298 6247; ul Kuusinena 19A; cover men/women R150/R300; 🕑 10pm-6am Fri & Sat;
Ⓜ Polezhayevskaya

The sheer size of this place is its most notable characteristic. This mammoth gay club offers nearly limitless entertainment possibilities: two dance floors – one techno, one pop – billiards, Internet and live entertainment. It's a chic place that is becoming popular with a mixed crowd, but the dark room is for men only.

GIFTS OF THE SEA Map pp248-9

Maly Gnezdnikovsky per; admission free;
🕑 2pm-midnight; Ⓜ Pushkinskaya or Tverskaya

This divey, smoky bar feels like the underground gay club it once was. The crowd is mostly made up of regulars – older than at most gay bars (or any Moscow bar for that matter). Cheap prices, red tablecloths and dirty, dingy bathrooms give it its retro Soviet feel. Enter through the courtyard behind the Meeting Place restaurant and look for the dark-brown door.

HERMITAGE GARDENS Map pp248-9

admission free; 🕑 10am-2am May-Sep;
Ⓜ Pushkinskaya or Tverskaya

On a mild evening, head to a *letny kafe*, or summer café, for a cold beer and a pile of peanuts. Sit outside under the stars and forget about 'face control' and thuggish bouncers. The informal beer tents at the Hermitage Gardens are all refreshingly democratic, meaning that everyone is welcome – an appropriately open atmosphere for a public park.

HUNGRY DUCK Map pp248-9

☎ 923 6158; Pushechnaya ul 9/6; admission varies;
🕑 noon-6am; Ⓜ Kuznetsky Most

This infamous bar is often described as the wildest in Europe. Its reputation is that most people lose most of their clothes by midnight, with every woman dancing on the bar. This may have something to do with the policy of free drinks for women till 11pm on some nights. Everybody agrees, for better or for worse, that this place is 'not the same as it used to be'. Enter from the courtyard next to the metro station.

KARMA BAR Map pp248-9

☎ 924 5633; Pushechnaya ul 3; cover R100-200;
🕑 7pm-6am Thu-Sat, 11pm-6am Sun;
Ⓜ Kuznetsky Most

The Karma Bar is home to a worldly mix of Asian food, Latin music and Russian

One way of avoiding face control

fun. Thursday night usually features live music, while the other nights are for DJs and dancing – there are free lessons from 9pm to 11pm on Friday and Saturday. Add to this mix happy hours and hookah pipes, and you've got one of Moscow's top expat clubs.

KEKS Map pp252-3

☎ 246 0864; ul Timura Frunze 11; meals R200-300; ⊙ 11am-last guest; Ⓜ Park Kultury

Finally, here's a trendy place that won't bust the budget. Converted from a former textile factory, this place now features black-and-white photos, deep, comfy armchairs, and a balcony ideal for watching the activity on the dance floor. And the dance floor is worth watching on Friday and Saturday night, when DJs spin cool music and young folks turn out in droves. The food does not exactly receive rave reviews, but the big salads and hearty grills are affordable and edible.

KULT Map p254

☎ 917 5706; Yauzskaya ul 5; admission free; ⊙ noon-midnight Sun-Wed, noon-6am Thu-Sat; Ⓜ Kitay Gorod

This hang-out for arty types comes complete with a big screen showing avant-garde films and a gallery featuring local artists. DJs spin all kinds of music, with an emphasis on jazz and bossa nova. Board games, hookah pipes and cool vibes make this one of Moscow's most chilled locations. Beware: just because it's bohemian doesn't mean you don't have to look good.

NEW AGE (THREE MONKEYS) Map p254

☎ 953 0909; www.gaycentral.ru, in Russian; Nastavnichesky per 11/1; no cover before midnight; ⊙ 10pm-7am Thu-Sun; Ⓜ Chkalovskaya

The newest and best club on the gay scene, New Age has a hopping dance floor, drag queens and go-go boys, an Internet café, and a cinema. The clientele comes dressed to kill.

NIGHT FLIGHT Map pp248-9

☎ 299 4165; Tverskaya ul 17; dinner R1000-2000, cover incl drink R650; ⊙ restaurant 6pm-4am, club 9pm-5pm; Ⓜ Pushkinskaya or Tverskaya

This continues to be one of Moscow's most popular spots for business travellers on

---

TOP FIVE NIGHTSPOTS

- **bilingua** (opposite), Chistye Prudy. Young, bohemian and friendly.
- **Karma Bar** (p141), Petrovsky District. Moscow's hottest expat club.
- **Keks** (left), Khamovniki. Hip and cheap – is that an oxymoron?
- **Propaganda** (below), Kitay Gorod. One of Moscow's longest-standing nightclubs.
- **16 Tons** (opposite), Barrikadnaya. Top spot to hear live music.

---

expense accounts, despite – or because of – its dubious reputation. Indeed, it's hard to miss the crowds of working women hanging around this club. Nonetheless, the restaurant continues to receive rave reviews, thanks to Swedish ingredients and chefs. And the dance floor is always hopping. There's no cover charge for restaurant guests.

PROPAGANDA Map pp248-9

☎ 924 5732; Bolshoy Zlatoustinsky per 7; meals R300-500; ⊙ noon-7am; Ⓜ Lubyanka

A long-time favourite, Propaganda looks like it's straight from the warehouse district, with exposed brick walls and pipe ceilings. By day it's a café with a popular business lunch, but at night the dance floor is cleared so the DJs can do their stuff. This is a gay-friendly place, especially on Sunday night.

ROSIE O'GRADY'S Map pp248-9

☎ 508 0752; ul Znamenka 9/12; meals R400-600, Guinness pints R200; ⊙ noon-last guest; Ⓜ Biblioteka imeni Lenina

One of a handful of friendly Irish pubs in town, Rosie's offers Guinness, Harp and Kilkenny on tap, the widest selection of Irish whiskeys, and the most extensive food menu. It's an old favourite of English-speaking expats, especially football fans.

SPORTLAND Map pp248-9

☎ 291 2041; Novy Arbat ul 21; cover R500; ⊙ 24hr; Ⓜ Smolenskaya or Arbatskaya

At Sportland there is nonstop sport on three giant screens and countless smaller plasma TVs around the bar. You will undoubtedly be able to catch your team's big game here, no matter who your team might be. Otherwise, there is no reason to frequent this casino-bar, unless you enjoy glaring lights, blaring slot machines and greasy food. The cover charge is subtracted from your bill.

POP & ROCK

Moscow is not Russia's top spot for home-grown bands, but the capital is nonetheless chock full of places to hear music. Live bands and DJs travel from other parts of Russia and all over Europe to play in this metropolis. For more information about Moscow's hottest acts, see p26. Tickets are usually available at the venue's box office in the hours leading up to the show. For big names, look for advertisements in *element* or in the *Moscow Times*; tickets for these events can be bought in advance.

16 TONS Map pp248-9

☎ 253 5300; www.16tons.ru; ul Presnensky val 6; cover R250-600; ☽ 11am-6am, concerts 10pm or 11pm; Ⓜ Ulitsa 1905 Goda
This club is widely believed to be the hottest live-music venue in the capital, attracting top local and foreign bands, which almost always play to a packed house. The brassy English pub-restaurant downstairs has an excellent house-brewed bitter.

BILINGUA Map p254

☎ 923 6683; Krivokolenny per 10/5; meals R200-500; ☽ 24hr; Ⓜ Chistye Prudy
Crowded with grungy student types, this café also sells books and funky clothing. If you can stand the smoke, it's a cool place to grab a bite to eat and listen to some music (nightly) or to peruse the literary offerings. Despite the name, there's not much in the way of foreign-language literature.

BUNKER Map pp248-9

☎ 200 1506; Tverskaya ul 12; admission varies; ☽ 24hr; Ⓜ Pushkinskaya or Tverskaya
The smaller, original version of B2 (see p140), this more intimate setting also has an impressive calendar of local bands and DJs. There's not too much room for dancing but those who want to manage to make do.

CHINESE PILOT DZHAO-DA Map pp248-9

☎ 924 5611; www.jao-da.ru, in Russian; Lubyansky proezd 25; cover R150-200; ☽ 10am-8pm Mon-Fri, noon-10pm Sat & Sun, music from 9pm; Ⓜ Kitay Gorod
A relaxed and relatively inexpensive place to hear live music, this divey basement place hosts lots of different kinds of bands from around Europe and Russia. Check out the website for details of upcoming shows.

TOP FIVE EXCLUSIVE CLUBS *Kathleen Pullum*

Conspicuous consumption is the name of the game in Moscow, and many clubs gain popularity not by providing amazing DJs, great atmosphere or a central location but by their levels of exclusivity. It's called face control. Unless you're superelite and have a beyond-beautiful face, expensive threads and someone even more beautiful on your arm there waits a tough group of implacable black-suited bouncers that you're going to have to pass to get in.

- **Billionaire** (Map pp252-3; ☎ 737 4100; 1-y Golutvinsky per 6, Zamoskvorechie; ☽ 11pm-last guest Fri & Sat; Ⓜ Polyanka) Word is that you have to show your last pay cheque and the figure has to be more than six digits for you to gain entry.
- **Leto** (Summer; ☎ 967 3620; Yauzskaya ul 1/15; ☽ 11.30pm-last guest Fri & Sat; Ⓜ Kitay Gorod)/**Osen** (Autumn; ☎ 921 9888; Teatralny pr 3; Ⓜ Teatralnaya)/**Zima** (Winter; ☎ 205 6216; Tryokhgorny val 6; Ⓜ Ulitsa 1905 Goda) This club rotates seasonally, changing name, location and concept every few months to ensure it will always be fresh and trendy. It also seems to get more exclusive with every incarnation.
- **First** (Map pp252-3; ☎ 951 3598; Sofiyskaya nab 34, Zamoskvorechie; ☽ restaurant noon-midnight, club noon-6am Fri & Sat; Ⓜ Novokuznetskaya) This club has posh written all over it. When Will Smith was in Moscow for the premier of *I, Robot* in 2004, he and his pal Jazzy Jeff spun a set here at the after party.
- **Penthouse No 1** (Map pp248-9; ☎ 299 8853; Hermitage Gardens, Karetny ryad 3, Tverskoy District; ☽ café noon-midnight daily, club midnight-6am Thu-Sat; Ⓜ Pushkinskaya or Tverskaya) Located in the picturesque Hermitage Gardens, Penthouse prides itself on its beautiful clientele and eclectic visual displays.
- **Cabaret** (Map pp248-9; ☎ 789 8315; Strastnoy bul 8A, Tverskoy District; ☽ 11pm-last guest Thu-Sun; Ⓜ Pushkinskaya or Tverskaya) As the name suggests, Cabaret is a fancy club with all the requisite luxury cars and drivers parked out the front. But don't feel bad about not getting in: upstairs in the same building is Sky Bar, which offers a fine rooftop patio with views of the capital and a smart, atmospheric interior.

TOP FIVE GAY MOSCOW

- **Body & Soul** (Chance; p141), West of the Centre. A huge club with multiple dance floors.
- **New Age** (Three Monkeys; p142), Chistye Prudy. The newest hot spot for gay Moscow.
- **911** (p140), Tverskoy District. A casual café attracting a mixed crowd.
- **Propaganda** (p142), Petrovsky District. A long-standing favourite on Moscow's gay scene.
- **12 Volts** (p140), Tverskoy District. A friendly gathering place for Moscow's gays and lesbians.

GORKY MOSCOW ART THEATRE
Map pp248-9
MKhAT; ☎ 203 8773; Tverskoy bul 22; admission R300-3000; ☼ box office noon-7pm; Ⓜ Pushkinskaya or Tverskaya
The huge brown block is the newly re-opened Moscow Art Theatre named after Maxim Gorky (not to be confused with the more renowned Moscow Art Theatre, or MKhT, which is named after Chekhov; see p147). This Soviet-style venue is home to its own theatre troupe, but it's more interesting for the big-name music acts that occasionally play here.

PROEKT OGI Map p254
☎ 229 5489; www.proektogi.ru, in Russian; Potapovsky per 8/12; cover R50-80; ☼ 8am-11pm; Ⓜ Chistye Prudy
This vaguely hippy (but definitely hip) place is for student types; enter through the unmarked door in the corner of the courtyard and descend into the underground –

literally and figuratively. Live music plays here most nights.

WOODSTOCK Map pp248-9
☎ 748 0343; 3/1 Pokrovsky bul; ☼ 10am-6am; Ⓜ Kitay Gorod
Comfy couches and busy billiard tables lend this club a low-key, loungey atmosphere. Weekends feature live music, usually blues and rock. This place is for the low-maintenance clubber – beer drinkers who enjoy a casual atmosphere and good music without expecting too much more.

JAZZ & BLUES
BB KING Map pp248-9
☎ 299 8206; Sadovaya-Samotechnaya ul 4/2; cover R200; ☼ noon-2am, concerts 8pm Wed-Sun; Ⓜ Tsvetnoy Bulvar
This old-style blues club hosts an open jam session on Wednesday night, acoustic blues on Sunday (at 7pm) and live performances at Friday and Saturday. The restaurant is open for lunch and dinner, when you can listen to jazz and blues on the old-fashioned jukebox. The place also organises the annual outdoor Putinka Blues Festival, which takes place in July.

CLUB FORTE Map pp248-9
☎ 202 8833; www.blues.ru/forte, in Russian; Bolshaya Bronnaya ul 18; cover R300-600; ☼ 2pm-midnight, concerts 9pm; Ⓜ Pushkinskaya or Tverskaya
Here the nightly concerts range from swing-jazz to Latin-jazz to golden oldies. The atmosphere is more formal than

Band performing at Jazztown (opposite)

at some of the other places, attracting a pseudo-intellectual crowd. Thursday and Friday are reserved for local band Arsenal, which plays rather uninspired big-band. Be sure to book.

JAZZTOWN Map p255
☎ 912 5726; www.jazztown.ru; Taganskaya pl 12; cover R200-2000; ⏰ 6pm-last guest, concerts 7pm; Ⓜ Taganskaya
Moscow's newest jazz venue is this flashy place, hosting Russian and international acts on most nights. The gigantic complex includes a restaurant and a casino. The 'jazzcothèque' makes for a fun night out, if you don't mind the Las Vegas–style atmosphere.

LE CLUB Map p255
☎ 915 1042; www.le-club.ru; Verkhnyaya Radishchevskaya ul 21; cover R300-3000; ⏰ concerts 8.30pm; Ⓜ Taganskaya
Moscow's number one venue for jazz is in the building of the Taganka Theatre (p148). Performers from all over the world come to play in this 1930s Chicago–style club. Tickets to international acts can be pricey, but they're the top names in the business.

CLASSICAL MUSIC

MOSCOW INTERNATIONAL HOUSE OF MUSIC Map p255
☎ 730 1011; www.mmdm.ru; Kosmodamianskaya nab 52/8; tickets R60-600; Ⓜ Paveletskaya
This new venue opened in 2003 in a graceful, modern, glass building. It has three halls, including Svetlanov Hall, which holds the largest organ in Russia. Needless to say, organ concerts held here are impressive. This is the usual venue for performances by the National Philharmonic of Russia (☎ 730 3778; www.nfor.ru, in Russian), a privately financed and highly lauded classical-music organisation. Founded in 1991, the symphony is directed and conducted by the esteemed Vladimir Spivakov.

MOSCOW TCHAIKOVSKY CONSERVATORY Map pp248-9
☎ 229 8183; Bolshaya Nikitskaya ul 13; Ⓜ Okhotny Ryad or Arbatskaya
The country's largest music school has two venues: the Great Hall (Bolshoy Zal) and the Small Hall (Maly Zal). Every four

years, hundreds of musicians gather at the Conservatory to compete for the titles of top pianist, singer, cellist and violinist at the prestigious International Tchaikovsky Competition. A competition is to be held in summer 2006.

TCHAIKOVSKY CONCERT HALL Map pp248-9
☎ 299 0378; www.philharmonia.ru, in Russian; Triumfalnaya pl 4/31; tickets R100-1000; Ⓜ Mayakovskaya
Home to the famous State Philharmonic (Moskovsky Gosudarstvenny Akademichesky Filharmonia), the capital's oldest symphony orchestra, the concert hall was established in 1921. It's a huge auditorium, with seating for 1600 people. This is where you can expect to hear the Russian classics such as Stravinsky, Rachmaninov and Shostakovich, as well as other European favourites.

OPERA & DANCE

The classical performing arts remain an incredible bargain in Moscow. Highly acclaimed professional artists stage productions in a number of elegant theatres around the city, and tickets in prime seats often cost only a few dollars. Of course, the Bolshoi is Moscow's most famous theatre. Other venues, however, host productions of comparable quality – tickets are a fraction of the price, and the venues themselves are often in better shape. Unfortunately for summer visitors, most theatres are closed between late June and early September. Most performances start at around 7pm.

TICKETS FOR THE BOLSHOI

If you have your heart set on going to the Bolshoi, it gets tricky. In theory, tickets can be reserved by phone or over the Internet, or (depending on the season) it is often possible to purchase tickets at the Bolshoi's box office if you go at least several days in advance. Otherwise, you are better off showing up shortly before the show and trying to buy tickets from a scalper. Scalpers are easy to find (they will find you); the trick is negotiating a price that is not several times the ticket's face value. Expect to pay upwards of R1000. Most importantly, make sure you examine the ticket and the date of the show (even the year) before money changes hands.

BOLSHOI THEATRE Map pp248-9

☎ 292 0050; www.bolshoi.ru; Teatralnaya pl 1; tickets R200-2000; ✆ box office 11am-3pm & 4-8pm, New Stage box office 11am-2pm & 3-7pm; Ⓜ Teatralnaya

An evening at the Bolshoi is still one of Moscow's most romantic and entertaining options, with an electric atmosphere in the glittering six-tier auditorium. Both the ballet and opera companies perform a range of Russian and foreign works here. Since the collapse of the Soviet Union the Bolshoi has been marred by politics, scandal and frequent turnover (see p24). Yet the show must go on – and it will.

At the time of research, however, the Bolshoi was preparing to close its main stage for long-needed renovations. It is expected to reopen for the 2008 season. In the meantime, the smaller New Stage (Novaya Stsena) – newly remodelled in 2003 – will continue to host performances.

See the boxed text on p145 for details on how to purchase tickets.

GELIKON OPERA Map pp248-9

☎ 290 5359; www.helikon.ru; Bolshaya Nikitskaya ul 19/16; tickets R50-500; Ⓜ Arbatskaya

Named after famous Mt Helicon, home to the muses and inspiration for musicians, this early 1990's opera company is unique in Moscow for its innovative – even experimental – opera performances. Director Dmitry Bertman is known for 'combining musical excellence with artistic risk', according to one local dramaturge. The Gelikon's 250-seat theatre provides an intimate setting that allows for interaction between the performers and the audience.

NEW BALLET Map p254

☎ 261 7603; www.newballet.ru; Novaya Basmannaya ul 25/2; ✆ box office 11am-7pm; Ⓜ Krasnye Vorota

If you can't stand to see another *Swan Lake*, you will be pleased to know that the New Ballet performs innovative contemporary dance. This performance art, called 'plastic ballet', incorporates elements of classic and modern dance, as well as pantomime and drama. The theatre is tiny, providing an up-close look at original, cutting-edge choreography.

NEW OPERA Map pp248-9

☎ 200 0868; www.novayaopera.ru; ul Karetny ryad 3; tickets R70-700; ✆ box office noon-3pm & 3.30-7.30pm; Ⓜ Mayakovskaya or Chekhovskaya

The theatre company was founded in 1991 by Mayor Luzhkov and artistic director Evgeny Kolobov. Maestro Kolobov himself stated 'we do not pretend to be innovators

Sign on the New Opera building (above)

in this beautiful and complicated genre of opera'. As such the New Opera stages the old classics, and does it well. The gorgeous, modern opera house is set amid the lovely Hermitage Gardens.

STANISLAVSKY & NEMIROVICH-DANCHENKO MUSICAL THEATRE

Map pp248-9

☎ 229 8388; www.stanislavskymusic.ru; Bolshaya Dmitrovka ul 17; Ⓜ Chekhovskaya

This is another opera and ballet company with a similar classical repertoire to the New Opera and high-quality performances. This historic theatre company was founded when two legends of the Moscow theatre scene – Konstantin Stanislavsky and Vladimir Nemirovich-Danchenko – joined forces in 1941. Their newly created theatre became a workshop for applying the innovative dramatic methods of the Moscow Art Theatre to opera and ballet (see the boxed text, below).

STATE KREMLIN PALACE Map p258

☎ 928 5232; www.kremlin-gkd.ru; ul Vozdvizhenka 1; tickets R100-1000; ☽ box office noon-8pm; Ⓜ Aleksandrovsky Sad

The Bolshoi doesn't have a monopoly on ballet in Moscow. Leading dancers also appear with the Kremlin Ballet and the Moscow Classical Ballet Theatre, both of which perform here. The Bolshoi is magical, but seeing a show inside the Kremlin is something special, too. The repertoire is similarly classical.

THEATRE

Moscow has around 40 professional and countless amateur theatres, staging a wide range of plays – contemporary and classic, Russian and foreign. Most performances are in Russian. An excellent resource for theatre buffs – with links to many Moscow theatres – is www.theater.ru.

Tickets are available at the theatre box offices, which are open from 11am or noon daily until showtime (normally about 7pm), usually with a break for lunch. The cheapest seats are usually less than R100, but even prime seats are usually less than R500. For more on Russian theatre, see p34.

CHEKHOV MOSCOW ART THEATRE

Map pp248-9

MKhT; ☎ 692 6748; http://art.theatre.ru, in Russian; Kamergersky per 3; ☽ box office noon-7pm; Ⓜ Teatralnaya

This is where method acting was founded over 100 years ago (see the boxed text, below). Besides the theatre itself and an acting studio-school, a small museum about the theatre's history is also onsite. Watch for English-language versions of Russian classics performed by the American Studio (☎ 292 3936).

LENKOM THEATRE Map pp248-9

☎ 299 0708; www.lenkom.ru, in Russian; Malaya Dmitrovka ul 6; tickets R50-1500; ☽ box office noon-3pm, 5-7pm; Ⓜ Pushkinskaya or Tverskaya

The Lenkom isn't the most glamourous theatre, but it's widely considered to have

---

STANISLAVSKY'S METHODS

In 1898, over an 18-hour restaurant lunch, actor-director Konstantin Stanislavsky and playwright-director Vladimir Nemirovich-Danchenko founded the Moscow Art Theatre as the forum for method acting. The theatre is known by its Russian initials MKhT, short for Moskovsky Khudozhestvenny Teatr.

More than just another stage, the Art Theatre adopted a 'realist' approach, which stressed truthful portrayal of characters and society, teamwork by the cast (not relying on stars), and respect for the writer. 'We declared war on all the conventionalities of the theatre...in the acting, the properties, the scenery, or the interpretation of the play', Stanislavsky later wrote.

This treatment of *The Seagull* rescued playwright Anton Chekhov from despair after the play had flopped in St Petersburg. *Uncle Vanya*, *Three Sisters* and *The Cherry Orchard* all premiered in the MKhT. Gorky's *The Lower Depths* was another success. In short, the theatre revolutionised Russian drama.

Method acting's influence in Western theatre has been enormous. In the USA Stanislavsky's theories are and have been the primary source of study for many actors, including such greats as Stella Adler, Marlon Brando, Sanford Meisner, Lee Strasberg, Harold Clurman and Gregory Peck.

MKhT, now technically called the Chekhov Moscow Art Theatre, still stages regular performances of Chekhov's work, among other plays.

the strongest acting troupe in the country. Flashy productions and lots of musicals keep non-Russian speakers entertained. The attached restaurant, Tram, is a fun spot for a post-performance bite to eat.

MALY THEATRE Map pp248-9

☎ 923 2621; Teatralnaya pl 1/6; tickets R50-500; Ⓜ Teatralnaya

'Maly' means small, meaning smaller than the Bolshoi across the street. This elegant theatre, founded in 1824, mainly features performances of 19th-century works by Ostrovsky and the like, many of which premiered here.

PUSHKIN DRAMA THEATRE

Map pp248-9

☎ 203 8582; www.pushkin.theatre.ru, in Russian; Tverskoy bul 23; Ⓨ box office noon-7pm; Ⓜ Pushkinskaya or Tverskaya

This 18th-century theatre sits in the heart of romantic Tverskoy bulvar. The strategy of artistic director Roman Kozak is to attract established directors to the large stage, while using the small stage to showcase young, up-and-coming names. The result is a diverse repertoire.

SATIRIKON THEATRE Map pp246-7

☎ 289 7844; www.satirikon.ru, in Russian; Sheremetyevskaya ul 8; tickets R50-1500; Ⓨ box office 11am-8pm; Ⓜ Rizhskaya

Boasting one of Moscow's most talented theatre producers, Konstantin Raikin, as well as a whole host of big-name directors, the Satirikon earned a reputation in the early 1990s with its outrageously expensive production of the *Threepenny Opera*. It has since broken its own record for expenditure with *Chantecler*, which featured ducks, cockerels and hens dancing on stage. From Rizhskaya metro take any trolleybus to the Kinoteatr Gavana stop and follow the crowds.

TABAKOV THEATRE Map p254

☎ 928 9685; www.tabakov.ru, in Russian; ul Chaplygina 1A; tickets R100-1000; Ⓨ box office 11am-7pm; Ⓜ Chistye Prudy

The theatre is named after its present director, Oleg Tabakov, a famous actor who is also the current director of the Checkhov Moscow Art Theatre (p147). Recent productions of *As I Lay Dying* and *Uncle Vanya* were highly praised.

TAGANKA THEATRE Map p255

☎ 915 1015; Zemlyanoy val 76/12; Ⓨ box office noon-8pm; Ⓜ Taganskaya

This legendary theatre is famous for its rebellious director, Yury Lyubimov, and the unruly actor Vladimir Vysotsky. During the 1980s, in response to his provocative plays, Lyubimov was exiled to London and had his citizenship revoked. These days, he's back in Moscow and continues to stage top-notch contemporary productions.

CHILDREN'S THEATRES

Cultural instruction starts at a young age in Moscow, with many companies and performances geared specifically towards young kids. Performances are almost always in Russian, but at that age the language of fun is universal. Performances are usually in the afternoons.

DUROV ANIMAL THEATRE Map pp248-9

☎ 971 3047; www.ugolokdurova.ru; ul Durova 4; tickets R30-150; Ⓨ showtimes vary, 11am-5pm Wed-Sun; Ⓜ Prospekt Mira

Dedushka Durov, or Grandpa Durov, founded this zany theatre for kids as a humane alternative to the horrible treatment of animals he saw at the circus. His shows

Posters for Chekhov Moscow Art Theatre (p147)

feature mostly domestic animals, including cats and dogs, farm animals, and the occasional bear. His most popular show is *Railway for Mice,* and guided tours of the museum give kids a closer look at the railway.

KUKLACHEV CAT THEATRE Map pp246-7
☎ 249 2907; Kutuzovsky pr 25; Ⓜ Kutuzovskaya
Here acrobatic cats do all kinds of stunts to the audience's delight. Director Yury Kuklachev says: 'We do not use the word 'train' here because it implies forcing an animal to do something; and you cannot force cats to do anything they don't want to. We *play* with the cats.'

MOSCOW CHILDREN'S MUSICAL THEATRE Map pp246-7
☎ 930 7021; www.sats.theatre.ru; pr Vernadskogo 5; tickets R50-150; Ⓢ shows 3pm Wed, 6pm Fri, noon & 6pm Sat, noon & 4pm Sun; Ⓜ Universitet
Founded by theatre legend Natalya Sats (the official name of the theatre is the Natalya Sats Moscow Children's Theatre) in 1965, this was the country's first children's theatre. Sats, apparently, was the inspiration for Prokofiev's famous rendition of *Peter and the Wolf,* which is still among the best and most popular performances at the children's theatre. All performances are highly entertaining and educational, as actors appear in costume before the show and talk with the children.

OBRAZTSOV PUPPET THEATRE & MUSEUM Map pp248-9
☎ 299 3310; www.puppet.ru; Sadovaya-Samotechnaya ul 3; adult R200-500, child R150-250; Ⓢ museum noon-3pm & 4-7pm, showtimes vary; Ⓜ Tsvetnoy Bulvar
Russia's largest puppet theatre performs colourful Russian folk tales and adapted classical plays. Kids can get up close and personal with the incredible puppets at the museum, which holds a collection of over 3000.

CIRCUS
The circus has long been a favourite form of entertainment for Russians, young and old (see p34 for more information). Visitors to Moscow can choose from two venues to see dancing bears and funloving clowns. Tickets are available at the circus box offices.

GREAT MOSCOW CIRCUS Map pp246-7
☎ 930 0300; www.circ.ru, in Russian; pr Vernadskogo 7; tickets R100-450; Ⓢ 7pm Wed, Fri & Sun; Ⓜ Universitet
This huge circus has five rings and holds 3400 spectators. The company includes literally hundreds of performers, from acrobats to animals. It is a great spectacle that is certain to entertain and amaze.

NIKULIN CIRCUS ON TSVETNOY BULVAR Map pp248-9
☎ 200 0668; www.circusnikulin.ru; Tsvetnoy bul 13; tickets R50-500; Ⓢ 7pm Thu & Fri, 2.30pm & 6pm Sat & Sun; Ⓜ Tsvetnoy Bulvar
Founded in 1880, this smaller circus is named for beloved actor and clown Yury Nikulin, who performed at the studio here for many years. Unlike a traditional circus, Nikulin's shows centre on a given theme, adding some cohesion to the production. But the gist is the same, with lots of trapeze artists, tightrope walkers and performing animals.

CINEMAS
Russia – as well as the Soviet Union before it – boasts a rich cinematic culture, and Moscow is its capital (see p32). These days, most theatres show the latest blockbusters from Hollywood, usually dubbed over in Russian. A few cinemas show more interesting Russian and foreign films, especially during Moscow's film festivals (see p10). Several cinemas also show films almost exclusively in English. Showtimes vary, so stop by the cinemas (or call) for the schedule.

AMERICAN CINEMA Map pp252-3
☎ 941 8747; www.america-cinema.ru; Radisson Slavyanskaya Hotel, Berezhkovskaya nab 2; tickets R200-350; Ⓢ shows 7pm & 9.30pm; Ⓜ Kievskaya
This huge theatre is where you can see the latest from Hollywood. Besides the two daily screenings, there are additional shows on Saturday and Sunday. Russian speakers can listen to voiceovers on headphones.

DOME THEATRE Map pp248-9
☎ 931 9000; www.domecinema.ru; Renaissance Moscow Hotel, Olympiysky pr 18/1; tickets R200-400; Ⓜ Prospekt Mira
This is one of Moscow's first deluxe American-style theatres. These days films are shown in

the original language – usually English – with dubs in Russian on the headphones.

ILLUZION Map p255

☎ 915 4353; Kotelnicheskaya nab 1/15; tickets R20-60; Ⓜ Taganskaya

The location inside one of Stalin's Seven Sisters (see p29) is appropriate for the repertoire, which focuses on old-school Soviet films. Foreign films are also sometimes shown.

MUSEUM CINEMA Map pp248-9

☎ 255 9095; Druzhinnikovskaya ul 15; tickets R20-100; Ⓜ Krasnopresnenskaya or Barrikadnaya

This art-house cinema is a favourite of film buffs and intellectual types for its selection of alternative films, including old classics and lesser-known contemporary films. Frequent festivals feature both Russian and foreign films, usually in the original language with Russian subtitles. The Kino Centre, in the same building, shows more mainstream fare, usually with subtitles.

NESCAFÉ IMAX CINEMA Map pp246-7

☎ 775 7779; www.nescafe-imaxcinema.ru, in Russian; Ramstore City, Leningradskoe sh; adult R300-500, child R200-300; Ⓜ Rechnoy Vokzal

Moscow's first IMAX theatre is just inside the MKAD ring. The theatre surrounds spectators with fantastic three-dimensional images of sharks, butterflies, astronauts, dinosaurs or whatever the subject of the day. The advantage here is that it doesn't matter what language the movie is in, as the dialogue isn't really the point. A free shuttle runs from Rechnoy Vokzal metro station.

ROLAN CINEMA Map p254

☎ 916 9190; Chistoprudny bul 12; tickets R100-400; Ⓜ Chistye Prudy

The two theatres – one large and one small – show art-house films and host interesting festivals, usually featuring contemporary Russian cinema. This place is popular with Moscow's bohemian crowd.

ACTIVITIES

Moscow is not a great choice for an 'active vacation', as you won't find many opportunities for rock climbing or river rafting. (It is commonly noted that if you see someone body out jogging, they are probably trying to catch a bus.) Skating and bicycle riding are becoming more popular in the capital, but equipment is still not available for rental, so you must bring or buy your own. That said, dodging traffic and stomping through snowdrifts will provide plenty of exercise for visitors. Otherwise, there are opportunities for swimming, skiing, skating and more. For the ultimate in bodily experiences, visit the Russian bathhouse, or *banya*.

BANYA

What better way to cope with Moscow than to have it steamed, washed and beaten out of you? There are traditional *bani* (Russian baths) all over town. If you aren't shy, shared facilities are cheaper than renting a private bath. Either way, the *banya* is a sensuous, exhilarating Russian experience.

BANYA ON PRESNYA Map pp248-9

☎ men 255 5306, women 253 8690; Stolyarny per 7; admission R500-600; ⊗ 8am-10pm Mon-Sat, 2-10pm Sun; Ⓜ Ulitsa 1905 Goda

Lacking the old-fashioned, decadent atmosphere of the Sanduny Baths (below), this new, clean, efficient place nonetheless provides a first-rate *banya* experience.

EXPEDITION SIBERIAN BANYA
Map p254

☎ 775 6075; Pevchesky per 6; 2-hr session R4800-6400; ⊗ 24hr; Ⓜ Kitay Gorod

In the basement of the Expedition restaurant (p124) is a small Siberian steam *banya* that's big enough for two guests. A professional *banshchik* is on hand to ladle water on the coals when the temperature starts to drop and to provide a healthy beating with birch branches.

SANDUNY BATHS Map pp248-9

☎ private rooms 925 4631, general 925 4633; www.sanduny.ru; Neglinnaya ul 14; private rooms per hr from R1200, general admission per hr R500-700; ⊗ 8am-10pm; Ⓜ Tsvetnoy Bulvar or Kuznetsky Most

Sanduny is the oldest and most luxurious *banya* in the city. The Gothic Room is like a work of art with its rich wood carving, and the main shower room has an aristocratic Roman feel to it. Recommended.

WELLNESS SPA Map pp246-7

☎ 709 5491; www.wellness-hall.ru, in Russian; Volgogradsky pr 54; private rooms R2300-2900; ☻ by appointment; Ⓜ Kuzminki

This distinctly New Russian place has private baths for groups of up to four people. Options include a Japanese sauna, a Greek bath and an ultra-fancy 'modern hall', in addition to the Russian *banya*.

BOWLING & BILLIARDS

CHAMPION BOWLING Map pp246-7

☎ 747 5000; www.champion.ru; Leningradskoe sh 16; bowling per hr R400-800, billiards per hr R100-350; ☻ 5pm-6am Mon-Fri, noon-6am Sat & Sun; Ⓜ Voykovskaya

Champion is a huge complex featuring 10-pin bowling, billiards, karaoke, sushi, big-screen TVs and more. It's easy to suffer from sensory overload, especially with the lights and whistles of nonstop slot machines and a dance floor packed with dooted-up *devushky* (young women).

COSMIC BOWLING Map pp252-3

☎ 246 3666, 246 4662; www.cosmik.ru, in Russian; ul Lva Tolstogo 18; bowling per hr R360-885, billiards per hr R240-600; ☻ noon-5am; Ⓜ Park Kultury

'Cosmic' refers to the psychedelically lit lanes – one of many hi-tech features at this supercool bowling alley. The separate billiards room offers both Russian and American pool, as well as snooker. This popular place is often packed: be prepared to hang out at the bar and wait for a lane or a table.

SWIMMING

Public pools are difficult places to take the plunge if you are a foreigner because attendants insist on a Russian doctor's certificate of your good health before they'll let you in. Fortunately, the pools generally have somebody on hand who can issue the certificate on the spot (for a small fee).

CHAIKA SWIMMING POOL Map pp252-3

☎ 246 1344; Turchaninov per 1/3; admission R350; ☻ 7am-10pm Mon-Sat, 8am-7pm Sun; Ⓜ Park Kultury

Boasting eight lanes and heated to a pleasant 29°C, this 50m open-air pool is an ideal place for swimming laps year-round. The entire facility, including locker rooms, is clean

and relatively easy to navigate. Kids under 16 are only welcome at designated times, so phone before bringing the little ones along.

LUZHNIKI Map pp252-3

☎ 201 0795; www.luzhniki.ru, in Russian; Luzhnetskya nab 24; per hr R130; ☻ 8.30am-8.30pm; Ⓜ Vorobyovy Gory

The vast complex built for the 1980 Olympic Games includes five swimming pools: two outdoor, two indoor and a kiddie pool. The pools are open year-round, and the water is heated to between 27°C and 29°C. The complex also includes a training room, sauna and tennis courts.

SILVER FOREST Map pp246-7
Serebryany bor

On a hot summer day, join many Muscovites and head to the beaches at this series of lakes and channels on the Moscow River, 20km north of the city centre. There are areas that are unofficially dedicated to families, gay people, nudists and even disco dancers. Take the metro to Sokol and then ride trolleybus No 65 to the end of the line.

WATCHING SPORT

Moscow is a great sports town, boasting Russia's top teams in football, hockey and basketball. See p17 for more information on these teams. Buy tickets at the stadiums.

DINAMO STADIUM Map pp246-7

☎ 212 3132; Leningradsky pr 36; Ⓜ Dinamo

Of the five Moscow teams that play in Russia's premier football league, Dinamo stadium hosts Dinamo, as well as TsSKA (see p152). In winter the stadium is home to Moscow's ice hockey team, also called Dinamo.

LOKOMOTIV STADIUM Map pp246-7

☎ 161 4283; Bolshaya Cherkizovskaya ul 125; Ⓜ Cherkizovskaya

Reconstructed in 2002, this smaller stadium hosts its namesake team, Lokomotiv, which plays in the premier football league.

LUZHNIKI STADIUM Map pp252-3

☎ 785 9717; www.luzhniki.ru, in Russian; Luzhnetskaya nab 24; Ⓜ Sportivnaya

Moscow's largest stadium seats up to 80,000 people and gleams from its recent

Entertainment

ACTIVITIES

151

reconstruction. Luzhniki is home to Torpedo and Spartak, both of which are teams in Russia's premier football league. This stadium is part of a larger complex that was the main venue for the 1980 Olympics. Besides the giant stadium, Luzhniki includes a collection of swimming pools (see p151), tennis courts and other facilities, which are used by casual and professional athletes alike.

TSSKA STADIUM Map pp246-7
☎ 213 2288; Leningradsky pr 39A; Ⓜ Aeroport
A top Moscow basketball team, TsSKA is a recent champion of the Russian league and also does well in the European league.

Some of the best games come from the TsSKA women's team, which plays from September to May.

WINTER SPORTS
There's no shortage of winter in Moscow, so take advantage of it. You can hire ice skates – usually for R50 to R100 per hour – and see where all those great Russian figure skaters come from at Gorky Park (Map pp252–3) or Chistye Prudy (Map p254). Bring your passport. Izmaylovsky Park (Map pp246–7) has both ski and skate rental. To get here, take bus No 7 or 131 from Partizanskaya metro and get off at the third stop.

Shopping

Shopping

Back in the old days, the only place to buy a tin of caviar or a painted box was at an elite Beriozka store. Entry was restricted to foreigners and people with foreign currency, every store carried the same dull stuff and prices were high. The only other options were the sad selections at the State Department Store (GUM) or the notorious black market. Russia has come a long way since then – basic toiletries are no longer luxuries, and one no longer need defy the law to bring home a decent souvenir.

That said, shopping is not among Russia's main attractions. Foreign goods cost the same as (if not more than) they do at home. If the item seems like a steal, then it's probably a bargain-basement counterfeit. Local items are often of low quality, although the situation is improving.

The selection of souvenir-type items is always changing and growing, as craftsmen unleash long-dormant creativity and collectors uncover long-hidden treasures. The speciality of Russian craftsmen is painted wooden knick-knacks. It starts with the traditional *matryoshki* (painted wooden nesting dolls) and takes off from there. Traditional wooden dishes and utensils are painted in decorative floral patterns. This style, called Khokhloma, is named for its village of origin, north of Nizhny Novgorod. Wooden spoons are the most common, but bowls, cups, nap-

CLOTHING SIZES

Measurements approximate only, try before buying.

Women's Clothing

Aus/UK	8	10	12	14	16	18
Europe	36	38	40	42	44	46
Japan	5	7	9	11	13	15
USA	6	8	10	12	14	16

Women's Shoes

Aus/USA	5	6	7	8	9	10
Europe	35	36	37	38	39	40
France only	35	36	38	39	40	42
Japan	22	23	24	25	26	27
UK	3½	4½	5½	6½	7½	8½

Men's Clothing

Aus	92	96	100	104	108	112
Europe	46	48	50	52	54	56
Japan	S		M	M		L
UK/USA	35	36	37	38	39	40

Men's Shirts (Collar Sizes)

Aus/Japan	38	39	40	41	42	43
Europe	38	39	40	41	42	43
UK/USA	15	15½	16	16½	17	17½

Men's Shoes

Aus/UK	7	8	9	10	11	12
Europe	41	42	43	44½	46	47
Japan	26	27	27½	28	29	30
USA	7½	8½	9½	10½	11½	12½

rings and salt-and-pepper shakers are also easy to find. Now that artists are free to create as they please, styles and patterns are more diverse, but the trend is still decidedly traditional.

Chess is extremely popular in Russia, and these days, chess sets in a variety of sizes and styles are available for sale. Owing to the shading and texture of materials used, the boards are often works of art in themselves. Pieces can be elaborately detailed, often based on some historical theme (eg the Russians versus the Tatars). Painted lacquer boxes – known as Palekh boxes – are usually black with a colourfully detailed scene. Prices are directly proportionate to the detail and skill with which they are painted.

Nobody leaves Russia without forming a decisive opinion about Gzhel porcelain, the curly white pieces with cobalt-blue floral design. Gzhel is a village 50km southeast of Moscow, known since the 14th century for its pottery. In 1972 the Gzhel Association set up porcelain workshops in the area and created its distinctive design, which now identifies all its pieces, including its tableware, vases, miniatures, toys and more. All the pieces are hand painted, making each one unique. Love it or hate it, nothing says 'Russia' like a Gzhel teapot.

The Soviet Union is gone but not forgotten. Old-timers continue to dig out of closets and basements all manner of stuff bearing the hammer and sickle, including military jackets and hats, *shapkas* (fur hats), flasks, pins, flags etc. There's a lot of it and nobody wants it anymore, so you can pick up this stuff cheaply. Many markets carry antique items, such as old stamps, books and posters, as well as some furniture and household items. See p219 for details on export restrictions concerning antiques and anything else more than 25 years old.

For details on shopping for food items, see p122.

Opening Hours

Gone are the days when Moscow's shops closed for a one- or two-hour *pereriv*, or break, in the middle of the day. Capitalism has arrived in the capital, and with it, plenty of hours for consumers to shop and spend. Most shops are open from 10am or 11am until 7pm or 8pm. Hours are usually shorter on Sunday, from about noon to 6pm. Larger stores and shopping centres are likely to stay open for longer hours; smaller shops and galleries may close early on some days or not open at all on Sunday.

CITY CENTRE

The City Centre is home to some of the capital's largest and most prominent shopping venues. The most historic occupies a prime locale on Red Square (Krasnaya ploshchad): the State Department Store, GUM, which is now among the capital's snazziest shopping malls. Within a 500m radius around Red Square, you will find two other shopping centres, a gigantic art exhibition centre, the city's largest bookstore and a Soviet throwback department store.

BIBLIO-GLOBUS Map pp248-9   Books
☎ 928 3567; Myasnitskaya ul 6; ☽ 9am-9pm Mon-Fri, 10am-9pm Sat, 10am-8pm Sun; Ⓜ Lubyanka
Moscow's favourite bookshop is huge, with lots of reference and souvenir books on language, art and history, and a good selection of maps and travel guides. This place is usually packed, not only with books but also with people.

CHAPURIN COUTURE
Map pp248-9   Clothing & Accessories
☎ 937 0528; Nautilus, Nikolskaya ul 25; ☽ 11am-9pm; Ⓜ Lubyanka
This boutique features clothing designed by renowned Moscow fashion designer, Igor Chapurin. Chapurin is somewhat of a fashion celebrity – not just in Russia, but

TOP FIVE SHOPPING STRIPS

- **Tretyakovsky proezd** (p66), City Centre. A veritable who's who of luxury goods, whether it's clothes (Prada, Gucci etc), cars (Ferrari Maserati) or couches (Armani Casa).
- **Tverskaya ulitsa** (p159), Tverskoy District. Moscow's main drag, lined with mainstream international chains.
- **Ulitsa Arbat** (p160), Arbat District. A long-standing tourist attraction, littered with souvenir stalls and antique shops.
- **Ulitsa Petrovka** (p157), Petrovsky District. A large department store, a fancy shopping centre and a bounty of boutiques. This shopping strip culminates in Stoleshnikov pereulok, a pedestrian strip given over to the most exclusive shops.
- **Izmaylovo (Vernisazh) Market** (p162), East of the Centre. Still the number one spot for souvenir shopping.

also in Europe – for his collections, which feature prominently at 'Fashion Week' (see p10) in Moscow.

DETSKY MIR Map pp248-9   Department Store
Children's World; ☎ 238 0096; Teatralny proezd 5; ☽ 9am-8pm Mon-Sat; Ⓜ Lubyanka
This mammoth shop – 'Children's World' in English – was the premier toy shop during Soviet times. Now Detsky Mir has a mix of imported and Russian-produced toys, along with well-stocked sporting goods and homeware departments (and other toys for adults). Detsky Mir is the only major Soviet-era department store that retains its old-school atmosphere. The service and products are okay, but the layout of this place is confusing and inconvenient. For a trip back in time, visit the *stolovaya* (cafeteria) on the 4th floor.

GUM Map p258   Shopping Mall
Gosudarstvenny Univermag; ☎ 921 5763; Red Square (Krasnaya pl) 3; ☽ 10am-10pm; Ⓜ Ploshchad Revolyutsii
On the eastern side of Red Square, this place has made the transition to a market economy in fine form: the 19th-century building is a sight in itself. It's often called a 'department store', but that's a misnomer as it's really a huge collection of individual shops spread over several floors.

TOP FIVE MOSCOW SOUVENIRS

- **Chocolate chess set** Perhaps you don't play chess, but there's no reason you can't indulge in Russia's most popular pastime. Get the sweet-tooth version at Confael (see p160).
- **Simpsons matryoshka** Choose your favourite sports team, rock band, TV show or political dynasty and you will undoubtedly find a set of nesting dolls in its honour at the Izmaylovo (Vernisazh) Market (p162).
- **Swan Lake Palekh box** The quintessential Russian souvenir is a painted lacquer box depicting one of the classics. Take your pick from the enormous selection at Izmaylovo Market (p162).
- **Polyot watch** This acclaimed brand of watch was worn by Yury Gagarin when he blasted into space. The famed First Moscow Watch Factory now produces a slew of different Polyot styles, some of which are pretty slick. Check out options at Zarya (p159).
- **Yuri Dolgoruki vodka** This ultra smooth vodka, produced by Moscow's Kristall factory, comes in a smooth bottle featuring an artistic rendition of St Basil's. Get it at Yeliseev Grocery (see p123) or Seventh Continent (see p123).

MANEZH EXHIBITION CENTRE

Map pp248-9   Art Gallery

☎ 292 4459; Manezhnaya ul; ⏰ 11am-8pm Tue-Sun; Ⓜ Alexandrovsky Sad, Borovitskaya or Biblioteka imeni Lenina

The long, low building on the southwestern side of the square houses ever-changing exhibits by local artists. It is newly renovated and reopened after a fire in 2004. See p65 for more information.

NAUTILUS Map pp248-9   Shopping Mall

☎ 937 2387; Nikolskaya ul 25; ⏰ 11am-9pm; Ⓜ Lubyanka

This oddly shaped four-storey building fronts Nikolskaya ulitsa and Teatralny proezd, with the entrance at the corner. Its bright interior houses a range of upmarket boutiques, including a very trendy luxury spa on the top floor. Take a break from shopping at the fantastic Loft Café (p124).

OKHOTNY RYAD

Map pp248-9   Shopping Mall

☎ 737 8449; Manezhnaya pl; ⏰ 11am-10pm; Ⓜ Okhotny Ryad

This zillion-dollar mall was built in the 1990s. Originally filled with expensive boutiques but with no people, times have changed. Now the stores cater to all income levels and they are usually packed. There is a big, crowded food court on the ground floor.

KITAY GOROD

Kitay Gorod is home to Moscow's oldest marketplace – the ancient trading arcades known as Gostinny Dvor. It is now a mini mall, filled with small shops and souvenir stalls. At the other end of the scale, Atrium is a shiny new shopping centre that looks like it could be in Anywhere, USA.

ATRIUM Map p254   Shopping Mall

☎ 970 1555; Zemlyanoy val 22; ⏰ 11am-11pm; Ⓜ Kurskaya

This slick new shopping arcade is made up of three storeys of useful shops, including clothing and accessories, sporting goods, toys and luggage. It is one of Moscow's more practical places to shop as it's not as exclusive as some more centrally located shopping malls. The mall contains a large Arbat Prestige outlet (see p159), a massive children's play centre and plenty of eateries.

GUS-KHRUSTALNY FACTORY STORE

Map pp248-9   Antiques & Souvenirs

☎ 232 5658; www.ghz.ru; Gostinny Dvor, ul Ilyinka 4; ⏰ 10am-8pm Mon-Fri, 10am-6pm Sat & Sun; Ⓜ Ploshchad Revolyutsii

Since the glass production factory was founded there in 1756, the town of Gus-Khrustalny (east of Moscow) has been known for its high quality and widely varied glassware. This factory store carries an excellent selection of beautiful and reasonably priced glassware and crystal. The speciality is coloured glass.

VOLOGDA LINEN

Map pp248-9   Antiques & Souvenirs

☎ 232 9463; www.linens.ru; Gostinny Dvor, ul Ilyinka 4; ⏰ 10am-8pm; Ⓜ Ploshchad Revolyutsii

Russia's cool, moist summers and fertile soil are ideal for producing flax, the fibre used to manufacture linen. This elegant, durable fabric is respectfully known in Russia as 'His Majesty Linen'. Some manufacturers claim that archaeologists have excavated linen pieces that have held up for more than 1000 years. High-quality linen products such as tablecloths, napkins, bed covers and even clothing are still manufactured in Russia – and prices are lower than for their Western counterparts.

CHISTYE PRUDY

Although Chistye Prudy's stores and services will satisfy most basic needs, this mostly residential neighbourhood does not have much to offer the serious shopper.

DIGITALBRAZ Map p254 Photography
☎ 928 6628; Chistoprudny bul 12; 🕙 10am-8pm; Ⓜ Chistye Prudy
This little shop should be able to take care of any photographic service you might need – developing and printing of film and digital photos, scanning photos to CD, colour copying etc.

MARKI Map p254 Clothing & Accessories
☎ 924 5047; ul Pokrovka 17; 🕙 11am-9pm; Ⓜ Chistye Prudy
This bright boutique carries clothing by dozens of Russian fashion designers, some better known than others. It's a great opportunity to witness the burgeoning Russian design scene. The prices are not outrageous.

PETROVSKY DISTRICT

Moscow's premier shopping district centres on posh ulitsa Petrovka. Trendy little boutiques and big fancy shopping centres line this centuries-old street. Nearby, the pedestrian-friendly Stoleshnikov pereulok contains more exclusive boutiques. If these digs are too rich for your blood, head over to Kuznetsky most, where more populist stores cater to Muscovites of more modest means.

ALPINE WORLD Map pp248-9 Sports Gear
☎ 200 2688; ul Petrovka 32/1-3; 🕙 10am-8pm Mon-Sat, 11am-8pm Sun; Ⓜ Chekhovskaya
It's the most centrally located sports store, with climbing boots and footwear for a wide range of activities, including skiing, skating and snowboarding. Western brands are well represented.

ATLAS Map pp248-9 Maps
☎ 928 6109; Kuznetsky most 9; 🕙 9am-8pm Mon-Fri, 10am-6pm Sat, 11am-5pm Sun; Ⓜ Kuznetsky Most
This little shop houses an impressive collection of maps, including city and regional maps covering the whole country. The walls are plastered with most of the maps that are for sale.

BIG STAR Map pp248-9 Clothing & Accessories
☎ 923 8560; ul Rozhdestvenka 5; 🕙 10am-8.30pm; Ⓜ Kuznetsky Most
Remember when you could bring one pair of jeans to Moscow and trade them

Couple looking at Central Asian carpets for sale at Izmaylovo (Vernisazh) Market (p162)

for enough roubles to last you all week? These days, Moscow has more jeans than Texas – and many of them are at Big Star. This place stocks new and used jeans in all colours, plus shorts, skirts and T-shirts.

BOLSHOI THEATRE STORE

Map pp248-9   Souvenirs & Antiques
☎ 292 0494; ul Petrovka 3; ☺ 10am-8pm Mon-Sat; Ⓜ Teatralnaya
This little boutique stocks dance costumes and equipment. Fun souvenirs include masks, boas and costume jewellery, or an old-fashioned Bolshoi Theatre T-shirt.

BUSTIERE Map pp248-9   Clothing & Accessories
☎ 209 2644; Kuznetsky most 3; ☺ 10am-8pm; Ⓜ Kuznetsky Most
Underwear is yet another measure of Russia's amazing transition to capitalism. Gone are the days of one-size-fits-all, baggy cotton briefs; sensational, sexy lingerie is now on sale all over Moscow (and often modelled by women on the street). Several top-of-the-line stores stock European designer lingerie that is devastatingly sensual and devastatingly expensive. Bustiere is more moderately priced, also featuring classy French and Italian styles.

GERTSEV GALLERY

Map pp248-9   Art Gallery
☎ 209 6665; www.gertsevgallery.ru; ul Karetny Ryad 5; ☺ 11am-8pm Mon-Fri, 11am-6pm Sat & Sun; Ⓜ Mayakovskaya
This innovative gallery showcases modern painting and sculpture by Russian and Western artists. With an additional location in Atlanta, Georgia, it is an attempt to create links between Russian and American artists.

HOUSE OF FOREIGN BOOKS

Map pp248-9   Books
☎ 928 2021; Kuznetsky most 18/7; ☺ 10am-8pm Mon-Sat, 11am-7pm Sun; Ⓜ Kuznetsky Most
This small shop specialises in foreign-language literature. Most books are in English, though there are smaller selections of German, French and other European languages. It's one of the few bookstores with a decent selection of guidebooks in English (although not about Russia, strangely).

TOP FIVE ART GALLERIES

- **Central House of Artists** (p161), Zamoskvorechie. A huge exhibition space that is home to dozens of smaller, commercial galleries.
- **Gertsev Gallery** (left), Petrovsky District. A Russian-American artistic partnership.
- **Guelman Gallery** (p161), Zamoskvorechie. Showcases some of the capital's most innovative contemporary art.
- **Kovcheg Gallery** (p162), North of the Centre. A rare glimpse at early Soviet art.
- **M'ARS** (below), Petrovsky District. Hosts both commercial and noncommercial shows by Russian and international artists.

MANTRAM Map pp248-9   Clothing & Accessories
☎ 925 4264; Kuznetsky most 11; ☺ 11am-9pm; Ⓜ Kuznetsky Most
This small boutique features Russian designs influenced by the mystic East. Clothes for men and women feature richly coloured fabrics and exotic patterns. Slippers, tapestries, pillows and other imported interior design elements are also on sale.

M'ARS CONTEMPORARY
ART CENTRE Map pp248-9   Art Gallery
☎ 923 5610; Pushkarev per 5; admission R50; ☺ noon-8pm Tue-Sun; Ⓜ Tsvetnoy Bulvar or Sukarevskaya
Founded by artists who were banned during the Soviet era, this cutting-edge gallery has recently moved into slick new quarters. The space includes 10 exhibit halls showing the work of top contemporary artists, as well as a cool club and café in the basement.

PETROVSKY PASSAGE

Map pp248-9   Shopping Mall
☎ 928 5012; ul Petrovka 10; ☺ 10am-9pm; Ⓜ Kuznetsky Most
This luxurious, light-filled arcade on Moscow's premier shopping strip houses a range of pricey shops, including La Perla, Max Mara, Bosco and others.

TEXAS Map pp248-9   Clothing & Accessories
☎ 200 0023; Tsvetnoy bul 25; ☺ 10am-8pm; Ⓜ Tsvetnoy Bulvar
Texas sells jeans in all shapes and sizes. Not just blue jeans. Not even just denim. Texas carries jeans in every colour and fabric

Shopping

PETROVSKY DISTRICT

158

imaginable, from a wide variety of designers. This is the place to come looking for those yellow velvet jeans you always dreamed of getting.

TSUM Map pp248-9 — Department Store
☎ 292 1157; ul Petrovka 2; ⊗ 9am-8pm Mon-Sat, 9am-6pm Sun; Ⓜ Teatralnaya

TsUM stands for Tsentralny Universalny Magazin (Central Department Store), and it was built in 1909 as the Scottish-owned Muir & Merrilees. It was the first department store aimed at middle-class shoppers. But it doesn't do this any more, as it is now filled with designer labels and luxury items.

ZARYA Map pp248-9 — Clothing & Accessories
☎ 208 9161; pr Mira 7; ⊗ 10am-8pm Mon-Fri, 10am-6pm Sat; Ⓜ Sukharevskaya

Zarya is one of several producers famed for high-quality Russian military watches. This boutique carries not only Zarya, but also Mayak, Vostok and the most celebrated brand, Polyot.

TVERSKOY DISTRICT

The Tverskoy District is among Moscow's busiest commercial districts, as evidenced by the traffic jams and crowded sidewalks along its namesake street. This busy thoroughfare is lined with shoes and clothing and jewellery shops – most of which you might find in London or Paris or New York. These same shops fill the slick shopping centre, the Actor Gallery, which overlooks the district's most prominent square.

ACTOR GALLERY Map pp248-9 — Shopping Mall
☎ 290 9832; Tverskaya ul 16/2; ⊗ 11am-9pm Mon-Sat, noon-9pm Sun; Ⓜ Pushkinskaya or Tverskaya

This three-storey shopping centre is at the hub of one of Moscow's busiest shopping streets. The stores are upmarket but not exclusive – Ecco, Levi's, Swatch and the like. Many of these same types of stores line Tverskaya ulitsa.

ANGLIA Map pp248-9 — Books
☎ 299 7766; Vorotnikovsky per 6; ⊗ 10am-7pm Mon-Fri, 10am-6pm Sat, 10am-5pm Sun; Ⓜ Mayakovskaya

One of Moscow's oldest English-language bookshops is now in a new convenient location off Tverskaya ulitsa. Some expats have complained that this place has 'gone downhill' since its move, but it still carries the capital's best selection of books in English, including contemporary literature and reference books. If you are not up for *Anna Karenina* in Russian, this is also a good place to pick up your English translation. Anglia also sponsors a used-book sale on Sunday afternoons.

ARBAT PRESTIGE Map pp248-9 — Cosmetics
☎ 777 7773; 1-ya Tverskaya-Yamskaya ul 26; ⊗ 11am-10.30pm; Ⓜ Belorusskaya

This fast-growing line of cosmetics boutiques is the indisputable leader in the Russian market. Large, bright stores carry the company's top-quality line of cosmetics and perfumes. This branch is one of 16 outlets around the city.

BARRIKADNAYA

Barrikadnaya is not much of a shopping district: its wide, busy roads are not conducive for strolling. These days, however, there is no corner of Moscow without a shiny new shopping centre, and Barrikadnaya is no exception.

NOVINSKY PASSAGE
Map pp248-9 — Shopping Mall
☎ 797 6200; Novinsky bul 31; ⊗ 10am-8pm; Ⓜ Barrikadnaya

This newish shopping centre is perhaps better for eating than for shopping; nonetheless, it contains a variety of mostly high-priced boutiques, with additional shops continuing to open.

TOP FIVE BOOKSHOPS

- **Anglia** (left), Tverskoy District. The oldest and best English-language bookstore in the capital.
- **Biblio-Globus** (p155), City Centre. Lose yourself for hours in this book warehouse.
- **Bookberry** (p160), Arbat District. Moscow's answer to Barnes & Noble.
- **Dom Knigi** (p160), Arbat District. An old Soviet institution – now with author talks, bestseller lists and frequent customer cards.
- **Shakespeare & Co** (p161), Zamoskvorechie. A good old-fashioned used-book shop.

Shop signs in GUM department store (p155)

ARBAT DISTRICT

The Arbat District has always been popular among shoppers in the capital. Novy Arbat ulitsa is lined with huge shopping centres on both sides (including the classic bookshop of Dom Knigi); while the pedestrian-friendly *stary* or 'old' Arbat (is perfect for scoping out antiques and other souvenirs.

ART POINT Map pp248-9   Clothing & Accessories
☎ 241 6717; ul Arbat 41; ☯ 11am-8pm;
Ⓜ Smolenskaya
This small boutique features creative clothing designed by two local models. On sale is mostly casual wear, including T-shirts, skirts, sweaters, scarves, handbags and watches, all with an innovative twist.

BOOKBERRY Map pp248-9   Books
☎ 291 8303; Nikitsky bul 17; ☯ 10am-11pm;
Ⓜ Arbatskaya
A slick new chain that includes not only an enormous bookshop, but also a café, à la Barnes & Noble. Bookberry undoubtedly carries the city's best selection of guidebooks and maps, not to mention a host of magazines, reference books and foreign-language literature.

CONFAEL CHOCOLATE
Map pp248-9   Confectionary
☎ 202 2937; Nikitsky bul 12; ☯ 10am-8pm;
Ⓜ Arbatskaya
This upmarket boutique and café is chock-full of mouth-watering chocolates, in every shape and size imaginable. Besides the boxes of truffles and chocolate-covered cherries, Confael also stocks themed chocolates related to holidays, hobbies and national events. Sample the goods in the attached café.

DOM KNIGI Map pp248-9   Books
☎ 789 3591; Novy Arbat ul 8; ☯ 9am-9pm Mon-Fri, 10am-9pm Sat, 10am-8pm Sun; Ⓜ Arbatskaya
The old Soviet bookstore is changing with the times, with a selection of foreign-language books to rival any in the city. This huge, crowded store that's filled with books holds regularly scheduled readings, children's programmes and other bibliophile activities.

IVAN TSAREVICH
Map pp248-9   Antiques & Souvenirs
☎ 951 7444; ul Arbat 4; ☯ 9.30am-8.30pm;
Ⓜ Arbatskaya
One of many souvenir shops on the old Arbat, with little to choose between them. This touristy area is probably not the best place to buy souvenirs, as prices are high and bargaining is nonexistent. But the selection here is decent, if you don't have time to go out to Izmaylovo Market (see p162).

SMOLENSKY PASSAGE
Map pp248-9   Shopping Mall
☎ 947 8015; Smolenskaya pl 3/5; ☯ 10am-10pm;
Ⓜ Smolenskaya
Besides the Finnish department store of Kalinka Stockmann, many other smaller shops are housed under the glass roof of this long-standing shopping mall.

WORLD OF NEW RUSSIANS
Map pp248-9   Antiques & Souvenirs
☎ 241 0081; www.newrussian.net; ul Arbat 36;
☯ 10am-9pm; Ⓜ Arbatskaya
It stocks a wide range of overpriced but amusing gifts, mostly traditional Russian items with a New Russian theme (the Gzhel mobile phone, for example).

ZAMOSKVORECHIE

Between the slew of galleries at the Central House of Artists and the smaller art houses littering the streets of Zamoskvorechie, this district is one of the top spots for shoppers interested in Moscow's contemporary art scene. Look for a developing 'art district' on the small island between the Moscow River and the Vodootvodny Canal (directly opposite the Cathedral of Christ the Saviour). There is talk of converting the old empty warehouses into studios and galleries.

ART STALLS Map pp252-3   Arts & Crafts Market
ul Krymsky Val; 🕒 **Sat & Sun;** Ⓜ **Park Kultury**
Many artists set up their stalls on ul Krymsky val opposite the entrance to Gorky Park, particularly on weekends. Unlike at Izmaylovo Market, this is more arts than crafts.

CENTRAL HOUSE OF ARTISTS
Map pp252-3   Art Gallery
☎ 238 9634; ul Krymsky val; adult/student & child R50/20; 🕒 11am-7pm Tue-Sun; Ⓜ Park Kultury
This huge building attached to the New Tretyakov contains studios and galleries, as well as exhibition space for rotating collections. Work is mostly contemporary, but includes photography, sculpture and painting.

GUELMAN GALLERY
Map pp252-3   Art Gallery
☎ 238 8492; www.guelman.ru; ul Malaya Polyanka 7/7, stroyenie 5; 🕒 noon-6pm Tue-Sat; Ⓜ Polyanka

Since the early 1990s, the Guelman Gallery has been working with young creative talent to showcase groundbreaking art and to push the boundaries of artistic acceptance in post-Soviet Russia. Besides exhibits at the gallery itself, Guelman often organises exhibits at the Central House of Artists and other venues around the city.

SHAKESPEARE & CO
Map pp252-3   Books
☎ 951 9360; Novokuznetsky 1-y per 5/7; 🕒 11am-7pm Mon-Sat, noon-6pm Sun; Ⓜ Novokuznetskaya or Paveletskaya
This tiny store occupies cramped quarters in the basement of an apartment block, giving it an old-school, underground, second-hand bookshop feel. It is, in fact, the only shop with a decent selection of used books, offering a welcome change to the standard English classics stocked by most Russian bookshops.

OUTER MOSCOW

Real estate is relatively cheap outside the city centre and the area around the centre. As a result, huge new hypermarkets are springing up on Moscow's outskirts, where Muscovites go in droves to take advantage of low prices and huge selections. Travellers are also drawn to the city's fringes for other kinds of markets. Besides the farmers' markets (p122), Gorbushka and Izmaylovo Markets are among the capital's top shopping spots.

Shopping   ZAMOSKVORECHIE

CLEAN THE WORLD OF CAPITALIST DEBRIS!

The most intriguing Soviet paraphernalia – both historically and artistically – are the old propaganda posters that touted the goals of the old Soviet Union and denounced the enemies of the day. The bold colours of the posters and even bolder messages provide a fascinating insight into Soviet culture.

Although printed in vast quantities, original Soviet posters are rare today. Most of them were posted, as they were meant to be, and eventually destroyed from wear and tear. The rarest posters feature political characters such as Trotsky or Kirov, who fell out of favour with the regime. In true Soviet style, evidence of these people was systematically destroyed.

Work by the most celebrated poster artists, such as Rodchenko, Lissitsky and Klutsis, might sell for as much as US$100,000. More recent posters – especially post-WWII – are available for a few hundred dollars or less, depending on their size and condition. Pick your favourite cause – abstinence, literacy, feminism, the military, anticapitalism etc – and soak up the propaganda. A few vendors with incredible collections hang out in the northwest corner of the Izmaylovo (Vernisazh) Market (p162).

The old propaganda posters are also now being reproduced and sold in bookshops. Interestingly, these are being marketed – not to tourists, as they are all in Russian – but to curious (younger) and nostalgic (older) Russians. Contemporary Moscow society regards public campaigns to stamp out capitalism and build communism a peculiar novelty. These reproductions are available for a few hundred roubles.

NORTH OF THE CENTRE

KOVCHEG GALLERY
Map pp246-7   Art Gallery
☎ 977 0044; ul Nemchinova 12; ⊗ noon-6pm Wed-Sun; Ⓜ Timiryazevskaya
This unique gallery is devoted to showcasing the work of early Soviet artists. Caught between the vibrant, early 20th century (post-impressionism and avant garde) and the stifling Soviet period (socialist realism), many of these artists were never able to exhibit their work, until recent efforts to uncover it.

UNEROID
Map pp246-7   Clothing & Accessories
2-ya Peshchyanaya ul 5; ⊗ noon-8pm; Ⓜ Sokol
This wacky, underground boutique features cosmos-inspired fashion modelled on alien mannequins. Look for lots of tie-dye, batik and other way-out motifs. Designers include Chillout Family, Space Tribe and Acid Dreams. Marijuana must have inspired the designers who have produced a collection of cool clothes reminiscent of the hippy era.

VDNKH CULTURE PAVILION
Map pp246-7   Souvenirs & Antiques
☎ 181 9481; VDNKh Pavilion No 66; Ⓜ VDNKh
It houses an art salon that features well-known and typically Russian products, such as Gzhel porcelain, Pavlovsky-Posad scarves, Palekh boxes and more.

EAST OF THE CENTRE

ALPINDUSTRY Map pp246-7   Sports Gear
☎ 165 9875; Pervomaiskaya ul 18; ⊗ 10am-9pm Mon-Fri, 10am-8pm Sat, 11am-7pm Sun; Ⓜ Partizanskaya or Izmaylovskaya
This sports store stocks a wide variety of basic camping equipment and outdoors wear. It's useful if you are planning some outdoor adventures, and also for seeking some extra protection against the Russian winter.

IZMAYLOVO MARKET
Map pp246-7   Art & Craft Market
admission R15; ⊗ 9am-6pm Sat & Sun; Ⓜ Partizanskaya
This sprawling area, also known as Vernisazh market, is packed with art, handmade crafts, antiques, Soviet paraphernalia and just about anything you might want for a souvenir. You'll find Moscow's biggest original range of matryoshki, Palekh and khokhloma ware, as well as less traditional woodworking crafts. There are also rugs from the Caucasus and Central Asia, pottery, linens, jewellery, fur hats, chess sets, toys, Soviet posters and much more.

Feel free to negotiate, but don't expect too much flexibility in prices. Vendors normally come down in price by about 10% with little or no argument; with some hard work you can get them down further. This place is technically open every day, but many vendors come out only on weekends, when your selection is greater.

Mayor Luzhkov has long threatened to raze this chaotic market and move the vendors indoors.

WEST OF THE CENTRE

GORBUSHKA MARKET
Map pp246-7   Electronics
Barklaya ul; ⊗ 10am-8pm; Ⓜ Bagrationovskaya
Now located in the former Rubin furniture factory, the Gorbushka market has electronics on the 1st floor, and music and movies on the 2nd floor. Despite increasing pressure from Western countries and continued attempts to crack down on the violation of copyright laws, pirated CDs and DVDs are still widely available here. A recent article on BBC News estimated that at Gorbushka market, 'a mere 40% of the goods are illegitimate.' As such, CDs cost from around R100. Also, you can also get movies that are not yet available on DVD in the West.

Sleeping

Sleeping

The optimal area to stay in Moscow is the city centre. Unfortunately, this privilege is reserved for travellers with either deep pockets or generous expense accounts. Fortunately for the rest of us, a few midrange options exist within the Garden Ring, which guarantees easy access to major sights and plenty of dining and entertainment options. The Tverskoy and Arbat districts are particularly lively, but Zamoskvorechie and Chistye Prudy are also very pleasant.

If you do find yourself far from the centre (which may be the case if you are on a tighter budget), look for easy access to the metro. An underground ride will whisk you from almost any stop into the centre in 20 minutes or less.

Accommodation Styles

There are no camping grounds around Moscow – but staying at many cheap hotels is much like camping! Hotels in this price range are grey places that were poor relations even in Soviet times. Midrange and budget hotels are primarily Soviet-era properties that have weathered the transition to a market economy with varying measures of grace. Many are huge labyrinths that lack any charm; however, with a bit of spirit, a stay in these places can be part of the Russian adventure. Many of these hotels have undertaken some degree of renovation. As a result, the quality of rooms can vary widely, and prices usually do, too (even within the same hotel).

The top-end hotels in Moscow provide international-standard comfort and service. Most are managed by Western hotel chains and cater mainly to businesspeople. Expect satellite TV, wireless access, air-con, minibar and room service in very comfortable modern rooms, as well as a range of expensive restaurants, shops, bars and services. Many top-end hotels have health clubs or exercise rooms with pool, sauna, massage and the like.

Price Ranges

Moscow doesn't provide much value for money when it comes to the hospitality industry. Luxury hotels are indeed top-notch, but they have prices to match. Expect to pay upwards of R8000 for a night at one of Moscow's top-end hotels. If you can forgo a degree of luxury, you can stay in a classy, comfortable and centrally located hotel for R4000 to R6000 for a double. Midrange travellers can choose from a range of hotels outside the centre, which offer decent rooms and amenities for R2500 to R3000 for a double. To stay in the centre at the same price, you will give up many of your creature comforts. A few budget options outside the city centre are available for less than R1500 per night. Most hotels accept credit cards.

Many hotels set their prices in *uslovie yedenitsiy* (often abbreviated as y.e.), or standard units, which is equivalent to euros or US dollars. Prices in this chapter are quoted in roubles, as you will always be required to pay in roubles. Prices listed here include the 20% value-added tax (VAT), but not the 5% sales tax, which is charged mainly at luxury hotels.

Happily, the dual-pricing system (whereby foreign visitors pay significantly higher rates than Russian citizens) has largely disappeared in Moscow. Be aware, however, that some cheaper hotels may charge a 'reservation fee' (as much as 50%) for the first night's stay.

Check-in and check-out times vary, but check-in is usually around 4pm and checkout is around 11am or noon.

TOP FIVE SLEEPS THAT WON'T BUST YOUR BUDGET

- **Altay Hotel** (p180), North of the Centre. Nice facilities near the Botanical Gardens.
- **Danilovsky Hotel** (p179), Zamoskvorechie. Moscow's holiest hotel.
- **Hotel Belgrad** (p170), Arbat District. Close to historic ulitsa Arbat.
- **Ozerkovskaya Hotel** (p179), Zamoskvorechie. A small, homey hotel near Paveletsky vokzal.
- **Warsaw Hotel** (p179), Zamoskvorechie. Brand new and bright blue.

FIND A FLAT

Hotels in Moscow can easily break your bank. In response to the shortage of affordable accommodation, some entrepreneurial Muscovites have begun renting out flats on a short-term basis. Flats are equipped with kitchens and sometimes with other useful amenities such as Internet access. Often, a good-sized flat is available for the price of a hotel room or less. It is an ideal solution for travellers in a group, who can split the cost.

Several websites provide information about apartments for rent. The quality of apartments varies widely of course but many have photos available online. The cost of renting is around US$80 to US$120 per night, with prices decreasing for longer stays. Expect to pay more for fully renovated, Western-style apartments.

www.apartmentres.com Bills itself as providing gay-friendly lodging. Most flats include free airport transfers and international phone calls.

www.enjoymoscow.com Apartments rented by Rick are off the Garden Ring between Sukharevskaya and Tsvetnoy Bulvar metro stations in Petrovsky.

www.flatmates.ru/eng A site for travellers looking for somebody to share short- or long-term accommodation in Russia.

www.hofa.ru Has apartments from US$50 per night and homestays from US$25 per night.

www.rentline.ru Offers online reservations for a variety of centrally located flats, starting from US$80 per night.

www.unclepasha.com Uncle Pasha is an unbelievable grouch, but his flat – at US$75 per night – is a great deal. He also maintains an extensive list of other budget accommodation options and will help you locate one.

CITY CENTRE

Within walking distance from Moscow's most famous sights, the city centre is certainly prime real estate. Unfortunately, with the reconstruction of the Hotel Moskva and the closing of the Hotel Rossiya, only top-end options remain in this area. And 'top end' in Moscow's means the tippety-top – prepare for prices to rival the world's most expensive cities.

ARARAT PARK HYATT

Map pp248-9   Hotel

☎ 783 1234; www.moscow.park.hyatt.com; Neglinnaya ul 4; r from R20,000; 🖳 🖳 🅿 🔀 ✕ ; Ⓜ Teatralnaya

Moscow's newest deluxe hotel is an archetype of contemporary design: its glass-and-marble façade is sleek and stunning, yet blends effortlessly with the classical and baroque buildings in the surrounding area. The graceful, modern appearance extends inside to the atrium-style lobby and the luxurious rooms. Guests enjoy every imaginable amenity, not the least of which is the Italian marble bathrooms, each with a separate shower and tub. The service in the Ararat Park is top-notch (twice-daily housekeeping!). Of the hotel's many restaurants, don't miss the Conservatory Lounge, which offers panoramic views of Teatralnaya ploshchad.

HOTEL METROPOL

Map pp248-9   Hotel

☎ 927 6000; www.metropol-moscow.ru; Teatralny proezd 1/4; s/d from R9900/11,500; 🖳 🖳 🔀 ✕ ; Ⓜ Teatralnaya

Nothing short of an Art Nouveau masterpiece, the historic Metropol brings an artistic touch to every nook and cranny, from the spectacular exterior (see the boxed text, p166) to the grand lobby and the individually decorated rooms. The overall effect is breathtaking, but the charm lies in the details such as stained-glass windows, Oriental rugs and the early-20th-century furnishings.

HOTEL SAVOY Map pp248-9   Hotel

☎ 929 8500; www.savoy.ru; ul Rozhdestvenka 3; 🖳 🖳 🅿 🔀 ✕ ; Ⓜ Lubyanka

Built in 1912, the Savoy is a historic hotel that maintains an atmosphere of prerevolutionary privilege for its guests. It is more intimate than the other luxury hotels, with just 70 elegant rooms. After a recent renovation, all rooms are equipped with marble bathrooms, king-sized beds and wi-fi access. The state-of-the-art health club includes a glass-domed 20m swimming pool, complete with geysers and cascades to refresh tired bodies. Postrenovation tariffs were not yet set at the time of research, but expect prices to rival neighbouring hotels.

LE ROYAL MERIDIEN NATIONAL
Map pp248-9   Hotel
☎ 258 7000; www.national.ru; Okhotny ryad 14/1; s/d from R10,240/11,840; 🖥 📺 ❎ ✖ ; Ⓜ Okhotny Ryad

For over a century, the National has occupied this choice location at the foot of Tverskaya ulitsa, opposite the Kremlin. The handsome building is somewhat of a museum from the early 20th century, displaying frescoed ceilings and antique furniture. The rooms are decorated and laid out uniquely – some have spectacular views into the Kremlin. While the place reeks of history, service and amenities are up to modern-day five-star standards.

CHISTYE PRUDY

The serene residential area surrounding Chistye Prudy is one of Moscow's most attractive neighbourhoods. Here, you will find a handful of affordable accommodation options within walking distance (or a quick metro ride) of the city's main attractions. But this area offers its own pleasant ambience, as well as some worthy dining and entertainment options, that make it enticing in its own right.

HOTEL SVERCHKOV Map p254   Hotel
☎ 925 4978; Sverchkov per 8; s/d with breakfast from R2600/3000; Ⓜ Chistye Prudy

On a quiet residential lane, this is a tiny 11-room hotel in a graceful 18th-century building. The hallways are lined with green-leafed plants, and paintings by local artists adorn the walls. Though the rooms are nothing special, this place is a rarity for its intimacy and hominess.

HOTEL VOLGA Map p254   Hotel
☎ 280 7729; www.hotel-volga.ru; Dokuchaev per 2; s/d from R3600/5000, ste with kitchen from R4700; Ⓟ ; Ⓜ Sukharevskaya

This characterless but comfortable hotel complex, run by Moscow's city government, is on a quiet corner northeast of the centre. The location isn't too convenient, except for its close proximity to the highly acclaimed restaurant Sirena (see p126). Most of the rooms are actually suites with several rooms and a kitchen, making the Volga ideal for small groups or families.

KAZAKH EMBASSY HOTEL
Map p254   Hotel
☎ 208 0994; Chistoprudny bul 3; s/d with breakfast R2700/3000; Ⓜ Chistye Prudy

This institution caters – as you might guess – to the guests and workers of the nearby Kazakh embassy. But anybody can stay at this imposing, modern building that fronts the Boulevard Ring. Kazakhstan may be independent, but its embassy hotel has not shed its Soviet mantle: rooms, however comfortable and clean, have no style. The whole place is well maintained and pleasant enough, in a post-Soviet sort of way.

LENINGRADSKAYA HOTEL
Map p254   Hotel
☎ 975 3032; fax 975 1802; Kalanchevskaya ul 21/40; s/d from R2800/3600; Ⓜ Komsomolskaya

This showpiece Soviet hotel is expected to re-open in early 2007 after an extensive renovation. Until its recent closure, it had retained its grand 1950s' style in its lobbies and staircases; the rooms also retained their 1950s' style, though there was not much grandeur there. This has always

---

MAMONTOV'S METROPOL

The Hotel Metropol, among Moscow's finest examples of Art Nouveau architecture, is another contribution by famed philanthropist and patron of the arts, Savva Mamontov. The decorative panel on the hotel's central façade, facing Teatralny proezd, is based on a sketch by the artist Vrubel. It depicts the legend of the *Princess of Dreams,* in which a troubadour falls in love with a kind and beautiful princess and travels across the seas to find her. He falls ill during the voyage and is near death when he finds his love. The princess embraces him, but he dies in her arms. Naturally, the princess reacts to his death by renouncing her worldly life. The ceramic panels were made at the pottery workshop at Mamontov's Abramtsevo estate (see p193).

The ceramic work on the side of the hotel facing Teatralnaya ploshchad is by the artist Golovin. The script is a quote from Nietzsche: 'Again the same story: when you build a house you notice that you have learned something.'

During the Soviet era, these wise words were replaced with something more appropriate for the time: 'Only the dictatorship of the proletariat can liberate mankind from the oppression of capitalism.' Lenin, of course.

Sleeping CHISTYE PRUDY

Mosaic at Hotel Metropol (p165)

been a convenient place to stay if you are arriving or departing by train, due to its proximity to three stations. Unfortunately, the seedy atmosphere that surrounds the train stations had seeped into the hotel. Let's hope the repairs result in improved atmosphere and amenities without greatly affecting affordability. This seems unlikely considering the hotel will sport a new moniker: Le Meridien Leningradskaya.

PETROVSKY DISTRICT

The Petrovsky District is home to some fancy digs – appropriate for this high-rent and swanky shopping district. If you want to save your money to spend at the boutiques, there are also one or two more affordable accommodation options.

AKVAREL Map pp248-9   Boutique Hotel
Watercolour hotel; ☎ 502 9430; www.hotelakvarel
.ru; Stoleshnikov per 12; s/d with breakfast
R6900/7500; 🖳 🅿 ⊠ ⊗ ; Ⓜ Chekhovskaya
Stoleshnikov pereulok is one of Moscow's most prestigious lanes, home to exclusive boutiques, upmarket restaurants and the grand Marriott Royal Aurora Hotel. Now it is also home to this more intimate business-class hotel, offering 23 simple but sophisticated rooms. The friendly Akvarel has a

small restaurant, a 'mini' fitness centre and a few meeting rooms, but the hotel is a far cry from the enormous enterprises that dominate Moscow's hospitality industry.

HOTEL BUDAPEST Map pp248-9   Hotel
☎ 923 1060; www.hotel-budapest.ru; Petrovs-
kie linii 2/18; s/d with breakfast R3850/5450;
🖳 ⊠ ; Ⓜ Kuznetsky Most or Teatralnaya
The chandelier-decked lounge and the marble lobby still retain an air of grandeur, albeit slightly faded. Unfortunately, the grandeur does not extend to the rooms, unless you dish out some extra cash for the deluxe rooms (from R5775). The Hotel Budapest is expanding: in early 2006 an additional wing will open with 136 new rooms, fitness centre and restaurant. Let's hope this doubling in size does not diminish the level of intimacy and service for which this place is known.

RENAISSANCE MOSCOW HOTEL
Map pp248-9   Hotel
☎ 931 9000; www.renaissancehotels.com/mowrn;
Olimpiysky pr 18/1; r Fri & Sat/Sun-Thu from
R6000/8400; 🖳 🖳 🅿 ⊠ ; Ⓜ Prospekt Mira
This gigantic complex, now operated by Marriott, was originally built for the 1980 Olympics, as was the enormous indoor Olympic Sports Complex next door. The hotel has more than 500 rooms, five different restaurants and the Dome Cinema, which shows films in English. Thanks to its athletic origins, the hotel also boasts one of the best fitness clubs in Moscow. While the Renaissance is a bit of a trek from the centre, it has a peaceful location and offers a complimentary shuttle bus to Pushkin-skaya ploshchad for easy access to the major sights.

CHEAP SLEEPS IN CHRISTYE PRUDY

Galina's Flat (Map p254; ☎ 921 6038; galinas.flat@
mtu-net.ru; ul Chaplygina 8, No 35; dm/s/d R300/
540/750; 🖳 ; Ⓜ Chistye Prudy) is just that – a private, Soviet-era flat with a few extra rooms that Galina rents out. Staying at Galina's feels like staying in your friend's crowded apartment – cosy, comfortable and convivial. She has a total of six beds, as well as kitchen and laundry facilities, but she does not provide visa support.

SRETENSKAYA HOTEL Map pp248-9 Hotel
☎ 933 5544; www.hotel-sretenskaya.ru;
ul Sretenka 15; s/d with breakfast R7260/7920;
P ⚡ ✕ ; M Sukharevskaya
Special for its relatively small size and
friendly atmosphere, the Sretenskaya
boasts a romantic, Russian atmosphere.
Rooms have high ceilings and tasteful,
traditional décor. This place is particularly
welcoming in winter, when you can warm
your bones in the sauna, or soak up some
sun in the tropical 'winter garden'. Discounts are available on weekends.

TVERSKOY DISTRICT

Busy, bustling Tverskaya ulitsa, and the
smaller streets around it, are home to a
whole slew of places to stay – from elegant
prerevolutionary palaces to Soviet-style
skyscrapers and cool and contemporary
boutique hotels. This neighbourhood also
offers Moscow's best selection of eating and
entertainment options, as well as easy access to the city centre.

EAST-WEST HOTEL
Map pp248-9 Boutique Hotel
☎ 290 0404; www.eastwesthotel.ru;
Tverskoy bul 14/4; s/d with breakfast R4800/6500;
⚡ ✕ ; M Pushkinskaya or Tverskaya
Located on the loveliest stretch of the
Boulevard Ring, this small hotel evokes the
atmosphere of the 19th-century mansion it
once was. Inside and out, architectural details and period furnishing are reminders of
an aristocratic lifestyle that once thrived on
this street. It is a kitschy but charming place
with 26 individually decorated rooms and
a lovely fountain-filled courtyard. Despite
the old-fashioned appeal, the East-West is
up-to-date with its amenities, offering satellite TV, Internet access and other services
associated with an upscale hotel.

GOLDEN APPLE Map pp248-9 Boutique Hotel
☎ 980 7000; www.goldenapple.ru;
ul Malaya Dmitrovka 11; r from R9000;
⚡ ✕ ; M Pushkinskaya or Chekhovskaya
While calling itself 'Moscow's first boutique
hotel' might be an exaggeration, this smallish, slick hotel is indeed a novelty. The location is excellent – in the heart of Moscow's
shopping district and just steps from the

serenity of Hermitage Gardens. A classical
edifice fronts the street, but the interior
is sleek and sophisticated. The rooms are
decorated in a minimalist, modern style –
subdued whites and greys punctuated by
contrasting coloured drapes and funky light
fixtures. Comfort is also paramount, with no
skimping on luxuries such as heated bathroom floors and down-filled duvets. This
is the best of New Russia: contemporary,
creative and classy.

MARCO POLO PRESNYA
Map pp248-9 Hotel
☎ 244 3631; www.visit-m.ru; Spiridonyevsky
per 9; s/d with breakfast from R6750/7425;
⚡ ✕ ; M Pushkinskaya
Once a prominent hotel for high-ranking
Communist Party officials, this small hotel is
now an excellent, straightforward business
hotel operated by the Moscow city government. It is situated in Moscow's most prestigious residential neighbourhood, home
to expats and diplomats. The restaurant
scene is lively, and Patriarch's Ponds is right
around the corner.

PEKING HOTEL Map pp248-9 Hotel
☎ 209 2215; www.hotelpekin.ringnet.ru, in
Russian; Bolshaya Sadovaya ul 5/1; r from R2800;
M Mayakovskaya
With renovation ongoing, this Stalinesque
building boasts a prime location towering
over Triumfalnaya ploshchad. It's hard to
see past the flashing lights and raucous-
ness of the casino, but this place is blessed
with high ceilings, parquet floors and a
marble staircase. The upgraded rooms
(R4800) – elegantly decorated in jewel
tones – are worth the investment.

BARRIKADNAYA

Mayor Luzhkov has big plans for this part
of town: skyscrapers are going up at lightning speed, and soon a new metro line will
make this a prime location.

ALEXANDER BLOK Map pp248-9 Boat Hotel
☎ 255 9278; www.nakorable.ru, in Russian;
Krasnopresnenskaya nab 12A; r R2500; ✕ ;
M Ulitsa 1905 Goda
You wanted to go on a cruise, but some-
how you ended up on vacation in Moscow

instead. If this is you, consider staying on board the good ship *Aleksandr Blok,* named after the esteemed Soviet poet. Restaurant, bar, nightclub, casino and hotel – all are housed within this cruise ship moored on the Moscow River. The cabins are clean but cramped – unless you spring for the captain's quarters (R6600). The *Alexander Blok* will occupy quite the hot spot once the new 'Moscow City' metro line opens up; whether it will survive this development remains to be seen.

HOTEL MIR Map pp248-9   Hotel
☎ 290 9504; www.otelmir.ru; Novy Arbat ul 36/9; s/d with breakfast R3500/5000; 🖳 P 🔀 ; M Krasnopresnenskaya
Steps from the White House, this futuristic building once hosted top-ranking officials from the far-flung Soviet empire. Now it is something of an anachronism: marble floors and crystal chandeliers adorn a grand lobby, but the rooms retain their bland, Soviet style. Clearly Hotel Mir was a posh place back in its day, but these days it is decidedly middle class. Nonetheless, reception at the hotel is warm and welcoming, without a hint of post-Soviet sourness.

MEZHDUNARODNAYA Map pp248-9   Hotel
☎ 258 2122; www.wtcmoscow.ru; Krasnoprenenskaya nab 12; r from R9000; 🖳 🍽 P 🔀 ✕ ; M Ulitsa 1905 Goda
Fondly called 'the Mezh', this huge hotel occupies the bulk of the World Trade Centre (WTC) Moscow. The complex contains a little bit of everything, from an expo centre to aqua park (room rates often increase during expositions), plus restaurants to suit every taste. (For a long time, it was neces-

sary for the WTC to provide so many services because it was rather isolated from the rest of the city.) With the opening of the new metro line, however, the complex will have its own metro stop, with the Mezh at the centre of it all.

ARBAT DISTRICT

While there aren't any hotels along the historic ulitsa Arbat itself, its namesake district offers a wide variety of accommodation, including a few surprisingly affordable options. Most of the hotels are located on the district's busiest streets and squares, but they still provide easy access to the quaint, quiet streets of this aristocratic area.

ARBAT HOTEL Map pp252-3   Hotel
☎ 244 7628; fax 244 0093; Plotnikov per 12; s/d with breakfast from R4320/5130; M Smolenskaya
One of the few hotels that manage to preserve some appealing Soviet kitsch – from the greenery-filled lobby to the mirrors behind the bar. For better or for worse, the guest rooms are decorated tastefully and comfortably. But the whole place has an anachronistic appeal. Its location is also very charming – on a quiet residential street, just steps from ulitsa Arbat.

GOLDEN RING HOTEL Map pp252-3   Hotel
☎ 725 0100; www.hotel-goldenring.ru; Smolenskaya ul 5; s/d R9240/9800; P 🔀 ✕ ; M Smolenskaya
At the foot of the Arbat, the Golden Ring Hotel overlooks busy Smolenskaya ploshchad. It doesn't look like much from the outside, but the interior is luxurious and modern. Rooms vary in size but they are all

Sleeping **ARBAT DISTRICT**

Winter garden at Sretenskaya Hotel (p168)

decorated in warm tones and rich fabrics. Soundproofed windows keep out the noise from the square. Of the hotel's four restaurants, the highlight is the Panorama, which – on the 22nd floor – boasts fantastic views of the city.

HOTEL BELGRAD Map pp252-3   Hotel
☎ 248 1643; www.hotel-belgrad.ru; Smolenskaya ul 8; s/d from R2560/2880; [P] ; [M] Smolenskaya
The big block on Smolenskaya ploshchad has no sign and a stark lobby, giving it a ghost-town aura. The rooms are similar – poky but functional – unless you pay for upgraded 'tourist' or 'business-class' accommodation (R4160 to R5280). The advantage is the location, which can be noisy but convenient to the western end of ulitsa Arbat.

HOTEL UKRAINA Map pp248-9   Hotel
☎ 933 5656; www.ukraina-hotel.ru; Kutuzovsky pr 2/1; s/tw from R4050/4650; [P] ; [M] Kievskaya
At 206m (including the steeple), this imposing Stalinist skyscraper was the tallest hotel in Russian when it was built in 1957. It sits majestically on the banks of the Moscow River, facing the White House, meaning fantastic vistas from some rooms. The hotel boasts that it has preserved the atmosphere of the 1950s, which is no empty assertion. It offers parquet floors and old wooden furniture, a vast lobby and banquet halls, and sometimes Soviet-style service – all reminiscent of bygone days. Rooms on the 28th floor, known as the 'business floor', have been wired for Internet access, a sign that the Ukraina may be moving into the 21st century.

RADISSON SLAVYANSKAYA HOTEL
Map pp252-3   Hotel
☎ 941 8020; www.radissonmoscow.com; Yevropeyskaya pl 2; r from R5600; [.][.][P][.][.] ; [M] Kievskaya
More like a shopping mall than a hotel, this huge complex includes a large business centre, loads of restaurants and shops and a movie theatre (see p149) – not to mention more than 430 guest rooms, all equipped with wireless Internet access. If you do venture out of the hotel (not that you need to), you can walk across the pedestrian bridge and over to the Arbat. Otherwise, the location next to Kievsky vokzal (Kyiv station) does not have much to offer.

KROPOTKINSKAYA & KHAMOVNIKI DISTRICT

Kropotkinskaya and Khamovniki – stretching southwest of the Kremlin along the Moscow River – are packed with Orthodox monuments and museums, but not hotels. Choose from one of two options.

HOTEL YUNOST Map pp252-3   Hotel
☎ 242 4860; www.yunost-hotel.ru; ul Khamovnichesky val 34; s/d from R2450/2800; [P] ; [M] Sportivnaya
Yunost – meaning 'youth' – looks very 1961, which is when it was built. The humourless security guard at the front and the slow-moving staff at reception also hearken back to these times. The Soviet-style rooms are clean and comfortable, but won't win any design awards. Nonetheless, this place is a decent option for the money. It's just around the corner from Novodevichy Convent.

TIFLIS HOTEL Map pp252-3   Hotel
☎ 733 9070; www.hoteltiflis.com; ul Ostozhenka 32; s/d with breakfast from R7100/9200; [.][.][.][.] ; [M] Park Kultury or Kropotkinskaya
Georgians know hospitality. The proof is in the fine restaurants – such as the landmark Tiflis (see p136) – and now also in this hotel of the same name. With only 30 rooms, this refined four-star place offers an intimate atmosphere and personalised service. Ask for a room with a balcony overlooking the fountain-filled patio.

ZAMOSKVORECHIE

The charming, old, narrow streets of Zamoskvorechie are lined with art galleries, old churches, trendy restaurants and more than a few places to stay. The area around Paveletskaya ploshchad, especially, is the target of development, with many new hotels – small and large – opening in the vicinity.

ALROSA ON KAZACHY Map pp252-3   Hotel
☎ 745 2190; www.alrosahotels.ru; 1-ya Kazachy per 4; s/d from R7000/8050; [.][.][.][.] ; [M] Polyanka
Set in the heart of Zamoskvorechie, one of the oldest and most evocative parts

(Continued on page 179)

СССР в 30-е годь

1 *Reflection in the windows of the metro station at Lubyanskaya ploshchad (p66), City Centre* 2 *1930s Soviet-era poster (p31)* 3 *Newlyweds at the Tomb of the Unknown Soldier (p61), City Centre* 4 *Guard at the Tomb of the Unknown Soldier (p61), City Centre*

1 *Interior of La Casa restaurant (p125), Chistye Prudy* 2 *Diners at the White Sun of the Desert (p128), Petrovsky District* 3 *Desserts at the White Sun of the Desert (p128), Petrovsky District* 4 *Cooking shashlyks at Noah's Ark restaurant (p125), Kitay Gorod*

1 *Interior of Noah's Ark restaurant (p125), Kitay Gorod* 2 *The bar at Beige Cafe (p127), Petrovsky District* 3 *Customers at Coffee Bean (p121), Tverskoy District* 4 *Relaxing under the arches of Kult bar (p142), Kitay Gorod*

1 *Matryoshka for sale at Izmaylovo (Vernisazh) Market (p162)* **2** *Fashion accessories on Tverskaya ulitsa (p159), Tverskoy District* **3** *Plaza in Okhotny Ryad shopping centre (p156), City Centre* **4** *Military souvenirs at Izmaylovo Market (p162)*

1 *Shopfront at Petrovsky Passage (p158), Petrovsky District* **2** *Inside view of the GUM department store (p155), City Centre* **3** *Shapka (fur hat) for sale, Petrovsky District (p157)* **4** *Shop window display, Tverskaya ulitsa (p159), Tverskoy District*

1 *Exterior of New Opera building (p146), Petrovsky District* **2** *'We Print History' banner on the Izvestia building (p111), Tverskoy District* **3** *Advertising for the New Opera (p146), Petrovsky District* **4** *Stained-glass window at Hotel Metropol (p66), City Centre*

1 *The sculpture garden at the Moscow Museum of Modern Art (p80), Petrovsky District* 2 *Poster promoting a display at the Manezh Exhibition Centre (p65), City Centre* 3 *Sculpture at the Tsereteli Gallery (p93), Kropotkinskaya* 4 *Front of Glazunov Gallery (p90), Kropotkinskaya*

1 *Monastery of St Jacob on Lake Nero, Rostov-Veliky (p198)*
2 *Hawkers selling glassware at the train station, Kostroma (p200)*
3 *Mosaic paying tribute to the heroes of Borodino, Borodino Panorama (p106)* **4** *View down to the Kotorosl River, Yaroslavl (p200)*

(Continued from page 170)

of Moscow, the Alrosa re-creates the atmosphere of an 18th-century estate. The light-filled atrium, bedecked with crystal chandelier, and 15 classically decorated rooms provide a perfect setting for old-fashioned Russian hospitality.

BALTSCHUG KEMPINSKI

Map pp248-9   Hotel

☎ 230 6500; www.kempinskimoscow.com; ul Baltschug 1; r Fri & Sat/Sun-Tue with breakfast from R9450/13,125; ▢ ▣ 🗙 ✕ ; Ⓜ Kitay Gorod or Ploshchad Revolyutsii

If you want to wake up to views of the sun glinting off the Kremlin's golden domes, this luxurious property on the Moscow River is the place for you. It is another historic hotel, built in 1898, with 230 high-ceilinged rooms that are sophisticated and sumptuous in design. The on-site restaurant is famous for its Sunday brunch, or 'Linner' if you prefer, as it's served from 12.30pm to 4.30pm. Russian champagne and live jazz accompany an extravagant buffet.

DANILOVSKAYA HOTEL

Map pp246-7   Hotel

☎ 954 0503; hotdanil@cityline.ru; s/d with breakfast from R3300/3900; ▢ ▣ ✕ ; Ⓜ Tulskaya

Moscow's holiest hotel is on the grounds of the 12th-century Danilovsky Monastery (see p98) – where the exquisite setting comes complete with 18th-century churches and well-maintained gardens. The modern five-storey hotel was built so that nearly all the rooms have a view of the monastery grounds. The rooms themselves are simple but clean; breakfast is modest: there's no greed, gluttony or sloth to be found here.

KATERINA-CITY HOTEL Map p255   Hotel

☎ 795 2444; www.katerina.msk.ru/eng/; Shlyuzovaya nab 6; s/d with breakfast R8000/11,000; ▢ ▣ ✕ ; Ⓜ Paveletskaya

Swedish-built and Russian-operated, this smallish hotel advertises 'European comfort and Russian hospitality'. It is indeed a delightful combination. The simple, stylish rooms feature bold colours and understated Scandinavian design, while the overall atmosphere is warm and welcoming. Perks available at the hotel include a fitness centre with both Finnish and Turkish saunas.

OZERKOVSKAYA HOTEL

Map p255   Boutique Hotel

☎ 951 9753; www.cct.ru; Ozerkovskaya nab 50; s/d from R3960/4220; Ⓟ ; Ⓜ Paveletskaya

This comfy, cosy hotel has only 25 rooms, including three that are tucked up under the mansard roof. The rooms are simply decorated, but parquet floors and comfortable queen-sized beds rank it above the standard post-Soviet fare. Add in attentive service and a central location (convenient for the express train to Domodedovo airport), and you've got an excellent-value accommodation option. Discounts are sometimes available, especially on weekends.

TATIANA HOTEL Map p255   Hotel

☎ 721 2500; www.tatiana-hotel.ru; Stremyanny per 11; r with breakfast R6500; ▢ Ⓟ 🗙 ✕ ; Ⓜ Paveletskaya

This attractive new business hotel is on a quiet street near Paveletsky vokzal – again, convenient for travellers flying in or out of Domodedovo. Built in 2002, the hotel features an airy, atrium-style lobby and 72 spacious rooms. They are all characterised by contemporary furnishings and warm pastels, not to mention perks such as heated bathroom floors.

WARSAW HOTEL Map pp252-3   Hotel

☎ 238 7701; warsaw@sovintel.ru; Leninsky pr 2; s/d/ste with breakfast R2500/3650/5000; Ⓜ Oktyabrskaya

The Warsaw sits at the centre of Oktyabrskaya ploshchad, voted by Muscovites as the ugliest square in the city. Nonetheless, the location is the main drawcard here: it offers lots of restaurants, easy access to the metro and a short walk into the heart of Zamoskvorechie. The hotel itself does not exactly add to the aesthetics of the square. However, the interior has recently undergone extensive renovations, as evidenced by the sparkling, space-age lobby, adorned with lots of chrome, blue leather furniture and spider-like light fixtures. The new rooms are surprisingly good value for the location.

OUTER MOSCOW

The majority of budget accommodation options are located on the outskirts of the city. Moscow is vast, but the places listed here are all within walking distance of the metro,

Sleeping

OUTER MOSCOW

which will whisk you into the centre in 15 to 20 minutes. And even Outer Moscow has its charms, including the lovely grounds of old country estates, a few museums, the city's best markets and the vast exhibition centre at VDNKh.

NORTH OF THE CENTRE

ALTAY HOTEL Map pp246-7   Hotel
☎ 482 5703; Botanicheskaya ul 41; altayhotel@comail.ru; s/d with breakfast R2200/2890; ▢ ✕ ; Ⓜ Vladykino
This is the classiest place to stay in the 'hotel district' near the Botanical Gardens. The hotel has been completely revamped, from the elegant lobby – with chandeliers and a fireplace – to the tastefully decorated guest rooms. Only a few old-style rooms remain (R800/1250) but they are often booked out.

HOTEL COSMOS Map pp246-7   Hotel
☎ 234 1206; www.hotelcosmos.ru; Prospekt Mira 150; s/d from R2240/2800; ▢ ▣ ✕ ; Ⓜ VDNKh
This gargantuan hotel opposite the All-Russia Exhibition Centre is a universe unto itself (appropriately enough for a place called 'Cosmos'). The avant-garde glass-and-steel structure houses more than 1700 rooms, countless restaurants and bars and a state-of-the-art fitness centre. Not surprisingly, a wide range of rooms is available, some with fantastic views.

OKSANA (DINAODA) HOTEL
Map pp246-7   Hotel
☎ 980 6100; www.dinaoda.ru; Yaroslavskaya ul 15/2; s/d from R3630/4300; ▢ ✕ ; Ⓜ VDNKh
A classical, six-storey building, the Oksana (also known as the Dinaoda) is a brand new hotel catering to business travellers. The rooms benefit from natural sunlight and spacious interiors; some are wheelchair accessible. The manicured miniature golf course is perhaps out of place in this elegant setting, but your children will appreciate it.

SOVIETSKY HOTEL Map pp246-7   Hotel
☎ 960 2000; www.sovietsky.ru; Leningradsky pr 32/2; r from R4960; ▢ ▣ ✕ ✕ ; Ⓜ Dinamo
Built in 1952, this historic hotel shows Stalin's tastes in all its architectural details, starting from the gilded hammer and sickle and the enormous Corinthian columns

flanking the front door. The sumptuous lobby is graced with grand sweeping staircases, crystal chandeliers and plush carpets, while even the simplest rooms have ceiling medallions and other ornamentation. The hotel's legendary restaurant 'Yar' (p138) – complete with old-fashioned dancing girls – is truly over-the-top. The location isn't super convenient, but this throwback is still a fun experience for a Soviet-style splurge.

Cheap Sleeps

HOSTEL SHERSTONE Map pp246-7   Hostel
☎ 711 2613; www.sherstone.ru; Gostinichny proezd 8/1, 3rd fl; dm/s/d R600/1200/1550; Ⓜ Vladykino
The name of this tree-lined street west of the Botanical Gardens means 'Hotel Way'. The Sherstone is a friendly hostel occupying one floor of a hotel by the same name. Its main advantage is the English-speaking staff, but rooms and services are also satisfactory.

HOSTEL TRAMP Map pp246-7   Hotel
☎ 771 0755, 551 2876; www.hostelling.ru; Selskohozyaistvennaya ul 17/2, Bldg 4, No 225; s/d R900/1000; Ⓜ Botanicheskaya Sad
Like most 'hostels' in Moscow, the Tramp is actually a travel agency affiliated with a budget hotel. In this case, it's the Hotel Turist, a pleasant, friendly hotel complex in its own right. Booking through Hostel Tramp, your room might be in any one of six red-brick buildings set amid shady grounds and located near the Botanical Gardens. Unfortunately, the place lacks the

---

AIRPORT ACCOMMODATIONS

Here are a couple of options for transit travellers who might need somewhere to crash between flights:

- **Aerotel Domodedovo** (☎ 795 3868; fax 795 3569; Domodedovo airport; r with breakfast from R3500; ▣ ✕ ✕) A brand new hotel within walking distance of its namesake airport; excellent value. The express train to Paveletsky vokzal links the airport to the city.
- **Sheremetevo-2** (☎ 578 5753/4; fax 739 4464; Sheremetevo-2 airport; r with breakfast from R3450; Ⓜ Rechnoy Vokzal, then minibus to airport) An option that's more affordable than the nearby Novotel. You can walk here from the airport, or use the Novotel's free shuttle.

rooms with new furniture and bathrooms are R2100/2700.

TRAVELLERS GUEST HOUSE

Map pp246-7   Hostel

☎ 631 4059; www.tgh.ru; Bolshaya Pereyaslavskaya ul 50, 10th fl; dm/s R690/1350, d with shared/private bathroom R1650/1800; ☐ ; Ⓜ Rizhskaya

This guesthouse calls itself Moscow's 'first and only' budget accommodation. Perhaps the first but no longer the only, this place is still one of the better options for budget travellers. Despite its location on the 10th floor of a drab hotel, it manages to maintain a vibrant, hostel-like atmosphere, thanks to the many travellers hanging out in the common room and also the services available through the affiliated Infinity Travel Agency (see p226). To get here from Rizhskaya metro, walk past the market and turn right to cross underneath the highway. Pass a church on the right-hand side, and continue south to the unmarked hotel on the left-hand side.

Lobby of the Hotel Ukraina (p170)

camaraderie of a traditional hostel, as there is no common area and you're not likely to run into other travellers unless you hang around the office.

HOTEL GLOBUS Map pp246-7   Hotel

☎ 286 4189; www.hotelglobus.ru; Yaroslavskaya ul 17; ste from R1700; ☐ 🖳 Ⓟ ✖ ; Ⓜ VDNKh

Just around the corner from Hotel Cosmos, this 'apartment-hotel' provides two-room suites with kitchen and bathroom – convenient for families and small groups. The kitchens are equipped with basic appliances such as fridges and electric kettles, but no stoves, limiting your cooking possibilities. The facility is sufficiently modern, but not particularly stylish or friendly. The 10 'pol-luks' suites (R2400) – with newer furnishings and facilities – are definitely worth the extra cash.

HOTEL ZARYA Map pp246-7   Hotel

☎ /fax 788 7277; Gostinichnaya ul 4/9; s/d from R1350/1500; Ⓜ Vladykino

The Zarya is a complex of short brick buildings, also located near the Botanical Garden. Renovation of the rooms is ongoing, so the cheapest ones are pretty plain. However, the receptionists are welcoming and the atmosphere is cosy. Upgraded

ZOLOTOY KOLOS Map pp246-7   Hotel

☎ 217 6356; www.zkolos.ru; Yaroslavskaya ul 15; s/d from R1090/1345; ✖ ; Ⓜ VDNKh

Outshined by its richer neighbour, the Oskana (aka the Dinaoda), this old-style hotel still has something to offer with its pleasant service and affordable rooms. Meaning 'Golden Grain', it once catered to agricultural types. Because of its location near the All-Russia Exhibition Centre, it is often booked by travelling businesspeople.

EAST OF THE CENTRE
Cheap Sleeps

G&R HOSTEL ASIA Map pp246-7   Guesthouse

☎ 378 0001; www.hostels.ru; Zelenodolskaya ul 2/3; s/d with shared bathroom from R875/1400; ☐ ; Ⓜ Ryazansky Prospekt

It calls itself a hostel, but it's really a travel agency hiding out in a big old Soviet hotel. Unlike at the other 'hostels', your room might be anywhere in this monolith. After your metro ride from the centre, exit the station and look for the 15-storey Hotel Asia, which houses this establishment. It has English-speaking staff (sort of) and a HI affiliation, but reviews from readers have been mixed.

HOTEL IZMAYLOVO
(GAMMA-DELTA) Map pp246-7   Hotel
☎ 737 7187, 737 7104; www.izmailovo.ru;
Izmaylovskoe sh 71; s/d from R1440/1540;
🖳 ; Ⓜ Partizanskyaya
Built for the 1980 Olympics, this hotel has
8000 beds, apparently making it Europe's
biggest hotel. Four of its five buildings
provide budget accommodation, but
the Gamma-Delta option is the snazziest
and most service-oriented. If you need to
escape the frenetic atmosphere that surrounds Izmaylovo Market, the hotel is just a
few steps from lovely Izmaylovsky Park.

SOUTH OF THE CENTRE
HOTEL ORLYONOK Map pp246-7   Hotel
☎ 939 8888; www.orlenok.ru; ul Kosygina 15; s/d
from R5250/5850; 🖳 Ⓟ ⌗ ; Ⓜ Vorobyovy Gory
The location, not far from Moscow State
University amid the Sparrow (Vorobyovy)

Hills, allows for fantastic views of the
Moscow city skyline from some rooms.
Otherwise, the rooms are sufficiently comfortable, if not luxurious. Security is tight,
but the attached casino still attracts prostitutes and gamers. There are several authentic Korean restaurants on the ground floor
(see p138). Room prices increase during
'exhibition period', which is one week out
of every month, so try to avoid these
times.

HOTEL SPUTNIK Map pp246-7   Hotel
☎ 930 3097; www.hotelsputnik.ru; Leninsky pr 38;
s/d from R1960/2660; Ⓜ Leninsky Prospekt
This hulk of a hotel is rather Soviet-style,
but its setting south of the centre has some
appeal. It's just a short walk to Sparrow
Hills and the leafy campus of Moscow State
University. Among the many services available, the on-site Indian restaurant Darbar
(p138) is one of Moscow's best.

Excursions

To Vologda (175km) — **M8**

Rybinsk Reservoir

Volga

Kostroma

Yaroslavl — A113

Volga

Ri

Ivanov

Uglich

Rostov-Veliky

R152

Teykovo

To Valdai (135km);
Novgorod (240km);
St Petersburg (390km)

M10

Volga River

Moscow Canal

Pereslavl-Zalessky

M8

Yurev-Polsky

Suzdal

A113

To Nizhi Novgorod (200kr

M7

A111

To Lake Seliger (150km)

Tver

A112

Volga River

Zavidovo

M10

A108

Khotkovo

Sergiev Posad

Alexandrov

Vladimir

Bogolyubov

Klin

Abramtsevo

Pestovo

Chernogolovka

Petushki

Gus Khrusta

To Riga (550km)

M9

Volokolamsk

Sheremetevo Airport 1

Sheremetevo Airport 2

Istra

M9

MKAD

★ **MOSCOW**

M7

A108

Arkhangelskoe

Moscow River

Moscow River

Gagarin

Borodino

Mozhaysk

M1

Peredelkino

Gorki Leninskie

Domodedovo Airport

M5

Gzhel

Oka River

Kolomna

A125

To Smolensk (230km);
Minsk (510km)

M1

A108

Chekhov

Melikhovo

Kashira

Oka River

M3

Serpukhov

Danki

Ryazan

Prioksko-Terrasny Reserve

M2

Kaluga

Oka River

M6

M5

To Pen Sama (575k

A132

M4

A126

Tula

Yasnaya Polyana

Ryazhsk

Oka River

M6

To Tambov; Volgograd (525km)

Bryansk

M13

M3

A141

Oryol

M4

M2

To Kyiv (600km)

To Kursk (150km)

To Voronezh (300km)

0 ——— 100 km
0 ——— 60 miles

Excursions

As soon as you leave Moscow, the fast-paced modern capital fades from view, while the slowed-down, old-fashioned countryside unfolds around you. The subtly changing landscape is crossed by winding rivers and dotted with peasant villages – the classic provincial Russia immortalised by artists and writers over the centuries.

Ancient Rus grew up in the clutch of towns northeast of Moscow that is now known as the Golden Ring. In many cases the whitewashed walls of these once-fortified cities still stand. The golden spires and onion domes of monasteries still mark the horizon, evoking medieval Rus. Bells ring out from towering belfries; robed holy men scurry through church doors; historic tales recall mysterious, magical times.

Moscow's elite have long escaped the heat and hustle of city life by retreating to the surrounding regions. Old aristocrats used provincial Russia as a location for grand palaces, extensive gardens and extravagant art collections. Artists and writers also sought inspiration in the countryside, usually in less extravagant quarters. Many of these retreats, from dacha to mansion, now house museums to inspire visitors.

TELEPHONE CODE CHANGES

In late 2005, the Russian Communications Ministry announced plans to change the area codes for 19 regions across Russia, including many towns in the Golden Ring. All codes that used to start with '0' should now start with a '4' instead, although be aware that there may be teething problems with this change. Also there are rumours that entirely new codes will be introduced for some localities. The new numbers are reflected in this chapter.

Should the planned changes be not operational when you use this book, the old telephone codes are: Abramtsevo ☎ 8254, Arkhangelskoe ☎ 095, Gorki Leninskie ☎ 095, Kostroma ☎ 0942, Moscow ☎ 095, Pereslavl-Zalessky ☎ 08535, Plyos ☎ 09339, Rostov-Veliky ☎ 08536, Sergiev Posad ☎ 8254, Suzdal ☎ 09231, Uglich ☎ 08532, Vladimir ☎ 0922, Yaroslavl ☎ 0852, Yasnaya Polyana ☎ 087, Zavidovo ☎ 095.

These days, most Muscovites do not have country estates, but they still need an occasional break from the urban madness. The lovely lakes district northwest of the capital provides plenty of opportunities for swimming, sunning and soaking up the tranquillity of rural Russia.

GOLDEN RING

The Golden Ring is the circle of ancient towns northeast of Moscow – so called for its wealth of architectural and artistic riches. Some of these spots are accessible from Moscow by day trip. But, if you have a few days to spare, it's worth leaving behind the big-city bustle to immerse yourself in the age-old allure of the Golden Ring.

The most visited destination in the Golden Ring is **Sergiev Posad** (p194), for its accessibility from Moscow and for its atmosphere of history and holiness. If you're willing to spend the night, you can continue north to **Pereslavl-Zalessky** (p196) and **Rostov-Veliky** (p198), charming villages with their own rich histories.

The Golden Ring's most enchanting destination is undoubtedly **Suzdal** (p190). The

The Assumption Cathedral (p188) in Vladimir

185

GETTING BACK TO NATURE

At least one-third of all Russian city dwellers own a small country home, or dacha. Often little more than a wooden hut, these retreats offer Russians refuge from city life. Dachas don't usually have electricity or running water, but they always have a fertile spot that's far away – at least psychologically – from the city. On weekends from May to September, many cities empty as people head for the country.

The dacha's most remarkable feature is its garden, which is usually bursting with flowering fruit trees and veggie plants. Families still grow all manner of vegetables and fruit, which are sold at the market or preserved for winter. Throughout winter, city dwellers can enjoy strawberry *kompot* (canned syrupy fruit) or pickled mushrooms, and fondly recall their time in the countryside.

After playing in the dirt, the next stop is undoubtedly the *banya*. While bathhouses exist in the city, the countryside *banya* experience cannot be replicated. Crowding into the tiny, wooden hothouse; receiving a beating with fragrant *veniki* (birch branches) straight from the forest; cooling down with a dip in the pond or – more extreme – a roll in the snow...now *that's* getting back to nature.

Nothing piques hunger like the Russian *banya,* and what better way to enjoy the fruits of your labour than with a hearty meal? Dacha cuisine evokes the peasant's kitchen: tasty soups that are the highlight of Russian food; *kasha,* or porridge, which sates any appetite; and coarse, black Russian bread. These dishes often use ingredients straight from the garden, coop or pasture. Simple to prepare, rich in flavour and nourishing to body and soul, dacha fare is exemplary of how Russians return to their rural roots for replenishment.

For an authentic dacha experience, visit **Uncle Pasha's Dacha** (☎ 910 932 5546, 916 117 1527; www.russian -horse-rides.com; d with meals R750) in the tiny village of Dubrovki (near Tver). The setting on the Volga is magnificent. The accommodation is rustic, as it should be (read: with outside toilet). Meals are included but leave something to be desired; guests are welcome to use the kitchen facilities to make their own. This place is hard to reach, so be sure to contact Uncle Pasha in advance.

---

distance from Moscow is best broken by stopping in historic **Vladimir** (opposite), the capital of ancient Rus. This excellent itinerary requires two or three days to do it justice.

The towns of the **Upper Volga** (p200), Yaroslavl and Kostroma, are obligatory destinations if you take the time to make a more complete circle around the ring. In its entirety, the Golden Ring could fill as much as a week, allowing time for some detours along the way.

COUNTRY ESTATES

The quintessential aristocratic getaway is Prince Nikolai Yusupov's palatial estate at **Arkhangelskoe** (p205). On a more modest scale, many artists, writers and musicians sought inspiration in the countryside around Moscow: Count Leo Tolstoy, at **Yasnaya Polyana** (p208); Pyotr Tchaikovsky, in **Klin**; and Anton Chekhov in **Melikhovo** (p207); not to mention the countless painters and sculptors that retreated to the artists' colony at **Abramtsevo** (p193). Even Lenin maintained a country estate on the outskirts of Moscow, at **Gorki Leninskie** (p206). All of these properties are now museums, accessible from Moscow by day trip.

HISTORIC SITES

The medieval towns of the Golden Ring and the country estates of the prerevolutionary elite are your main choices for historic sites around Moscow. If you easily overload on ancient churches and opulent art collections, however, you may prefer an excursion to the **Borodino Battlefield** (p205), the site of turning-point battles in the War of 1812 as well as WWII. Literary buffs will also appreciate this destination, which features prominently in *War & Peace*.

NATURAL ATTRACTIONS

For outdoor activities for all seasons – from swimming to skiing – you can't beat the lakes district northwest of Moscow. Resorts such as **Zavidovo** (p203) and **Istra** (p203) are beautifully located and easily reached from Moscow. You can go for a day, but will want to stay longer. Providing a unique variation on the nature theme, the **Priyosko-Terrasny Nature Reserve** (p207) will delight animal-lovers of all ages. For a truly Russian experience, see the boxed text, above.

VLADIMIR ВЛАДИМИР

☎ 4922 / pop 360,000

High up the slope from the Klyazma River sits the solemnly majestic Assumption Cathedral, built to announce Vladimir's claim as capital of Rus. These days, Vladimir – 178km east of Moscow – feels more like a modern, provincial town than an ancient capital. Nonetheless, the grandeur of medieval Vladimir shines through the commotion of this busy industrial town.

The exquisite examples of Russia's most formative architecture, along with some entertaining museums, make Vladimir one of the jewels in the Golden Ring.

In the early 12th century, Prince Vladimir Monomakh founded the fortress city of Vladimir as the eastern outpost of his domain. He entrusted these lands to his youngest son, Yury Dolgoruky; when Yury became Grand Prince, the region emerged as the political centre of the northern Slavs. In 1157 Yury's son, Andrei Bogolyubsky moved the throne from Kyiv to the city-state of Vladimir. Andrei and his brother Vsevolod III (1176–1212) brought builders and artists from as far away as Western Europe to give Vladimir a Kyiv-like splendour.

The city recovered from devastating attacks by nomadic raiders in 1238 and 1293. But its realm disintegrated into smaller principalities, with Moscow (then called Muscovy) increasingly dominant. The head of the Russian Church resided in Vladimir from 1300 to 1326, but then moved to Moscow. Worldly power finally shifted to Moscow around this time too. Even so, the rulers remained nominally Grand Princes of Vladimir until the 15th century.

Vladimir's main street is Bolshaya Moskovskaya ulitsa, although it sometimes goes by its former name, ulitsa III Internatsionala. To make matters more confusing, other segments of the street go by different names, including simply Moskovskaya ulitsa, which is just west of the Golden Gate. Bolshaya Moskovskaya ulitsa is where you'll find the city's main attractions such as the Golden Gate and the Cathedrals of the Assumption and St Dmitry.

TRANSPORT

The daily express train between Moscow's Kursky vokzal (Kursk station; R208, 2½ hours) and Nizhny Novgorod (R290, 2½ hours) stops in Vladimir, as do many slower trains. Privately run buses (R100, three hours) also leave regularly from Kursky vokzal and Kazansky vokzal (Kazan station) to Vladimir. They do not run on a timetable, but leave as they fill up.

There are also scheduled buses to/from Moscow's Shchyolkovsky bus station (Shchyolkovsky avtovokzal), beside the Shchyolkovskaya metro station to Kostroma (R150, five hours, three daily), Yaroslavl (R160, 5½ hours, twice daily), and Suzdal (R20, one hour, half-hourly). There are also six buses a day to Nizhny Novgorod (five hours).

Excursions

VLADIMIR

VLADIMIR

SIGHTS & INFORMATION
Assumption Cathedral
  Успенский собор 1 C1
Cathedral of St Dmitry
  Дмитриевский собор.........................2 C1
Chambers Палаты...............................3 C1
Crystal, Lacquer Miniatures & Embroidery
  Exhibition Выставка хрусталя,
  лаковой миниатюры и вышивки4 A1

Golden Gate Золотые ворота........5 A1
History Museum
  Исторический Музей 6 C1
Internet@Salon Интернет-Салон.7 B1
Nativity Monastery
  Рождественский Монастырь 8 C1
Old City Wall
  Старая стена города...................9 B1
Old Vladimir Exhibition
  Выставка Старый Владимир10 B1
Post & Telephone Office Почтамт и
  переговорный пункт...............11 B1
St George Church
  Георгиевская Церковь 12 B1
Sberbank Сбербанк 13 C1

EATING
Old Town Старый Город...............14 C1

SLEEPING
Golden Gate Hotel Гостиница
  У Золотых Ворот 15 B1
Hotel Vladimir
  Гостиница Владимир.............16 D1

TRANSPORT
Bus Station Автовокзал................17 D1

The train and bus stations are on Vokzalnaya ulitsa at the bottom of the slope and 500m east of the cathedrals.

Begun in 1158, the **Assumption Cathedral** is a white-stone version of Kyiv's brick Byzantine churches. Its simple but majestic form is adorned with fine carving, innovative for the time. The cathedral was extended on all sides after a fire in the 1180s, when it gained the four outer domes.

The cathedral used to house the *Vladimir Icon of the Mother of God,* brought from Kyiv by Andrei Bogolyubsky. A national protector bestowing supreme status to its city of residence, the icon was moved to Moscow in 1390 and is now kept in the Tretyakov Gallery.

Inside the working church, a few restored 12th-century murals of peacocks and prophets holding scrolls can be deciphered about halfway up the inner wall of the outer north aisle; this was originally an outside wall. The real treasures are the *Last Judgment* frescoes by Andrei Rublyov and Daniil Chyorny, painted in 1408 in the central nave and inner south aisle, under the choir gallery towards the west end.

The church also contains the original coffin of Alexander Nevsky of Novgorod, the 13th-century military leader who was also Prince of Vladimir. He was buried in the former **Nativity Monastery** northeast of here, but his remains were moved to St Petersburg in 1724 when Peter the Great allotted him Russian hero status. Adjoining the cathedral on the northern side are an 1810 bell tower and the 1862 St George's Chapel.

A quick stroll to the east of the Assumption Cathedral is the smaller **Cathedral of St Dmitry** (1193–97), where the art of Vladimir-Suzdal stone carving reached its pinnacle. The church is permanently closed, but the attraction is its exterior walls, covered in an amazing profusion of images.

The top centre of the north, south and west walls all show King David bewitching the birds and beasts with music. The Kyivan prince Vsevolod III, who had this church built as part of his palace, appears at the top left of the north wall, with a baby son on his knee and other sons kneeling on each side. Above the right-hand window of the south wall, Alexander the Great ascends into heaven, a symbol of princely might; on the west wall are the labours of Hercules.

The grand building between the cathedrals is known as the **Chambers**, containing a children's museum, art gallery and historical exhibit. The former is a welcome diversion for the little ones, who may well be suffering from old-church syndrome on this trip. The art gallery features art since the 18th century, with wonderful depictions of the Golden Ring towns.

Across the small street, the **History Museum** displays many remains and reproductions of the ornamentation from the Assumption and St Dmitry cathedrals.

Vladimir's **Golden Gate** – part defensive tower, part triumphal arch – was modelled on the very similar structure in Kyiv. Originally built by Andrei Bogolyubsky to guard the main western entrance to his city, it was later restored under Catherine the Great. Now you can climb the narrow stone staircase to check out the military museum inside. It is a small exhibit, the centrepiece of which is a diorama of old Vladimir being ravaged by nomadic raiders. Across the street to the south you can see a remnant of the **old wall** that protected the city.

The red-brick building opposite was built in 1913 to house the Old Believers' Trinity Church. Now it is a **Crystal, Lacquer Miniatures & Embroidery Exhibition**, which features the crafts of Gus-Khrustalny and other nearby towns.

The red-brick water tower atop the old ramparts houses the **Old Vladimir Exhibition**, a nostalgic collection of old photos, advertisements and maps, including a photo of a very distinguished couple taking a ride in Vladimir's first automobile in 1896. The highlight is the view from the top. The nearby **St George Church** houses the Vladimir Theatre of Choral Music, where performances are often held on summer weekends.

Monastery of the Deposition of the Holy Robe (p192) in Suzdal

Sights & Information

Assumption Cathedral (☎ 325 201; Sobornaya pl; admission R100; ⊙ 1.30-4.30pm Tue-Sun)

Chambers (☎ 323 320; Bolshaya Moskovskaya 58; admission R150; ⊙ 10am-5pm Tue-Sun) Contains a children's museum, art gallery and exhibits.

Crystal, Lacquer Miniatures & Embroidery Exhibition (☎ 324 872; Moskovskaya ul 2; admission R50; ⊙ 10am-4pm Wed-Mon)

History Museum (☎ 322 284; Bolshaya Moskovskaya ul 64; admission R50; ⊙ 10am-4pm Tue-Sun)

Internet@Salon (cnr uls Gagarina & Bolshaya Moskovskaya; per hr R30; ⊙ 9am-9pm)

Military Museum (☎ 322 559; Golden Gate; admission R50; ⊙ 10am-4pm Fri-Wed)

Old Vladimir Exhibition (☎ 325 451; Kozlov val; admission R40; ⊙ 10am-4pm Tue-Sun)

Post & Telephone Office (ul Podbelskogo; ⊙ 8am-8pm Mon-Fri)

St George Church (Georgievskaya tserkov; ul Georgievskaya 2A)

Sberbank (Bolshaya Moskovskaya ul 27; ⊙ 9am-7pm Mon-Fri, 9am-5pm Sat) Has exchange facilities and ATM.

Sleeping & Eating

Golden Gate Hotel (☎ 323 116; www.golden-gate .ru; Bolshaya Moskovskaya ul 17; s/d with breakfast R1800/2300; ⊙ restaurant noon-midnight; meals R200-400) There are 14 spacious rooms, with large windows overlooking the activity on the main street – or a central courtyard if you prefer. The attached restaurant is among the town's best, and popular with tour groups.

Hotel Vladimir (☎ 323 042; tour@gtk.elcom.ru; Bolshaya Moskovskaya ul 74; s/d with bathroom & breakfast from R950/1300, r with shared bathroom per person from R350; P) Has acceptable rooms at a range of prices, including upgraded singles/doubles for R1150/1600. It's a friendly place with lots of services, including a restaurant and bar.

Old Town (☎ 325 101; Bolshaya Moskovskaya ul 41; meals R300-400; ⊙ 11am-2am) It's one of two side-by-side restaurants on the main drag. Choose from the cosy bar, the elegant dining room or – if weather is fine – the lovely terrace with views of the Cathedral of St Dmitry.

DETOUR: BOGOLYUBOVO (БОГОЛЮБОВО)

According to legend, when Andrei Bogolyubsky was returning north from Kyiv in the late 1150s, his horses stopped where Bogolyubovo now stands, 11km east of Vladimir. Apparently they wouldn't go another step, so Andrei decided to establish his capital in Vladimir, and not his father's old base of Suzdal.

Whatever the reasoning, between 1158 and 1165, Andrei built a stone-fortified palace at this strategic spot near the meeting of the Nerl and Klyazma Rivers. A tower and arch from Andrei Bogolyubsky's palace survive amid a dilapidated but reopened 18th-century monastery (by the Vladimir–Nizhny Novgorod road in the middle of Bogolyubovo). The dominant buildings today are the monastery's 1841 **bell tower** beside the road, and its 1866 **Assumption Cathedral**. Just east of the cathedral is an arch and tower, on the stairs of which – according to a chronicle – the much-disliked Andrei was assassinated by hostile *boyars* (nobles). The arch abuts the 18th-century **Church of the Virgin's Nativity**.

Nearby, Andrei Bogolyubsky built what is considered to be the most perfect of all old Russian buildings, the **Church of the Intercession on the Nerl**. To reach this famous little church, go 200m towards Vladimir from the monastery-palace complex and turn on to ulitsa Frunze, which winds downhill and under a railway bridge. Take the path to the left that runs along the side of a small wood. The church, built in 1165, appears across the meadows, about 1.3km from the bridge. This walk can be precarious in spring, when this area is often flooded from the rising river.

The church's beauty lies in its simple but perfect proportions, a brilliantly chosen waterside site (floods aside) and sparing use of delicate carving. If it looks a mite top-heavy, it's because the original helmet dome was replaced by a cushion dome in 1803.

Legend has it that Andrei had the church built in memory of his favourite son, Izyaslav, who was killed in battle against the Bulgars. As with the Cathedral of St Dmitry in Vladimir, King David sits at the top of three façades, the birds and beasts entranced by his music. The interior has more carving, including 20 pairs of lions. If the church is closed, try asking at the house behind.

The buildings in the village have been converted to museums.

To get to Bogolyubovo, take trolley bus 1 east from Vladimir and get off at Khimzavod. Walk along the main road for 100m to the bus stop, where you can catch a *marshrutka* (fixed-rate minibus) to Bogolyubovo (second stop). Drivers from central Vladimir should head straight out east along the main road. From Suzdal, turn left when you hit Vladimir's northern bypass and continue for 5km.

SUZDAL СУЗДАЛЬ

☎ 49231 / pop 12,000

The winding Kamenka River, flower-drenched meadows and dome-spotted skyline make this medieval capital the perfect fairytale setting. Suzdal, 35km north of Vladimir, has earned a federally protected status, which has limited development in the area. As a result, its main features are an abundance of ancient architectural gems and a decidedly rural atmosphere. Judging from the spires and cupolas, Suzdal may have as many churches as people.

Although the town's history dates to 1024, Yury Dolgoruky made Suzdal the capital of the Rostov-Suzdal principality in the first half of the 12th century. Andrei Bogolyubsky

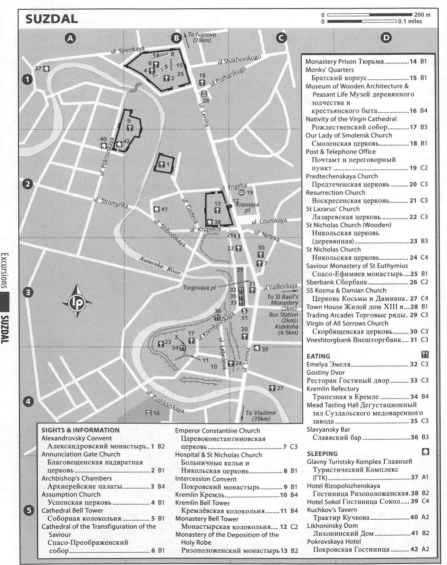

SUZDAL

Monastery Prison Тюрьма	14 B1
Monks' Quarters	
Братский корпус	15 B1
Museum of Wooden Architecture &	
Peasant Life Музей деревянного	
зодчества и	
крестьянского быта	16 B4
Nativity of the Virgin Cathedral	
Рождественский собор	17 B3
Our Lady of Smolensk Church	
Смоленская церковь	18 B1
Post & Telephone Office	
Почтамт и переговорный	
пункт	19 C2
Predtechenskaya Church	
Предтеченская церковь	20 C3
Resurrection Church	
Воскресенская церковь	21 C3
St Lazarus' Church	
Лазаревская церковь	22 C3
St Nicholas Church (Wooden)	
Никольская церковь	
(деревянная)	23 B3
St Nicholas Church	
Никольская церковь	24 C4
Saviour Monastery of St Euthymius	
Спасо-Ефимиев монастырь	25 B1
Sberbank Сбербанк	26 C2
SS Kosma & Damian Church	
Церковь Косьмы и Дамиана	27 C4
Town House Жилой дом XIII в	28 B1
Trading Arcades Торговые ряды	29 C3
Virgin of All Sorrows Church	
Скорбященская церковь	30 C3
Vneshtorgbank Внешторгбанк	31 C3

EATING	🍴
Emelya Эмеля	32 C3
Gostiny Dvor	
Ресторан Гостиный двор	33 C3
Kremlin Refectory	
Трапезная в Кремле	34 B4
Mead Tasting Hall Дегустационный	
зал Суздальского медоваренного	
завода	35 C3
Slavyansky Bar	
Славянский бар	36 B3

SLEEPING	🛏
Glavny Turistsky Komplex Главный	
Туристический Комплекс	
(ГТК)	37 A1
Hotel Rizopolozhenskaya	
Гостиница Ризоположенская	38 B2
Hotel Sokol Гостиница Сокол	39 C4
Kuchkov's Tavern	
Трактир Кучкова	40 A2
Likhoninsky Dom	
Лихонинский Дом	41 B2
Pokrovskaya Hotel	
Покровская Гостиница	42 A2

SIGHTS & INFORMATION
Alexandrovsky Convent
Александровский монастырь .. 1 B2
Annunciation Gate Church
Благовещенская надвратная
церковь 2 B1
Archbishop's Chambers
Архиерейские палаты 3 B4
Assumption Church
Успенская церковь 4 B1
Cathedral Bell Tower
Соборная колокольня 5 B1
Cathedral of the Transfiguration of the
Saviour
Спасо-Преображенский
собор 6 B1

Emperor Constantine Church
Царевоконстантиновская
церковь 7 C3
Hospital & St Nicholas Church
Больничные кельи и
Никольская церковь 8 B1
Intercession Convent
Покровский монастырь 9 B1
Kremlin Кремль 10 B4
Kremlin Bell Tower
Кремлёвская колокольня 11 B4
Monastery Bell Tower
Монастырская колокольня 12 C2
Monastery of the Deposition of the
Holy Robe
Ризоположенский монастырь 13 B2

190

moved the capital to Vladimir in 1157, from whence the principality was known as Vladimir-Suzdal. Set in a fertile wheat-growing area, Suzdal remained a trade centre even after the Mongol-led invasions. Eventually, it united with Nizhny Novgorod until both were annexed by Moscow in 1392.

Under Muscovite rule, Suzdal became a wealthy monastic centre, with incredible development projects funded by Vasily III and Ivan IV (the Terrible) in the 16th century. In the late 17th and 18th centuries, wealthy merchants paid for 30 charming churches, which still adorn the town.

The main street, ulitsa Lenina, runs from north to south through Suzdal. The bus station is 2km east along ulitsa Vasilevskaya.

The 1.4km-long earth rampart of Suzdal's **kremlin**, founded in the 11th century, today encloses a few streets of houses and a handful of churches, as well as the main cathedral group on Kremlyovskaya ulitsa. The **Nativity of the Virgin Cathedral**, its blue domes spangled with gold, was founded in the 1220s, but only its richly carved lower section is original white stone, the rest being 16th-century brick. The inside is sumptuous with 13th- and 17th-century frescoes and 13th-century damascene (gold on copper) west and south doors. Unfortunately, the cathedral was under restoration when we visited and has been closed indefinitely.

The **Archbishop's Chambers** houses the Suzdal History Exhibition. The exhibition includes the original 13th-century door from the cathedral, photos of its interior and a visit to the 18th-century Cross Hall (Krestovaya palata), which was used for receptions. The tent-roofed 1635 **bell tower** on the east side of the yard contains additional exhibits.

Just west of this group stands the 1766 wooden **St Nicholas Church**, brought from Glatovo village near Yuriev-Polsky. There's another **St Nicholas Church**, one of Suzdal's own fine small 18th-century structures, just east of the cathedral group.

The open-air **Museum of Wooden Architecture & Peasant Life**, illustrating old peasant life in this region of Russia, is a short walk across the river south of the kremlin. Besides log houses, windmills, a barn and lots of tools and handicrafts, its highlights are the 1756 Transfiguration Church (Preobrazhenskaya tserkov) and the simpler 1776 Resurrection Church (Voskresenskaya tserkov).

At the opposite end of town, the **Saviour Monastery of St Euthymius** was founded in the 14th century to protect the town's northern entrance. Suzdal's biggest monastery grew mighty in the 16th and 17th centuries after Vasily III, Ivan the Terrible and the noble Pozharsky family funded impressive new stone buildings and big land and property acquisitions. It was girded with its great brick walls and towers in the 17th century. Inside, the **Annunciation Gate-Church** houses an interesting exhibit on Dmitry Pozharsky (1578–1642), leader of the Russian army that drove the Polish invaders from Moscow in 1612.

A tall 16th- to 17th-century **bell tower** stands before the seven-domed **Cathedral of the Transfiguration of the Saviour**. Every 90 minutes from 10.30am to 4.30pm, a short concert of chimes is given on the tower's bells. The cathedral was built in the 1590s in 12th- to 13th-century Vladimir-Suzdal style. Inside, restoration has uncovered some bright 1689 frescoes by the school of Gury Nikitin from Kostroma. On summer weekends, a short but heavenly live a cappella concert takes place once an hour. The **tomb** of Prince Dmitry Pozharsky is by the cathedral's east wall.

The 1525 **Assumption Church** facing the bell tower adjoins the old Father Superior's chambers, which houses a display of Russian icons. The **monks' quarters** across the compound contain a museum of artistic history.

At the north end of the complex is the old monastery **prison**, set up in 1764 for religious dissidents. It now houses a fascinating exhibit on the monastery's military history and

TRANSPORT

Buses run every 30 minutes to/from Vladimir (R20, one hour). Otherwise, most of the buses to Suzdal originate elsewhere. Buses from Vladimir go to Yaroslavl (R164, five hours, twice daily) and Kostroma (R142, 4½ hours, daily), but it is often easier to go to Ivanovo (R80, two hours, four daily) and change there. One daily bus goes directly to/from Moscow's Shchyolkovsky bus station (R145, 4½ hours).

Some long-distance buses continue past Suzdal's bus station, located on the east of town, into the centre; otherwise, a *marshrutka* will take you there.

Excursions

SUZDAL

prison life, including displays of some of the better-known prisoners who stayed here. The combined **hospital** and **St Nicholas Church** (1669) contains a rich museum of 12th- to 20th-century Russian applied art, much of it from Suzdal itself.

Across ulitsa Lenina from the southeastern corner of the monastery is the **Our Lady of Smolensk Church** (built 1696–1707), along with Suzdal's only surviving early-18th-century **townhouse**.

Southwest of the monastery, the **Intercession Convent** is once again home to a small community of nuns, after being closed during the Soviet period. The Intercession Cathedral (built 1510–18), with its three domes, holds regular services in the centre. Founded in 1364, the convent was originally a place of exile for the unwanted wives of tsars.

Among them was Solomonia Saburova, first wife of Vasily III, who was sent here in the 1520s because of her supposed infertility. The story goes that she finally became pregnant too late to avoid being divorced. A baby boy was born in Suzdal. Fearing he would be seen as a dangerous rival to any sons produced by Vasily's new wife, Solomonia secretly had him adopted, pretended he had died and staged a mock burial. This was probably just as well for the boy since the new bride, Yelena, did indeed produce a son – Ivan the Terrible.

The legend received dramatic corroboration in 1934 when researchers opened a small 16th-century tomb beside Solomonia's, in the crypt underneath the Intercession Cathedral. They found a silk-and-pearl shirt stuffed with rags – and no bones. The crypt is closed to visitors.

The little white **Alexandrovsky Convent** at the top of the river embankment stands out for its simple, quiet beauty. Reputedly founded in 1240 by Alexander Nevsky for noble women whose menfolk had been killed by nomadic raiders, its present Ascension Church (Voznesenskaya tserkov) and bell tower date from 1695.

Back on ulitsa Lenina, the **Monastery of the Deposition of the Holy Robe** was founded in 1207 but the existing buildings date from the 16th to 19th centuries. The monastery is now pretty dilapidated. Still, its two pyramidal entrance turrets (1688) on the south gate are exquisite. Suzdal's tallest structure, a 72m **bell tower** (built 1813–19), rises from the east wall. The central 16th-century Deposition Cathedral (Rizopolozhensky sobor) is reminiscent of the Moscow Kremlin's Archangel Cathedral with its three helmet domes.

Suzdal's Torgovaya ploshchad (Trade Sq) is dominated by the pillared Trading Arcades (built 1806–11) along its western side. Although the four churches in the immediate vicinity are closed, the five-domed 1707 **Emperor Constantine Church** in the square's northeastern corner is a working church with an ornate interior. Next to it is the smaller 1787 **Virgin of All Sorrows Church**.

Almost every corner in Suzdal has its own little church with its own charm. Some other gems include the simple **Resurrection Church** dating from 1719, on Torgovaya ploshchad; the shabby but graceful **Predtechenskaya Church**, built in 1720 on ulitsa Lenina; and the slender, multicoloured tower of **St Lazarus' Church**, from 1667, on Staraya ulitsa. The **SS Kosma & Damian Church** (1725) is placed picturesquely on a bend in the river east of ulitsa Lenina. Suzdal's fifth monastery is the 17th-century **St Basil's** (Vasilevsky monastyr) on the Kideksha road. No doubt you will find your own favourite.

Modern frescoe in the Trinity Monastery of St Sergius (p195), Sergiev Posad

Sights & Information

Intercession Convent (☎ 20 889; ul Pokrovskaya; admission free; ⏰ 9.30am-4.30pm Thu-Mon)

Museum of Wooden Architecture & Peasant Life (ul Pushkarskaya; admission R50; ⏰ 9.30am-3.30pm Wed-Mon May-Oct)

Post & Telephone Office (Krasnaya pl; ⏰ 8am-8pm) Open 24 hours for phone calls.

Saviour Monastery of St Euthymius (☎ 20 746; ul Lenina; admission to exhibits R40-50 each or all-inclusive R280; ⏰ 10am-6pm Tue-Sun)

Sberbank (ul Lenina; ⏰ 8am-4.30pm Mon-Fri) Foreign-exchange office.

Suzdal History Exhibition (☎ 21 624; Archbishop's Chambers, Nativity of the Virgin Cathedral; admission R30; ⏰ 10am-5pm Wed-Mon)

Vneshtorgbank (Kremlyovskaya ul; ⏰ 10am-5pm Tue-Fri, 10am-3.30pm Sat-Sun) Centrally located bank with ATM.

Eating

Emelya (☎ 21 011; ul Lenina 84; meals R200-300; ⏰ 11am-midnight) Enjoy the lovely vista from the outside tables, especially at sunset.

Gostinny Dvor (☎ 21 778; trading arcades; meals R200-300; ⏰ 11am-midnight) A popular spot among locals to drink and socialise.

Kremlin Refectory (☎ 21 763; kremlin; meals R300-500; ⏰ 11am-11pm) An atmospheric location inside the Archbishop's Chambers. This place has been serving tasty, filling Russian favourites for 300 years.

Mead Tasting Hall (☎ 20 803; reading arcades; tasting menu R120-150; ⏰ 10am-5pm Mon-Fri, 10am-8pm Sat & Sun) Hidden in the back of the trading arcades, this hall is done up like a church interior – frescoes, arched ceilings and stained-glass windows. The menu features different varieties of *medovukha,* a mildly alcoholic honey ale that was consumed by the princes of old.

Slavyansky Bar (☎ 20 062; Kremlyovskaya ul 6; meals R100-200; ⏰ 10am-8pm) A pleasant and convenient stop for a quick refresher.

Sleeping

Hotel Rizopolozheskaya (☎ 24 314; ul Lenina; s/d with breakfast R620/1000) Suzdal's cheapest place to stay, housed in the decrepit Monastery of the Deposition.

Hotel Sokol (Hotel Falcon; ☎ 20 088; www.hotel-sokol .ru; Torgovaya pl 2A; s/d with breakfast from R1300/2200) This is an attractive new hotel ideally located opposite the trading arcades. Its 40 rooms are simply decorated and fully equipped with new wooden furniture and modern bathrooms. The elegant, bi-level restaurant is also recommended. Prices decrease significantly between October and April.

Hotel Suzdal (☎ 21 530; www.suzdaltour.ru; s/d with breakfast from R1580/1800; 🖥 🛁 🐕) One of three hotels in the 'Hotel Tourist Centre' (Gostinichny Turistsky Kompleks), this place is low on charm but high on facilities: the complex includes a fitness centre, a bowling alley, several restaurants, and a cheaper 'motel' (s/d R1120/1340).

Kuchkov's Tavern (☎ 20 252; fax 21 507; ul Pokrovskaya 35; s/d with breakfast R1650/2000) On a quiet street opposite the Intercession Convent, this guesthouse has a 'New Russian' ambience that doesn't fit in with old-fashioned Suzdal, but it's not a bad option. Its 17 rooms are comfortable but overdecorated; it has a nice *banya* and an excellent restaurant.

Likhoninsky Dom (☎ 21 901; aksenova-museum@rnt .vladimir.ru; ul Slobodskaya 34; s/d with breakfast R1500/1800) Suzdal's most charming place to stay. The 17th-century merchant's house has five charming rooms and a pretty garden. This place feels like home, thanks to the kindly ladies that run it.

Pokrovskaya Hotel (☎ 20 908; www.suzdaltour.ru; s/d with breakfast R1820/2400) Offers cosy wooden cabins on the grounds of the Intercession Convent. The old-fashioned wooden furniture, rag rugs and fluffy quilts provide a welcoming atmosphere. A restaurant is also expected to open in the convent refectory.

ABRAMTSEVO АБРАМЦЕВО

☎ 254 from Moscow, ☎ 49654 from elsewhere

Artists' colony and country estate, Abramtsevo was a font of artistic inspiration for the renaissance of traditional Russian painting, sculpture and architecture.

In 1870 Savva Mamontov – railway tycoon and patron of the arts – bought this lovely estate 45km north of Moscow. Here, he hosted a whole slew of painters, who sought inspiration in the gardens and forests: the much-loved Ilya Repin (see p31); landscape artist Isaak Levitan; portraitist Valentin Serov; and the quite un-Slavonic painter and ceramicist Mikhail Vrubel. Other artists came to dabble at the woodworking and ceramics workshop, and musicians (including Fyodor Shalyapin, who made his debut here) performed in the private opera.

The **Abramtsevo Estate Museum-Preserve** (☎ 32 470; admission R100; ⏰ 10am-5pm Wed-Sun) is a delightful retreat from Moscow or addition to a trip to Sergiev Posad (see p194). Apart from the highlights below, arts and crafts exhibits occupy the other buildings on the grounds, which cost extra to enter.

Several rooms of the **main house** have been preserved intact, complete with artworks by various resident artists. The main attraction is the dining room, featuring Repin's portraits of the patron and his wife, and Serov's luminous *Girl with Peaches*. A striking majolica bench by Vrubel is in the garden.

The prettiest building in the grounds is the **Saviour Church 'Not Made by Hand'** (Tserkov Spasa Nerukotvorny). The structure epitomises Mamontov's intentions: it's a carefully researched homage by half a dozen artists to 14th-century Novgorod architecture. The iconostasis is by Repin and Vasily Polenov. The tiled stove in the corner, still working, is exquisite.

The Slavophile painter Viktor Vasnetsov conjured up the fairy tale of Baba Yaga the witch, with his rendition of her **Hut on Chicken Legs**.

TRANSPORT

Suburban trains run every half hour from Moscow's Yaroslavsky vokzal (Yaroslavl station; 1½ hours, R50). Most – but not all – trains to Sergiev Posad or Alexandrov stop at Abramtsevo. There are regular buses between Abramtsevo and Sergiev Posad (R20, 20 minutes).

By car, turn west off the M8 Moscow–Yaroslavl highway just north of the 61km post (signs to Khotkovo and Abramtsevo mark the turn-off) and continue over the train tracks.

SERGIEV POSAD СЕРГИЕВ ПОСАД

☎ 254 from Moscow, ☎ 49654 from elsewhere / pop 100,000

According to old Russian wisdom, 'there is no settlement without a just man; there is no town without a saint.' And so the town of Sergiev Posad is a tribute to St Sergius of Radonezh, founder of the local Trinity Monastery and patron saint of all of Russia. The monastery – today among the most important and active in Russia – exudes Orthodoxy. Bearded priests bustle about; babushkas fill bottles of holy water; and crowds of believers light candles to St Sergius, Keeper of Russia. This mystical place is a window into the age-old belief system that has provided Russia with centuries of spiritual sustenance.

Often called by its Soviet name Zagorsk, Sergiev Posad is 60km from the edge of Moscow on the Yaroslavl road. It's an easy day trip from Moscow – a rewarding option for travellers who don't have time to venture further around the Golden Ring.

St Sergius of Radonezh began his calling as a hermit monk in the forest wilderness. In 1340 he founded a monastery at Sergiev Posad, which soon became the spiritual centre of Russian Orthodoxy. Prince Dmitry Donskoy's victory in battle against the Mongols in 1380 was credited to the blessing of Sergius. Soon after his death at the age of 78, Sergius was named the patron saint of all of Russia. Since the 14th century, pilgrims have been journeying to this place to pay homage to him.

Although the Bolsheviks closed the monastery, it was reopened after WWII as a museum, residence of the patriarch and working monastery. The patriarch and also the Church's administrative centre moved to the Danilovsky Monastery (see p98) in Moscow in 1988, but the Trinity Monastery of St Sergius remains one of the most important spiritual sites in Russia. Its concentrated artistry and its unique role in the interrelated histories of the Russian Church and State make it is well worth a visit.

TRANSPORT

The fastest transport option is the daily express train from Moscow's Yaroslavsky vokzal (Yaroslavl station) to Rostov-Veliky (one hour from Moscow). Suburban trains also run every half-hour (R55, 1½ hours); take any train bound for Sergiev Posad or Alexandrov. To travel onwards to Rostov-Veliky (3½ hours) or Yaroslavl (five hours), you may have to change at Alexandrov.

Bus services to Sergiev Posad from Moscow's VDNKh metro station depart every 30 minutes from 8.30am to 7.30pm (R50, 70 minutes).

Three daily buses start at Sergiev Posad and run to Pereslavl-Zalessky (1½ hours). Nine daily northbound buses stop here in transit to Yaroslavl, Kostroma or Rybinsk; all these will take you to Pereslavl-Zalessky, Rostov-Veliky or Yaroslavl if you can get a ticket.

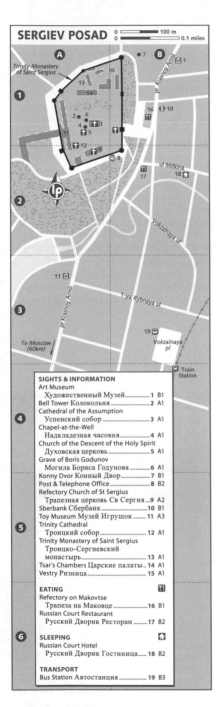

SERGIEV POSAD

0   100 m
0   0.1 miles

Trinity Monastery
of Saint Sergius

To Moscow
(60km)

Vokzalnaya ul

ul Mitkina

1-ya Rybnaya ul

Pr Krasnoy Armii

Vokzalnaya
pl

Train
Station

SIGHTS & INFORMATION
Art Museum
  Художественный Музей...............1 B1
Bell Tower Колокольня 2 A1
Cathedral of the Assumption
  Успенский собор..............................3 A1
Chapel-at-the-Well
  Надкладезная часовня...................4 A1
Church of the Descent of the Holy Spirit
  Духовская церковь..........................5 A1
Grave of Boris Godunov
  Могила Бориса Годунова...............6 A1
Konny Dvor Конный Двор 7 B1
Post & Telephone Office.....................8 B2
Refectory Church of St Sergius
  Трапезная церковь Св Сергия ...9 A2
Sberbank Сбербанк..........................10 B1
Toy Museum Музей Игрушек 11 A3
Trinity Cathedral
  Троицкий собор.............................12 A1
Trinity Monastery of Saint Sergius
  Троицко-Сергиевский
  монастырь.....................................13 A1
Tsar's Chambers Царские палаты..14 A1
Vestry Ризница..................................15 A1

EATING
Refectory on Makovtse
  Трапеза на Маковце.....................16 B1
Russian Court Restaurant
  Русский Дворик Ресторан 17 B2

SLEEPING
Russian Court Hotel
  Русский Дворик Гостиница..........18 B2

TRANSPORT
Bus Station Автостанция 19 B3

Prospekt Krasnoy Armii is the main street, running north-south through the town centre. The train and bus stations are on opposite corners of a wide square to the east of prospekt Krasnoy Armii. The monastery is about 400m north of here.

The **Trinity Monastery of St Sergius** is an active religious centre with a visible population of monks in residence; visitors should refrain from photographing them. Female visitors should wear headscarves, and men are required to remove hats in the churches.

Built in the 1420s, the squat, dark **Trinity Cathedral** is the heart of the Trinity Monastery. The tomb of St Sergius stands in the southeastern corner, where a memorial service for St Sergius goes on all day, every day. The icon-festooned interior, lit by oil lamps, is largely the work of the great medieval painter Andrei Rublyov and his students.

The star-spangled **Cathedral of the Assumption** was modelled on the cathedral of the same name in the Moscow Kremlin. It was finished in 1585 with money left by Ivan the Terrible in a fit of remorse for killing his son. It is closed to the general public but included as a part of guided tours. Outside the west door is the **grave of Boris Godunov**, the skilled 'prime minister' whose tsar-like rule led to the Time of Troubles in the early 17th century.

Nearby, the resplendent **Chapel-at-the-Well** was built over a spring that is said to have appeared during the Polish siege. The five-tier baroque **bell tower** took 30 years to build in the 18th century, and once had 42 bells, the largest of which weighed 65 tonnes.

The **Vestry**, behind the Trinity Cathedral, displays the monastery's extraordinarily rich treasury, bulging with 600 years of donations by the rich and powerful – tapestries, jewel-encrusted vestments, solid-gold chalices and more.

The huge block with the 'wallpaper' paint job is the **Refectory Church of St Sergius**, so called because it was once a dining hall for pilgrims. Now it's the Assumption Cathedral's winter counterpart, with morning services in cold weather. It's closed apart for services, except for guided tours. The green building next door is the metropolitan's residence.

The miniature imitation of the Trinity Church is the 15th-century **Church of the Descent of the Holy Spirit**. It's used only on special occasions. It contains, among other things, the grave of the first Bishop of Alaska.

Several other museums around town showcase the monastery's rich artistic traditions. See local artists' works in the two exhibition halls of the **Art Museum**, while toys from throughout history and around the world are on display at the **Toy Museum**. The so-called **Konny Dvor** exhibits the ethnological and archaeological history of Sergiev Posad.

Sights & Information

Art Museum (☎ 45 356; pr Krasnoy Armii 144; ☽ 10am-5pm Tue-Sun)

Konny Dvor (Horse Yard; ☎ 45 356; ul Udarnoy Armii; ☽ 10am-5pm Wed-Sun)

Post & Telephone Office (pr Krasnoy Armii 127A) Find it just outside the southeastern wall of the monastery.

Sberbank (pr Krasnoy Armii; ☽ 9am-4pm Mon-Fri) Exchange facilities available, but no ATM.

Toy Museum (☎ 44 101; pr Krasnoy Armii 123; ☽ 11am-5pm Tue-Sat)

Trinity Monastery of St Sergius (Troitse-Sergieva Lavra; ☎ 45 350; admission free, guided tour R600, photos R150; ☽ 10am-6pm)

Vestry (Trinity Monastery of St Sergius; admission R160; ☽ 10am-5.30pm Wed-Sun)

Eating & Sleeping

Russian Court hotel (☎ 75 392; www.zolotoe-koltso .ru/hoteldvorik; ul Mitkina 14/2; s/d with breakfast from R1500/1900 Sun-Thu, R1700/2100 Fri & Sat) Some rooms at this delightful hotel boast views of the onion domes peeking out above whitewashed walls. The place is quite modern, despite the rustic style. The fanciest room has a Jacuzzi.

Russian Court restaurant (☎ 45 114; pr Krasnoy Armii 134; meals R500-800; ☽ 10am-9pm) Not to be confused with the hotel by the same name, this restaurant is decorated like a Russian dacha. Appropriately enough, it features staff in peasant dress and hearty country cuisine. The place is popular with tour groups in summer.

Trapeza na Makovtse (☎ 41 101; pr Krasnoy Armii 131; meals R500-800; ☽ 10am-9pm) Location, location, location. The highlight of this 'refectory' is alfresco dining in the shadow of the spires and cupolas. It's also pleasant inside, where there's live music nightly.

PERESLAVL-ZALESSKY
ПЕРЕСЛАВЛЬ-ЗАЛЕССКИЙ

☎ 48535 / pop 45,000

On the shore of Lake Pleshcheyevo, almost halfway between Moscow and Yaroslavl, Pereslavl-Zalessky is a popular dacha destination for Muscovites who enjoy the peaceful village atmosphere. The southern half of the town is characterised by narrow dirt lanes lined with carved wooden *izbay* (cottages) and blossoming gardens.

Pereslavl-Zalessky – 'Pereslavl Beyond the Woods' – was founded in 1152 by Yury Dolgoruky. The town's claim to fame is as the birthplace of Alexander Nevsky. Its earthen walls and the little Cathedral of the Transfiguration are as old as the town.

Pereslavl is pretty much a one-street town, with the bus station at the southwestern end, 2km from the centre. Apart from the few churches in the kremlin area, most of the historic sights are out of the centre.

The walls of Yury Dolgoruky's kremlin are now a grassy ring around the central town. Inside is the 1152 **Cathedral of the Transfiguration of the Saviour**, one of the oldest buildings in Russia. A bust of Alexander Nevsky stands out in front, while three additional churches across the grassy square make for a picturesque corner. These include the tent-roofed **Church of Peter the Metropolitan**, built in 1585 and renovated in 1957, and the 18th-century twin churches fronting the road.

The Trubezh River, winding 2km from the kremlin to the lake, is fringed by trees and narrow lanes. You can follow the northern riverbank most of the way to the lake on paths and streets. The **Forty Saints' Church** sits picturesquely on the south side of the river mouth.

TRANSPORT

Pereslavl is not on the train line, but buses travel frequently to Moscow's Shchyolkovsky bus station (2½ hours). Not all of these stop at Sergiev Posad (one hour, three daily). Other buses travel to Kostroma (four hours, two daily) and Yaroslavl (three hours, two daily) via Rostov-Veliky (1½ hours).

Bus 1 runs up and down the main street from just south of the bus station; heading out from the centre, you can catch it just north of the river. Taxis wait at Narodnaya ploshchad.

Southwest of the kremlin, the **Nikolsky Women's Monastery** has undergone massive renovation. Since its founding in 1350, this monastery has been on the brink of destruction – whether from Tatars, Poles or Communists – more than seems possible to survive. In 1994 four nuns from the Yaroslavl Tolga Convent came to restore the place, and today it looks marvellous. Rumour has it that the rebuilding is being bankrolled by a wealthy Muscovite businessperson who has benefited from the nuns' blessings.

Founded in 1010, the **Nikitsky Monastery** received its current name in the 12th century, after the death of the martyr St Nikita. To punish himself for his sins, Nikita had clasped his limbs in chains and spent the end of his days in an underground cell in the monastery. The handcuffs, which now hang in the main **cathedral**, are said to help cure addictions and other worldly vices. Behind the cathedral, a small chapel is being built around the dank cell where Nikita died. The monastery is about 3km north of the centre on the west side of the main road. Buses 1, 3 and 4 go most of the distance, or you can catch a taxi from Narodnaya ploshchad.

South of the centre, the **Goritsky Monastery** was founded in the 14th century, though today the oldest structures are the 17th-century gates, gate-church and belfry. The centrepiece is the baroque **Assumption Cathedral** (Uspensky sobor) with its beautiful carved iconostasis. The other buildings hold a variety of art and history exhibits.

The 1785 **Purification Church of Alexander Nevsky** is a working church across the main road from the Goritsky. To the west, on a hillock overlooking fields and dachas, is the **Danilovsky Monastery**, whose tent-roofed Trinity Cathedral (Troitsky sobor) dates to the 1530s. There's another 16th-century walled monastery, the **Fyodorovsky Monastery**, 2km south on the Moscow road.

Besides being the birthplace of Alexander Nevsky, Pereslavl also claims to be the birthplace of the Russian Navy: Lake Pleshcheyevo is one of the places where Peter the Great developed his obsession with the sea. As a young man, he studied navigation here and built a flotilla of over 100 little ships by the time he was 20.

Four kilometres along the road past the Goritsky Monastery, at the southern end of the lake, is the small **Botik Museum**. Its highlight is the sailboat *Fortuna*, one of only two of Peter the Great's boats to survive fire and neglect; the other is in the St Petersburg Naval Museum.

SIGHTS & INFORMATION
Cathedral of the Transfiguration of the Saviour
Спасо-Преображенский собор 1 C1
Church of Peter the Metropolitan
Церковь Петра митрополита..................................2 C1
Danilovsky Monastery
Даниловский монастырь 3 A3
Forty Saints' Church
Сорокосвятская церковь.....4 A1
Goritsky Monastery
Горицкий монастырь.............5 A3

Nikolsky Women's Monastery
Никольский женский монастырь 6 B2
Purification Church of Alexander Nevsky
Церковь Александра Невского Сретенского 7 B3
Sberbank Сбербанк .... (see 10)
Yartelekom Service Centre
Яртелеком сервисный центр...............................8 D1

EATING
Tavern on the Lake
Трактир на Озерной................9 D1

SLEEPING
Hotel Pereslavl
Гостиница Переславль.........10 C1

TRANSPORT
Bus Station Автостанция 11 A3
Taxi Stand Станция такси.......12 C1

To Market;
Nikitsky Monastery (2km);
Yaroslavl (70km);
Rostov-Veliky (125km)

Lake Pleshcheyevo

Footbridges

Narodnaya pl

Trubezh River

Sovetskaya ul

Podgornaya ul

To Botik Museum (4km);
Cafe Botik (4km)

Train Station

ul Kardovskogo

To Fyodorovsky Monastery (2km);
Sergiev Posad (65km);
Moscow (125km)

PERESLAVL-ZALESSKY

0 ——— 1 km
0 ——— 0.5 miles

Excursions

PERESLAVL-ZALESSKY

Sights & Information

Assumption Cathedral (Goritsky Monastery; admission R40; ☽ 10am-6pm May-Oct, 9am-5pm Nov-Apr)

Botik Museum (☎ 22 788; Podgornaya ul; admission R40; ☽ 10am-5pm Tue-Sun)

Goritsky Monastery (☎ 38 100; http://museum .pereslavl.ru; admission R50; ☽ 10am-6pm May-Oct, 9am-5pm Nov-Apr)

Nikitsky Monastery (admission free; ☽ 10am-5pm)

Sberbank (Rostovskaya ul 27; ☽ 9am-7pm Mon-Sat) Exchange facility in the lobby of Hotel Pereslavl.

Yartelekom Service Centre (☎ 31 595; Rostovskaya ul 20; Internet per hr R50) Has Internet and telephone facilities.

Eating & Sleeping

Cafe Botik (☎ 98 085; Podgornaya ul; meals R200-300; ☽ 11am-11pm) This fun, waterfront café (also shaped like a boat) is in a prime location opposite the Botik Museum. Stop for lake views and lunch before or after your excursion.

Hotel Pereslavl (☎ 31 788; fax 32 687; Rostovskaya ul 27; s/d from R650/1000) Although this hotel is only 20 years old, it is badly in need of the renovation that is ongoing. The cheapest rooms are very drab, but you can upgrade if you are willing to pay the price (R1300/1600).

Tavern on the Lake (☎ 94 264; Rostovskaya ul 27; meals R150-300; ☽ 9am-midnight) Gnaw on shashlyk (meat kebab) to your heart's desire at this Georgian eatery. Pork, chicken, beef and sturgeon – all are grilled up and served hot and spicy.

ROSTOV-VELIKY РОСТОВ-ВЕЛИКИЙ

☎ 48536 / pop 40,000

For a place called Rostov-Veliky, or 'Rostov the Great', this place gives the impression of a sleepy village. Perhaps for this reason, the magnificent Rostov kremlin catches visitors off guard when its silver domes and whitewashed stone walls appear amid the dusty streets. Rostov is among the prettiest of the Golden Ring towns, idyllically sited on shimmering Lake Nero. It is also one of the oldest, first chronicled in 862.

Rostov's main attraction is its unashamedly photogenic **kremlin**. Although founded in the 12th century, nearly all the buildings here date from the 1670s and 1680s. With its five magnificent domes, the **Assumption Cathedral** dominates the kremlin, although it is just outside its north wall. The cathedral was here a century before the kremlin, while the **belfry** was added in the 1680s. Each of 15 bells in the belfry has its own name; the largest, weighing 32 tonnes, is called Sysoi. The monks play magnificent bell concerts, which can be arranged through the excursions office, in the west gate, for R250.

The west gate (the main entrance) and north gate are straddled by the **Gate-Church of St John the Divine** and the **Gate-Church of the Resurrection**, both of which are richly decorated with 17th-century frescoes. Enter these churches from the monastery walls, which you can access from the stairs next to the north gate. Like several other buildings within the complex, these are only open from May to September. Between the gate-churches, the **Church of Hodigitria** houses an exhibition of Orthodox Church vestments and paraphernalia.

The metropolitan's private chapel, the **Church of the Saviour-over-the-Galleries**, has the

TRANSPORT

Rostov-Veliky is about 220km northeast of Moscow. The fastest train from Moscow is the express service from Yaroslavsky vokzal (Yaroslavl station; R180, three hours). Otherwise, some long-distance trains stop at Rostov-Veliky en route to Yaroslavl. You can also catch a suburban train, which requires changing at Alexandrov.

The most convenient option to get to Yaroslavl (R52, 1½ hours, seven daily) is by bus, either transit or direct. Transit buses also pass through on their way to Moscow (four to five hours, hourly), Pereslavl-Zalessky (two hours, six daily) and Sergiev Posad (four to five hours, three daily). One lone bus goes to Uglich (three hours).

The train and bus stations are together in the drab modern part of Rostov, 1.5km north of the kremlin. Bus 6 runs between the train station and the town centre.

most beautiful interior of all, covered in colourful frescoes. These rooms are filled with exhibits: the **White Chamber** displays religious antiquities, while the **Red Chamber** shows off *finift* (enamelware), a Rostov artistic speciality.

Although the ticket office is in the west gate, you can also enter the kremlin through the north gate. Don't leave without stopping into the gift shop behind the Metropolitan's House to shop for *finift* souvenirs and to sample the homebrewed *medovukha*.

The restored **Monastery of St Jacob** is the fairy-tale apparition you'll see as you approach Rostov by road or rail. To get there you can take buses 1 or 2 west 1.5km from the kremlin, although it's very pleasant to walk there alongside Lake Nero. Heading east of the kremlin, bus 1 will also bring you to the dilapidated **Monastery of St Avraam,** with a cathedral dating from 1553.

Named after a pagan sun god, **Khors** is a private gallery on the lakeshore behind the kremlin. The eclectic collection includes some antique household items, models of

Sidewalk vendor in Uglich (p201)

wooden churches and some exquisite enamel work by local artist Mikhail Selishchev. The two small rooms are available for rent to 'artists passing through'. The artist who runs the place also hosts workshops on enamel and Rostov artistry.

For a different perspective on this panorama, board the ferry *Zarya* for a float around Lake Nero. The hour-long trip leaves from the pier near the western gate of the kremlin, and cruises past both monasteries.

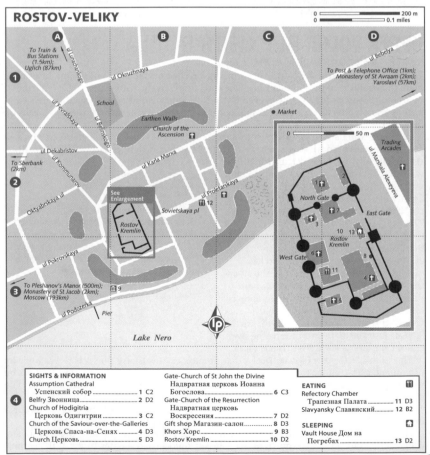

SIGHTS & INFORMATION

Assumption Cathedral
Успенский собор 1 C2
Belfry Звонница 2 D2
Church of Hodigitria
Церковь Одигитрии 3 C2
Church of the Saviour-over-the-Galleries
Церковь Спаса-на-Сенях 4 D3
Church Церковь 5 D3

Gate-Church of St John the Divine
Надвратная церковь Иоанна
Богослова 6 C3
Gate-Church of the Resurrection
Надвратная церковь
Воскресения 7 D2
Gift shop Магазин-салон 8 D3
Khors Хорс 9 B3
Rostov Kremlin 10 D2

EATING

Refectory Chamber
Трапезная Палата 11 D3
Slavyansky Славянский 12 B2

SLEEPING

Vault House Дом на
Погребах 13 D2

Sights & Information

Khors (☎ 62 483; www.khors.org; ul Podozerka 30; admission free; ⊙ 3-8pm Mon-Fri, 10am-9pm Sat & Sun)

Kremlin (☎ 61 717; admission grounds R5, exhibits R15-25 each; ⊙ 10am-5pm)

Post & Telephone Office (ul Severnaya 44) About 1km east of the kremlin.

Sberbank (ul Dekabristov, ⊙ 9am-2pm & 3-5pm Mon-Fri, 9am-2pm Sat)

Zarya (☎ 61 717; tickets R250; ⊙ 10am, 11.30am, 1pm, 2.30pm, 4pm Tue-Sun)

Eating

Refectory Chamber (☎ 62 871; Rostov kremlin; meals R200-400; ⊙ 9am-5pm, til later in summer) The draw to dining at the refectory is the atmospheric location inside the kremlin, near the Metropolitan's House. The grand dining room is often crowded with tour groups supping on traditional Russian fare.

Slavyansky (☎ 62 228; Sovietskaya pl 8) About 100m east of the kremlin, this semi-swanky place gets recommendations from the locals.

Sleeping

Pleshanov's Manor (Usadba Pleshanova; ☎ 76 440; www.hotel.v-rostove.ru; Pokrovskaya ul 34; r with breakfast Sun-Thu/Fri & Sat R1200/1500; ▢ 🖳) This 19th-century manor house – once the residence of a merchant and philanthropist family – is now a welcoming inn with a nice restaurant, cosy library and wood sauna. The charm of the common areas does not extend to the rooms, which are modern and fresh, but bland.

Vault House (☎ 31 244; s/d with shared bathroom R350/600, d with bathroom R1400-1600) It's inside the kremlin, near the east gate. The clean, wood-panelled rooms vary in size and view.

UPPER VOLGA ВЕРХНЯЯ ВОЛГА

☎ 4852 / pop 680,000 (Yaroslavl); ☎ 4942 / pop 280,000 (Kostroma)

Yaroslavl (Ярославль) and Kostroma (Кострома), perched on the banks of the mighty Volga, mark the far curve of the Golden Ring. They are, respectively, 250km and 300km northeast of Moscow – too far for a day trip, even if you have your own wheels. Both cities are rich in history and architecture, offering ample rewards for the traveller who has time to venture further from the capital.

Yaroslavl is the urban counterpart to Suzdal. This is the biggest place between Moscow and Arkhangelsk, and it has a more urban feel than anywhere else in the Golden Ring. Its big-city skyline, however, is dotted not with smoke stacks and skyscrapers, but with onion domes and towering spires. As a result of a trade boom in the 17th century, churches are hidden around every corner. The poet Grigoriev wrote: 'Yaroslavl is a town of unsurpassed beauty; everywhere is the Volga and everywhere is history.' And everywhere, everywhere, are churches.

Founded in the 12th century, the **Monastery of the Transfiguration of the Saviour** was one of Russia's richest and best-fortified monasteries by the 16th century. The oldest surviving structures, dating from 1516, are the **Holy Gate** near the main entrance by the river, and the austere **Cathedral of the Transfiguration**.

TRANSPORT

There are three or four daily suburban trains between Kostroma and Yaroslavl (three hours), as well as about 20 daily trains from Moscow's Yaroslavsky vokzal to Yaroslavl (R350, five hours). An overnight train to/from Moscow's Yaroslavsky vokzal goes to Kostroma (8½ hours). Buses also ply these routes.

The best way to get between Kostroma and Yaroslavl in summer is by hydrofoil, which runs twice a day in either direction.

The exquisite **Church of Elijah the Prophet** that dominates Sovetskaya ploshchad was built by prominent 17th-century fur dealers. It has some of the Golden Ring's brightest frescoes by the ubiquitous Yury Nikitin of Kostroma and his school, and detailed exterior tiles. The church is closed during wet spells.

The Volga and Kotorosl embankments make for an enjoyable 1.5km walk. Look for a myriad of churches, as well as the **Music & Time** museum and the **Yaroslavl Art Museum**.

Historic Kostroma is located where its namesake river converges with the Volga. The delightful historic centre – known as Susaninskaya ploshchad – dates to the 18th century,

DETOUR: UGLICH (УГЛИЧ)

Uglich is a quaint but shabby town on the Volga 90km northwest of Rostov-Veliky. Here the son of Ivan the Terrible, Dmitry (later to be impersonated by the string of False Dmitrys in the Time of Troubles), was murdered in 1591, probably on the orders of Boris Godunov.

Within the waterside **kremlin** (☎ 48532-53 678; each exhibit R34; 🕙 9am-1pm & 2-5pm), the 15th-century Prince's Chambers (Knyazhyi palaty) house a historical exhibit that tells this sordid tale. The star-spangled Church of St Dmitry on the Blood (Tserkov Dmitria-na-krovi) was built in the 1690s on the spot where the body was found. Its interior is decorated with bright frescoes and the bell that was used to mourn Dmitry's death. (In 1581 the bell was used to call an insurrection on the murder of the *tsarevich*. In response, Godunov ordered the 300kg bell to be publicly flogged and its tongue to be ripped out before it was banished for many years to the Siberian town of Tobolsk.) The impressive five-domed Transfiguration Cathedral (Preobrazhensky sobor) and an Art Museum are also in the kremlin.

When you tire of Dmitry, visit the **Vodka Museum** (☎ 48532-23 558; ul Berggolts 9; admission R60; 🕙 10am-5pm). The price of admission includes samples! Another fun stop is the **Museum of City Life** (☎ 48532-24 414; www.uglich.ru; admission R60; 🕙 timed to ferry schedule), an interactive museum with costumes and musical instruments. Reservations are recommended.

If you get stuck in Uglich, you can stay at the **Assumption Hotel** (Uspenskaya Gostinitsa; ☎ 48532-51 870; www.uspenskaya.yaroslavl.ru; pl Uspenskaya; s/d 500/700), opposite the kremlin. It's a cheery place with comfortable rooms and a small café.

Uglich is a regular stop for tour boats plying the Volga. Landlubbers can come by bus from Yaroslavl (R96, three hours, six daily). Buses to Rostov-Veliky run sporadically, so you may have to travel via Borisoglebsk. Otherwise, taxis wait outside the tiny bus station.

when the old wooden structures were demolished by fire. Clockwise around the northern side are a 19th-century **fire tower** (still in use and under Unesco protection); a former military **guardhouse**, housing a small literature museum; an 18th-century **hotel** for members of the royal family; the **palace** of an 1812 war hero, now a courthouse; and the **town hall**. In the streets between are many merchants' townhouses, including the elaborate neo-Russian **Art Museum**.

But the pride of Kostroma is the 14th-century **Monastery of St Ipaty**, which poses majestically on the right bank of the Kostroma River. In 1590 the Godunovs built the monastery's **Trinity Cathedral** (Troitsky sobor), which now contains more than 80 old frescoes by a school of 17th-century Kostroma painters, headed by Gury Nikitin (plus some 20th-century additions).

The monastery's more recent history is closely tied to the Godunov and Romanov families, fierce rivals in high-level power games before the Romanovs established their dynasty.

Suzdal's St Nicholas Church (p191) with the onion-domed Nativity of the Virgin Cathedral (p191) in the background

In 1600 Boris Godunov exiled the head of the Romanov family, Fyodor, and his son Mikhail to this monastery. Mikhail Romanov was here in 1613, when the all-Russia Council came to insist that he accept his position as tsar, thus ending the Time of Troubles. In honour of the event, all successive Romanov rulers came here to visit the monastery's red **Romanov Chambers** (Palaty Romanova), opposite the cathedral.

The monastery is 2.5km west of the town centre. Take bus 14 from the central ploshchad Susaninskaya and get off once you cross the river. Behind the monastery is an attractive outdoor **Museum of Wooden Architecture**.

Sights & Information
YAROSLAVL

Alfa Bank (☎ 4852-739 177; ul Svobody 3; ☻ 9am-6pm Mon-Thu, 9am-4.30pm Fri) Exchange office and ATM facilities.

Church of Elijah the Prophet (Sovetskaya pl; admission R60; ☻ 10am-1pm & 2-6pm Thu-Tue May-Sep)

Internet Club (☎ 4852-726 850; pr Lenina 24; per hr R32; ☻ 9am-11pm) A dark club in the Dom Kultury.

Monastery of the Transfiguration of the Saviour (☎ 4852-303 869; www.yarmp.yar.ru; Bogoyavlenskaya pl 25; grounds R10, each exhibit R20-30, all-inclusive Mon-Wed R50, Thu-Sun R130; ☻ grounds 8am-8pm daily Oct-May, exhibits 10am-5pm Tue-Sun year-round)

Music & Time (☎ 4852-328 637; Volzhskaya nab 33A; admission R50; ☻ 10am-7pm)

Post & Telephone office (ul Komsomolskaya 22; per hr R33; ☻ 8am-8pm Mon-Sat, to 6pm Sun) Also offers Internet services.

Sberbank (☎ 4852-729 518; ul Kirova 6; ☻ 8.30am-4pm Mon-Sat) Changes money and gives credit card advances.

Yaroslavl Art Museum (☎ 4852-303 504; Volzhskaya nab 23; admission R25, special exhibits R10-30; ☻ 10am-5pm Tue-Sun)

KOSTROMA

Guardhouse & Literary Museum (☎ 4942-516 027; ul Lenina 1; admission R20; ☻ 9.30am-5pm)

Kostroma Art Museum (☎ 4942-513 829; pr Mira 5 & 7; admission to each building R40; ☻ 10am-6pm)

Monastery of St Ipaty & Trinity Cathedral (☎ 4942-312 589; admission R50; ☻ 9am-5pm)

Museum of Wooden Architecture (☎ 4942-577 872; admission R20, photos R30; ☻ 9am-5pm May-Oct)

Post & Telephone Office (cnr uls Sovetskaya & Podlipaeva; ☻ 9am-9pm)

Sberbank (Sovetskaya ul 9; ☻ 9am-4pm Mon-Fri) Conveniently located bank with ATM.

Telecom Centre (☎ 4942-621 020; cnr uls Sovetskaya & Podlipaeva; per hr R50; ☻ 9am-9pm) Internet access in the same complex as the post office.

Eating
YAROSLAVL

Actor (☎ 4852-727 543; ul Kirova 5; meals R100-200, beers R60; ☻ 10am-2am) It has a trattoria ambience, without the fresh air. The walls are covered with whimsical frescoes and theatre posters, and the air is filled with sounds of live rock, jazz and blues.

Bristol Restaurant (☎ 4852-729 408; ul Kirova 10; meals R200-500; ☻ noon-midnight Sun & Mon, noon-2am Fri & Sat) Sunlit café downstairs; a formal dining room upstairs.

Poplavok (☎ 4852-314 343; Kotorosl River; meals R500-800; ☻ noon-1am) Kostroma's only truly waterside dining (on a boat). Seafood specials are skilfully prepared and artfully presented.

KOSTROMA

Horn & Hoof Cafe (☎ 4942-315 240; Sovetskaya ul 2; meals R150-200; ☻ 9am-midnight) A coffee shop that also harkens back to eras past. Wrought-iron furniture and B&W photos set the atmosphere.

White Sun (☎ 4942-579 057; Lesnaya ul 2; meals R400-600) This restaurant serves spicy central-Asian food and has a prime location next to the river station.

Sleeping
YAROSLAVL

Hotel Volga (☎ 4852-731 111; fax 728 276; ul Kirova 10; s with shared bathroom R600, s/d with bathroom R1500/1800) A throwback to prerevolutionary Russia.

Hotel Yubileynaya (☎ 4852-309 259; www.yubil.yar.ru; Kotoroslnaya nab 26; s/d with breakfast from R1800/2600; ☒ ☐) The usual concrete-slab building located in a prime spot overlooking the Kotorosl River. The rooms are completely renovated, simply decorated and comfortably furnished.

Ring Premier Hotel (☎ 4852-581 058; fax 581 158; ul Svobody 55; s/d with breakfast R4500/5000; ☒ ☐) A slick new business hotel.

KOSTROMA

Hotel Mush (☎ 4942-312 400; www.mush.com.ru; Sovetskaya ul 29; r with breakfast R1300-2100) It has

Excursions UPPER VOLGA

a central location and hospitable atmosphere. The four rooms are spacious and elegantly furnished. Enter through the courtyard.

Ipatievskaya Village (☎ 4942-577 179; fax 319 444; Beregovaya ul 3A; d R1500-2300) A wooden house opposite the monastery entrance. The quaint rooms feature modern amenities but old-fashioned style. Highlights

include the authentic Russian *banya* and the small beach fronting the Kostroma River.

Rus Tourist Complex (☎ 4942-546 163; russ@kmtn.ru; Yunosheskaya ul 1; s/d with breakfast from R1000/1500) This is Kostroma's Soviet-standard block hotel overlooking the Volga. It's about 2km southeast of the centre, near the bridge.

ZAVIDOVO ЗАВИДОВО
☎ 495

At a beautiful spot at the confluence of the Volga and Shosha Rivers, the village of Zavidovo is midway between Klin and Tver on the road to St Petersburg. On the outskirts, the **Zavidovo Holiday Complex** (☎ 937 9944; www.zavidovo.ru; d incl breakfast from R5000/5500; 🖳 🐾 🐴) offers all kinds of recreational activities, such as horse riding, water skiing, tennis, boating and fishing. Afterwards, soothe your weary body in the tiled Turkish bath or the lakeside Russian *banya*. In addition to the hotel complex, comfortable cottages (Sun-Thu/Fri & Sat R8100/9800) sleeping four to eight people replicate various architectural styles, including Finnish cabins, Alpine chalets and Russian dachas.

TRANSPORT
Suburban trains from Moscow's Leningradsky vokzal (Leningrad station) to Tver stop in Zavidovo (R75, two hours, hourly).

ISTRA ИСТРА
☎ 231

A steady stream of pilgrims makes the journey to this village, 50km west of Moscow. Their motives are diverse, as they come to worship at the grandiose New Jerusalem Monastery, or to worship the gods of sun and fun at the nearby holiday resorts.

In the 17th century, Nikon, the patriarch whose reforms drove the Old Believers from the Russian Orthodox Church, decided to show one and all that Russia deserved to be the centre of the Christian world by building a little Holy City right at home, complete with its own Church of the Holy Sepulchre. Thus, the grandiose **New Jerusalem Monastery** (Novo-Iyerusalimsky monastyr; ☎ 49 787; each exhibit adult/child R40/20, guided tour R500; 🕙 10am-4pm Tue-Sun) was founded in 1656 near the picturesque Istra River. The abrasive Nikon lost his job before the church was completed.

Unlike other monasteries around Moscow, this one had no military use. In WWII the retreating Germans blew it to pieces, but it's gradually being reconstructed. After years as a museum, the monastery is now in Orthodox hands and attracts a steady stream of worshippers.

In the centre of the monastery grounds is

TRANSPORT
Suburban trains run from Moscow's Rizhsky vokzal (Riga station) to Istra (R42, 1½ hours, hourly), from where buses run to the Muzey stop by the monastery. If the weather is fine, a 3km walk from the Istra train station is a pleasant alternative.

the **Cathedral of the Resurrection** (Voskresensky sobor) intended to look like Jerusalem's Church of the Holy Sepulchre. Like its prototype, it's really several churches under one roof. The main building is still under restoration, but it's possible to enter the detached **Assumption Church** (Uspensky tserkov) in the northern part of the cathedral. Here, pilgrims come to kiss the relics of the holy martyr Tatyana, the monastery's patron saint.

Reconstruction is also complete on the unusual underground **Church of SS Konstantin & Yelena** (Konstantino-Yeleninskaya tserkov), with only its belfry peeping up above the ground. Nikon was buried in the cathedral, beneath the **Church of John the Baptist** (Tserkov Ioanna Predtechi).

DETOUR: PLYOS (ПЛЁС)

Plyos is a tranquil town of wooden houses and hilly streets winding down to the Volga waterfront, halfway between Ivanovo and Kostroma. Though fortified from the 15th century, Plyos' renown stems from its role as a late-19th-century artists' retreat. Isaac Levitan, Russia's most celebrated landscape artist, found inspiration here in the summers of 1888 to 1890. The playwright Chekhov commented that Plyos 'put a smile in Levitan's paintings'. During the three summers he lived here, Levitan completed around 200 works, including 23 paintings.

The oldest part of town is along the river, as evidenced by the ramparts of the old fort, which date from 1410. The hill is topped by the simple 1699 **Assumption Cathedral** (Uspensky sobor), one of Levitan's favourite painting subjects.

The **Levitan House Museum** (Dom-Muzey Levitana; ☎ 49339-43 782; ul Lunacharskogo 4; admission R50; ⏱ 9am-5pm Tue-Sun) in the eastern part of the town, across the small Shokhonka River, displays works of Levitan and other artists against the background of the Volga.

Plyos is easy to reach in summer, when hydrofoils ply the Volga from Kostroma and Yaroslavl. Otherwise, buses run occasionally from Kostroma (weekends only).

The **refectory** exhibits weapons, icons and artwork from the 17th century, including personal items belonging to the patriarch, Nikon. In the monastery walls, there is additional **exhibit space** displaying 20th-century drawings and handicrafts from around the Moscow region. On weekends you can sample freshly brewed tea and homemade pastries in the **tearoom**.

Just outside the monastery's north wall, the Moscow region's **Museum of Wooden Architecture** is a collection of picturesque peasant cottages and windmills, set along the river. It is open May to September.

On the shores of the lovely Istra water reserve, sits a collection of quaint wooden cottages known as the **Istra Holiday Country Hotel** (☎ 495-739 6198; www.istraholiday.ru; Trusovo; d Sun-Thu/Fri & Sat from R4000/7100; 🛒 ❄). The place offers all the sports and outdoor activities you could hope for, from skiing to swimming to lounging on the beach. The resort is all-inclusive, with two restaurants, several cafés and bars, as well as sports facilities and a spa.

Museum of Wooden Architecture (p202) in Kostroma

ARKHANGELSKOE АРХАНГЕЛЬСКОЕ

☎ 495

In the 1780s, the wealthy Prince Nikolai Yusupov bought this grand palace on the outskirts of Moscow and turned it into a spectacular **estate** (☎ 495-363 1375; www.arkhangelskoe .ru; admission grounds R150, colonnade R80; ☺ grounds 10am-6pm daily, exhibits 10am-4pm Wed-Sun).

During several ambassadorships and as Director of the Imperial Museums, Prince Nikolai accumulated a private art collection that outclassed many European museums. The **palace** consists of a series of elegant halls that display his paintings, furniture, sculptures, glass, tapestries and porcelain.

> ### TRANSPORT
> The estate is 22km west of central Moscow. Take *marshrutka* 151, 285 or 549 from Moscow's Tushin-skaya metro station to Arkhangelskoe (R20, 30 minutes).

The multilevel, Italianate **gardens** are full of 18th-century copies of classical statues. The majestic **colonnade** on the eastern side was meant to be a Yusupov mausoleum, but the family fled Russia after the revolution. In summer months, this is the exquisite setting for live classical music **concerts** (☎ 501 453 8229; tickets R300; ☺ 5pm Sat & Sun May-Sep).

Prince Nikolai also organised a troupe of serf actors that eventually became one of the best known of its kind, and built them a **theatre** just west of the gardens. Predating everything else is the little white **Church of the Archangel Michael** (Arkhangelskaya tserkov) built in 1667.

BORODINO БОРОДИНО

☎ 238

In 1812 Napoleon invaded Russia, lured by the prospect of taking Moscow. For three months the Russians retreated, until on 26 August the two armies met in a bloody battle of attrition at the village of Borodino, 130km west of Moscow. In 15 hours, more than one-third of each army was killed – more than 100,000 soldiers in all. Europe would not know fighting this devastating again until WWI.

The French seemed to be the winners, as the Russians withdrew and abandoned a Moscow set ablaze. But Borodino was in fact the beginning of the end for Napoleon, who was soon in full, disastrous retreat.

The entire battlefield – covering more than 100 sq km – is now the **Borodino Field Museum-Preserve**, basically vast fields dotted with dozens of memorials to specific divisions and generals (most erected at the centenary of the battle in 1912). Start your tour at the **museum** (☎ 51 546; www.borodino .ru; ☺ 10am-6pm Tue-Sun), where you can study a diorama of the battle before setting out to see the site in person.

> ### TRANSPORT
> Suburban trains leave in the morning from Moscow's Belorussky vokzal (Belarus station) to Borodino (R45, two hours). A few trains return to Moscow in the evening, but be prepared to spend some time waiting. If you miss the train, you may be able to catch a bus or a car to nearby Mozhaysk, from where there are frequent trains and buses.
>
> As the area is rural, visiting by car is more convenient and probably more rewarding. If driving from Moscow, stay on the M1 (Minskoe shosse) till the Mozhaysk turn-off, 95km beyond the Moscow outer ring road. It's 5km north to Mozhaysk, then 13km west to Borodino village.

The front line was roughly along the 4km road from Borodino village to the train station: most of the monuments are close to this road. The hilltop monument around 400m in front of the museum is the **grave of Prince Bagration**, a heroic Georgian infantry general who was mortally wounded in the battle.

Further south, a concentration of monuments around Semyonovskoe village marks the battle's most frenzied fighting; here Bagration's heroic Second Army, opposing far larger

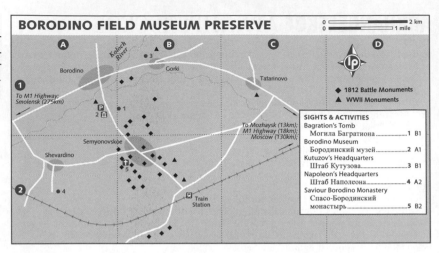

BORODINO FIELD MUSEUM PRESERVE

SIGHTS & ACTIVITIES
Bagration's Tomb
   Могила Багратиона 1 B1
Borodino Museum
   Бородинский музей.........................2 A1
Kutuzov's Headquarters
   Штаб Кутузова...............................3 B1
Napoleon's Headquarters
   Штаб Наполеона.............................4 A2
Saviour Borodino Monastery
   Спасо-Бородинский
   монастырь 5 B2

French forces, was virtually obliterated. Apparently, Russian commander Mikhail Kutuzov deliberately sacrificed Bagration's army to save his larger First Army, opposing lighter French forces in the northern part of the battlefield. **Kutuzov's headquarters** are marked by an obelisk in the village of Gorki. Another obelisk near Shevardino to the southwest, paid for in 1912 with French donations, marks **Napoleon's camp**.

This battle scene was re-created during WWII, when the Red Army confronted the Nazis on this very site. Memorials to this battle also dot the fields, and WWII trenches surround the monument to Prince Bagration. Near the train station are two WWII mass graves.

The **Saviour Borodino Monastery** (☎ 51 057; admission R15; ☷ 10am-5pm Tue-Sun) was built by the widows of the Afghanistan conflict. Among its exhibits is a display devoted to Leo Tolstoy and the events of *War and Peace* that took place at Borodino.

The rolling hills around Borodino and Semyonovskoe are largely undeveloped, due to their historic status. Facilities are extremely limited; be sure to bring a picnic lunch.

GORKI LENINSKIE ЛЕНИНСКИЕ ГОРКИ
☎ 495

In Lenin's later years, he and his family spent time at the lovely 1830s manor house on this wooded estate, 32km southeast of the Kremlin. Now it is an interesting and well-maintained **museum** (☎ 495-548 9309; admission to each exhibit R50, guided tour R350; ☷ 10am-4pm Wed-Mon).

The house was redesigned in neoclassical style by the Art Nouveau architect Fyodor Shekhtel. It is largely furnished with the incredible collection of custom-designed furniture that was commissioned by the wealthy Morozov family, who owned the estate prior to the revolution. It is set amid lovely landscaped grounds – reason enough to visit this spot on a summer afternoon.

TRANSPORT

Bus 439 (30 minutes) leaves every 90 minutes for the estate from the Domodedovskaya metro station in Moscow. By car, follow the M4 (Kashirskoe shosse) to 11km beyond the Moscow outer ring road, then turn left to Gorki Leninskie.

Many of the rooms are maintained as when Lenin's family lived here. A special exhibit re-creates his office in the Kremlin, with many of his personal items on display. The highlight, however, is his vintage Rolls Royce – one of only 15 of its type in the world. Other buildings on the grounds house exhibits about 20th-century political history and peasant life in the region.

MELIKHOVO МЕЛИХОВО

☎ 272

'My estate's not much,' wrote playwright Anton Chekhov of his home at Melikhovo, south of Moscow, 'but the surroundings are magnificent'. Here, Chekhov lived from 1892 until 1899 and wrote some of his most celebrated plays, including *The Seagull* and *Uncle Vanya*. When in residence Chekhov flew a flag above his home, notifying peasants that they could come for medical assistance.

Today the estate houses the **Chekhov museum** (☎ 23 610; admission R10, tour R50; ⏰ 10am-4pm Tue-Sun) dedicated to the playwright and his work. Visitors today can examine his personal effects, wander around the village and peek into the 18th-century **wooden church**.

Theatre buffs should visit in May, when the museum hosts **Melikhovo Spring** (tickets R100-150), a week-long theatre festival. Theatre groups from all over the world descend on the village to perform their interpretations of the great playwright's work.

TRANSPORT

Suburban trains (R50, 1½ hours) run frequently from Moscow's Kursky vokzal (Kursk station) to the town of Chekhov, 12km west of Melikhovo. Bus 25 makes the 20-minute journey between Chekhov and Melikhovo, with departures just about every hour. By car, Melikhovo is about 7km east of the dual carriageway that parallels the old M2 Moscow–Oryol road, signposted 50km south of Moscow's outer ring road.

PRIOKSKO-TERRASNY NATURE RESERVE
ПРИОКСКО-ТЕРРАСНЫЙ ЗАПОВЕДНИК

The **Prioksko-Terrasny Nature Reserve** (☎ 27-707 145; http://online.stack.net; admission R50, guided tour R150-350; ⏰ 9am-4pm) covers 50 sq km bordering the northern flood plain of the Oka River, a tributary of the Volga. The reserve is a meeting point of northern fir groves and marshes with typical southern meadow steppe. It has a variety of fauna, though you're unlikely to see many of the species.

The nature reserve's pride, and the focus for most visitors, is its European bison nursery *(pitomnik zubrov)*. Two pairs of bison, one of Europe's largest mammals (some weigh over a tonne), were brought here from Poland in 1948. Now there are about 60 and more than 200 have been sent out to other parts of the country. The best opportunity to see the bison is during feeding time.

You cannot wander freely around the reserve by yourself, so it's useful to make advance arrangements for an informative tour. Otherwise, you might tag on to a prescheduled group tour. There is also a small **museum** near the office with stuffed specimens of the reserve's fauna, typical of European Russia, including beavers, elk, deer and boar.

TRANSPORT

Public transport is difficult. If you leave by 8am, you can take a suburban train from Moscow's Kursky vokzal (Kursk station) to Serpukhov (two hours), then a rare bus (No 25, 31 or 41) to the reserve. You might also be able to negotiate a ride from Serpukhov.

Drivers from Moscow should follow Simferopolskoe shosse (the extension of Varshavskoe shosse). At 98km, look for the sign to the reserve or to the village of Danki.

Produce market in Suzdal (p190)

YASNAYA POLYANA ЯСНАЯ ПОЛЯНА

☎ 487

Located 14km south of central Tula and around 240km from Moscow, **Yasnaya Polyana** (☎ 238 6710, 517 6081; www.yasnayapolyana.ru; admission R100; ✆ 10am-5pm Tue-Sun May-Oct, 9.30am-3.30pm Tue-Sun Nov-Apr) is the estate where the great Russian writer Count Leo Tolstoy was born and buried.

Tolstoy spent much of his life in this house, which is a simple place filled with many of his possessions. Of Yasnaya Polyana, he wrote: 'All [my grandfather] had built here was not only solid and comfortable, but also very elegant. The same is true about the park he laid out near the house.' Tolstoy's nearby **grave** is unmarked except for the bouquets of flowers left by newlyweds. **Cafe Preshpekt** (meals R200 to R250) features hearty home-cooked Russian fare. House specialities are prepared according to recipes of Sofia Andreevna, Leo's devoted wife.

TRANSPORT

The easiest way to get to Yasnaya Polyana is the express train from Moscow's Kursky vokzal (Kursk station; R180, three hours, departs 9am, returns 4.36pm). While waiting for the shuttle bus to the museum, you can amuse yourself by perusing the exhibit on the railway during Leo Tolstoy's time. Otherwise, you can take the *elektrichka* to Tula (R130, three hours), then take bus 261 to Yasnaya Polyana (R10, 20 minutes).

If you're driving from Moscow, it's easiest to follow Tula's western bypass all the way to its southern end and then turn back north towards Tula.

Directory ∎

Directory

TRANSPORT
AIR
International fares fluctuate dramatically, depending on the season, economy and other factors. Russian domestic fares tend to be more stable. Some domestic fares and schedules appear in the boxed text, opposite.

For general information on international airfares, as well as some tips for budget travellers, see www.waytorussia.net/transport /international/air.html.

Airlines
The former Soviet state airline, Aeroflot, has been decentralised into hundreds of smaller airlines ('baby-flots'), most with a regional focus. The upshot of this orgy of aerobatic entrepreneurship is relatively unregulated skies. Tales of Russian-airline safety lapses are commonplace, so do some research before booking your flight on one of the regional airlines. Aeroflot and Transaero are two national airlines that serve all major domestic destinations and meet international standards for safety and service.

See p226 for a list of agents who sell domestic- and international-flight tickets, or you can deal directly with the airlines themselves. Airline offices of international companies in Moscow include:

Aeroflot (Map pp248–9; ☎ 753 5555; www.aeroflot.com /eng/; ul Petrovka 20/1, Petrovsky District; Ⓜ Chekhovskaya)

Air France (Map pp252–3; ☎ 937 3839; www.airfrance .com; ul Korovy Val 7, Zamoskvorechie; Ⓜ Oktyabrskaya)

Alitalia (Map pp248–9; ☎ 967 0110; www.alitalia.com; World Trade Centre, Krasnopresnenskaya nab 12, poezd 7, Barrikadnaya; Ⓜ Ulitsa 1905 Goda)

Austrian Airlines (Map pp252–3; ☎ 995 0995; www .aua.com; Korovy Val 7, Zamoskvorechie; Ⓜ Oktyabrskaya)

British Airways (Map pp248–9; ☎ 363 2525; www .britishairways.com; Business Centre Parus, 1-ya Tverskaya Yamskaya ul 23, Tverskoy District; Ⓜ Belorusskaya)

Delta Air Lines (Map pp252–3; ☎ 937 9090; www.delta .com; Gogolevsky bul 11, Kropotkinskaya; Ⓜ Kropotkinskaya)

Finnair (Map pp252–3; ☎ 933 0056; www.finnair.ru; Kropotinsky per 7, Khamovniki; Ⓜ Park Kultury)

KLM Royal Dutch Airlines (Map pp252–3; ☎ 258 3600; www.klm.com; ul Usachyova 33/2, Khamovniki; Ⓜ Sportivnaya)

LOT Polish Airlines (Map pp248–9; ☎ 775 7737; www .lot.com; Trubnaya ul 21/11, 3rd floor, Petrovsky District; Ⓜ Tsvetnoy Bulvar)

Lufthansa (Map pp248–9; ☎ 737 6400; www.lufthansa .com; Renaissance Moscow Hotel, Olimpiysky pr 18, Petrovsky District; Ⓜ Prospekt Mira)

Malév-Hungarian Airlines (Map pp248–9; ☎ 202 8416; www.malev.hu; Povarskaya ul 21, Barrikadnaya; Ⓜ Barrikadnaya)

SAS (Map pp248–9; ☎ 775 4747; www.scandinavian .net; 1-ya Tverskaya Yamskaya ul 5, Tverskoy District; Ⓜ Mayakovskaya)

Swiss Air (Map p255; ☎ 937 7767; www.swiss.com; Paveletskaya pl 2, Zayauzie; Ⓜ Paveletskaya)

Transaero (Map pp252–3; ☎ 241 4800; www.transaero .ru/english; 2-y Smolensky per 3, Arbat District; Ⓜ Smolenskaya)

Airports
Moscow's five airports serve a range of destinations. For information on flights in and out of all airports, call ☎ 941 9999 (Russian only). The easiest and surest way to get from any airport into the city is to book your transfer in advance through a travel agent (see p226). The driver will meet your flight with a sign and drive you straight from the airport to your destination in the city.

BYKOVO
The little-used **Bykovo airport** (code BKA; ☎ 558 4933) is about 30km southeast of

---

THINGS CHANGE...
The information provided in this section is particularly vulnerable to change. Check directly with the airline or a travel agent to make sure you understand how a fare (and ticket you may buy) works and shop carefully. Be aware of the security requirements for international travel. The details given in this chapter should be regarded as pointers and are not a substitute for your own careful, up-to-date research.

DOMESTIC FLIGHTS FROM MOSCOW

Destination	Flights daily	Duration	One-way fare
Arkhangelsk	4	1¾hr	R4200-4600
Astrakhan	4	2½hr	R4850
Irkutsk	2	5hr	R8500-9000
Kaliningrad	7	2hr	R2800-3000
Krasnodar	6	2hr	R3200-3900
Murmansk	4	2hr	R4400-5090
Novosibirsk	6	3hr	R3600-6800
Sochi	5-6	2hr	R2900-4000
St Petersburg	20	50min	R2800-3500
Yekaterinburg	11	2½hr	R5300-5400
Vladivostok	3-4	7hr	R12,500-13,800
Volgograd	4	2hr	R3400-3600

the city centre on Novoryazanskoe shosse. *Prigorodnye* trains run from Kazansky vokzal (Kazan train station) to Bykovo vokzal, 400m from the airport (R30, one hour, every 20 minutes). You can also pick this train up at Vykhino, near Vykhino metro. A taxi to/from the city centre is about R800 and can take 1½ hours.

DOMODEDOVO

Moscow's second airport, **Domodedovo** (code DME; ☎ 933 6666; www.domodedovo.ru, in Russian), has undergone extensive upgrades in recent years in order to service more international flights. Most notably, all British Airway flights now fly in and out of Domodedovo. It's about 40km south of the centre.

A super-convenient express train leaves Paveletsky vokzal (Pavelets station) for Domodedovo airport (R100, 45 minutes, every 30 minutes). This route is particularly handy, as you can check-in to your flight at the Paveletsky vokzal. Taxi fare to/from the city centre is R700 to R800, with the trip taking up to 1½ hours, depending on traffic.

SHEREMETEVO-1&2

Sheremetevo (code SVO; www.sheremetyevo-airport.ru) has two terminals. Moscow's main international airport is **Sheremetevo-2** (☎ 956 4666), 30km northwest of the city centre. It services most flights to/from places outside the former Soviet Union. From the smaller terminal, **Sheremetevo-1** (☎ 232 6565), most flights are to/from St Petersburg, the Baltic States, Belarus and northern European

Russia. Bus No 517 and airport shuttle buses run between the two terminals.

Minibuses travel between Rechnoy Vokzal metro station and Sheremetevo-1, with Sheremetevo-2 the middle stop in both directions. They make the journey as soon as they are full, which is about every 30 minutes or less. At Rechnoy Vokzal, leave the metro platform by the exit at the front end of the train. Minivans wait at the road, 100m from the station. The combined metro and minivan trip to/from Sheremetevo-2 takes about one hour; to/from Sheremetevo-1 is about 10 minutes extra. City bus No 551 also follows this route, but takes much longer. At Sheremetevo-2, minibuses leave from a stop 200m in front of the terminal (just to the right of the car park). Make certain your shuttle is going in the right direction.

A taxi arranged on the spot between Sheremetevo airport and the city centre takes about 45 minutes and should not cost more than R800. A better bet is to arrange one in advance through one of the taxi companies listed on p214).

VNUKOVO

About 30km southwest of the city centre, **Vnukovo** airport (code VKO; ☎ 436 2813; www.vnukovo-airport.ru/eng/index.htm) serves the Caucasus, Moldova and Kaliningrad. New high-speed trains run between Kievsky vokzal and Vnukovo (R76, 35 minutes). They run every hour between 7am and noon and between 5pm and 8pm. Outside these hours, you can take a *marshrutka* (minibus) from Yugo-Zapadnaya metro (R30, 30 minutes). A taxi to/from the city centre can take over an hour and costs about R800.

BOAT

Around Moscow

For new perspectives on Moscow neighbourhoods, fine views of the Kremlin, or just good old-fashioned transportation, a boat ride on the Moscow River is one of the city's highlights. The main route runs between the Kievsky boat landing station (Map pp252–3) and the Novospassky Most landing (Map p255), near Novospassky Monastery (adult/child R200/100, 1½ hours, every 20 minutes).

There are six intermediate stops: at the foot of Sparrow Hills (Vorobyovy Gory landing; Map pp246–7); Frunzenskaya near the southern end of Frunzenskaya naberezhnaya; Gorky Park (Map pp252–3); Krimean Most; Bolshoy Kamenny Most opposite the Kremlin (Map pp252-3); and Ustinsky Most, east of Red Square (Map p254).

The boats seat about 200 people (most Muscovites are actually going somewhere, not just out for the ride) and are operated by the **Capital Shipping Company** (☎ 458 9624). Boats run from mid-April to mid-October.

To/From Moscow

In summer, passenger boats from Moscow ply the rivers and canals of Russia all the way north to St Petersburg, and south to Astrakhan or Rostov-on-Don. The navigation season is generally May to September.

The St Petersburg route follows the Moscow Canal and then the Volga River to the Rybinsk Reservoir; then the Volga-Baltic Canal to Lake Onega; the Svir River to Lake Ladoga; and the Neva River to St Petersburg.

The main southbound route takes the Moscow Canal north to the Volga. It then follows the Volga east before heading south all the way downstream to Astrakhan (which

is nine days from Moscow), via Uglich, Yaroslavl, Kostroma, Nizhny Novgorod, Kazan, Ulyanovsk, Samara and Volgograd.

The Moscow terminus for these sailings is the **Severny Rechnoy Vokzal** (Northern River Station; Map pp246–7; ☎ 457 4050; Leningradskoe shosse 51; Ⓜ Rechnoy Vokzal). Take the metro to Rechnoy Vokzal, then walk 15 minutes due west, passing under Leningradskoe shosse and then through a nice park.

Some cruise companies:

Capital Shipping Company (Map pp246–7; ☎ 458 9624; www.cck-ship.ru, in Russian; Severny Rechnoy Vokzal, Leningradsky sh 51; Ⓜ Rechnoy Vokzal) Operates cruise ships departing regularly from Moscow's Severny Rechnoy Vokzal.

Cruise Company Orthodox (Map pp246–7; ☎ 943 8560; www.cruise.ru; ul Alabyana 5; Ⓜ Sokol) A Russian company that also caters to foreigners, meaning English-speaking staff and upgraded accommodation. Cruises go all the way down the Volga River to Rostov-on-Don, through the locks of the Rostov-Don Canal.

Cruise Marketing International (☎ 800 578 7742; www.cruiserussia.com; 3401 Investment Blvd, Ste 3, Hayward CA USA) Offers a series of 11- and 15-day cruises between Moscow and St Petersburg, with stops in little villages and Golden Ring towns.

BUS & TRAM

Around Moscow

Buses, trolleybuses and trams are useful along a few radial or cross-town routes that the metro misses, and sometimes they are necessary for reaching sights away from the city centre. Tickets (*talony*; R10) are usually sold on the vehicle by a *provodnitsa* (conductor). Some offer good sightseeing:

No 1 From Dobryninskaya metro in Zamoskvorechie, the route goes along ulitsa Bolshaya Polyanka and across Bolshoy Kamenny most, which has a good Kremlin view. Succeeding sights include Pashkov House, the old Moscow

BUSES FROM MOSCOW

The following buses depart from Moscow's Shchyolkovsky bus station. For St Petersburg, take the train (see the boxed text, p215).

Destination	Buses daily	Duration	One-way fare
Nizhny Novgorod	5	9hr	R300
Pereslavl-Zalessky	2	6hr	R236
Suzdal	1	4½hr	R145
Vladimir	4	3½hr	R120

State University, Le Royal Meridien National and scenic Tverskaya ulitsa to Belorussky vokzal.

No 2 Makes a big circle around the Kremlin and Kitay Gorod, offering great views, then goes past the Polytechnical Museum, Lubyanskaya ploshchad, Bolshoi Theatre, Hotel Metropol, Le Royal Meridien National, Manezhnaya ploshchad and old Moscow State University. The route then turns on to ulitsa Vozdvizhenka and heads west to Kutuzovsky prospekt, the Triumphal Arch and Victory Park.

No 8 Offers views of Zamoskvorechie and its many churches. From Dobryninskaya metro, it heads north along Pyatnitskaya ulitsa and returns south along ulitsa Bolshaya Ordynka.

To/From Moscow

INTERNATIONAL SERVICES

International bus services offer the cheapest means of getting to Russia, although services to Moscow are limited.

Berlin Linien Bus (☎ 975 3309; www.berlinlinienbus.de; Leningradsky vokzal) Operates a daily bus service between Berlin and Moscow (€66, 12 hours).

Eurolines (☎ 975 2574 or 737 6743; www.eurolines .com; Leningradsky vokzal) Offers a bus service between St Petersburg and various Western European capitals.

DOMESTIC SERVICES

Buses run to a number of towns and cities within 700km of Moscow. Fares are similar to *kupeny* (2nd-class) train fares. In general, travelling by bus is not as reliable or as comfortable as travelling by train, so it is best only for destinations with poor train services, including some Golden Ring towns. They tend to be crowded, although they are usually faster than the *prigorodnye* trains.

Book domestic tickets at Moscow's long-distance bus terminal, the **Shchyolkovsky bus station** (Map pp246–7; Ⓜ Shchyolkovskaya), 8km east of the city centre. Queues can be bad, so it's advisable to come here and book ahead, especially for travel on Friday, Saturday or Sunday. Sample fares are provided in the boxed text, opposite.

CAR & MOTORCYCLE

There's little reason for travellers to rent a car for getting around Moscow, as public transport is quite adequate, but you might want to consider car rental for trips out of the city. Beware that driving in Russia is truly an unfiltered Russian experience. Poor roads, maddeningly inadequate signposting, low-quality petrol and keen highway patrolmen can lead to frustration and dismay.

Driving

To drive in Russia, you must be 18 years old and have a full driving licence. In addition, you'll need an International Driving Permit with a Russian translation of your licence, or a certified Russian translation of your full licence (you can certify translations at a Russian embassy or consulate).

For your own vehicle, you will also need registration papers and proof of insurance. Be sure your insurance covers you in Russia. Finally, a customs declaration, promising that you will take your vehicle with you when you leave, is also required.

The maximum legal blood-alcohol content is 0.04%, but in practice it is illegal to drive after consuming *any* alcohol at all. This is a rule that is strictly enforced. The normal way of establishing alcohol in the blood is by a blood test, but apparently you can be deemed under its influence even without any test.

Officers of the State Automobile Inspectorate (Gosudarstvennaya Avtomobilnaya Inspektsia), better known as GAI, skulk about on the roadsides all around Moscow waiting for miscreant drivers. They are authorised to stop you (by pointing their striped stick at you and waving you towards the side), to issue on-the-spot fines and, worst of all, to shoot at your car if you refuse to pull over. The GAI also hosts the occasional speed trap – the road to Sheremetevo airport is infamous for this. If you are required to pay a fine, pay in roubles only – and make sure you get a receipt.

Moscow has no shortage of petrol stations that sell all grades of petrol. Most are open 24 hours, are affiliated with Western oil companies and can be found on the major roads in and out of town. See the *Moscow Business Telephone Guide* for listings of parts, and service and repair specialists for many Western makes of car.

Rental

Car rental is usually only considered for trips out of the city.

Be aware that many firms won't let you take their cars out of the city, and others will only rent a car with a driver. This latter option is not necessarily a bad one as cars with drivers aren't always more expensive. Also you can avoid the trouble of coping with Russian roads and police.

The major international car-rental firms have outlets in Moscow. Generally it is best to reserve your car before you arrive – advance reservations and special offers can reduce the price by 50% or more. Prices for on-the-spot hire with basic insurance start at €80 per day. The major car-rental agencies will usually pick up or drop off the car at your hotel:

Avis (☎ 578 7179; www.avis-moscow.ru/en/; Sheremetyevo-2)

Europcar (☎ 363 6418; www.europcar.ru/eng/; Domodedovo)

Hertz (Map pp246–7; ☎ 937 3274; www.hertz.ru; Smolnaya ul 24; Ⓜ Rechnoy Vokzal)

METRO

The metro is the easiest, quickest and cheapest way of getting around Moscow. Many of the elegant stations are marble-faced, frescoed, gilded works of art (see the Underground Odyssey tour, p117). The trains are generally reliable: you will rarely wait on the platform more than two minutes. Nonetheless, trains get packed during rush hour. Up to nine million people a day ride the metro, more than the London and New York City systems combined. Sometimes it feels like all nine million are trying to get on one train.

The 150-plus stations are marked with large 'M' signs. Magnetic tickets are sold at ticket booths (R13). It's useful to buy a multiple-ride ticket (10 rides for R120, 20 for R195), which saves you the hassle of queuing up every time.

Stations have maps of the system and signs on each platform showing the destination. Interchange stations are linked by underground passages, indicated by *perekhod* (underground crossing) signs, usually blue with a stick figure running up the stairs. The carriages now have maps inside that show the stops for that line in both Roman and Cyrillic letters. The system is fairly straightforward. The biggest confusion you may find is that often when two or more lines meet, each line's interchange station has a different name.

A map of the Moscow's metro system appears on pp256–7.

In late 2005, the first station of a new mini-metro line opened, serving the up-and-coming area known as Moscow-City (Moskva-City). This area, west of the Krem-

lin, along the north bank of the Moscow River, will be served by two new stations (Delovoy Tsentr and Mezhdunarodnaya).

TAXI

Almost any car in Moscow can be a taxi, so get on the street and stick your arm out. Many private cars cruise around as unofficial taxis, known as 'gypsy cabs', and other drivers will often take you if they're going in the same direction. Expect to pay R100 to R150 for a ride around the city centre.

Official taxis – recognisable by their chequerboard logo on the side and/or a small green light in the windscreen – charge about the same. No driver uses a meter (even if the cab has one), and few will admit to having change.

Don't hesitate to wave on a car if you don't like the look of its occupants. As a general rule, it's best to avoid riding in cars with more than one person. Problems are more likely to crop up if you take a street cab waiting outside a nightclub, or a tourist hotel or restaurant at night. Women need to be particularly careful.

If you book a taxi over the phone (hotel staff will do this for you if you don't speak Russian), the dispatcher will normally ring back within a few minutes to provide a description and license number of the car. It's best to provide at least an hour's notice before you need the taxi. Some reliable taxi companies (with websites in Russian only):

Central Taxi Reservation Office (Tsentralnoe Byuro Zakazov Taxi; ☎ 927 0000; www.cbz-taxi.ru)

RUSSIAN STREET NAMES

We use the Russian names of all streets and squares in this book to help you when deciphering Cyrillic signs and asking locals the way. The following abbreviations are used on the maps and for presenting practicalities information:

bul (*bulvar;* бульвар) – boulevard

nab (*naberezhnaya;* набережная) – embankment

per (*pereulok;* переулок) – lane or side street

pl (*ploshchad;* площадь) – square

pr (*prospekt;* проспект) – avenue

ul (*ulitsa;* улица) – street

sh (*shosse;* шоссе) – road

Directory

TRANSPORT

Eleks Polyus (☎ 707 2707; www.taxi-14.ru)

MV Motors (☎ 775 6775; www.7756775.ru)

New Yellow Taxi (☎ 940 8888; www.nyt.ru)

Taxi Bistro (☎ 327 5144; www.taxopark.ru)

Taxi Blues (☎ 105 5115; www.taxi-blues.ru)

TRAIN

Moscow has rail links to most parts of Russia, most former Soviet states, numerous countries in Eastern and Western Europe, and China and Mongolia. Sample fares and schedules are listed in the boxed texts. Prices are for a *kupe* (2nd-class in a four-seat couchette) ticket on a *skory* (fast) train.

Confusingly, the whole Russian rail network runs on Moscow time. You'll usually find timetables and station clocks on Moscow time, but if in doubt confirm these details carefully. The only general exception is suburban rail services, which stick to local time.

Tickets

For long-distance trains it's best to buy your tickets in advance. Tickets on some trains may be available on the day of departure, but this is less likely in summer. Always take your passport along when buying a ticket.

Tickets are sold at the train stations themselves, but it is much easier to buy tickets from a travel agent (see p226) or *kassa zheleznoy dorogi* (train-ticket office). These are often conveniently located in hotel lobbies. One agent selling airplane and train tickets is GlavAgentstvo, with the following outlets:

Belorussky vokzal (Belarus station; Map pp248–9)

Leningradsky vokzal (Leningrad station; Map p254)

Lubyanka ploshchad (Map pp248–9; ☎ 924 8728; Detsky Mir, Teatralny proezd 5/1; Ⓜ Lubyanka)

Pushkinskaya ploshchad (Map pp248–9; ☎ 290 2771; Tverskoy bul 14/5; Ⓜ Pushkinskaya)

Sheremetyevo-1 airport

Classes

On long-distance trains, your ticket will normally give the numbers of your carriage (*vagon*) and seat (*mesto*). For more details of travelling on Russian trains, see Lonely Planet's *Russia & Belarus* or *Trans-Siberian Railway*.

Compartments in a 1st-class carriage, also called soft class (*myagky*) or sleeping car (*spalnyy vagon, SV* or *lyux*), have upholstered seats and also convert to comfortable sleeping compartments for two people. Not all trains have a 1st-class carriage. Travelling 1st class costs about 50% more than a 2nd-class ticket.

Compartments in a 2nd-class carriage, usually called 'compartmentalised' (*kupeny* or *kupe*), are four-person couchettes.

Reserved place (*platskartny*), sometimes also called hard class or 3rd class, has open bunk accommodation. Groups of hard bunks are partitioned, but not closed off, from each other. This class is low on comfort, privacy and security.

Types of Train

The regular long-distance service is a fast train (*skory poezd*). It stops more often than an intercity train in the West and rarely gets up enough speed to merit the 'fast' label. Foreigners booking rail tickets through agencies are usually put on a *skory* train.

Generally, the best of the *skory* trains (*firmenny*) have cleaner cars, more polite attendants and much more convenient arrival and departure hours; they sometimes also have fewer stops, more 1st-class accommodation or functioning restaurants.

TRAINS FROM MOSCOW TO ST PETERSBURG

Train no & name	Departure	Duration	Fare
2 Krasnya Strela	11.55pm	8hr	R1700 (kupe)
4 Ekspress	11.59pm	8hr	R1700 (kupe)
6 Nikolaevsky Ekspress	11.30pm	8hr	R1700 (kupe)
24 Yunost	12.30pm	8hr	R1300 (seat)
160 Avrora	4.30pm	5½hr	R1300 (seat)
164 ER200	6.28pm	4½hr	R1700 (seat)

Directory

TRANSPORT

INTERNATIONAL TRAINS FROM MOSCOW

Destination & train no	Departure	Station	Duration	Fare (kupe)
Beijing 004	9.51pm	Yaroslavsky	132hr	R6413
Kyiv (Kiev) 001	8.23pm	Kievsky	14hr	R1033
Minsk 001	10.25pm	Belorussky	10hr	R654
Riga 001	7.11pm	Rizhsky	16hr	R2030
Tallinn 034	6.15pm	Leningradsky	15hr	R1560
Vilnius 005	7.01pm	Belorussky	15hr	R1588
Warsaw 009	3.52pm	Belorussky	20hr	R2200

A passenger train *(passazhirsky poezd)* can take an awfully long time to travel between cities. They are found mostly on routes of 1000km or less, clanking and lurching from one small town to the next.

SUBURBAN TRAINS

When taking trains from Moscow, note the difference between long-distance and 'suburban' trains. Long-distance trains run to places at least three or four hours out of Moscow, with limited stops and a range of classes. Suburban trains, known as *prigorodnye poezdy* or *elektrichka*, run to within 100km or 200km of Moscow, stop almost everywhere, and have a single class of hard bench seats. You buy your ticket before the train leaves, and there's no capacity limit.

Most Moscow stations have a separate ticket hall for suburban trains, usually called the *prigorodny zal*, which is often tucked away at the side or back of the station building. Suburban trains are usually listed on separate timetables and may depart from a separate group of platforms.

Stations

Moscow's nine main train stations *(vokzal):*

Belorussky (Belarus; Map pp248–9; Tverskaya Zastava pl; Ⓜ Belorusskaya) For trains heading west, including trains to/from Belarus, Lithuania, Poland and Germany, and some trains to/from the Czech Republic.

Kazansky (Kazan; Map p254; Komsomolskaya pl; Ⓜ Komsomolskaya) The start and end point for trains to/from the southeast, including Kazan and Central Asia.

Kursky (Kursk; Map p254; pl Kurskogo Vokzala; Ⓜ Kurskaya) Serves points south and east, including Vladimir, the Caucasus, eastern Ukraine, Crimea, Georgia, Azerbaijan.

Kievsky (Kyiv, or Kiev; Map pp252–3; pl Kievskogo Vokzala; Ⓜ Kievskaya) Serves points southwest, including Kyiv, western Ukraine, Moldova, Slovakia, Hungary, Austria, Romania, Bulgaria and Venice, as well as some trains to/from the Czech Republic.

Leningradsky (Leningrad; Map p254; Komsomolskaya pl; Ⓜ Komsomolskaya) For trains heading to/from the northwest, including St Petersburg, Vyborg, Estonia, Helsinki.

Paveletsky (Pavelets; Map pp252–3; Paveletskaya pl; Ⓜ Paveletskaya) For trains to/from points south, including the express train to Domodedovo airport.

DOMESTIC TRAINS FROM MOSCOW

Destination & train no	Departure	Station	Duration	Fare
Irkutsk 002	9.22pm	Yaroslavsky	77hr	R6200
Kazan 028	7.28pm	Kazansky	11hr	R1150
Murmansk 382	7.28pm	Leningradsky	34hr	R1860
Nizhny Novgorod 062*	4.55pm	Kursky	4½hr	R300 (seat)
Pskov 010	7.55pm	Leningradsky	12hr	R1120
Samara 010	6.50pm	Kazansky	15hr	R1888
Tver	10 daily	Leningradsky	2hr	R400
Vladimir 816*	6.04pm	Kursky	2½hr	R208 (seat)
Yaroslavl	14 daily	Yaroslavsky	4hr	R340
Yekaterinburg 122	4.50pm	Yaroslavsky	28hr	R2300

Fares are for *kupe,* unless stated otherwise. *Express train; other slower trains also available.

Rizhsky (Riga; Map pp246–7; Rizhskaya pl; Ⓜ Rizhskaya) Serves Latvia.

Savyolovsky (Savyolov; Map pp246–7; pl Savyolovskogo Vokzala; Ⓜ Savyolovskaya) For trains to/from the north-east including Yaroslavl.

Yaroslavsky (Yaroslavl; Map p254; Komsomolskaya pl; Ⓜ Komsomolskaya) Serves Yaroslavl and the longest-distance trains, including those to Mongolia, China, Russian Far East and anything east of the Urals.

LEFT LUGGAGE

You can check your bags at most hotels and train and bus stations. Look for signs for Камера Хранения *(kamera khraneniya)* or Автоматические Камеры Хранения *(avtomaticheskie kamery khraneniya)*. The latter refers to left-luggage lockers. Both options are usually secure, but be sure to note the opening and closing hours. To utilise the lockers:

1 Buy two tokens *(zhetony)* from the attendant.

2 Find an empty locker and put your luggage in.

3 Decide on a combination of one Russian letter and three numbers, and write it down.

4 Set the combination on the inside of the locker door.

5 Put one token in the slot.

6 Close the locker.

To open the locker, set your combination on the outside of the door. After you've set your combination, put the second token in the slot, wait a second or two for the electrical humming sound, and pull open the locker.

PRACTICALITIES

ACCOMMODATION

Moscow's accommodation options included in the Sleeping chapter are organised according to geographic location. Within each neighbourhood, they are listed in alphabetical order, with a few options for budget travellers listed under 'Cheap Sleeps' at the end of the listing for some neighbourhoods.

The hotel market in Moscow caters primarily to business travellers. As a result, prices are higher than you might expect. It also means that accommodation is harder to find during the week than on weekends, and prices may be lower on Friday and Saturday nights. Prices do not generally fluctuate seasonally, although there are certainly exceptions.

One such exception is that prices at the large, Western, chain hotels fluctuate dramatically, from weekday to weekend, from month to month, from season to season. Discounted rates are often available through booking services or through the hotel's website. By contrast, Russian hotels tend to publish one set of rates, which apply to anyone who walks through the door.

Reservations are highly recommended. Although Moscow has plenty of hotel rooms, there is a definite shortage of affordable rooms, and a veritable dearth of affordable, comfortable rooms. Unfortunately, some old-style hotels still charge a reservation fee – usually 20% but sometimes as much as 50% of the first night's tariff.

Russia does not have much of a bargaining culture. Haggling over the price of a hotel room – even in low season – will likely elicit confused stares. Keep in mind that the person at the reception probably does not have the authority to offer you any deal.

Most hotels will allow you to check-in as early as you arrive, as long as the room is available. Check-out is usually at noon, unless you pay for a *sutki* (24-hour period), in which case you can check-out at the same time that you checked-in, whether at 6am or at 6pm.

Booking Services

Many on-line booking services advertise discounted rates for hotels in Moscow. They are not all the same, so it pays to shop around. Moscow-specific online booking services:

www.destinationrussia.com

www.hotels-moscow.ru

www.moscowcity.com

www.moscow-hotels.net

www.moscow-hotels-russia.com

Rental Accommodation

Renting a flat in Moscow usually requires going through an agency. Check out the classified section in the *Moscow Times* or the listings on www.expat.ru for advertisements. Keep in mind, however, that most of these ads are placed by agencies that will charge a fee – usually equivalent to one month's rent.

The other option is to rent via a website catering to travellers (see p165). The disadvantage here is that these sites offer mostly short-term rentals, with small discounts for longer-term stays. This option turns out to be very pricey over the long haul.

BUSINESS HOURS

Government offices open from 9am or 10am to 5pm or 6pm weekdays. Hours for banks and other services vary. Large branches in busy commercial areas are usually open from 9am to 4.30pm or 5pm weekdays, with shorter hours on Saturday. Smaller branches have shorter hours, often closing for a one-hour break (*pereriv*) in the middle of the day.

The consumer culture is developing rapidly in Russia, and one place it is evident is hours of operation. Most shops are open daily, often from 10am to 8pm. Smaller shops might close on Sunday. Department stores and food shops are also usually open from 8am to 8pm daily. These days, many larger food shops stay open *kruglosutochno* (around the clock).

Restaurants typically open from noon to midnight, although – again – it is not unusual for them to stay open 24 hours a day.

Museum hours change often, as do their weekly days off. Most shut entrance doors 30 minutes or an hour before closing time. Many museums close for a 'sanitary day' during the last week of every month.

CHILDREN

You will know that Russia has made its transition to capitalism when you see the supermarkets well stocked with nappies, formulas and every other product your children might need.

Moscow does not present any particular hazards to your kids, save for ornery babushkas. (Even they seem to have a soft spot for kids, though.) While the Russian capital – filled with museums, churches and theatres – might not seem like the most appealing destination, it is surprisingly well equipped for youngsters. See the boxed text, p53 for a list of kid-friendly sights. In addition to these suggestions, children's theatre is a carry-over from the Soviet period that continues to thrive in Moscow (see p148). Purely capitalist innovations are the playrooms and kids' parties that are now offered

by many restaurants and bars, to attract their parents for lunch or dinner (see p126).

The concept of babysitting services has not yet developed in Moscow, although some upmarket hotels offer this service. Lonely Planet's *Travel with Children* contains useful advice on how to cope with kids on the road and what to bring to make things go more smoothly.

CLIMATE

Moscow enjoys an extreme continental climate, meaning hot summers and cold, cold winters. Spring and autumn are the most pleasant seasons to visit, but don't let the climate scare you away. See p21 for more information about climate. Refer to the City Calendar on p9 for events in the city.

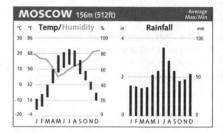

COURSES
Cooking

Russian cooking classes are hard to come by, but Dom Patriarshy (see p54) does offer an occasional half-day course. Learn to whip up some *bliny* (crepes) for lunch.

Language

Check the *Moscow Times* for advertisements for Russian tutors and short-term courses.

Center for Russian Language & Culture (Map pp246–7; ☎ 939 1463; www.ruslanguage.ru; Moscow State University, or MGU; 20-hour course per week €110; Ⓜ Universitet) Caters mostly to students, offering semester-long courses and dorm lodging.

Liden & Denz Language Centre (Map pp248–9; ☎ 254 4991; Gruzinsky per 3, no 181; www.lidenz.ru; 20 lessons for €255 per week – minimum two weeks; Ⓜ Belorusskaya) Has more expensive courses that service the business and diplomatic community with less-intensive evening courses.

Russian Village (☎ 721 7294; www.rusvillage.com; weekend/week/month course from €320/770/2380 including lodging and meals) An upscale 'country resort' language school located in the village of Pestovo, north of Moscow.

Ziegler & Partner (Map pp246–7; ☎ /fax 939 0980; www .studyrussian.com; MGU; Ⓜ Universitet) A Swiss group offering individually designed courses, from standard conversation to specialised lessons in business, literature etc.

CUSTOMS

When you enter Russia, you'll have the option to fill out a declaration form (dekla-ratsia). If you have more than US$10,000 in goods and currency, you are required to fill out this form and go through the red lane, to have your form stamped. This process may require having your luggage checked.

If you have less than US$10,000 you are not required to get your customs form stamped and you can proceed through the green line. However, if you have any valuable items (such as expensive jewellery or electronics) it may be useful to declare it, to protect yourself and your stuff when you are leaving the country. In this case, make sure you get a stamp on your customs declaration form on your arrival.

Travellers may leave Russia with up to US$3000 in goods and currency without submitting declaration forms. In order to ensure your ability to leave with valuable items from home, follow the advice earlier. Stamped declaration forms will have to be submitted upon exit from Russia. Your stamped form cannot show that you are leaving with more than you brought in. The system is antiquated – considering the reality of credit-card purchases and ATM access to cash – but nonetheless it is still in place.

Look after your stamped customs declaration. If you lose it you will need a police report confirming the loss, which you have to present to customs when you leave Russia.

What You Can Bring In

You may bring in modest amounts of anything for personal use except, obviously, illegal drugs and weapons. Less obviously, visitors are banned from bringing in GPS devices. If you're travelling with hypodermic needles, bring in a prescription for them and declare them under the line 'Narcotics and appliances for use thereof'.

Up to 1000 cigarettes and 5L of alcohol are allowed (note that prices for such items

in Russia will almost certainly be cheaper than abroad), but large amounts of anything saleable are suspect. Food is allowed (except for some fresh fruit and veggies).

What You Can Take Out

You can take anything bought from a legitimate shop or department store, but save your receipts.

Items more than 100 years old cannot be taken out of the country. Anything vaguely 'arty', such as manuscripts, instruments, coins, jewellery, antiques or antiquarian books (meaning those published before 1975) must be assessed by the Committee for Culture (Map pp248–9; ☎ 244 7675; ul Arbat 53, Arbat District; ⊙ 10am-2pm & 3-6pm Mon-Fri; Ⓜ Smolenskaya). Bring your item (or a photograph, if the item is large) and your receipt. The bureaucrats there will issue a receipt for tax paid, which you show to customs on your way out of the country.

A painting bought at a tourist art market, in a department store, or from a commercial gallery should be declared and receipts should be kept. Generally speaking, customs in airports is much more strict and thorough than at any border crossing.

It is technically illegal to take roubles out of the country, so it's best to change any large sums before you depart.

DISABLED TRAVELLERS

Inaccessible transport, lack of ramps and lifts, and no centralised policy for people with physical limitations make Russia a challenging destination for wheelchair-bound visitors. More mobile travellers will have a relatively easier time, but keep in mind that there are obstacles along the way. Toilets are frequently accessed from stairs in restaurants and museums; distances are great; public transport is extremely crowded; and many footpaths are in a very poor condition.

This situation is changing (albeit very slowly), as buildings undergo renovations and become more accessible. Most upscale hotels (especially those belonging to Western chains) offer accessible rooms.

Some local organisations that might be useful for disabled travellers:

All-Russian Society for the Blind (Map pp248–9; ☎ 928 1374; www.vos.org.ru; Novaya pl 14, Kitay Gorod; Ⓜ Kitay Gorod) Provides info and services for visually impaired people, including operating holiday and recreation centres.

All-Russian Society for the Deaf (Map pp248–9; ☎ 252 1043; ul 1905 goda 10A, Barrikadnaya; Ⓜ Ulitsa 1905 Goda) Organises cultural activities and has recreational facilities for its members.

All-Russian Society of Disabled People (Map pp246–7; ☎ 935 0064; ul Udaltsova 11; Ⓜ Prospekt Vernadkogo) Does not offer any services to travellers, but may provide publications (in Russian) on legal issues or local resources.

ELECTRICITY

Standard voltage is 220V, 50Hz AC, though some places still have an old 127V system. Sockets require a continental or European plug with two round pins. Look for voltage (V) and frequency (Hz) labels on your appliances. Some trains and hotel bathrooms have 110V and 220V shaver plugs.

EMBASSIES

It's wise to register with your embassy, especially if you'll be in Russia for a long stay. For more embassies check www.themoscow times.ru/travel/facts/embassies.html.

Australia (Map p254; ☎ 956 6070; www.australianembassy .ru; Podkolokolny per 10A/2, Kitay Gorod; Ⓜ Kitay Gorod)

Canada (Map pp252–3; ☎ 105 6000; Starokonyushenny per 23, Kropotkinskaya; Ⓜ Kropotkinskaya)

France (Map pp252–3; ☎ 937 1500; www.ambafrance.ru; ul Bolshaya Yakimanka, Zamoskvorechie; Ⓜ Oktyabrskaya)

Germany (Map pp246–7; ☎ 937 9500; www.germany .org.ru; Mosfilmovskaya ul 56; Ⓜ Universitet, then bus No 119) Consular Section (☎ 933 4312; Leninsky pr 95A; Ⓜ Prospekt Vernadskogo, then bus Nos 616 or 153)

Ireland (Map p254; ☎ 937 5911; Grokholsky per 5, Chistye Prudy; Ⓜ Prospekt Mira)

Netherlands (Map pp248–9; ☎ 797 2900; Kalashny per 6, Arbat District; Ⓜ Arbatskaya)

UK (Map pp248–9; ☎ 956 7200; www.britemb.msk.ru; Smolenskaya nab 10, Arbat District; Ⓜ Smolenskaya)

USA (Map pp248–9; ☎ 728 5000; www.usembassy .state.gov/moscow; Bol Devyatinsky per 8, Barrikadnaya; Ⓜ Barrikadnaya)

EMERGENCY

Ambulance ☎ 03, in Russian

Crisis hotline ☎ 244 3449, in English ☎ 937 9999

Emergency ☎ 766 0601, in English ☎ 245 4387

Fire ☎ 01, in Russian

Police ☎ 02, in Russian

GAY & LESBIAN TRAVELLERS

Moscow is the most cosmopolitan of Russian cities, and the active gay and lesbian scene reflects this attitude. Newspapers such as the *Moscow Times* feature articles about gay and lesbian issues, as well as listings of gay and lesbian clubs. The newest publication of note is the glossy magazine *Queer* (Квир), which offers up articles and artwork.

For details on venues, see the boxed text, p144. Some other useful resources:

www.gay.ru/english Includes updated club listings, plus information on gay history and culture in Russia.

www.gaytours.ru While Dmitry is no longer working as a tour guide, his site is still a wealth of information about gay life in Moscow.

www.lesbi.ru An active site for lesbian issues; in Russian only.

Cracks in the Iron Closet: Travels in Gay & Lesbian Russia, by David Tuller and Frank Browning, is a fascinating account of the gay and lesbian scene in modern Russia. A combination of travel memoir and social commentary, it reveals an emerging homosexual culture that is surprisingly different from its US counterpart.

Queer Sites, by Dan Healy, traces the history of seven world cities, including Moscow, focusing on sexual mores, the homosexual experience, and how they have changed over time.

HOLIDAYS

During major holidays, Moscow empties out, as many residents retreat from the city for much-needed vacations: the first week in January (between New Year's Day and Orthodox Christmas), and the first week or two of May (around May Day and Victory Day). Transport is difficult to book around these periods, though accommodation is usually not a problem. While many residents leave, the city is a festive place during these times, usually hosting parades, concerts and other events. The downside is that many museums and other institutions have shortened hours or are closed altogether during holiday periods.

INTERNET ACCESS

Besides the plethora of Internet cafés, wireless access (wi-fi) is also becoming more common around Moscow. Take advantage of free wi-fi access at several upscale hotels,

PUBLIC HOLIDAYS

New Year's Day 1 January
Russian Orthodox Christmas 7 January
International Women's Day 8 March
International Labour Day/Spring Festival 1 and 2 May
Victory (1945) Day 9 May
Russian Independence 12 June
Day of Reconciliation and Accord (formerly Revolution Day) 7 November

anyone who remotely looks as if they come from the Caucasus, and other people with darkish skin, but the *militsiya* have the right to stop anyone. Technically, everyone is required to carry their *dokumenty*, or passport, on their person at all times. Unfortunately, some readers have complained about police pocketing their passports and demanding bribes. The best way to avoid such unpleasantness is to carry a photocopy of your passport, visa and registration, and present that when an officer demands to see your *dokumenty*. A photocopy is sufficient, despite what the officer may argue.

as well as NetLand or Time Online listed here. A more complete listing of clubs and cafés with wi-fi access is at http://wifi.yandex .ru, in Russian – click on Где ето (*gde eto*).

Internet Club (Map pp248–9; ☎ 292 5670; Kuznetsky most 12, Petrovsky District; per hr R60; ☼ 9am-8pm Mon-Fri, 10am-midnight Sat &Sun; Ⓜ Kuznetsky Most) Small, simple and very central. It lacks the hip atmosphere of its competitors, but gets the job done.

Netcity (Map pp248–9; ☎ 292 0111; Kamergersky per 6, Kitay Gorod; per hr R60; ☼ 10am-11pm; Ⓜ Teatralnaya) Work stations at this trendy café offer form more than function, but they are sufficient to surf the net or check email. It has good coffee and fresh-squeezed juice. There is another branch (Map p255; ☎ 969 2125; Paveletskaya pl 2/1, Zamoskvorechie; per hr R60; ☼ 9.30am-midnight; Ⓜ Paveletskaya).

NetLand (Map pp248–9; ☎ 781 0923; Teatralny pr 5, City Centre; per hr R40-60; ☼ 24hr; Ⓜ Kuznetsky Most or Lubyanka) A loud, dark club that fills up with kids playing computer games. You may want to take advantage of the more peaceful VIP room. It's inside the Detsky Mir building; enter from ulitsa Rozhdestvenka.

Phlegmatic Dog (Map pp248–9; ☎ 995 9545; Okhotny Ryad, ground level; ☼ 10am-1am; Ⓜ Okhotny Ryad) Recently voted 'Most Stylish' Internet café in the world by Yahoo! Mail. Cool music and cold beers are nice, but the real draw is free Internet access with the purchase of food or drink.

Time Online (Map pp248–9; ☎ 363 0060; Okhotny Ryad, basement; per hr R65-75; ☼ 24hr; Ⓜ Okhotny Ryad) Offers copy and photo services, and over 200 zippy computers or free wi-fi access. Besides the original outlet in Okhotny Ryad, there is a branch near Belorussky vokzal (Map pp248–9; ☎ 363 0060; Bolshoy Kondretevsky per 7, Tverskoy District; per hr R65-75; ☼ 24hr; Ⓜ Belorusskaya).

LEGAL MATTERS

It's not unusual to see police officers, or *militsiya*, randomly stopping people on the street to check their documents. In recent years, this checking has tended to focus on

LIBRARIES & CULTURAL CENTRES

British Council Resource Centre (Map p254; ☎ 782 0200; www.britishcouncil.org/ru; Nikoloyamskaya ul 1, Zayauzie; ☼ noon-7pm Mon-Fri, 10am-6pm Sat; Ⓜ Taganskaya) Located at the Foreign Literature Library; take your passport.

Foreign Literature Library (Map p254; ☎ 915 3669; Nikoloyamskaya ul 1, Zayauzie; ☼ 10am-8pm Mon-Fri, 10am-6pm Sat; Ⓜ Taganskaya) Home to several international libraries and cultural centres, including the American Cultural Center Library, the French Cultural Centre and the British Council Resource Centre.

Russian State Library (Map pp248–9; Vozdvizhenka ul 3; ☼ 9am-9pm; Ⓜ Biblioteka imeni Lenina) On the corner of Mokhovaya ulitsa, this is one of the world's largest libraries, with over 20 million volumes. Take your passport and one passport photo, and fill in some forms at the information office to get a free *chitatelsky bilet* (reader's card).

MAPS

An excellent, up-to-date map in English is *Moscow Today*, published by Atlas Print Company. It is usually available at Atlas (see p157) and other bookstores around Moscow including Biblio-Globus (see p155). Or, see http://en.atlas-print.ru/. Accurate maps in Cyrillic are easily available in Moscow.

MEDICAL SERVICES

Before purchasing travel insurance, make sure the policy will be recognised by Russian medical facilities.

For a list of pharmacies, see p223.

American Medical Center (Map p254; ☎ 933 7700; www.amcenters.com; Grokholsky per 1, Chistye Prudy; Ⓜ Prospekt Mira) Offers 24-hour emergency service, consultations and a full range of specialists, including paediatricians and dentists. It has an onsite pharmacy with English-speaking staff.

Botkin Hospital (Map pp246–7; ☎ 237 8338, 945 7533; 2-y Botkinsky proezd 5, North of the Centre; Ⓜ Begovaya) The best Russian facility.

European Medical Center (Map pp248–9; ☎ 933 6655; www.emcmos.ru; Spirodonovsky per 5, Tverskoy District; Ⓜ Mayakovskaya) Includes medical and dental facilities, which are open around the clock for emergencies. The staff speaks 10 different languages.

MONEY

Russian currency is the rouble, written as рубль or abbreviated as руб. There are 100 kopecks (копеек or коп) in the rouble, and these come in small coins that are worth one, 10 and 50 kopecks. Roubles are issued in coins in amounts of one, two and five roubles. Banknotes come in values of 10, 50, 100, 500 and 1000 roubles. Small stores, kiosks and many other vendors have difficulty changing large notes, so save those scrappy little ones.

The rouble has been relatively stable since it was revalued in 1998 (see p19 for more details). Exchange rates are listed in Quick Reference inside the front cover. See www.oanda.com/convert/classic for more up-to-date rates.

Alfa Bank (⊘ 8.30am-8pm Mon-Sat) has many branches around Moscow that usually change travellers cheques. ATMs at the branches listed dispense either roubles or US dollars. You will also see branches of the affiliated Alfa-Express, which have ATMs:

Arbat District (Map pp248–9; ul Arbat 4/1; Ⓜ Arbatskaya)

Petrovsky District (Map pp248–9; Kuznetsky Most 7; Ⓜ Kuznetsky Most)

Tverskoy District (Map pp248–9; Marriott Grand Hotel, ul Tverskaya 26; Ⓜ Mayakovskaya)

ATMs

Automatic teller machines (ATMs), linked to international networks such as AmEx, Cirrus, Eurocard, MasterCard and Visa, are now common throughout Moscow. Look for signs that say bankomat (Банкомат). Using a credit or debit card, you can always obtain roubles and often US dollars.

Changing Money

US dollars and euros are now widely accepted at exchange bureaus around Moscow. Other currencies will undoubtedly cause more hassle than they are worth. Whatever currency you bring should be in pristine condition. Banks and exchanges do not accept old, tatty bills with rips or tears. For US dollars make certain that besides looking and smelling newly minted, they are of the new design, with the large off-set portrait.

When you visit the exchange office, be prepared to fill out a lengthy form and show your passport. Your receipt is for your own records, as customs officials no longer require documentation of your currency transactions. As anywhere, it's always worth shopping around for the best rates.

Credit Cards

Credit cards, especially Visa and Master-Card, are becoming more widely accepted, not only at upmarket hotels, restaurants and stores. You can also use your credit card to get a cash advance at most major banks in Moscow.

Travellers Cheques

Travellers cheques are still relatively difficult to change. The process can be lengthy, involving trips to numerous different cashiers in the bank, each responsible for a different part of the transaction. Expect to pay 1% to 2% commission.

Not all travellers cheques are treated as equal by Russian establishments willing to handle them. You'll have little or no luck with any brands other than AmEx, Thomas Cook and Visa. The most reliable place to cash AmEx travellers cheques is **American Express** (Map pp252–3; ☎ 933 6636; ul Usachyova 33, Khamovniki; Ⓜ Sportivnaya). It also offers ATM, mail holding and travel services for AmEx card holders.

NEWSPAPERS & MAGAZINES

All of the following English-language publications can be found at hotels, restaurants and cafés around town that are frequented by tourists. Numerous other publications seem to appear at random, lasting a few issues and then vanishing. *Afisha* is a glossy magazine in Russian that comes out bi-weekly with lots of information about pop culture and entertainment events.

element (www.elementmoscow.ru) This oversized weekly newsprint magazine has restaurant reviews, concert listings and art exhibits. It also publishes a seasonal supplement highlighting Moscow's hottest restaurants.

Exile (www.exile.ru) An irreverent, free weekly, with extensive entertainment listings. It is hard not to be offended by this rag, which may be why it is not as widely distributed as it used to be.

Go (www.go-magazine.ru) The *Moscow Times'* monthly entertainment guide.

Moscow News (www.moscownews.ru) This long-standing, Russian news weekly recently reappeared as an English-language publication, focusing on domestic and international politics and business.

Moscow Times (www.themoscowtimes.com) The undisputed king of the hill in locally published English-language news is this first-rate daily, which covers Russian and international issues, as well as sports and entertainment. The Friday edition is a great source for what's happening at the weekend.

PHARMACIES

A chain of 24-hour pharmacies called 36.6 has many branches all around the city, including the following:

Arbat District (Map pp248–9; Novy Arbat ul 15; Ⓜ Smolenskaya)

Kitay Gorod (Map p254; ul Pokrovka 1; Ⓜ Kitay Gorod)

Petrovsky District (Map pp248–9; Kuznetsky Most 18; Ⓜ Kuznetsky Most)

Tverskoy District (Map pp248–9; Tverskaya ul 25; Ⓜ Tverskaya or Mayakovskaya)

POST

Although the service has improved dramatically in recent years, the usual warnings about delays and disappearances of incoming and outgoing mail apply to Moscow. Airmail letters take two to three weeks from Moscow to the UK, and three to four weeks to the USA or Australasia.

Incoming mail is so unreliable that many companies, hotels and even individuals prefer to use private services that have their addresses in either Germany or Finland. The mail completes its journey to its Russian destination with a private carrier. Unfortunately, alternative options do not really exist.

Should you decide to send mail to Moscow or try to receive it, note that addresses should be written in reverse order: Russia, postal code, city, street address, and then name.

Central Telegraph (Map pp248–9; Tverskaya ul 7, Tverskoy District; ✆ post 8am-10pm, telephone 24hr; Ⓜ Okhotny Ryad) This convenient office also offers telephone, fax and Internet services.

Main Post Office (Map p254; Myasnitskaya ul 26, Chistye Prudy; ✆ 8am-8pm Mon-Fri, 9am-7pm Sat & Sun; Ⓜ Chistye Prudy) Moscow's main post office is on the corner of Chistoprudny bulvar.

Express Services

All the following operate air courier services. Call for information on drop-off locations and to arrange pick-ups.

DHL Worldwide Express (☎ 956 1000)

FedEx (☎ 234 3400)

TNT (☎ 797 2777)

UPS (☎ 961 2211)

RADIO
Russian-Language

Radio in Russia is broken into three bands: AM, UKV (the lower band of FM from 66–77MHz) and FM (100–107MHz). Western-made FM radios usually won't go lower than 85MHz.

Some of the more popular radio stations include the following:

Ekho Moskvy (91.2FM) Interviews, news, jazz and some Western and local pop music.

Love Radio (106.6FM) Russian and Western pop featuring, you guessed it, love songs.

Radio Maximum (103.7FM) European rock and pop, Russian…intellectual pop, if this is not a contradiction in terms.

Radio Rossii Nostalgie (FM 100.5) Western retro rock from the USA, Britain and France.

Radio-7 (FM 104.7) Mainly Western pop and rock plus some Russian rock from bands such as Aquarium and DDT.

Silver Rain (FM 100.1) Mellow Western pop music, sometimes retro.

Ultra (FM 100.5) Alternative Western music.

English-Language

The clearest BBC World Service shortwave (SW) frequencies in the morning, late evening and at night are near 9410kHz and 12,095kHz (the best), although the exact setting varies with your location in Russia. The BBC broadcasts at the following times and frequencies:

Time	Frequency
2-5am	9410kHz
3-9pm	9410kHz
2-5am	6195kHz
6-8pm	6195kHz
5am-9pm	12,095kHz
6am-3pm	15,565kHz
7am-3pm	17,640kHz
8pm-midnight	5930kHz
	6180kHz
	7325kHz

SAFETY

Unfortunately, street crime targeting tourists has increased in recent years, although Moscow is not as dangerous as paranoid locals might have you think. As in any big city, be on your guard against pickpockets and muggers. Be particularly careful at or around metro stations, especially at Kurskaya and Partizanskaya, where readers have reported specific incidents. Always be cautious about taking taxis late at night, especially near bars and clubs that are in isolated areas. Never get into a car that already has two or more people in it.

Watch out for gangs of children (generally referred to as 'gypsy kids'), who are after anything they can get their hands on.

Some policemen can be bothersome, especially to dark-skinned or some foreign-looking people. Practical advice from a Moscow synagogue is 'cover your kippa (skullcap)'. Other members of the police force target tourists. Reports of tourists being hassled about their documents and registration have declined. However, it's still wise to carry a photocopy of your passport, visa and registration stamp. If stopped by a member of the police force, do not hand over your passport! It is perfectly acceptable to show a photocopy instead.

The most common hazards are violent or xenophobic drunks, and overly friendly drunks.

TAX & REFUNDS

The value-added tax (VAT, in Russian NDS) is 20% and is usually included in the price listed for purchases. Moscow also has a 5% sales tax that is usually only encountered in top hotels.

TELEPHONE

The telephone country code for Russia is ☎ 7. The new Moscow city code is ☎ 495, which is the area code for phone numbers listed in this book, unless otherwise stated. If calling Moscow from abroad, dial the entire code.

To call internationally from Moscow, dial ☎ 8, wait for the second tone, then dial ☎ 10 plus the country code, city code and phone number. The method of placing international calls is also expected to change in 2007 or 2008 (see the boxed text, opposite).

Hotel Phones

At most traditional Russian hotels, local calls are free. Placing a long-distance call may or may not be possible, but check with the hotel administration. Calls from expensive Western hotels are, well, expensive. Most hotel-room phones provide a direct-dial number for incoming calls, which saves having to be connected through the switchboard. How-

WHERE THE STREETS ARE PAVED WITH MONEY

Beware of well-dressed people dropping wads of money on the streets of Moscow.

A common scam in Moscow involves a respectable-looking person who 'accidentally' drops some money on the footpath as he passes by an unsuspecting foreigner – that's you. Being an honest person, you pick up the money to return it to the careless person, who is hurrying away. A second guy sees what is happening and tries to stop you from returning it, proposing that you split the money and, well, split. He may try to lure you off the busy street to a private place to broker the deal.

This is a no-win situation. These guys are in cahoots. While you are negotiating about how to split the money – or arguing about returning it – the first guy suddenly realises he is missing his cash. He returns to the scene of the crime. But lo and behold, the cash you return to him is not enough: some money is missing and you are culpable. This leads to a shakedown or any number of unpleasantries.

The moral of the story is that the streets of Moscow are not paved with money. Resist the temptation to pick up money lying on the sidewalk.

CHANGING PHONE NUMBERS

Russian authorities have an annoying habit of frequently changing telephone numbers, particularly in cities. We've tried our best to list the correct telephone number at the time of research but it's likely that some will change during the lifetime of this book. As of December 2005 Moscow's telephone code has been 495, though in some areas, mainly suburbs, it is 499. Moscow Region (the countryside just outside Moscow) is changing to 496, and there are plans to change all city codes that start with 0, generally substituting 4 for the initial 0. The reason for this is that in 2007/2008 intercity and international connection codes will be changed to 0 and 00 respectively (from the current 8 and 8 + 10).

ever, this can lead to unwanted disturbances, namely unsolicited calls from prostitutes.

Mobile Phones

Mobile (or cell) phones (*sotovye telefony*) are now ubiquitous in the capital, as Muscovites bypass the antiquated landline system. It is often possible to use your phone that you bring from home, but you should check with your provider before departure because this can be prohibitively expensive.

In some cases it's necessary to dial ☎ 8 when trying to reach a mobile phone (as when making an intercity/international call).

Alternatively, it is a simple procedure to set up a 'pay-as-you-go' account with a local provider. Phone cards are sold at stores and kiosks all over the city for 50, 100, 200 or 500 units. The cards provide instructions on how to enter a secret code and credit the units to your account. Instructions are in Russian, so you might ask for assistance when you purchase your phone. Units are consumed faster or slower depending on whether you call domestic or international numbers or within the same mobile-phone network. Note that you spend your units both when you dial and when you receive calls.

Several companies offer such services, with rates varying significantly; some of the service providers offer surprisingly low rates for international calls:

Euroset (Map pp248–9; ☎ 777 7710; www.euroset.ru; Tverskaya ul 4, City Centre; Ⓜ Okhotny Ryad) A large salon that carries many different brands of phones, and sells subscriptions to any provider.

Megafon (Map pp248–9; ☎ 507 7777; Malaya Sukharevskaya pl 1, Petrovsky District; Ⓜ Sukharevskaya) Offers the cheapest rates for 'pay-as-you-go' service.

MTS (Map p255; ☎ 915 2110; Marksistskaya ul 4, Zayauzie; www.mts.ru; Ⓜ Taganskaya) Another prominent service provider.

Pay Phones

Most pay phones require prepaid phonecards, which are available from metro token booths and from kiosks. Cardphones can be used for local and domestic or international long-distance calls. Cards in a range of units are available; international calls require at least 100 units. The only trick is to remember to press the button with the speaker symbol when your party answers the phone.

Telephone Offices

The **Central Telegraph** (Map pp248–9; Tverskaya ul 7, Tverskoy District; ⓨ 24hr) is convenient for phone calls and doubles as a post office. For calls, you leave a deposit with an attendant and are assigned a private booth where you dial your number directly as outlined on opposite. Again, you might have to press the button with the speaker symbol or ответ (answer) when your party answers the phone.

In some other offices, you may have to give your number to an attendant who dials the number and then sends you to a booth to take the call. You can collect change from your deposit when you leave. Rates are similar to home services.

The post or telegraph office is also the place to send a fax.

TIME

Russians use the 12-hour clock and the 24-hour clock interchangeably. From the end of September to the end of March, Moscow time is GMT/UTC plus three hours. So when it is noon in Moscow it is:

9am in London

4am in New York

1am in San Francisco

7pm in Vladivostok

From the last Sunday in March to the last Sunday in September, 'summer time' is in force and the time becomes GMT/UTC plus four hours.

Directory

PRACTICALITIES

TIPPING

Tipping is becoming increasingly common in restaurants, especially in upmarket establishments. Plan to leave 10% of your bill. Tipping your guide – generally R100 to R300 per day – is also an accepted practice. Small gifts, such as a box of chocolates, a CD or a souvenir from home are also appropriate and appreciated.

TOILETS

Pay toilets are identified by the words платный туалет (platny tualet). In any toilet Женский or Ж stands for women's (zhensky), while Мужской or M stands for men's (muzhskoy).

Plastic-cabin portable loos are scattered around Moscow in public places, but other public toilets are rare. Where they do exist, they are often dingy and uninviting. These days, though, the oilets in hotels, restaurants and cafés are usually modern and clean, so public toilets need only be used for emergencies.

Toilet paper is not the rarity it once was. But it's still wise to carry your own supply, as there is no guarantee it will be there when you need it.

TOURIST INFORMATION

Moscow has no tourist-information centre. However, plenty of information is available either at hostels and upscale hotels, through travel agents or through the print media (see p18). Other useful resources available include:

http://eng.menu.ru Reviews and menus from hundreds of Moscow restaurants.

http://eng.moscowout.ru Provides a full calendar of events in the capital, with links to restaurant and movie reviews, nightlife and activities for kids.

www.expat.ru Run by and for English-speaking expats living in Russia, this site provides useful information about real estate, children in Moscow, social groups and more.

www.mbtg.ru The free Moscow Business Telephone Guide is an invaluable, bilingual phonebook.

www.moscow-taxi.com Viktor the virtual taxi driver provides extensive descriptions of sites in and outside of Moscow, as well as hotel booking and other tourist services.

www.waytorussia.net Lists restaurant and accommodation options and has lots of information about local events, sights and transport.

TRAVEL AGENCIES

If you're just interested in getting train or plane tickets, in addition to the following agencies you can also try GlavAgentstvo (see p215). The following agencies offer more services, including tours:

G&R International (Map pp246–7; ☎ 378 0001; www .hostels.ru; ul Zelenodolskaya 3/2, 5th fl; Ⓜ Ryazansky Prospekt) Operates the Hostel Asia, as well as organising tour itineraries, providing visa support and selling transport tickets.

Infinity Travel (Map pp252–3; ☎ 234 6555; www.infin ity.ru; Komsomolsky pr 13, Khamovniki; Ⓜ Park Kultury) Affiliated with the Travellers Guest House, this on-the-ball travel company is a great source of airline tickets and also offers rail tickets, visa support and trans-Siberian and Central Asia packages.

VISAS

All foreigners visiting Russia need visas. A Russian visa can either be a passport-sized paper document that is separate from your passport or a sticker in your passport. The visa lists entry/exit dates, your passport number, any children travelling with you and visa type. It's an exit permit too, so if you lose it (or overstay), leaving the country can be harder than getting in.

There are five types of visa available to foreign visitors, as listed below.

Business Visas

Far more flexible and desirable for the independent traveller is a business visa. A single-entry business visa is valid for up to three months, while a multiple-entry visa may be valid for up to 12 months. Both of these allow complete freedom of movement once you arrive in Russia.

A business visa requires the same documentation listed in the boxed text (see opposite), but the invitation from a Russian company is usually more expensive. Also, the Russian consulate may require the original copy of this invitation. In addition to these documents, travellers applying for a visa for more than three months must submit an HIV-AIDS test certificate.

Note that your visa registration may or may not be included in the price of your invitation. If you are not planning to stay at a hotel, be sure that the company issuing your invitation can register your visa once you arrive in Moscow.

Tourist Visas

These are the most straightforward but inflexible visas available and allow a stay of up to 30 days in Russia. In theory, you're supposed to have prebooked accommodation for every night in Russia, but in practice you can often get away with only booking a few, perhaps even just one. Once your visa has been registered at your hotel, you can move freely in Russia and stay where you like.

Extending a tourist visa is a hassle and the extension, if granted, will usually be only for a short time. So, tourist visas are best for trips when you know exactly what you're doing and when, where and for how long you'll be doing it. In addition to the items listed in the boxed text, above, you will also need a voucher issued by the travel agency that provided your invitation. Note that Russian consulates reserve the right to see your return ticket or some other proof of onward travel when you apply for a visa.

Transit Visas

This is for 'passing through', which is loosely interpreted. For transit by air it's usually good for 48 hours. For a nonstop Trans-Siberian Railway journey it's valid for 10 days, giving westbound passengers a few days in Moscow; those heading east, however, are not allowed to linger in Moscow. To obtain a transit visa, you will need to show the itinerary for your entire trip, as well as any visa needed for your onward journey.

'Private' Visas

This is the visa you get for a visit by personal invitation, and it's also referred to as an 'ordinary' visa by some authorities. The visa itself is as easy to get as a tourist visa, but getting the invitation is a complex matter.

The person who is inviting you must go to their local visa office of the Russian Ministry of Internal Affairs (RMIA) – sometimes still referred to as OVIR – and fill out an invitation form for approval of the invitation. Approval, which takes several weeks, comes in the form of a notice of permission *(izveshchenie)*, good for one year, which the person inviting you must send to you. You will need this invitation approval notice, together with the standard application form, to apply for the visa, which is valid for up to 60 days in your host's town. On arrival in Russia you will also have to go to the local visa office to register your visa (see p228).

Student Visas

Student visas are flexible, extendable and even entitle you to pay Russian prices for items affected under the country's dual-pricing system (see p20). You'll need an invitation from the Ministry of Internal Affairs, which the Russian school or university will help you obtain (after paying upfront for the tuition, no doubt). To obtain a visa valid for more than three months, you must submit an HIV-AIDS test certificate.

How & When to Apply

Apply for a visa as soon as you have all the documents you need (but not more than two months ahead). Business, tourist, private and student visas all take the same amount of time to process once you have the paperwork. Processing time ranges from 24 hours to two weeks, depending on how much you are willing to pay. Transit visas normally take seven working days, but may take as little as a few hours at the Russian embassy in Beijing.

It's possible to apply at your local Russian consulate by dropping off all the necessary documents with the right payment, or by mailing it all (along with a self-addressed, postage-paid envelope). When you receive the visa, be sure to check it carefully – especially the expiry, entry and exit dates and any restrictions on entry or exit points.

Registration

When you check in at a hotel, camping ground or hostel, you surrender your passport and visa so the hotel can register you with the local visa office. You'll get your documents back the next morning, if not the same day. Alternatively, the tourist agency that issued your visa is responsible for your registration. *All* Russian visas must be registered with the local visa office within three business days of your arrival in Russia. No 'ifs' or 'buts' about it. You may have to pay a registration fee, especially if the registration is provided by an agency, not a hotel.

The company or organisation that invites you to Russia is responsible for your initial registration – and no other company can support your visa. If you're not sure which organisation invited you, the simplest option is to spend a night at one of the major hotels, which will register your visa for you at the front desk. There may be a fee involved, but usually the cost of the room will suffice.

Extending a visa that's not registered can be impossible, and getting out of the country with an unregistered visa could be a very expensive proposition.

WOMEN TRAVELLERS

Although sexual harassment on the streets is rare, it is common in the workplace, in the home and in personal relations. Discrimination and domestic violence are hard facts of life for many Russian women. Some estimate that as many as 12,000 to 16,000 women throughout Russia die at the hands of their partners every year. Alcoholism and unemployment are related problems.

Activists ridicule as hypocritical the 8th of March Women's Day celebrations in Russia (see p10) while such problems con-

tinue. Others say it is the one day in the year that men have to be nice to their mates.

Foreign women are likely to receive some attention, mostly in the form of genuine, friendly interest. An interested stranger may approach you out of the blue and ask: *'Mozhno poznokomitsa?'* (May we become acquainted?). The easiest answer is a gentle, but firm, *'Nyet'*. The conversation usually goes no further, although drunken men may be more persistent. The best way to lose an unwelcome suitor is to enter an upmarket hotel or restaurant, where ample security will come to your aid. Women should avoid taking private taxis alone at night.

Russian women dress up and wear lots of make-up on nights out. If you are wearing casual gear, you might feel uncomfortable in an upmarket restaurant, club or theatre.

The following websites provide useful information about women's organisations in Moscow:

www.members.tripod.com/IWC_Moscow The International Women's Club is an active group of expat women. They are involved in organising social and charity events.

www.womnet.ru The Women Information Network (WIN) site, in Russian only, is updated regularly. It has news items, local events, book reviews and information on grants for women's organisations.

www.womnet.ru/db/english/english.html WIN also has this extensive database of women's organisations throughout Russia. Search by name, location or area of interest.

WORK

Working in Russia can be an exciting, rewarding, enlightening, frustrating insanity-inducing experience. The opportunities for employment have lessened since Russia's economic crash of August 1998, but there are still loads of Westerners employed by multinational and local companies.

If you are interested in working in Russia, Jonathan Packer's book *Live & Work in Russia and Eastern Europe* is a good reference. English-language publications such as the *Moscow Times* also have job listings.

The following groups can provide a wealth of information and important contacts for doing business in Moscow:

American Chamber of Commerce (☎ 961 2141; www .amcham.ru)

European Business Club (☎ 721 1760; www.ebc.ru)

Russian-British Chamber of Commerce (☎ 961 2160; www.rbcc.co.uk).

Language ▮

Language

It's true – anyone can speak another language. Don't worry if you haven't studied languages before or that you studied a language at school for years and can't remember any of it. It doesn't even matter if you failed English grammar. After all, that's never affected your ability to speak English! And this is the key to picking up a language in another country. You just need to start speaking.

Learn a few key phrases before you go. Write them on pieces of paper and stick them on the fridge, by the bed or even on the computer – anywhere that you'll see them often.

You'll find that locals appreciate travellers trying their language, no matter how muddled you may think you sound. So don't just stand there, say something! If you want to learn more Russian than we've included here, pick up a copy of Lonely Planet's comprehensive but user-friendly *Russian Phrasebook*.

It's relatively easy to find English speakers in Moscow, but your travels will be far more interesting if you at least take the time to learn a few basic words and phrases, and the Cyrillic alphabet – so that you can at least read maps and street signs.

THE CYRILLIC ALPHABET

Russian uses the Cyrillic alphabet, which is not as tricky as it looks. It's well worth the effort to familiarise yourself with it.

The list below shows the letters used in the Russian Cyrillic alphabet with the Roman-letter equivalents that have been used for the transliterations in this book. In some instances, direct letter-for-letter transliterations have not been used if this would render inaccurate pronunciation. If you follow the pronunciation guides included with the words and phrases below, you should have no trouble making yourself understood.

Cyrillic	Roman	Pronunciation
А а	a	as in 'father' when stressed; as in 'ago' when unstressed
Б б	b	as in 'but'
В в	v	as in 'van'
Г г	g	as in 'go'
Д д	d	as in 'dog'
Е е	ye	as in 'yet' when stressed; as in 'yeast' when unstressed
Ё ё	yo	as in 'yore'
Ж ж	zh	as the 's' in 'measure'
З з	z	as in 'zoo'
И и	i	as in 'police'
Й й	y	as in 'boy'
К к	k	as in 'kind'
Л л	l	as in 'lamp'
М м	m	as in 'mad'
Н н	n	as in 'net'
О о	o	as in 'more' when stressed; as the 'a' in 'ago' when unstressed
П п	p	as in 'pig'
Р р	r	as in 'rub', but rolled
С с	s	as in 'sing'
Т т	t	as in 'ten'
У у	u	as in 'rule'
Ф ф	f	as in 'fan'
Х х	kh	as the 'ch' in 'Bach'
Ц ц	ts	as in 'bits'
Ч ч	ch	as in 'chin'
Ш ш	sh	as in 'shop'
Щ щ	shch	as 'fresh chips'
ъ		'hard' sign (rarely used)
Ы ы	i	as the 'i' in 'ill'
ь	-'	like a faint 'y' sound
Э э	e	as in 'end'
Ю ю	yu	as in 'Yukon'
Я я	ya	as in 'yard'

PRONUNCIATION

The sounds of the Russian letters a, o, e and я are 'weaker' when the stress in the word doesn't fall on them, eg in вода (*voda*, water) the stress falls on the second syllable, so it's pronounced 'va-da', with the unstressed pronunciation for o and the stressed pronunciation for a. Russians usually print the letter ё without the dots, a source of confusion in pronunciation.

The 'voiced' consonants б, в, г, д, ж and з are not voiced at the end of words or before voiceless consonants. For example, хлеб (bread) is not pronounced 'khlyeb', as written, but 'khlyep'. The letter r in the common adjective endings -eгo and -oгo is pronounced 'v'.

SOCIAL
Meeting People
Hello.
zdrastvuitye
Здравствуйте.
Hi.
privyet
Привет.
Goodbye.
da svidaniya
До свидания.
Please.
pazhalsta
Пожалуйста.
Thank you (very much).
(bal'shoye) spasiba
(Большое) спасибо.
You're welcome. (ie don't mention it)
nye za shta
Не за что.
Yes/No.
da/nyet
Да/Нет.
Do you speak English?
vi gavarite pa angliyski?
Вы говорите по-английски?
Does anyone here speak English?
kto-nibud' gavarit pa-angliyski?
Кто-нибудь говорит по-английски?
Do you understand?
vi panimayete?
Вы понимаете?
I (don't) understand.
ya (nye) panimayu
Я (не) понимаю.
Please repeat that.
paftarite pazhalsta
Повторите, пожалуйста.
Please speak more slowly.
gavarite pa-medleneye pazhalsta
Говорите помедленнее, пожалуйста.
Please write it down.
zapishyte pazhalsta
Запишите, пожалуйста.

Going Out
What's on ...?
Shto praiskhodit interyesnava ...?
Что происходит интересного ...?
  locally
  pablizasti   поблизости
  this weekend
  na etikh   на этих выходных
    vikhadnikh
  today
  syevodnya   сегодня
  tonight
  vyecheram   вечером

Where are the ...?
gdye nakhodyatsa ...?
Где находятся ...?
  clubs
  klubi, diskoteki   клубы, дискотеки
  gay venues
  gey klubi   гей клубы
  places to eat
  kafe ili restarani кафе или рестораны
  pubs
  bari   бары (or irlandskii bari
                      for 'Irish pubs')

Is there a local entertainment guide?
yest' abzor myest kuda paiti v gazete?
Есть обзор мест куда пойти в газете?

PRACTICAL
Question Words

Who?	kto?	Кто?
What?	shto?	Что?
When?	kagda?	Когда?
Where?	gdye?	Где?
How?	kak?	Как?

Numbers & Amounts

0	nol'	ноль
1	adin	один
2	dva	два
3	tri	три
4	chitiri	четыре
5	pyat'	пять
6	shest'	шесть
7	sem'	семь
8	vosem'	восемь
9	devyat'	девять
10	desyat'	десять
11	adinatsat'	одиннадцать
12	dvenatsat'	двенадцать
13	trinatsat'	тринадцать
14	chetirnatsat'	четырнадцать

15	petnatsat'	пятнадцать
16	shesnatsat'	шестнадцать
17	semnatsat'	семнадцать
18	vosemnatsat'	восемнадцать
19	devitnatsat'	девятнадцать
20	dvatsat'	двадцать
21	dvatsat' adin	двадцать один
22	dvatsat' dva	двадцать два
30	tritsat'	тридцать
40	sorak	сорок
50	pedesyat	пятьдесят
60	shesdesyat	шестьдесят
70	semdesyat	семьдесят
80	vosemdesyat	восемьдесят
90	devenosta	девяносто
100	sto	сто
1000	tisyacha	тысяча
2000	dvye tisachi	две тысячи

Days

Monday	panidel'nik	понедельник
Tuesday	ftornik	вторник
Wednesday	srida	среда
Thursday	chetverk	четверг
Friday	pyatnitsa	пятница
Saturday	subota	суббота
Sunday	vaskrisen'e	воскресенье

Banking

I'd like to ...
mne nuzhna ...
Мне нужно ...
  cash a cheque
  abnalichit' chek
  обналичить чек
  change money
  abmenyat' den'gi
  обменять деньги
  change some travellers cheques
  abmenyat' darozhniye cheki
  обменять дорожные чеки

Where's the nearest ...?
gdye blizhayshiy ...?
Где ближайший ...?
  automatic teller machine (ATM)
  bankamat
  банкомат
  foreign exchange office
  abmenni punkt
  обменный пункт

Post

Where is the post office?
gdye pochta?
Где почта?

I want to send a ...
khachu paslat'
Хочу послать ...
  fax
  faks   факс
  parcel
  pasilku   посылку
  small parcel
  banderol'   бандероль
  postcard
  atkritku   открытку

I want to buy ...
khachu kupit' ...
Хочу купить ...
  an envelope
  kanvert   конверт
  a stamp
  marku   марку

Phones & Mobiles

I want to buy a phone card.
ya khachu kupit' telefonnuyu kartachku
Я хочу купить телефонную карточку.

I want to make a call (to ...)
ya khachu pazvanit' (v ...)
Я хочу позвонить (в ...)
  Europe/America/Australia
  yevropu/ameriku/avstraliyu
  европу/америку/австралию

Where can I find a/an ...?
gdye ya mogu naiti ...?
Где я могу найти ...?
I'd like a/an ...
mnye nuzhen ...
Мне нужен ...
  adaptor plug
  peryehadnik dlya razetki
  переходник для розетки
  charger for my phone
  zaryadnaye ustroistva dlya telefona
  зарядное устройство для телефона
  mobile/cell phone for hire
  mabil'ni telefon
  мобильный телефон напрокат
  SIM card for your network
  sim-karta dlya mestnoi seti
  сим-карта для местной сети

Internet

Where's the local Internet café?
Gde zdyes' internet kafe?
Где здесь интернет кафе?

I want to ...
ya khachu ...
Я хочу ...
  check my email
  praverit moi imeil
  проверить мой имэйл
  get online
  padsayedinitsa k internetu
  подсоединиться к интернету

Transport
What time does the ... leave?
f katoram chasu pribivaet ...?
В котором часу прибывает ...?
What time does the ... arrive?
f katoram chasu atpravlyaetsa ...?
В котором часу отправляется ...?

bus	aftobus	автобус
fixed-route	marshrutnaye	маршрутное
minibus	taksi	такси
train	poyezt	поезд
tram	tramvay	трамвай
trolleybus	tralleybus	троллейбус

When is the ... bus?
kagda budet ... aftobus?
Когда будет ... автобус?

first	pervi	первый
last	pasledniy	последний
next	sleduyushchiy	следующий

Are you free? (taxi)
svaboden?
Свободен?
Please put the meter on.
vklyuchite pazhalsta schetchik
Включите пожалуйста счетчик.
How much is it to ...?
skol'ka stoit daekhat' do ...?
Сколько стоит доехать до ...?
Please take me to ...
atvezite menya pazhalsta v ...
Отвезите меня, пожалуйста в ...

FOOD

breakfast	zaftrak	завтрак
lunch	abed	обед
dinner	uzhyn	ужин
snack	peryekusit'	перекусить
eat	est'/s'yest'	есть/съесть
drink	pit'/vipit'	пить/выпить

Can you recommend a ...
Nye mogli bi vi parekamendavat' ...
Не могли бы вы порекомендовать ...

bar/pub
bar/pivnuyu   бар/пивную
café
kafe   кафе
restaurant
restaran   ресторан

Is service/cover charge included in the bill?
absluzhivanye vklucheno v schet?
Обслуживание включено в счет?

For more detailed information on food and dining out, see pp13–16 and pp119–38.

EMERGENCIES
Help!
na pomashch'!/pamagite!
На помощь!/Помогите!
I'm lost.
ya zabludilsya/zabludilas' (m/f)
Я заблудился/заблудилась.
I'm sick.
ya bolen/bal'na (m/f)
Я болен/больна.
Where's the police station?
gdye militsiya?
Где милиция?

Call ...!
pazvanite ...!
Позвоните ...!
  the police
  v militsiyu   в милицию
  a doctor
  doktoru   доктору
  an ambulance
  v skoruyu pomosch'   в скорую помощь

HEALTH
Where's the nearest ...?
gde blizhaishaya ...?
Где ближайшая ...?
  chemist (night)
  apteka (dezhurnaya) аптека (дежурная)
  dentist
  zubnoy vrach   зубной врач
  doctor
  vrach   врач
  hospital
  bal'nitsa   больница

I need a doctor (who speaks English).
mne nuzhen vrach (anglagavaryaschii)
Мне нужен врач (англоговорящий).

I have (a) ...		headache	
u menya ...	У меня ...	galavnaya bol'	головная боль
diarrhoea		pain	
panos	понос	bol'	боль
fever		stomachache	
temperatura	температура	balit zheludak	болит желудок

GLOSSARY

avtovokzal – bus terminal

bankamat – ATM
banya – Russian bathhouse, similar to a sauna
bilet – ticket
bliny – crepes
borscht – beetroot soup
boyar – high-ranking noble
bufet – snack bar
buterbrod – open-faced sandwich

dacha – country cottage or summer house
devushka – young woman
duma – parliament

elektrichka – slow, suburban train

firmenny poezd – a fancy, fast train, often with a special name

GAI (Gosudarstvennaya Avtomobilnaya Inspektsia) – State Automobile Inspectorate
glasnost – literally 'openness'; used in reference to the free-expression aspect of the Gorbachev reforms
gostinitsa – hotel

ikra – caviar

kamera khraneniya – left-luggage
kasha – porridge
kassa – cash register or ticket office
kefir – yogurt-like sour milk
khram – cathedral
korpus – building, often used in addresses
kremlin – fort, usually a town's foundation
kupenyy or **kupe** – 2nd class on a train; usually four-person couchettes
kvas – mildly alcoholic fermented juice

luks or **lyux** – luxury or 1st class; often refers to a sleeping car on a train or rooms in a hotel

maly – small
matryoshka – painted wooden nesting doll
mesto – place, as in seat on a train
most – bridge
muzey – museum

naberezhnaya – embankment

passazhirskiy poezd – slow, intercity passenger train
pelmeni – dumplings filled with meat or vegetables
perekhod – cross walk, often underground
pereriv – break period, often in the middle of the day, when stores close
perestroika – literally 'restructuring'; refers to Gorbachev's economic reforms of the 1980s
pirozhek – deep-fried meat or vegetable turnover
ploshchad – square
platskartnyy – 3rd class, general seating on an intercity train
prigorodny poezd – slow, suburban train
proezd – passage
prospekt – avenue
provodnitsa – conductor

rynok – market

sad – garden
samizdat – underground publishing during the Soviet period
samovar – urn used to heat water for tea
shampanskoe – Russian sparkling wine
shapka – fur hat
shashlik – meat kebab
shosse – highway
shtuka – piece or item; often used as a unit of sale
skory poezd – fast train
spalny vagon (SV) – sleeping car
stolovaya – canteen or cafeteria

taksofon – pay phone
tramvay – tram which runs on tracks above ground, usually outside the city centre
tsarina – wife of the tsar
tserkov – church

ulitsa – street
uslovnye yedensitsy (y.e.) – standard unit; used to quote prices in upmarket restaurants and hotels

vagon – train carriage
val – rampart
vokzal – train station

zakuski – appetisers
zheton – metal token; used for some older pay phones or left-luggage lockers

Behind the Scenes

THE LONELY PLANET STORY

The story begins with a classic travel adventure: Tony and Maureen Wheeler's 1972 journey across Europe and Asia to Australia. There was no useful information about the overland trail then, so Tony and Maureen published the first Lonely Planet guidebook to meet a growing need.

From a kitchen table, Lonely Planet has grown to become the largest independent travel publisher in the world, with offices in Melbourne (Australia), Oakland (USA) and London (UK). Today Lonely Planet guidebooks cover the globe. There is an ever-growing list of books and information in a variety of media. Some things haven't changed. The main aim is still to make it possible for adventurous travellers to get out there – to explore and better understand the world.

At Lonely Planet we believe travellers can make a positive contribution to the countries they visit – if they respect their host communities and spend their money wisely. Every year 5% of company profit is donated to charities around the world.

THIS BOOK

This third edition of *Moscow* was written by Mara Vorhees, as was the previous edition. Ryan ver Berkmoes wrote the first edition. Jerry Easter, Kathleen Pullum, Leonid Ragozin, Clementine Cecil, Kevin O'Flynn, and Alan and Julia Thompson wrote some of the boxed texts for this edition. This edition was commissioned in Lonely Planet's London office and produced in the Melbourne office by the following people:

Commissioning Editors Fiona Buchan, Alan Murphy, Imogen Hall

Coordinating Editor Evan Jones

Coordinating Cartographer Anthony Phelan

Coordinating Layout Designer John Shippick

Managing Cartographer Mark Griffiths

Assisting Editors Lucy Monie, Sarah Bailey, Lutie Clark, Helen Koehne

Assisting Layout Designers Jim Hsu, Jacqui Saunders, Laura Jane

Cover Designer Marika Kozak

Project Manager Ray Thomson

Language Content Coordinator Quentin Frayne

Thanks to Sally Darmody, Bruce Evans, Mark Germanchis, Rebecca Lalor, Nick Stebbing, Dave Burnett, Suzannah Shwer, Wayne Murphy, Valentina Kremenchutskaya, Imogen Bannister, Adriana Mammarella, Brigitte Ellemor, Gabbi Wilson

Cover photographs Student at the Moscow Academic Ballet School, Dean Conger/APL/Corbis (top); Metro station, Moscow, Dynamic Graphics (UK) Ltd/Photolibrary (bottom); Detail of St Basil's Cathedral, Jonathan Smith/Lonely Planet Images (back).

Internal photographs by Lonely Planet Images and Jonathan Smith except for the following: p206 Graham Bell; p188, p192 Christina Dameyer; p186 Martin Moos; p201, p207 Simon Richmond. All images are the copyright of the photographers unless otherwise indicated. Many of the images in this guide are available for licensing from Lonely Planet Images: www.lonelyplanetimages.com.

SEND US YOUR FEEDBACK

We love to hear from travellers – your comments keep us on our toes and help make our books better. Our well-travelled team reads every word on what you loved or loathed about this book. Although we cannot reply individually to postal submissions, we always guarantee that your feedback goes straight to the appropriate authors, in time for the next edition. Each person who sends us information is thanked in the next edition – and the most useful submissions are rewarded with a free book.

To send us your updates – and find out about Lonely Planet events, newsletters and travel news – visit our award-winning website: www.lonelyplanet.com/feedback

Note: We may edit, reproduce and incorporate your comments in Lonely Planet products such as guidebooks, websites and digital products, so let us know if you don't want your comments reproduced or your name acknowledged. For a copy of our privacy policy visit www.lonelyplanet.com/privacy.

THANKS

Of all the places to stay in Moscow, none is so comfortable, convenient and completely welcoming as Tommo and Julia's flat, where accommodation comes with good company and a fat cat. Thanks to Jimmy and Belen (et al), who demonstrated first hand what to do with kids in Moscow. Special thanks to Dmitry Menshikov and Anna Lebedeva, and contributors to the boxed texts Jerry Easter, Kevin O'Flynn, Kathleen Pullum, Clementine Cecil, Leonid Ragozin, and Alan and Julia Thompson. Jerz, thanks for being my creative inspiration, even when you're thousands of miles away. This book is dedicated to the memory of Olivia, who made homecomings all the happier.

OUR READERS

Many thanks to the travellers who used the last edition and wrote to us with helpful hints, useful advice and interesting anecdotes.

Kevin Allen, Ian Barclay, Alan Buckley, Eleanor Crook, Arjan de Brujin, Fernando Ferreira Lima, Sarah Harding, Barbara Jani, James Kinneir, Jon Inge Kjernlie, Peter Klein, Karen Koblitz, John Landry, Alexander Leonov, Jay & Carolyn MacInnes, Maureen & Jason Mayland, Ginny Muller, Anita Newcourt, Peter Nickol, Paul Ozorak, Peter Pladet, Karen & John Reilly, Gregory Rose, Craig & Mel Scutchings, Laura Sheahen, Fred Thornett, Nils Wiemer, Peter Wilson, Andrew Young.

Index

See also separate indexes for Eating (p243), Entertainment (p243), Shopping (p244) and Sleeping (p244).

Index

Index

Index

240

Index

242

Index

000 map pages
000 photographs

MAP LEGEND

ROUTES

Tollway	One-Way Street
Freeway	Mall/Steps
Primary Road	Tunnel
Secondary Road	Walking Tour
Tertiary Road	Walking Tour Detour
Lane	Walking Trail
Under Construction	Walking Path
Track	Pedestrian Overpass
Unsealed Road	

TRANSPORT

Ferry	Rail
Metro	Rail (Underground)
Bus Route	Monorail

HYDROGRAPHY

River, Creek	Canal
Intermittent River	Water

BOUNDARIES

International	Regional, Suburb
State, Provincial	Ancient Wall

AREA FEATURES

Airport	Forest
Area of Interest	Land
Building, Featured	Mall
Building, Information	Park
Building, Other	Sports
Building, Transport	Urban
Cemetery, Christian	Cemetery, Other

POPULATION

CAPITAL (NATIONAL)	CAPITAL (STATE)
Large City	Medium City
Small City	Town, Village

SYMBOLS

Sights/Activities	Entertainment	Information
Christian	Entertainment	Bank, ATM
Jewish	**Shopping**	Embassy/Consulate
Monument	Shopping	Hospital, Medical
Museum, Gallery	**Sleeping**	Information
Other Site	Sleeping	Internet Facilities
Swimming Pool	**Transport**	Police Station
Zoo, Bird Sanctuary	Airport, Airfield	Post Office, GPO
Eating	Parking Area	**Geographic**
Eating	Taxi Rank	Lookout
Drinking	Bus Station	Mountain, Volcano
Drinking		National Park
Café		River Flow

Maps

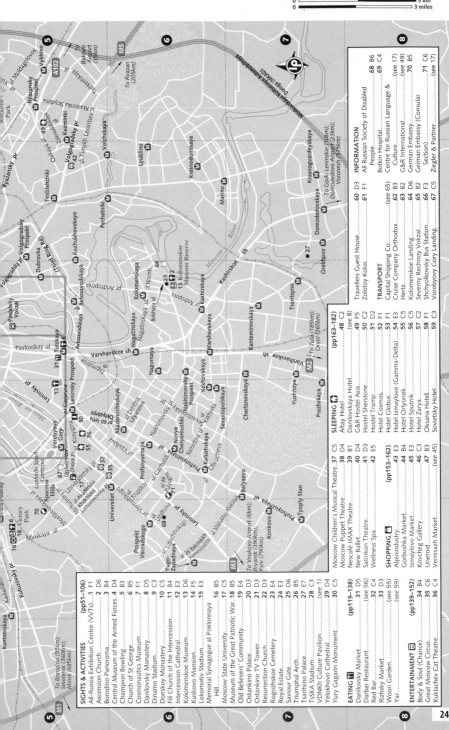

0	5 km
0	3 miles

SIGHTS & ACTIVITIES   (pp51–106)
All-Russia Exhibition Centre (VVTs)...1 F1
Ascension Church..................................2 D6
Borodino Panorama...............................3 B4
Central Museum of the Armed Forces..4 D4
Champion Bowling.................................5 B3
Church of St George..............................6 B5
Cosmonautics Museum..........................7 F1
Danilovsky Monastery............................8 D5
Dinamo Stadium....................................9 C3
Donskoy Monastery.............................10 C5
Fili Church of the Intercession.............11 B4
Intercession Cathedral..........................12 E3
Kolomenskoe Museum..........................13 D6
Kuskovo Mansion.................................14 F5
Memorial Synagogue at Poklonnaya......15 E3
  Hill...16 B5
Moscow State University.......................17 C5
Museum of the Great Patriotic War....18 B5
Old Believers' Community......................19 E4
Ostankino Palace..................................20 D3
Ostankino TV Tower.............................21 D3
Resurrection Church..............................22 D3
Rogozhskoe Cemetery..........................23 E4
Royal Estate...24 E3
Saviour Gate..25 D6
Triumphal Arch....................................26 B5
Tsaritsino Palace..................................27 E7
TsSKA Stadium....................................28 C3
VDNKh Culture Pavilion.......................(see 1)
Yelokhovo Cathedral............................29 D4
Yury Gagarin Monument.......................30 C5

EATING 🍴   (pp119–138)
Danilovsky Market................................31 D5
Darbar Restaurant................................(see 56)
Red Bar...32 C4
Rizhsky Market.....................................33 D3
Woori Garden.......................................(see 55)
Yar...(see 59)

ENTERTAINMENT 🎭   (pp139–152)
Body & Soul (Chance)...........................34 B4
Great Moscow Circus............................35 C6
Kuklachev Cat Theatre..........................36 C4

Moscow Children's Musical Theatre..37 C5
Moscow Puppet Theatre.......................38 D4
Nescafé IMAX Theatre..........................39 B1
New Ballet..40 D4
Satirikon Theatre..................................41 D3
Wellness Spa..42 E5

SHOPPING 🛍   (pp153–162)
Alpindustry...43 E3
Gorbushka Market................................44 B4
Izmaylovo Market.................................45 E3
Kovcheg Gallery....................................46 C3
Uneroid...47 B3
Vernisazh Market..................................(see 45)

SLEEPING 🛏   (pp163–182)
Altay Hotel...48 C2
Danilovskiy Hotel.................................(see 8)
G&R Hostel Asia...................................49 F5
Hostel Sherstone..................................50 C2
Hostel Tramp.......................................51 D2
Hotel Cosmos......................................52 F1
Hotel Globus..53 D2
Hotel Izmaylovo (Gamma-Delta)..........54 E3
Hotel Orlyonok....................................55 C5
Hotel Sputnik.......................................56 C5
Hotel Zarya..57 D2
Oksana Hotel.......................................58 F1
Sovietsky Hotel....................................59 C3

Travellers Guest House.........................60 D3
Zolotoy Kolos.......................................61 F1

INFORMATION
All Russian Society of Disabled
  People...68 B6
Botkin Hospital.....................................69 C4
Centre for Russian Language &
  Culture..(see 17)
G&R International................................(see 49)
German Embassy...................................70 B5
German Embassy (Consular
  Section)...71 C6
Ziegler & Partner..................................(see 17)

TRANSPORT
Capital Shipping Co..............................(see 65)
Cruise Company Orthodox....................62 B3
Hertz...63 B2
Kolomenskoe Landing...........................64 D6
Severny Rechnoy Vokzal.......................65 C5
Shchyolkovsky Bus Station....................66 F3
Vorobyovy Gory Landing.......................67 C5

247

TVERSKOY, PETROVSKY, ARBAT & BARRIKADNAYA

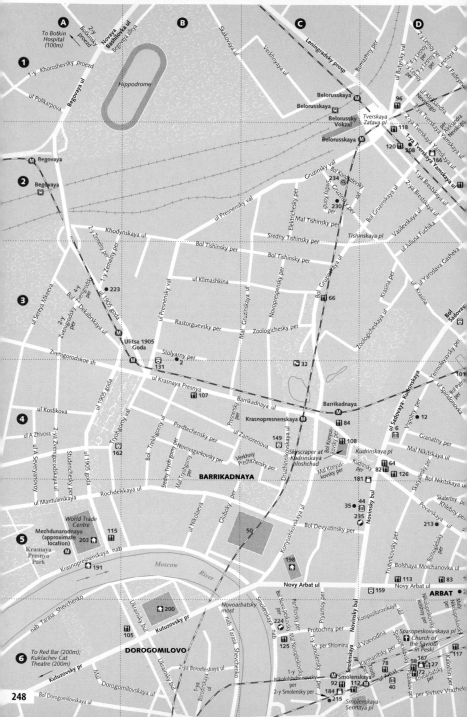

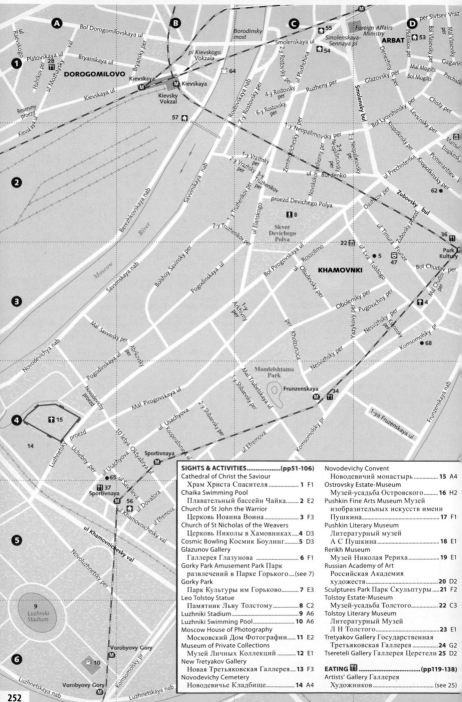

KHAMOVNIKI, KROPOTKINSKAYA & ZAMOSKVORECHIE

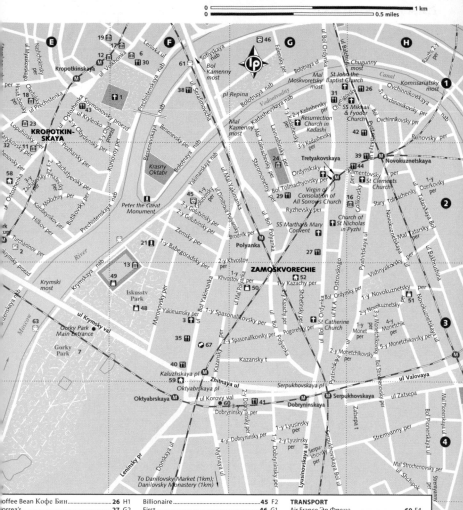

0 _____ 500 m
0 _____ 0.3 miles

SIGHTS & ACTIVITIES .... (pp51-106)
Andronikov Monastery 1 D6
Choral Synagogue
    Хоральная Синагога 2 A5
Menshikov Tower
    Башня Меньшикова 3 A4
Rublyov Museum of early Russian
    Culture & Art Музей Древнерусской
    Культуры и Искусства
    им Рублёва .... (see 1)

Sakharov Museum
    Музей А Д Сахарова 4 C6
Saviour's Cathedral
    Спасский собор 5 D6
Skating Rink Зимний каток 6 B4

EATING .... (pp119-138)
American Bar & Grill
    Американский Бар
    и Гриль 7 C6
Avocado Авокадо 8 A4
Cheese Hole Сырная Дырка 9 B5
Cibo e Vino 10 B4
Coffee Bean Кофе Бин 11 B4
Drova Дрова 12 A4
Expedition Экспедиция 13 A6
Khodzha Nasredin in Khiva
    Ходжа Насредин в Хиве 14 B5
Maharaja Махараджа 15 A5
Noah's Ark Ноев Ковчег 16 A5
Nostalgie Art Club 17 A4
Prisoner of the Caucasus
    Кавказская Пленница 18 A1
Ramstore Рамстор 19 C2
Shokolodnitsa Шоколадница ....(see 12)
Sirena 20 A2
Tent Шатёр 21 B4
Vapiano Вапиано 22 A1

ENTERTAINMENT .... (pp139-152)
bilingua 23 A4
Chinese Pilot Dzhao-Da Китайский
    Лётчик Джао-Да 24 A5
Kult Культ 25 B6
Leto (Summer) Лето 26 A6
New Age (Three Monkeys)
    Три Обезьяны 27 C6
Proekt OGI Проект ОГИ 28 A4
Rolan Cinema Ролан ....(see 17)
Sovremennik Theatre
    Театр Современник 29 B4
Tabakov Theatre Театр под
    управлением Олега
    Табакова 30 B4
Woodstock 31 B4

SHOPPING .... (pp153-162)
Atrium Атриум 32 C5
digitalbraz 33 A4
Marki Марки 34 B4

SLEEPING .... (pp163-182)
Galina's Flat Квартира Галины 35 B4
Hotel Sverchkov
    Гостиница Сверчков 36 A4
Hotel Volga
    Гостиница Волга 37 A2
Kazakh Embassy Hotel Гостиница
    Посольства Казахстана 38 A4
Leningradskaya Hotel Гостиница
    Ленинградская 39 B2

TRANSPORT
Ustinsky Most Landing
    Пристань Устинский мост 40 A6

INFORMATION
36.6 ....41 A5
American Medical Center Американский
    Медицинский Центр 42 A1
Australian Embassy Посольство
    Австралии 43 A6
British Council Resource Centre ...... (see 44)
Foreign Literature Library
    Библиотека иностранной
    литературы 44 B6
Irish Embassy
    Посольство Ирландии 45 A1
Main Post Office
    Московский главпочтамт 46 A3

ZAYAUZIE

0 ——————————— 500 m
0 ——————————— 0.3 miles

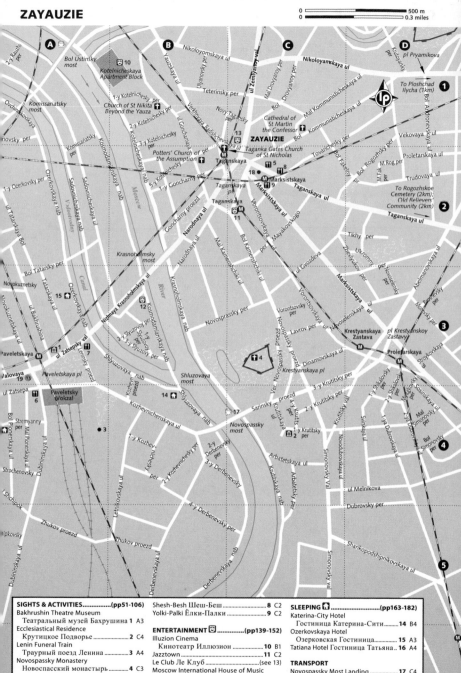

255

MOSCOW METRO

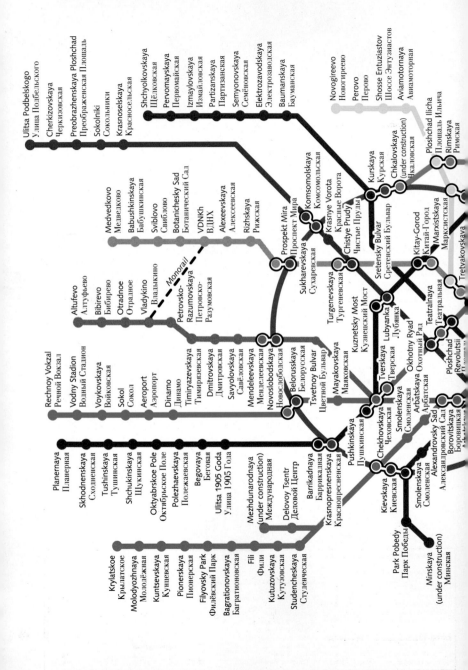

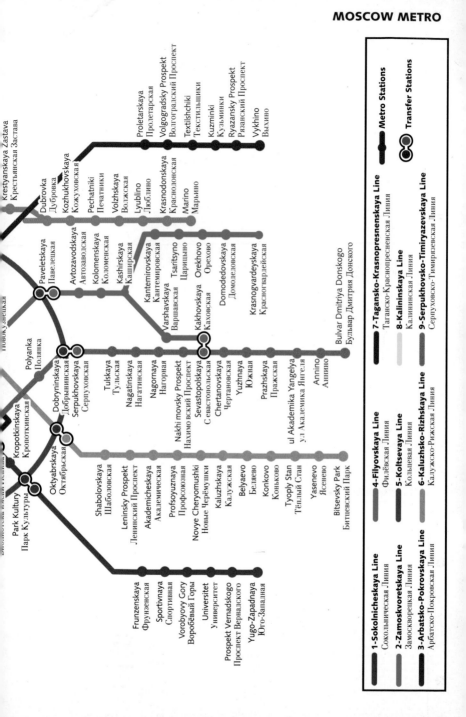

MOSCOW METRO

● Metro Stations

◎ Transfer Stations

1-Sokolnicheskaya Line
Сокольническая Линия

2-Zamoskvoretskaya Line
Замоскворецкая Линия

3-Arbatsko-Pokrovskaya Line
Арбатско-Покровская Линия

4-Filyovskaya Line
Филёвская Линия

5-Koltsevaya Line
Кольцевая Линия

6-Kaluzhsko-Rizhskaya Line
Калужско-Рижская Линия

7-Tagansko-Krasnopresnenskaya Line
Таганско-Красиопресненская Линия

8-Kalininskaya Line
Калининская Линия

9-Serpukhovsko-Timiryazevskaya Line
Серпуховско-Тимирязевская Линия

Krestyanskaya Zastava
Крестьянская Застава

Dubrovka / Дубровка
Kozhukhovskaya / Кожуховская
Pechatniki / Печатники
Volzhskaya / Волжская
Lyublino / Люблино
Krasnodonskaya / Краснодонская
Marino / Марьино

Proletarskaya / Пролетарская
Volgogradsky Prospekt / Волгоградский Проспект
Textilshchiki / Текстильщики
Kuzminki / Кузьминки
Ryazansky Prospekt / Рязанский Проспект
Vykhino / Выхино

Paveletskaya / Павелецкая
Avtozavodskaya / Автозаводская
Kolomenskaya / Коломенская
Kashirskaya / Каширская

Kantemirovskaya / Кантемировская
Tsaritsyno / Царицыно
Orekhovo / Орехово
Domodedovskaya / Домодедовская
Krasnogvardeyskaya / Красногвардейская

Polyanka / Полянка
Dobryninskaya / Добрынинская
Serpukhovskaya / Серпуховская
Tulskaya / Тульская
Nagatinskaya / Нагатинская
Nagornaya / Нагорная
Nakhimovsky Prospekt / Нахимовский Проспект
Sevastopolskaya / Севастопольская
Chertanovskaya / Чертановская
Yuzhnaya / Южная
Prazhskaya / Пражская
Annino / Аннино

Varshavskaya / Варшавская
Kakhovskaya / Каховская

Bulvar Dmitriya Donskogo
Бульвар Дмитрия Донского

ul Akademika Yangelya
ул Академика Янгеля

Kropotkinskaya / Кропоткинская
Oktyabrskaya / Октябрьская
Park Kultury / Парк Культуры

Shabolovskaya / Шаболовская
Leninsky Prospekt / Ленинский Проспект
Akademicheskaya / Академическая
Profsoyuznaya / Профсоюзная
Novye Cheryomushki / Новые Черёмушки
Kaluzhskaya / Калужская
Belyaevo / Беляево
Konkovo / Коньково
Tyoply Stan / Тёплый Стан
Yasenevo / Ясенево
Bitsevsky Park / Битцевский Парк

Frunzenskaya / Фрунзенская
Sportivnaya / Спортивная
Vorobyovy Gory / Воробёвый Горы
Universitet / Университет
Prospekt Vernadskogo / Проспект Вернадского
Yugo-Zapadnaya / Юго-Западная

257

THE KREMLIN & RED SQUARE

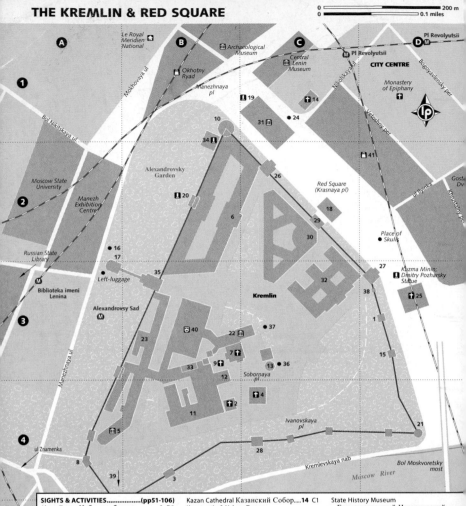